THE BLUE GUIDES

Austria
Belgium
Channel
China*
Corsica
Crete
Cyprus
Egypt
England
France
Germany
Greece
Holland
Hungary*
Ireland
Northern Italy
Southern Italy
Morocco
Portugal
Scotland
Sicily
Spain
Switzerland
Turkey: Bursa to Antakya
Wales
Yugoslavia

Boston and Cambridge
Florence
Istanbul
Jerusalem
London
Moscow and Leningrad
New York
Oxford and Cambridge
Paris and Versailles
Rome and Environs
Venice

Cathedrals and Abbeys of England and Wales
Literary Britain and Ireland
Museums and Galleries of London
Victorian Architecture in Britain

*in preparation

The W Portal of the Jerónimos, Belém

BLUE GUIDE

PORTUGAL

IAN ROBERTSON

A. & C. Black
London

W. W. Norton
New York

Third edition 1988
Reprinted with corrections 1989

Published by A & C Black (Publishers) Limited
35 Bedford Row, London WC1R 4JH

Published in the United States of America by
WW Norton & Company, Inc.
500 Fifth Avenue, New York, NY 10110

Published simultaneously in Canada by
Penguin Books Canada Limited
2801 John Street, Markham, Ontario LR3 1B4

British Library Cataloguing in Publication Data
Robertson, Ian, Campbell, 1928-
    Portugal. — 3rd ed. — (Blue guide).
    I. Portugal — Description and travel —
    1981- — Guide-books
    I. Title II. Series
    914.69′0444 DP516

    ISBN 0-7136-2966-5

ISBN 0-393-30477-9   USA

Ian Robertson was born in Tokyo and educated in England. After spending several years in publishing and bookselling in London, he began working on *Blue Guides* when he was commissioned to rewrite *Blue Guide Spain* in 1970. He has since revised the Blue Guides to Ireland, France, Paris, Portugal and Switzerland, as well as writing *Blue Guide Austria* and *Blue Guide Cyprus.* He has also written introductions to reprints of Richard Ford's *Handbook for Travellers in Spain,* Joseph Baretti's *Journey from London to Genoa* and Gleig's *The Subaltern.*

Printed and bound in Great Britain by
Courier International Ltd, Tiptree, Essex

PREFACE

This third edition of *Blue Guide Portugal* follows the successful pattern set by the previous editions, the demand for which confirmed the revival of interest in that country among discriminating travellers. Several factors had affected its accessibility in previous decades, although the Algarve was beginning to be exploited: the Spanish Civil War; the Second World War; the dictatorship of Salazar, with which few found sympathy; the Revolution of 25 April 1974, and subsequent 'troubles', caused it to be avoided by those following more popular tracks beaten through the cities and along the shores of some other European countries, and—let it be said—often to its advantage.

The new 'democratised' generation, now integrated with modern Europe, has already done much to bring about a revival of interest, and travellers will still find much in this very beautiful and individual country which has been elsewhere commercialised or otherwise dissipated.

The long association of England with the Kingdom of Portucale began perhaps in 1147, when a body of Crusaders sailing from Dartmouth to the Holy Land put in at Oporto and, at the invitation of Afonso Henriques, participated in the conquest of Lisbon, where Gilbert of Hastings became its first bishop. Trading prospered between the two countries; in 1294 the first of a number of commercial treaties was signed. Some 600 years have now passed since another treaty of importance between the two crowns was sealed in 1373, confirmed in 1386 by the Treaty of Windsor. The following year Philippa of Lancaster, daughter of John of Gaunt, married João I, the first of the Avis dynasty, one of whose sons was Henry the Navigator; while a later marriage was that of Charles II with Catherine of Braganza, daughter of João IV. English 'Factories' were founded at Lisbon and Oporto, and the Methuen Treaties of 1703 followed. In 1808 Wellington first landed in Portugal, which he made his base of operations against the French during the Peninsular War: indeed Portugal has every reason to be known as 'England's oldest ally', even if there have been occasional and understandable differences.

This Guide is devoted entirely to the mainland: Madeira and the Azores are *not* included, as it was thought that most travellers to those islands would prefer separate and slighter guides than one concentrating on peninsular Portugal. Following the conventional formula adopted for the *Blue Guides*, the country is described in a series of routes following its network of roads. These are in general much improved, although there are still some areas through which, for physical reasons, it is not easy to travel at any great speed. But it must be emphasised that this does not pretend to be a fast motorists' guide, nor one describing the sophisticated delights of crowded beaches (not yet so crowded in Portugal) and international 'night-life'. It is intended for those who wish to take a closer look at the country, its architecture and monuments, the very diversity of which should satisfy the demands of the most enthusiastic tourist.

Towns are described for sightseeing on foot, almost always the most convenient and enjoyable way of getting about, while unless one deliberately breaks away from the beaten track onto rougher winding roads one will miss much of the enjoyment which the exploration of less frequented districts can give. Not all routes are necessarily intended to be travelled in a day, but they indicate a general direction which may be followed. The complement of town and site plans has been corrected and extended.

Particular reference must be made here to the masterly Introduction to Portuguese Art and Architecture by **J.B. Bury**; to the valuable Introduction to the History of Portugal, by **Richard Robinson**, and to the Introduction to Port and the Wines of Portugal, by **David Francis**, providing insight into the complexities of the country's architecture and history, and aspects of her commerce. A selective Bibliography is also included, in which the reader will find Murray's 'Hand-Book for Portugal', edited by John Mason Neale, published in the 1850s, and the direct forerunner, with Richard Ford's great 'Hand-Book for Spain' of 1845, of the first *Blue Guides* to the Peninsula.

A very considerable area of Portugal has been covered in person in the compilation and revision of this Guide, and thus a substantial proportion of the descriptions has been written in the light of observation on the spot and familiarity with actual conditions. Nevertheless, even when revising, it is not always possible to revisit every locality, and the readers' assistance is therefore solicited, and any constructive suggestions for correction or improvement will be gratefully welcomed, and acknowledged by the Editor, who alone is responsible for all inexactitudes, shortcomings, inconsistencies, and solecisms. No one is better aware of the difficulty of avoiding errors both of omission and commission. But an attempt has been made to provide a balanced account of most aspects of Portugal without intentionally neglecting any which might appeal to the discerning traveller and without being so exhaustive as to leave no opportunities of discovering additional pleasures.

The Editor should perhaps emphasise here that the traveller must realise that Portugal is still recovering from a revolution, which although 'bloodless', shook the country to its foundations, and some years may pass before its economic and political stability is ensured, but there are many signs of progress. Some hundreds of thousands of Portuguese have sought to settle in Portugal after being forced to leave her late colonies, and their employment and accommodation continues to be a problem. There is less excuse for the lack of taste in too many houses erected there by Portuguese workers in the more affluent countries of Europe, but at least they have a home rather than a hovel in which to live, even if adjacent streets remain strewn with refuse. It is frequently heard that the towns were cleaner before 25 April 1974; certainly the fly-posted walls since then have not improved their appearance, but it is hoped that more forceful attempts will be made to reduce the eyesores. It is likewise hoped that there might be some official campaign to counteract the offensive habit of spitting in public, but no doubt there are more urgent demands on the public purse, such as the reduction of the still-high illiteracy rate—mostly among elderly people—which is a sad reflection on late regimes, who considered it expedient to let the impoverished priest-ridden peasantry so remain.

It is easy to criticise apparently uncontrolled speculative building, but it is sincerely hoped that those responsible for the preservation of the environment will be able to protect the country's shores and forests from the further encroachments of a materialistic age; certainly every encouragement should be given to those entrusted with the task of conservation and restoration of the nation's cultural heritage: there is much work to be done. In the past much of this was unskilful or misplaced. The Church has regrettably already ruined too many buildings in its care, particularly by the application of 'gold' paint to gilded woodwork; but no doubt the erection of tasteless statuary in the 'dictatorial style' in the close proximity of monuments will cease.

The continuing practice of 'starring' the highlights may come in for some criticism, but although the system is subjective and inconsistent, such asterisks do help the hurried traveller to pick out those things which the general consensus of opinion (modified occasionally by the Editor's personal prejudice, admittedly) considers should not be missed. In certain cases a museum has been starred, rather than individual objects among those described, when the standard of its contents is remarkably high.

A number of museums and collections in Portugal are likely to be closed to the public for reorganisation or rearrangement, often overdue; some are unaccountably shut. Others have taken advantage of the siting of the 17th Council of Europe Exhibition in Lisbon in 1983 to make radical changes. While the majority of the more important museums were visited by the Editor, it is likely that in certain cases the Guide will be describing *what may be seen* rather than indicating the exact position of the objects listed. Unfortunately many collections lack any form of published catalogue or leaflet, a situation, while at present understandable, it is hoped will be improved with time.

Porchester (later Lord Carnarvon), when travelling in the Peninsula in 1827–28, remarked that if he could divest himself of every national partiality, 'and suppose myself an inhabitant of the other hemisphere, travelling solely for my amusement, noting men and manners, and were asked in what country society had attained its most polished form, I should say in Portugal....Portuguese politeness is delightful, because it is by no means purely artificial, but flows in a great measure from a natural kindness of feeling'. In this respect the country has little changed. The Editor has experienced more disinterested help and hospitality in Portugal than anywhere else he has travelled; the kindness of the Portuguese on numerous occasions being in noticeable contrast to the negative and off-hand attitudes taken in some other countries which may have a higher standard of living but which are less civilised. Such innate politeness is getting progressively rarer in the world, and to experience it makes a visit to Portugal that much more pleasant.

To acknowledge all the hospitality and assistance the Editor has received would therefore swell these paragraphs inordinately, for many others have gone out of their way to offer advice or otherwise ease his path. Reading between the lines of Murray's *Hand-Book*, not all compilers in the past have been so lucky, particularly when applying to British official sources. In Lisbon, J.M. Neale noted: 'The English Consul is Mr Smith....The Vice-Consul, Mr Meagher....From the latter gentleman every kind of courtesy will be experienced'.

In addition to those many people providing facilities or offering advice who were listed at this point in previous editions, the following must be mentioned: *Maria Alice Faria* and *José Miguel Pestana de Mello Moser* (Instituto Português do Património Cultural); *Margarida Alçada* (Direcção dos Serviços dos Monumentos Nacionais); *Benjamim Enes Pereira* (Museu de Etnologia, Lisbon); *Dulce Helena Gonçalves Santos Pires Antunes Borges* (Museu da Guarda); *António Pestana de Vasconcellos* (Museu de Évora); *Maria Teresa Cristelo de Almeida d'Eça* (Museu dos Biscainhos, Braga); *Salete da Ponte* (Museu de Conímbriga); and several curators of the Museu Nacional de Arqueologia e Etnologia, Lisbon; and again, *José Luis Porfirio* (Museu de Arte Antiga, Lisbon).

Thanks are due to *Alberto Marques*, to *Luís Cancella de Abreu*, Direcção-Geral do Turismo in Lisbon, and to *João Custódio* in London; *Ana-Maria Horta* (ENATUR, Lisbon); *José Joaquim Valentim (Câmara Municipal de Lisboa); Maria de Céu Gonçalves da Rocha Sá Lima* (Ponte de Lima); and to the owners of the Paços de Calheiros, de S. Cipriano, and do Ameal, for their generous practical assistance and for their hospitality.

Teresa Marques, Luís Vasco, Elisabete Correia Vicente, and *Álvaro José Barbosa* (at Tomar), *Isabel Silva* (at Viana do Castelo), *Rosa Vala* (at Óbidos), the staff of the tourist office at Vila do Conde, not forgetting *Maria Manuela Pessoa Ferreira da Silva* (at Évora), have gone out of their way with providing information and other assistance. Among those who have eased his path in several ways, or have suggested the inclusion of additional material, are *Eugénio Lisboa* (Cultural Counsellor, Portuguese Embassy, London); *Nicolas Sapieha, Francisco Hipolito Raposa, Paulo Lowndes Marques; Bruce K. Heyman;* and *Gregory V. Jones.*

Note. In August 1988 a serious fire caused widespread damage to the area of the *Chiado* in Lisbon (see p 119), and some of the old houses were gutted. It is expected that the damaged buildings will be restored or rebuilt to their original condition with the help of grants from the EEC. The progress of this extensive work will be described in the next edition of this Guide, which will also include a revised description of the *Museu Nacional de Arte Antiga* in Lisbon (see pp 130–136) in which several paintings have been repositioned in recent months.

A NOTE ON BLUE GUIDES

The Blue Guide series began in 1918 when Muirhead Guide-Books Limited published 'Blue Guide London and its Environs'. Finlay and James Muirhead already had extensive experience of guide-book publishing: before the First World War they had been the editors of the English editions of the German Baedekers, and by 1915 they had acquired the copyright of most of the famous 'Red' Handbooks from John Murray.

An agreement made with the French publishing house Hachette et Cie in 1917 led to the translation of Muirhead's London Guide, which became the first 'Guide Bleu'—Hachette had previously published the blue-covered 'Guides Joanne'. Subsequently, Hachette's 'Guide Bleu Paris et ses Environs' was adapted and published in London by Muirhead. The collaboration between the two publishing houses continued until 1933.

In 1931 Ernest Benn Limited took over the Blue Guides, appointing Russell Muirhead, Finlay Muirhead's son, editor in 1934. The Muirheads' connection with Blue Guides ended in 1963 when Stuart Rossiter, who had been working on the Guides since 1954, became house editor, revising and compiling several of the books himself.

The Blue Guides are now published by A & C Black, who acquired Ernest Benn in 1984, so continuing the tradition of guide-book publishing which began in 1826 with 'Black's Economical Tourist of Scotland'. The Blue Guide series continues to grow: there are now more than 30 titles in print with revised editions appearing regularly and many new Blue Guides in preparation.

'Blue Guides' is a registered trademark.

CONTENTS

MAPS AND PLANS

TOWN PLANS

GROUND AND SITE PLANS

EXPLANATIONS

Smaller type is used for sub-routes and excursions, for historical and preliminary paragraphs, and (generally speaking) for descriptions of greater detail or minor importance.

Asterisks indicate points of special interest or excellence.

Distances, total and intermediate, are measured in kilometres, and total route distances are also given in miles. Road distances along the routes themselves record the approx. distance between the towns and villages, etc., described, but it should be noted that with the realignment of many roads it is almost certain that these distances will vary slightly from those measured by motorists on their milometers. Measurements of buildings are given in metres (m). **Altitudes** are likewise expressed in metres.

Place-names, and anglicisations. Most place names and personal names have been given their Portuguese form, except in a few cases where the English form is much more familiar, such as *Lisbon* (Lisboa); *Oporto* (Porto); *Braganza* (Bragança); *Busaco* (Buçaco); and the river *Tagus* (Tejo), etc. When the place itself is being described, the Portuguese is given in brackets, as above. Likewise, certain names of persons have been given their English equivalent, such as Henry the Navigator, for instance, rather than Henrique, and Camoens rather than Camões. Some other names are not always obvious, for example: Duarte (Edward), and João (John). Note that Arthur Wellesley is called Wellington throughout, although he did not receive his title until after the Battle of Talavera (1809).

The **Population** figures printed in this Guide, based on those of the last census (1981), are given in round figures, and should be sufficient to give an idea of the likely amenities of a town. Figures are not usually given for towns and villages with fewer than 10,000 inhabitants.

Abbreviations. In addition to generally accepted and self-explanatory abbreviations, the following occur in the guide:

C = Century
N.S. = *Nossa Senhora*, Our Lady
PT = *Posto de Turismo*, Tourist Office
Rte = Route
Note that *Esq.* is left in Portuguese and *Dto.* is right.

INTRODUCTION TO THE HISTORY OF PORTUGAL

By *Richard Robinson*

Portugal emerged as an independent kingdom in the 12C, and its frontiers were established in the following century, so that the country can properly boast of being one of the oldest countries in Europe. The history of this territory before that period is open to much conjecture, while its prehistory is likewise largely speculative.

The Romans, and before. Traces of habitation in the W and SW of the Iberian peninsula date back to Palaeolithic times. After the last glaciation the area would seem to have been host to primitive shell-gathering folk (c 7000 BC), but settled communities only developed in Neolithic times. Evidence remains of a dolmen culture, most prevalent in coastal districts, in the 2nd millennium BC. Especially in the N, this megalithic culture was succeeded by a *castro* culture, apparently originating in Neolithic times, but surviving through to the Roman era.

Based on fortified hill-top settlements, some of which appear to have fought shy of the Copper Age and the Bronze Age, this culture would seem to have merged during the Iron Age with that of *Celtic* invaders (c 700–600 BC). An excellent example survives in the *citânia* of *Briteiros* (in the Minho), although from the evidence of place-names it is suggested that Celtic settlements extended much further S. In the far S there were settlements, possibly from Africa, by people known as *'Iberians'*, who founded *Tharsis*. The relationship of these people, as indeed that of the Celts or the *Ligurians*, to the warrior tribe of the *Lusitani*, based between the Tagus and Douro, is obscure. Like the *Bracari*, living N of the Douro, they were probably Celts. In the earlier part of the 1st millennium BC *Phoenicians* were active as traders, setting up coastal stations in the S and exploiting the metals mined inland. They were joined by *Greek* traders in the 6C BC, but from c 535 the *Carthaginians* held sway, possibly recruiting mercenaries here in the 3C during their wars with Rome.

The peninsula as a whole passed from Carthaginian to *Roman* domination as a result of the Second Punic War (218–202 BC). What was later to become Portugal formed part of their province of HISPANIA ULTERIOR, but it took some time for the Romans to overcome resistance. A general rising of the Lusitani in 154 BC led to massacres, and a prolonged guerrilla war in which the Lusitanian leader *Viriatus* was assassinated by three of his followers who had been bribed by the Romans (139 BC). The Consul *Decimus Junius Brutus* then set up a 'capital' at *Olisipo* (Lisbon), and embarked on a campaign to pacify the N.

Lisbon was likewise *Julius Caesar's* capital in 60 BC, and it was he who was really responsible for incorporating the area into the Empire. Colonists were settled at *Scallabis* (Santarém), and *Pax Julia* (Beja) was founded. Other major centres were *Ebora* (Évora), *Myrtilis* (Mértola), and *Bracara Augusta* (Braga). Pacification was not entirely achieved until 19 BC, by which time Hispania Ulterior had already been divided by *Augustus* (27 BC) into *Baetica* (Andalucía) and *Lusitania* (covering the territory of future Portugal S of the Douro, and Spanish Extremadura), with its capital at *Emerita Augusta* (Mérida). The area between the Douro and the Minho became the *conventus bracarum* of the province of *Tarraconensis* (created in 2 BC), which in the 3C was to be combined with the NW corner of the peninsula to form the new province of *Gallaecia*. Although the boundaries of the provinces had little similarity with the frontiers of what was to become Portugal, the area covered by four of the lesser administrative units (*conventus*) largely conformed to its future extension.

While the effects of Roman rule over this area should not be overestimated, nearly four centuries of their presence left a most important legacy: their language (modern Portuguese being derived from Latin); their traditions of urban civilisation; a network of main roads; precedents for the exploitation of minerals; a legal system; and the establishment of farms on a large scale (*latifundia*) in the S. Evidence of their occupation can be seen at *Conímbriga*, *Évora*, *Miróbriga* (Santiago do Caćem), and elsewhere.

The last century of Roman rule saw the establishment of bishoprics at Braga, Évora, Faro, and Lisbon (the last three dependent on the see of Mérida); and also the appearance of the Arian and Priscillian heresies.

Suevi, Visigoths, and Moors. With the demise of the Empire, the Peninsula was invaded after 409 by four groups of 'barbarians', all from beyond the Pyrenees. The *Vandals* settled in N Gallaecia, and Baetica; the *Alans* occupied Lusitania, later (in 429) moving across to Africa on the arrival of the Arian Christian *Visigoths*, who c 415 had entered as agents of the Romans. The other group, who remained in the Peninsula, were the *Suevi* (or Swabians), who c 411 had settled between the Minho and Douro, as confirmed by the evidence of place-names. Strongest in the countryside, the Suevi co-existed and eventually merged with the urban Hispano-Romans, notably in Braga and *Portucale* (Oporto). *Rechiarus*, their king (448–57), although converted to Christianity, was attacked and killed by the Arian Visigoths. The Suevi were reconverted by *St. Martin of Dume* after 550, but their kingdom was suppressed by the Visigothic king *Leovigild* in 585, whose successor, *Recared*, was converted to Catholicism. What happened then is unclear, as with most things concerning the Suevi.

Nevertheless, the unstable elective monarchy of the Visigoths went unchallenged until internal disputes led to the invitation into the Peninsula of Muslim forces from Africa, commanded by *Tarik* (Tariq ibn Ziyād; 711). They advanced rapidly, probably occupying the S half of the country up to the Mondego by 714/16. Settlement followed c 750, with Egyptians in the Beja-Faro region and Syrians between Faro and Seville, jointly known as *al-Gharb al-Andalus*, the W part of Muslim Andalucía, from which it became autonomous after a rebellion in the 9C. This area S of the Douro was relatively prosperous under the Muslims, but that to the N, being a battle zone, suffered depopulation.

The Moors introduced new forms of irrigation; rice-fields and fruit-farms were established in the *Algarve* (al-Gharb); mineral resources were exploited; handicrafts flourished. And the land, although theoretically owned by the State, or by mosques, continued to be worked by Christian smallholding peasants paying rent to urban landlords, who were in turn taxed by the State. These subject Christians (known as *Mozárabs*), together with the Jews, lived in semi-autonomous quarters, and in comparative tranquillity, at least until c 1099, when a further wave of Muslims, the *Almoravids* (who had landed in the Peninsula from N Africa in 1086) reached the Algarve, to be followed in 1146 by the more fanatical *Almohads*. Meanwhile the Muslims were faced by Christian incursions from the N, before which a proportion of the upper and middle class fled;

others were enslaved or were obliged to congregate in Moorish quarters, or *mourarias*, where they could be more easily taxed. During the next three centuries they were absorbed, but in turn left a legacy of some hundreds of Arabic words to enrich the language.

Reconquest, and the emergence of Portugal. The Christian reconquest may be said to have commenced in 718 with *Pelayo's* symbolic 'victory' over a small force of Moors at Covadonga, in the Asturias. During the next 150 years the kings of Asturias-León made further incursions into Gallaecia (Galicia) and the 'land of Portucale' between the Minho and the Douro. Oporto fell to them in 868. By the 11C *Portucale* had become established as a county in its own right, although those who ruled it were dependent on Asturias-León. In 1050 *Fernando I* of Castile (1036–65, who had become king of León in 1037) commenced the consolidation of his empire. An incipient 'dynasty' of Portucale was ousted, and in 1064 Coimbra was put under the control of *Davidiz*, a Mozárab.

In 1065 *Alfonso VI* succeeded his father, Fernando; by 1073 he was also king of Castile, Galicia, and Portugal. Among foreign crusaders who answered his call for support after his defeat by the Almoravids in 1086, was *Raymond of Burgundy*, who later married Alfonso's daughter *Urraca*. By 1095 Raymond was also lord of Galicia and count of Coimbra. In 1097, *Henry*, Raymond's cousin, was given the County of Portucale, and Coimbra, as *tenente* (feudal possessor).

On the death of Alfonso, a war of succession broke out. Galicia went to Urraca and her son *Alfonso Raimúndez* (later Alfonso VII). Henry of Burgundy retained Portugal until his death (1112/14), when his wife *Teresa* (illegitimate daughter of Alfonso VI) became 'regent' for their son, *Afonso Henriques*. Teresa fell out with local barons and veered towards subjection to Galicia, which since 1126 had been ruled by *Alfonso VII*. Young Afonso was more independent, and in 1128, at the battle of *São Mamede*, near his capital, Guimarães, he defeated his mother's faction. By 1137 his authority in the Minho was recognised by Alfonso VII (*Pact of Túy*), although Afonso Henriques acknowledged his vassalage; and in 1143 this was confirmed by the *Treaty of Zamora*, in which Alfonso recognised Afonso Henriques title as *rex* (king) of Portugal.

Complete independence came with the break-up of León-Castile at Alfonso's death, and this was formally recognised by Pope Alexander III in 1179 (on payment of an increased tribute). Afonso Henriques was also supported by *João Peculiar*, Archbishop of Braga, whose right to a diocese independent of Toledo and Santiago de Compostela had been won by his predecessor, *St. Gerald of Moissac*.

In Portugal, the Reconquest took a century and a half to complete, far faster than in the rest of the Peninsula. Santarém and Lisbon had been first captured in the 11C, but the Christians had been pushed back to the Mondego by the Almoravids; and the pattern of advances followed by reverses repeated itself during the reign of Afonso Henriques, who in 1139 inflicted a decisive defeat on the Moors at *Ourique* during one of his periodic raids. Santarém was retaken in 1147, while Lisbon likewise fell to him with the assistance of crusaders from northern Europe en route via Dartmouth to the Holy Land. *Gilbert of Hastings* was the first bishop of Lisbon, but dependent on Braga. *Alcácer do Sal* was captured in 1158, and in 1162 and 1165 both Beja and Évora were seized by *Fernão Gonçalves* and *Gerald the Fearless* (sem Pavor); but in 1171 the Almohads pushed the Christians back to Santarém.

The Western Algarve was invaded by *Sancho I* (1185–1211), who captured the Moorish capital at Silves in 1189 with the help of another contingent of passing crusaders, but all this territory S of the Tagus, except for Évora, was lost to him during *al-Mansur*'s campaign the following year. *Afonso II* (1211–23) recaptured Setúbal and Alcácer do Sal, likewise with the assistance of crusaders, while during the anarchic reign of *Sancho II* (1223–48) the Alentejo and E Algarve were incorporated into the expanding kingdom. *Afonso III* (1248–79) moved the capital from Coimbra to Lisbon, and occupied Faro and the W Algarve in 1249. Definitive recognition by Castile of the frontiers of the Portuguese kingdom was endorsed by the *Treaty of Alcañices* in 1297.

Political and Social Organisation. The new kingdom had a population estimated at 400,000, with the N half of the country much more heavily populated than the reconquered area. Internal colonisation followed in the wake of the reconquest. Communities were planted in Trás-os-Montes and Beira, and much land S of the Tagus passed into the hands of the military orders, the *Templars*, and the *Hospitallers* (from c 1128), and from the 1170s into those of *Santiago* and *Calatrava*. The religious orders also played an important part. The *Cistercians* were given land at Alcobaça in 1153, and did much to develop the area immediately to the S. By 1263 the Algarve was settled, and the towns of Covilhã, Guarda, and Idanha were founded to guard the frontier with León; while stock-rearing, the cultivation of olives and vines, and the growing of cereal crops took the place of more belligerent activities.

The kings of the Burgundian line, advised by rudimentary royal councils, began to consult the opinion of assembled nobles and clergy, the first of such *cortes* being held at Coimbra in 1211. Municipal representation was conceded at the cortes of Leiria (1254), called to agree to an increase in taxation and to a devaluation of the coinage. Royal power was only theoretically limited by the Cortes, which was summoned more frequently in times of financial stringency. Although a free peasantry was the dominant characteristic of society, the rights of subjects, particularly those in the towns, were defined by the king in a charter or *foral* (Pl. *forais*). Moors were still segregated in their *mourarias*, and Jews in their *judarias*, which were both under royal jurisdiction.

The next most powerful body in the emergent country was the Church. The clergy, who were extremely wealthy, were at first dominant in the society of orders, and were in theory immune from taxation; they collected their own 'tenths' (*dízimos*), and from 1210 held their own courts. The king appointed bishops and abbots, and could prevent Papal decisions being applied in his realm. There were constant disputes over the extent of jurisdictions, and the king inhibited the acquisition of property by ecclesiastics and nobles by instituting periodic inquiries (*inquirições*), which might result either in confiscations or in the reconfirmation of title. The concordat of 1289 settled most outstanding conflicts, and to the king's advantage.

Lay society was controlled by about one hundred *ricos homens*, an aristocratic warrior class possessing estates, dependents, and jurisdictions. Then came perhaps one thousand *infanções*, or lesser nobles (without jurisdictions), apart from more numerous *fidalgos*, men-at-arms attached to the king or to nobles. Among the Commons (or 'third estate'), free peasants predominated. The better-off (*homens bons*) represented the municipalities (*concelhos*) at the cortes, whose power grew with the growth of the economy, and provided the villein-knights (*cavalheiros vilãos*), who defended the newly-established frontier. Although juridically free, many peasants were tied to their lord's demesne or were long-term tenants. The need to repopulate the S blurred existing distinctions between Christian serfs and free settlers, and serfdom would seem to have disappeared by the 13C, except for numbers of Moorish slaves.

Apogee and Decline of the Afonsin Dynasty. First among the last four Burgundian kings to perfect the administrative system, to boost agriculture and trade, and generally to consolidate Portuguese independence, was *Dinis* (1279–1325), by then ruling over about one million subjects. The judicial systems, both lay and ecclesiastical, were brought under royal control; silver-mines, and those of tin, sulphur, and iron, were exploited; and his progressive afforestation schemes won him the nickname of 'El-Rei lavrador', the Husbandman King. He also cultivated music and poetry. The military orders were 'nationalised'. The Templars, suppressed by the Papacy in 1312, were re-founded as the *Order of Christ* in 1319. Fifty forts were built along the frontier. The promotion of 'free fairs' encouraged internal trade, while Portugal's geographical position made her an ideal intermediary between the maritime powers of northern Europe and the Mediterranean. Both Lisbon (provided with a university in 1290, but transferred to Coimbra in 1308) and Oporto flourished.

The country was ravaged by the 'Black Death' during the reign of *Afonso IV* (1325–57), which decimated the population in 1348–49. In 1355 took place the murder of *Inês de Castro* (the Galician mistress of the Infante Pedro), whose family was suspected of furthering Castilian interests.

Pedro I's reign (1357–67) saw further centralisation of the judicial system; by now Portuguese was the language of the law and administration. His successor, *Fernando* (1367–83), while continuing to encourage maritime trade, attempted to combat the growing agricultural crisis, accelerated if not caused by the Black Death, for the demand for labour in the cities had attracted the peasantry away from the land and led to food shortages by the 1370s. The *Law of the Sesmarias* (1375) was accordingly promulgated, which sought to bring more land under cultivation and to control the movement of labour. Portugal had become involved in the Hundred Years' War. Castilian legitimists assumed that Fernando would succeed to the Castilian throne on the death of *Pedro the Cruel*, but in the event it was seized by *Enrique de Trastámara* (*Enrique II*), who invaded Portugal and in February 1373 sacked Lisbon. Portugal was at this time allied with *John of Gaunt, Duke of Lancaster*, who also claimed the Castilian throne (for both he and *Edmund, Earl of Cambridge*, had married daughters of Pedro the Cruel).

Partly owing to the failure of the English to send troops, Fernando was obliged to make peace with Castile at the *Treaty of Santarém* (March 1373), ostensibly switching his allegiance to Enrique, although he remained in touch with John of Gaunt. On Enrique's death in 1379, Fernando started parallel negotiations, promising *Beatriz* (or *Brites*), his ten-year-old heiress, to *Edward*, six-year-old son of Edmund of Cambridge, at the same time suggesting that she might marry the infant son of *Juan I*, Enrique's successor. Edmund of Cambridge arrived at Lisbon in June 1381 with 3000 men to assist in the planned attack on Juan.

Edward was betrothed to Beatriz. But the troops were not supplied with the promised mounts and the campaign collapsed. Edmund and his son returned to England late in 1382. Meanwhile Fernando, disappointed and much debilitated, and by now under the thumb of his wife *Leonor Teles de Meneses* (who had taken as her lover a Galician knight, *Juan Fernández Andeiro*, Count of Ourém), continued to play a double game. Beatriz was now to marry Juan I himself, who had recently become a widower. Portugal would be governed by a council of regency until any child of the marriage was old enough to succeed, while should they remain childless, the Castilian king would guarantee the autonomy of Portugal. Beatriz left for Castile in May 1383 and in October Fernando died, aged 38. Leonor Teles, his unpopular widow, attempted to govern the country with Andeiro, but some six weeks later her lover was assassinated by *João*, an illegitimate son of Pedro I.

João, who was also Grand Master of the *Order of Avis* (formerly Calatrava), became regent; Leonor, although she had the backing of the majority of the nobility and bishops (but not the archbishop) being driven out by a revolt of the mercantile and lower orders of Lisbon. João rewarded the citizens by allowing representatives of their guilds to form a committee—later known as the *House of the 24*—to share in the administration of the capital.

In the face of another Castilian invasion, Portugal again sought English aid in her defence. Another siege of Lisbon was only raised by plague spreading through the invader's ranks. In the countryside a sense of national independence was intensified by grievances against the pro-Castilian nobles who had acquired crown lands in previous decades. Few of the latter were to survive the decisive battle fought near *Aljubarrota* on 14 August 1385, when *Nun'Álvares Pereira*, the 'Holy Constable', aided by some English archers, defeated the army of Juan of Castile. João of Avis was shortly after crowned at Coimbra, the first ruler of the new dynasty.

The Duke of Lancaster dining with Dom João I

The House of Avis. The revolution of 1383 led to the replacement of the old nobility by a new landed aristocracy dependent on *João I* (1385–1433), a change of personnel rather than a social revolution. Mutual interest led to the signing of the *Treaty of Windsor* in 1386, formally confirming the *Anglo-Portuguese Alliance* of 1373, which was still being invoked in the 20C.

Part of the Treaty of 1386 read: 'There shall be inviolate and endure forever between the above Kings now reigning and their heirs and successors, and between the subjects of both kingdoms a solid, perpetual and real League, Amity, Confederacy and Union, not only on behalf of themselves and their Heirs and Successors, their Subjects, Vassals, Allies and Friends whatsoever, so that either of them shall be bound to succour and afford aid to the other against all men that may live and those who shall attempt to violate the Peace of the other, or injure his state in any way'. The substance of this article has been re-affirmed in a number of Anglo-Portuguese treaties during the intervening six centuries.

João married *Philippa of Lancaster*, daughter of John of Gaunt, Duke of Lancaster, in 1387. The struggle against Castile continued until 1411, after which João kept some of his closer supporters happy by adopting an aggressive policy in Morocco, and Ceuta was taken in 1415. His successor *Duarte* (Edward; 1433–38), hoping to capture Tangier in 1437, met with disaster.

An attempt by Duarte to revoke some titles to land, promulgated by the *Lei Mental* of 1434 (decreeing that in the absence of a son to inherit, estates would revert to the crown) not unnaturally brought about a reaction from the nobility, which continued during the minority of *Afonso V* (1438–81). In 1440 the *Duke of Coimbra*, associated with the 'peace party', seized the Regency from Afonso's mother, *Eleanor of Aragón*, to the chagrin of the Duke of Braganza's party, who sought to undermine royal power. Afonso, however, supported the Braganza faction, and the Duke of Coimbra was killed at the internecine battle of *Alfarrobeira* in 1449.

Although there had been some unification of legal codes during Afonso's minority, the young king was more concerned with martial glory to be gained by crusading in N Africa. In 1471 Tangier was eventually taken. On the death of his Castilian brother-in-law *Enrique IV* in 1474, Afonso supported *Juana* (Enrique's daughter, whom he hoped to marry), in her claim to the throne, but, defeated at *Castro Queimado* and failing to enlist French support, Afonso had to concede to the Catholic Kings his own pretentions to the Canary Islands at the peace treaty of *Alcáçovas* (1479).

The Making of the Maritime Empire. In the 15C Portugal was in the vanguard of European overseas exploration and expansion, although it had little naval or ocean-going tradition, even if Dom Dinis had employed a Genoese admiral to found a navy, and his successor Afonso IV had encouraged non-Portuguese voyages to the Canaries. The activities of *Prince Henry* (a younger son of João and Philippa), administrator of the property of the Order of Christ, and known to history as '*the Navigator*' (although he never ventured beyond Tangier in person), were an extension of his dual concern with crusading and profit. In the wake of the capture of Ceuta, he built up at Lagos an international team of pilots, cartographers, and astronomers, etc. The motives of Henry and subsequent expansionists were mixed: was it to spread the Faith; to outflank Islam in Morocco; to become purveyors of gold, spices and slaves (long the role of the

Infidel); to win renown by the conquest of more territory; or mere curiosity?

The 'adjacent islands' of *Madeira* and the *Azores* were discovered (or re-discovered) in 1419 and 1427 respectively, and both were subsequently colonised. The psychological barrier represented by *Cape Bojador* was rounded in 1434, and a trading-post set up at *Arguim* in the 1440s became a prime source of slaves. The *Cape Verde Islands*, later colonised by the Order of Christ, were discovered c 1457, while *Sierra Leone* had been reached by Henry's death in 1460. There followed a significant lull in the process of exploration until the reign of *João II* (1481–95). That maritime enterprise paid off was strikingly confirmed when the Crown's revenue doubled with the establishment of *São Jorge da Mina* (1482), source of Sudanese gold. In 1487 *Bartolomeu Dias* rounded the *Cape of Good Hope*. After Papal arbitration, Spain and Portugal divided the world at the *Treaty of Tordesillas* (1494) at a line 370 leagues W of the Cape Verdes.

Manuel I (1495–1521) and *João III* (1521–57) promoted such expansion as part of a royal enterprise, the Crown taking its 'royal fifth' of the trading profits, which made Manuel for a time the richest ruler in Europe. *Vasco da Gama* opened the sea route to *India* in 1497–98; *Newfoundland, Greenland* and *Labrador* were reached and *Brazil* discovered in 1500, although the exploration of Brazilian resources hardly started until the second half of the 16C, its sugar plantations stimulating the S Atlantic slave trade and leading to the foundation of *Luanda* in 1575. Morocco was not forgotten—Dom Manuel campaigned there in 1513–15, and João III continued to hold Tangier, Ceuta and *Mazagan*—but the main target was Asia. By 1513 the Portuguese had reached *Timor* and *China*, and sailed on to *Japan* in the 1540s.

It was the monopoly of maritime trade which was now their primary concern, and the Asian empire therefore depended on the founding of key trading-posts (from which missionaries could also operate) and strategically placed forts. *Goa* grew in importance from 1510; *Malacca* was occupied in 1511, and *Ormuz* in 1515. A trading-post was set up at *Macau* in 1557.

Yet the growth of this impressive maritime empire did not in fact improve economic conditions at home, for the profits of trade got no further than the royal household, some of the quiescent nobility, and a few foreign merchants. What was essentially a royal project did not lead to the emergence of an entrepreneurial class, as had happened in N European countries. But although overseas trade was estimated to constitute two-thirds of Portuguese revenue in the 16C, the cost was such that even the Crown fell into debt. Falling prices in Europe brought about a deficit in the spice and allied trades from the 1520s, and the royal trading monopoly, the *Casa da Índia*, was bankrupt by 1560; more and more of the proceeds of empire went to pay foreign debts. By the 1570s the picture was one of exhaustion. Although agricultural production had picked up after 1450, by the 1540s shortages of meat and cereals were again experienced, partially as a result of the continuing drift to the cities. Despite the essentially commercial nature of the empire, the heavy drain on population and the high cost of the material upkeep of its fleets were among its negative consequences.

The Decline of the House of Avis. When 'the perfect prince', João II, ascended the throne, he set about reversing his predecessor's profligacy in granting land to the nobility. In 1483 the *Duke of Braganza*, head of a family whose estates covered a third of the kingdom, was executed, and his possessions seized by the Crown. In the following year the queen's brother, the *Duke of Viseu*, was also eliminated. The nobility remained submissive as royal power thus asserted became more centralised and bureaucratic. João II turned the complaints of the commons with regard to Jews against the nobles in the cortes, but the nobility were not arraigned there by the king; and under *Dom Manuel, 'the Fortunate'* both cortes and nobility were eclipsed. The taxation of the *concelhos* was regulated and the *forais* reformed, while the exercise of justice was brought completely under royal control. In 1521 the promulgation of a legal code, the *Ordenações manuelinas*, brought all separate jurisdictions to an end. Royal patronage of the *misericórdias* (charitable institutions ministering to the sick and the needy) encouraged their spread both at home and overseas during the 16C.

In the Middle Ages Portugal's treatment of its Jewish minority was, by international standards, lenient, but by 1490 popular resentment of their tax-gathering and money-lending activities was being voiced in the cortes. When the Catholic Kings expelled the Spanish Jews in 1492 some 60,000 of them took refuge in Portugal, but four years later Dom Manuel also decreed their expulsion. Although a minority left for the Netherlands, most of them ostensibly submitted to baptism as 'New Christians'. Anti-Jewish rioting in Lisbon in 1504 was followed by a pogrom in 1506. Although Dom Manuel had given the forcibly converted a 20-year period of grace before investigating their religious convictions, it was not until 1531, prompted by the threat of the Protestant Reformation, that João III personally introduced the Inquisition into Portugal, encouraged, it is said, by his younger brother, the Cardinal-infant Dom Afonso. This was established with Papal permission in 1536, but was not properly organised until 1547, and then was as much an instrument to control the growing middle classes (particularly those intermarried with 'New Christians') as a tool for rooting out heresy. Of 24,522 people investigated over the next two centuries, 1454 were condemned to death; others suffered lesser fates.

The late 15th and 16C witnessed a flowering of the arts and literature under the centralised monarchy. Printing was introduced c 1487, and there were many contacts with the humanism of the Renaissance. Portugal escaped the Reformation, but not the Counter-Reformation. From the 1560s the control of education passed into the hands of the Jesuits. A number of colleges were founded in the 1530s and 1540s, and in 1537 the University was reorganised at Coimbra. This was the epoch of the dramatist *Gil Vicente*, while in 1572 *Luís de Camões* published his national epic, 'The Lusiads'. The arts and 'Manueline' architecture of this period are described in the following article.

The reign of *Dom Sebastião* (1557–78) saw a disastrous reversion to the crusading ideals of Afonso V. Morocco was the obsession of this unstable, chivalric dreamer, who came of age in 1568. Sensing his opportunity when the succession to the sultanate of Fez was in dispute, he raised a force of 18,000 (including a contingent commanded by Sir Thomas Stukely), and in 1578 set sail from the Algarve with high expectation. Sebastião himself was killed, and his army decisively defeated by a superior force at *Alcácer-Quibir* (al-Qasr al-Kabir), some 8000 Portuguese, including the flower of the nobility, being left on the field. Only 100 or so escaped capture.

The raising of ruinous ransoms for the rest was the primary preoccupation of Cardinal Henrique, Sebastião's elderly great-uncle.

Habsburg Domination. The succession to the childless *Cardinal-king Henrique* (1578–80) was disputed, and *António, Prior of Crato*, a royal bastard, had himself proclaimed king, but he failed to emulate the precedent of 1383. A Spanish army under the *3rd Duke of Alba*, supporting the claim of Sebastião's uncle, Philip (Felipe)II of Spain, defeated the prior's troops at *Alcântara*, and in 1581 the Cortes at Tomar proclaimed the Habsburg king as *Felipe I* (1581–98). Although the Crowns were thus united, Portuguese autonomy was to be 'respected'.

An attempt by the Prior of Crato to regain the throne in 1589 with the support of *Drake* (taking his revenge for the 'Armada' of the previous year, a proportion of which had set sail from Lisbon), was unsuccessful. Felipe suppressed the challenges of various 'false Sebastians' who presented themselves. (There was a popular messianic belief that Dom Sebastião was still alive, and would on his return inaugurate a 'fifth empire' of Portuguese dominance, there being some confusion with earlier prophecies with regard to the advent of a *rei encoberto* or 'hidden king'.)

The union with Spain brought some short-term advantages. Spanish wheat made up for Portugal's deficiency, and Portugal found a protector for her vulnerable empire, while Habsburg generosity in granting titles benefited those few who could afford them. But the Spaniards were unpopular with the lower orders, who blamed them for the country's decline. The closure of Lisbon to Philip's Dutch rebels was held responsible for Dutch attacks in the East, but the defence of their maritime empire was by the 17C beyond the capacity of the Portuguese alone. During the 'Spanish captivity' Ormuz was lost to the English (1622), while the Dutch invaded both Ceylon, and African territories. After the return to independence, *Salvador de Sá* chased the Dutch from Luanda and São Tomé (1648), and although Brazil was recovered by 1652, the Asian empire continued to shrink: the Dutch took Malacca in 1641, and Ceylon in the 1650s.

Although Felipe I carried out certain administrative reforms, he respected Portuguese autonomy, but his successor, *Felipe II* (III of Spain; 1598–1621) violated these undertakings by appointing Spaniards to the Council of Portugal in Madrid. Nevertheless, the Cortes gave him a tolerably warm welcome in 1619, and agreed that his son should succeed, but under *Felipe III* (IV of Spain; 1621–40) the erosion of Portuguese autonomy continued. During the Thirty Years' War Spain's lack of men and money led to increasing centralisation under the *Count-Duke of Olivares*, which provoked discontent in Portugal and elsewhere, even if the need for cash necessitated a more lenient attitude towards the 'New Christians'.

Hispanicisation of the élite; the absorption of the army and navy into the Spanish forces; increased taxation: all lent force to the latent spirit of independence in Portugal. Popular disturbances occurred at Évora in 1637, while in June 1640 Catalonia revolted. Olivares attempted to use Portuguese resources to crush this rising, which partially provoked the coup of 1 December 1640 in Lisbon. The *Duchess of Mantua*, the governor, was overthrown, and *Miguel de Vasconcelos*, her strongman, was defenestrated. The nobility, officeholders, and the clergy, were divided in their loyalties, but with popular support the movement for independence succeeded under the leadership of the reluctant but powerful Duke of Braganza, grandson of a female claimant of 1580, who became *João IV* (1640–56).

Restoration. The continuing revolt of the Catalans enabled the Portuguese to consolidate their newly won independence, and in the context of the Thirty Years' War Spain was also preoccupied with France until the Treaty of the Pyrenees in 1659. Meanwhile the English had renewed their old alliance with Portugal regardless of changes of regime: to the pledges of Charles I (1642) and Oliver Cromwell (1654) was added the Treaty of 1661, by which *Charles II* married *Catherine of Braganza* and Portugal ceded Tangier and Bombay. In 1659 Spain attacked and captured Elvas, but the Portuguese army, reorganised by the *Duke of Schomberg*, with a modest English contingent, won the battles of *Ameixial, Castelo Rodrigo* and *Montes Claros* (1663–65). In 1668 Spain, while retaining Ceuta, recognised Portuguese independence at the *Treaty of Lisbon* and the Papacy followed the Spanish lead.

Internally, João IV endeavoured to create a centralised and bureaucratic administration run by secretaries of state. The demands of war had enabled him to force the Cortes to agree to a high level of taxation and to provide a defence levy, while the 'New Christians' and others were won over by the return of property confiscated by the Inquisition. His allies among the nobility were rewarded with lands, and some gained considerable power, which they attempted to consolidate during the confused reign of the paralytic *Afonso VI* (1656–83). In 1667 the king's brother, *Pedro*, was persuaded by the Queen-mother and the French to oust the Regent, *Castelo Melhor*. Pedro ruled as Prince Regent, marrying his brother's former wife, *Maria-Francesca d'Aumale*, her marriage having been formally annulled. From 1683 to 1706 he ruled as *Pedro II*, during which years royal authority was strengthened. Portugal was reconciled with the Papacy, and little recourse was had to the Cortes, summoned for the last time in 1697. For more than a century the Crown was financially independent of that body.

The Age of Mercantilism. Pedro II's most notable appointment was that of the *3rd Conde de Ericeira* to the post of Superintendent of Finance in 1675. For the next 15 years, until his suicide in 1690, this exponent of mercantilist ideas did much to improve the country's prosperity, by boosting exports and restricting the importation of luxury goods. Her commerce prospered, being protected by tariffs, ranging from the textiles of Covilhã, Portalegre and Fundão to the production of hats and glass. But after his death the economy again deteriorated.

With a view to balancing trade as Brazilian sugar lost its markets, the famous *Methuen Treaty* of December 1703 was signed (called after its negotiator, *John Methuen*), not to be confused with the *Anglo-Portuguese Treaty* of May 1703 (signed by his son *Sir Paul Methuen*). England admitted Portuguese wines on preferential terms, which benefited Portugal in the short run. In the longer term it stimulated the port-wine trade, but arguably misdirected attention from the necessity of growing more wheat. English textiles were assured of a permanent market in Portugal, but the dominance of English goods, at first imported on the same terms as French and Dutch, was a product of the boom in Anglo-Portuguese trade made possible by the gold of Brazil. English merchants ran the carrying trade, and English competition adversely affected Portuguese industry in coastal areas, although not in the interior. The Methuen Treaty did not in itself prevent industrialisation in Portugal, although coupled with strategic factors it did in the long term increase Portugal's dependence on Britain. The Treaty was not revoked until 1842.

Portugal sided with Britain during the *War of the Spanish Succession* (1702–13) in supporting the Habsburg claimant to the Spanish throne in preference to a Bourbon. A Franco-Spanish invasion was repelled, and an Anglo-Portuguese force commanded by the *Marquês das Minas* entered Spain, even occupying Madrid briefly in the summer of 1706, but they were defeated at *Almansa* in 1707. But with the accession of *João V* (1706–50) the country took little further part in the conflict.

The absolutist monarchy built up by Dom João and his successors was made possible by the exploitation and influx of gold from Brazil, which began in the 1690s and reached its peak c 1740. The Crown's revenue soared as it took its fifth, and every attempt was made to ensure that none was smuggled direct from Brazil to Britain, but as this gold had to pay for foreign imports, it had little direct beneficial effect on the country's economic development. João V's ministers still followed Ericeira's practice in endeavouring to protect national industries, but measures such as the ban on buying foreign silk proved ineffective. Evidence of the 18C gold boom survives in the richly gilded woodwork adorning most Baroque churches, and in the gigantic Germanic palace of Mafra, on whose construction perhaps as many as 50,000 workmen were employed between 1717 and 1735.

Although the devout king had early in his reign sent a fleet to help the Papacy against the Turks, a fleet victorious at the battle of *Matapan* in 1717, the general tendency of policy was towards increasing royal control over ecclesiastical affairs. Dom João favoured clerical reform and was opposed to the ossified educational practices of the long-dominant Jesuits. He therefore determined that the Papacy should agree to all bishops of Lisbon being Cardinal-Patriarchs, and a breach with the Papacy opened in 1728 was only healed in 1748 with Papal compliance to the king's wish. Reconciliation was complete when the Pope conferred on Dom João the title of *El-Rei fidelíssimo* (Most Faithful King). Meanwhile, he had exhibited a desire for cultural improvement by founding the Royal Academy of History in 1720; but the intellectual élite came increasingly under the influence of progressive ideas current in Britain and France, gaining for themselves the nickname *estrangeirados* ('foreignised ones').

Dom João's successor, *Dom José* (1750–77) was more interested in the opera, introduced from Italy in the 1730s, and management of affairs of state was left in the hands of his ruthless minister, *Sebastião José de Carvalho e Melo*, 1st *Marquês de Pombal*, who had been ambassador in London in the 1740s. Pombal's policies were initially pragmatic responses to circumstances. He endeavoured to improve the administration in order to extract the maximum profit from the colonies, and smuggling was inhibited. He created a tax-collecting bureaucracy and, in 1761, the Royal Treasury. State monopoly companies were founded to control the tobacco and port-wine industries, whaling, fishing, and the Asian and Brazil trades. It was the economic depression of the 1760s which prompted a more deliberate strategy for economic development. As Brazilian gold and diamond production declined, Pombal sought to boost agriculture and to build up industry at home, especially in the Lisbon area.

Like his father, Dom José was personally devout, but the *estrangeirado* Pombal went further down the road towards secular autocracy and

Enlightened Despotism. He incurred the hostility of the Jesuits by emancipating their Indian protégés in Brazil, to the advantage of the settlers, while his methods for dealing with any opposition to reform became clear when the anti-monopolistic merchant association of the *Mesa do Bem Comum* was dissolved, and the taverners' (or Tipplers') revolt in Oporto was brutally put down in 1757.

On 1 November 1755 Lisbon was convulsed by an earthquake, in which a large part of the capital collapsed, and perhaps as many as 30–40,000 people died, not only in the earthquake itself but in the epidemics and famine that followed. During and after this calamity Pombal's position of power was supreme. For while Jesuits preached that the tremors represented Divine Judgement on the dictator's wayward policies, this, together with a mysterious attempt on the king's life in 1758, gave the minister an opportunity of neutralising any potential opposition. The Jesuits themselves, together with certain nobles, were held by Pombal to have been responsible for the attempted assassination, and the execution of members of the powerful *Távora* family followed, while *Fr Malagrida*, a leading Jesuit, was burned at the stake. In 1759 the Society of Jesus was dissolved and its members exiled. (In 1773 the Papacy was persuaded to suppress it altogether: at least for some decades.)

The rational principle of uniformity was applied to the juridical sphere. Slavery was abolished in mainland Portugal in 1761; Royal censorship replaced ecclesiastical; the Inquisition became a Department of State; and all distinctions between old and 'New' Christians were abolished. The Papal Nuncio was expelled. This secularisation of the State was accompanied by university reforms, and faculties of science were established. Royal schools were founded along the lines advocated by the exiled Portuguese philosopher *Luís António Verney*, and included one specifically for the nobility. In his authoritarian way, by dragging the country into the century of Enlightenment, Pombal laid the foundation of the modern Portuguese state. He was also responsible for the laying out of the present Baixa quarter of Lisbon, built in a Neo-classical style, and his rational attempts at town-planning can also be seen on a smaller scale at Vila Real de Santo António in the Algarve. Military reforms were also undertaken, supervised by the *Count of Schaumburg-Lippe*, after Portugal had been again invaded following opposition to the Bourbon Family Compact of 1761 during the Seven Years' War (1756–63).

On the succession of *Maria I* (1777–1816), Pombal was immediately dismissed, tried, and confined to his considerable estates. Under this excessively devout queen (who also suffered from melancholia), his religious legislation was repealed, a concordat signed with the Vatican, and censorship again made an ecclesiastical concern. Although some monopoly companies were abolished, Pombal's economic policies were nevertheless implemented. Roads and canals were built, shipbuilding and mineral prospecting were encouraged, the textile industry was modernised, and attempts were made to improve agricultural methods. The Royal Academy of Sciences was established in 1779, as were various technical academies. Full advantage was taken of Portugal's position as a middleman between Brazil (where cotton was replacing gold as a major export) and Britain, with which a trade balance was achieved. Dependence on Britain was offset by diversification of trade, and a trading and diplomatic alliance was entered into with Russia. Portugal seemed at last to be on the road to prosperity when in 1789 Europe was convulsed by the French Revolution.

The Napoleonic Era. The reign of Maria I united material progress with political conservatism. One of her ministers, the Intendant-General of Police, *Pina Manique*, brought security and street-lighting to Lisbon and founded an orphanage. But at the same time he was zealous in persecuting potential subversives, such as Freemasons, particularly after 1789, until to appease the French, he was retired. Fearful that revolution might be contagious and spread to Brazil, Portugal sent troops to fight revolutionary France on the Catalan front (1793), but after 1795 she stood alone with England against the Directory, and in 1801 was invaded by Spain during the so-called *'War of the Oranges'*, being compelled to cede the district around Olivença. Dependent for half her trade on Britain, and on British sea-power to protect her trade routes, more so after *Trafalgar* (1805), Portugal could hardly comply with Napoleon's demands that she close her ports to British shipping; and invasion by the French was the inevitable consequence.

Géneral Junot entered Lisbon in 1807, but the royal family (with João as Prince Regent since 1799) had already embarked for Brazil, where they set up court. The Portuguese invoked the British alliance, and an expeditionary force, at first commanded by *Sir Arthur Wellesley*, later landed near the mouth of the Mondego. In August 1808 the French were defeated at *Roliça* and *Vimeiro*. By the reprehensible *Convention of Cintra*, signed soon after, the French were repatriated (with their booty) in English ships. *Marshal Soult* then invaded the N of Portugal, but on 12 May 1809 was driven out of Oporto by Wellesley, who had returned to Portugal. After his victory at *Talavera* that July, he was known as Viscount *Wellington*. Meanwhile, he had ordered the construction of lines of defence near *Torres Vedras* to protect Lisbon from possible future incursions, and *William Carr Beresford* was organising and imparting discipline to Portuguese forces, who at *Busaco* (27 September 1810) were able to take their place beside Wellington's seasoned troops in inflicting severe losses on the invading army of *Marshal Masséna*. The French settled before the *Lines of Torres Vedras*, until in the following spring they were forced by starvation to retire, when hostilities were carried into Spain (*Fuentes de Oñoro*; May 1811). Portuguese forces continued to be integrated with the British until the end of the Peninsular War. It should be remembered that numerous units of the British army were stationed along the Spanish frontier for several winters, mostly between the Douro and Guadiana.

At the peace settlement, Olivença should have been restored to Portugal, but the decision of the Powers was conveniently forgotten by the Spaniards. The consequences of the French invasion and occupation were very much graver than this slight loss of territory. The process of industrialisation had been interrupted, and the vital links with Brazil (proclaimed a kingdom on equal terms with Portugal in 1815) were fatally weakened, although the court remained in Rio de Janeiro until 1821. Portuguese affairs were left meanwhile in the hands of Marshal Beresford, respected but not popular. Britain had preserved Portuguese independence, but the Anglo-Portuguese treaty of 1810, which allowed Britain to trade freely and directly with Brazil, removed the mainstay of the homeland's economy. The country was deep in debt and trade was bad. From 1808 until 1821 Portugal was in effect a British protectorate and a colony of Brazil.

João VI succeeded his deranged mother on her death in 1816.

Constitutionalism. The growth of liberal ideas was for long associated with those who had served Napoleon. In 1817 a former commander of Napoleon's Portuguese Legion, and a Masonic Grand Master, *Gomes Freire de Andrade*, and 11 accomplices, were executed by Beresford for conspiracy, but this act of repression had little influence on the course of events. The large military establishment had not yet been disbanded and three-quarters of the national revenue was still spent on the army. Even so, officers resented not being paid regularly, and—as is their wont—complained of lack of promotion. In August 1820, while Beresford was visiting Brazil, soldiers in Oporto in touch with the Sinédrio lodge established by the liberal reformer, *Manuel Fernandes Tomás*, 'pronounced' against the government, ushering in 30 years of political turmoil, which did little to help the parlous economic situation.

As with similar risings in Spain, the rebel officers called a constituent *Cortes*, which proceeded to pass reforms, drawing up a constitutional document much influenced by Fernandes Tomás and the Spanish liberal constitution of 1812. Although ostensibly seeking a return to pre-absolutist times, the Constitution of 1822 was based on the ideals of the Enlightenment. Seigneurial rights and the *forais* were abolished, as were clerical privileges and the Inquisition: provisions which offended the Church. Despite a desire to promote agriculture in a climate of free enterprise, corporations and monopoly companies were not dissolved. Administrative and judicial decentralisation was decreed, and a single-chamber parliament instituted. The king, who eventually returned to Portugal in 1821, having been absent for 14 years, accepted the constitution which allowed him to suspend laws but not to dissolve the assembly. This was chosen every two years by an electorate excluding illiterates, women, and the clergy. Attempts by the Constituent Cortes to restrict Brazilian autonomy led to independence being declared by Crown Prince *Pedro* on behalf of the creole élite in 1822, but Portugal only accepted the loss of Brazil in 1825.

In 1823 a rural reaction against liberal constitutionalism began, headed by Pedro's younger brother, *Miguel*, and his mother *Carlota Joaquina* (sister of the Spanish king, Fernando VII). The constitution was suspended, but João VI sent his son Miguel into exile. On João's death in 1826, his son Pedro (constitutional Emperor of Brazil) was appointed king by the Regency Council and, as *Pedro IV*, he promulgated the Royal Charter (1826), the fundamental constitutional text of 19C Portugal—but a less advanced document than the Constitution of 1822—in which a Chamber of Deputies was partly elected on a restricted suffrage and partly nominated; an upper chamber consisted of hereditary peers. Pedro conditionally abdicated in favour of his young daughter, *Maria da Glória*. It was planned that she would marry his brother, Miguel, who was appointed Regent. But immediately on his return from exile, Miguel abolished the constitution and convoked the traditional cortes, and appears to have enjoyed considerable popular support for this move, although only the United States and Mexico recognised him when he proclaimed himself king.

Prior to his return, *Saldanha*, the War Minister, and a grandson of Pombal, had promoted a number of liberal officers, who were to lead military uprisings in Oporto and Coimbra. Saldanha himself, together with the *Duke of Palmela*, went into exile in England. In 1830 Pedro IV was proclaimed Regent in the Azores, and with the backing of English and Spanish liberals, set up a government led by Palmela and *José Xavier Mousinho da Silveira*. Encouraged by France and England, a liberal expedition landed near Oporto in 1832, where it was besieged. The deadlock was only broken when the *Duke of Terceira* landed in the Algarve, under the protection of *Charles Napier's* naval squadron, and marched on Lisbon (1833). Miguel's forces then laid siege to the capital, but were defeated by Terceira and Saldanha and forced to capitulate at *Évora-Monte* in May 1834. Miguel was again exiled, his supporters purged, and a liberal regime imposed on the indifferent population by the *Quadruple Alliance* (Britain, France, and Spanish and Portuguese liberals). During the 1840s liberalism remained dependent for its survival on this foreign support.

The Age of Revolution. Steps were taken to reduce the enormous debts accumulated during the 'War of the Two Brothers' or Miguelite War. Mousinho da Silveira produced another blueprint for the regeneration of Portugal along the lines pioneered by Fernandes Tomás. The adminstrative and judicial systems were reformed on the Napoleonic bureaucratic model; tithes, forais, corporations, and monopoly companies were abolished. *Joaquim António de Aguiar* dissolved the religious orders, removed Miguelite bishops from their posts and seized ecclesiastical property, a move which naturally led to a breach with the Papacy. Most of the seized property was not distributed, but was sold to supporters of Dom Pedro in a desperate attempt to improve Portugal's financial situation. The land was mostly acquired by existing landowners or by commercial bourgeoisie, some of whom were further gratified by receiving titles from the liberals. Thus ended the *ancien régime* in Portugal.

Maria II (1834–53) ascended the throne at the age of fifteen, at the death of her father. The prevailing state of political tension and confusion was exacerbated by her headstrong behaviour and by the poor advice she received, particularly from relations such as Leopold of the Belgians. The liberals soon divided into conservatives and progressives. The more radical of the latter became known as *Septembrists*, named for the revolt of September 1836 in Lisbon by the army and general populace, following the election victory in Oporto of the Passos brothers. Septembrists were mostly artisans and lower middle class, especially in Oporto; they demanded a return to the Constitution of 1822 and favoured protection and reform. *Manuel Passos* established a new educational system, modelled on French examples, and *Sá da Bandeira* took steps to end slavery throughout the Portuguese empire.

The Septembrists survived opposition from Terceira and Saldanha – who had supported the Charter of 1826 – and in 1837 drew up yet another constitution. It was more advanced than that of 1826, but still alienated some Septembrists by not keeping to the principles of the proposals of 1822.

In 1842 the Septembrist Constitution of 1838 was replaced by the Charter of 1826. The *Chartists* (supporters of the Charter of 1826) had come to the fore in the late 1830s under *António Bernardo da Costa Cabral*, an authoritarian ex-Septembrist backed by the queen. He purged the National Guard—a paramilitary citizens' force—of leftists, re-established free trade, resumed relations with the Papacy, and reformed the administrative code, thus fostering a return to prosperity after 1839.

Discontent returned when *Costa Cabral's* sanitary regulations forbidding further burials *in* churches provoked popular reaction in the countryside (the revolt 'of Maria da Fonte'). Economic recession returned, reviving urban discontent, and by 1846 the country was again on the verge of civil war. Radical Septembrists supported the *patuleia* (their popular junta in Oporto) and co-operated with Miguelites against Maria II and the Chartists. Peace was imposed by Anglo-Spanish intervention at the *Convention of Gramido* (1847), but there was still general resentment at the vengeful policies of Costa Cabral, who was returned to power.

An era of relative stability, coinciding with improvements in international economics, began in 1851 when the Duke of Saldanha ousted Costa Cabral, a fellow Chartist but also a personal enemy.

Liberalism. Under Saldanha progressive and conservative liberals reached a new understanding based on the Charter of 1826 and the electoral reform of 1852. These restricted the suffrage to 36,000 electors. Queen Maria was succeeded by *Pedro V* (1853–61), followed by his brother, *Luís* (1861–89), who was a model constitutional monarch. The new political system was operated by an agreed rotation of power between the 'Regenerators' of Saldanha and *Fontes Pereira de Melo*, and the 'Historicals' of the *Duke of Loulé* (heirs of the Septembrists). It functioned smoothly enough until the end of the century, despite another revolt by Saldanha (an advocate of Iberian unity) and the creation of a Reformist party under Sá da Bandeira (who was intent on reducing public expenditure and the bureaucracy).

In 1876 the Reformists joined the Historicals to form the *Progressists*, under *Anselmo José Braamcamp*. Their programme emphasised gradual democratisation, administrative decentralisation and the development of primary education. The Regenerators gave priority to the country's economic development. The latter policies, known as 'Fontismo', were associated with Fontes de Melo, who created the Ministry of Public Works. He was responsible for the building of roads, bridges, and ports; the creation of an electric telegraph network; and for encouraging the construction of railways (the first line, Lisbon—Carregado, was opened in 1856).

The infrastructure of improved communications and the investment of foreign capital allowed a general expansion of the economy from the 1870s. Nevertheless, Portugal lagged behind the rest of western Europe. The growth of her industry was slow. Although interest had been shown in British engines from 1780, steam power was not used until the 1830s. Portuguese private banking developed only in the 1840s, but the State was always saddled with debts, and governments usually failed to balance budgets. An improvement in the balance of payments was largely due to the remittances received from emigrants from the Minho and the islands, who left for Brazil in large numbers from the 1880s. By 1900 a quarter of Portugal's trade and industry was foreign-controlled, and one sixth of industry was foreign-owned, half of this being in British hands.

The population of about three million in 1820 had risen to five million by 1900. The effect of the new industrialisation coincided with a quadrupling of Oporto's population, and a doubling of Lisbon's. In 1822 there were some 15,000 workers in the country; this figure had risen to 200,000 (a quarter of them in textiles) by 1914. Tobacco manufacture and sardine canning also became major industries in the late 19C, but the wine trade suffered from the ravages of phylloxera. Tariffs were raised in 1892, by which time the country was in the midst of a cork boom.

The drift of people from the land to the cities continued. Agriculture showed signs of improvement only towards the end of the century: more potatoes and rice were cultivated; and there was a fall in wheat imports. Agriculture may have also benefited from the eventual abolition of entailed lands (*morgados*) in 1863, the regulation of tenancy laws, and the abolition of primogeniture in the Civil Code of 1867. Under the new laws at least two thirds of an estate had to be divided equally between the heirs. It also permitted civil marriages, and abolished the death penalty for civil crimes.

The 19C also witnessed a certain cultural regeneration, symbolically connected with political regeneration by the appointment to office of *Almeida Garrett*, poet and dramatist, by Saldanha in 1852. Other major Romantics included the novelists *Júlio Dinis* and *Camilo Castelo Branco*, and the historian *Alexandre Herculano*. A reaction set in from c 1865, manifested most obviously in realist novels by *Eça de Queirós*. Noteworthy among his contemporaries were the poets *Cesário Verde* and *Antero de Quental*, and the historian and reformer *Oliveira Martins*.

From Monarchy to Republic. After the loss of Brazil in 1825, the Portuguese empire consisted of a number of islands, enclaves, and coastal settlements: Goa, Macau, part of Timor; and in Africa, the Cape Verde Islands, Guiné, São Tomé and Príncipe, Angola, and Mozambique. From the 1830s Sá da Bandeira was a constant advocate of the development of the African territories, but a revival of interest in imperial affairs only came during the last quarter of the century. This was especially true after 1885, when the international *Conference of Berlin* made effective occupation (rather than historical association) the criterion for ownership in the 'scramble for Africa'. In 1887 the Portuguese announced their intention to bring all the land between the Angolan and Mozambican coasts under their control. This conflicted with British interests, however, by pre-empting British plans to link-up their African possessions from Cairo to the Cape; and the Portuguese government of *Dom Carlos* (1889–1908) was humiliated by being forced to give way to *Lord Salisbury*'s veto of the scheme in 1890. But the scheme did promote the 'pacification' of Angola and Mozambique by a generation of proconsuls such as *António Enes* and *Mousinho de Albuquerque*.

Britain renewed her pledge to defend the integrity of Portuguese possessions in the *Treaty of Windsor* (1899). During the late 19C and early 20C São Tomé became the chief cacao producer, but it was also notorious for the use of contract labour: outsiders considered the practice to be slavery in effect, despite Portugal's formal abolition of slavery throughout her territories in 1869.

Despite the progress described above, the liberal monarchy was in crisis from c 1890. The state was virtually bankrupt, surviving on loans against the tobacco monopoly and on emigrants' remittances. From the 1880s there had been a decline in real wages, causing urban discontent. Industrialisation proceeded without legislation to protect the worker: trade unions were harassed by government and strikes were declared illegal. Socialist theories had begun to enter Portugal from France in the 1850s, but it was not until the 1870s that socialist organisations were founded. These remained small, and they were hopelessly divided into reformist, revolutionary, Marxist, and Anarcho-Syndicalist factions, and therefore did not represent a serious threat to the government.

The real threat to the Monarchist establishment came from *Republicanism*, a radical and nationalist movement of the urban lower-middle class. This movement attacked government for its corruption and inefficiency and held them responsible for the resurgence of clerical influence in society, led by the Jesuits. Troubles began with the Republican military revolt of 31 January 1891 in Oporto, protesting the government's submission to British political pressure. It failed. The crisis reached a head when the system of alternating parties—-allowing bankers, industrialists, traders and landowners to share political power—collapsed during the 1890s.

In rural areas elections were largely controlled by landowners or government officials, despite the extension of the suffrage to 500,000 by 1910. Nevertheless Republicans gained strength in the cities with the growth of popular discontent. Governments vacillated between firm and conciliatory action. While the Regenerators and Progressists fragmented, Liberal-Regenerators, Dissident-Progressists, and Nationalist parties emerged with the new century.

In 1906 Dom Carlos placed the government in the hands of *João Franco*. Franco used dictatorial methods to put the regime back on its feet, but these proved counter-productive, driving more liberals into the Republican camp. The failure of another Republican revolt in January 1908 was followed by the assassination of the King and the Crown Prince on 1 February. Attempts to appease the Republican challenge by the ministers of *Manuel II* (1908–10) also proved futile and the Monarchy was violently overthrown on 5 October 1910 by a combined force of Republican military and naval personnel and by the popular but clandestine Masonic-led organisation known as the Carbonária. Dom Manuel, 'The Unfortunate', went into exile in England, where he died in 1932.

The Republic. The Republicans gained an overwhelming victory in the elections for the Constituent Assembly of 1911. Although they promised universal suffrage, literacy requirements actually reduced the male electorate to less than it had been under the previous regime. There was only minimal popular support for the fallen monarchy during minor monarchist incursions from Spain in 1911–12. The Republicans created a bi-cameral parliament, but did not give the President of the Republic the power of dissolution. It legalised the right to strike, with the result that ensuing strikes alienated the protesting urban and rural workers who were sympathetic to the regime. Parliament also dissolved the Jesuits and passed the *Law of Separation* (1911), dividing Church and State. In effect this was an attempt to put the Catholic church under State control and led to Portugal's second breach with the Papacy as well as widespread passive popular opposition. The introduction of military service was also unpopular, but it was the religious issue which was the key to political alignments. In the absence of social reform (impossible economically) anticlericalism was used as a means to retain popular urban support. *Afonso Costa* became leader of the majority Republican faction, the *Democrats*, largely because of his intransigence on this issue. The less radical minority Republican groups were led by *Brito Camacho* (Unionists), and *A.J. de Almeida* (Evolutionists).

Costa retained control largely by the manipulation of patronage, but the havoc this practice brought to the economy by 1914 ended any hope of financial stability. Discontent among Republicans and non-Republicans, both inside and outside the armed forces, increased. As the President could not dissolve parliament, and the Democratic party machine could win elections by patronage and intimidation, military intervention became the accepted way to change governments. There were 45 such interventions between 1910 and 1926.

In 1915 *General Pimenta de Castro* took power and sought to appease the opposition. He was overthrown by a Democratic revolution within four months. Costa returned to power, but economic conditions worsened and class conflicts became more acute. In 1916 Portugal officially entered the war on the Allied side, although it had been fighting in Africa since 1914. Costa formed a short-lived coalition with Almeida. *Sidónio Pais*, heading another coalition of the discontented, led a coup in December 1917. His 'New Republic', based on a strong presidency and universal male suffrage, was soon opposed by his Unionist and trade union allies and forced to rely increasingly on Monarchist and Catholic goodwill.

Sidónio Pais was assassinated in December 1918. There followed a confused period in which the Monarchist *Admiral Canto e Castro* became President and opposed attempts to restore the Monarchy by force. The Democrats returned in 1919. The years 1919–26 were marked by political instability, inflation and insolvency, and aggravated by the effects of the war, by frequent outbursts of violence, and by military interventions. Workers organised themselves into Anarcho-Syndicalist unions, conservative Republican groups and Monarchists. Members of the officer corps and the hitherto staunchly pro-Democratic urban lower-middle class were utterly weary of politics; while in the universities French anti-Republican theories became fashionable. On 28 May 1926 a bloodless coup was launched in Braga, overthrowing the Democratic government. Power passed first to *Commander Mendes Cabeçadas*, a leader of the revolution of 1910; then to *General Gomes da Costa*, who had commanded troops in Flanders; and finally to *General Óscar Carmona*. These changes reflected divisions within the anti-Democratic coalition. By 1928 Republican institutions were consolidated, following the failure of the Monarchist *General Sinel de Cordes* to improve the financial situation. Carmona then became President.

The New State. In 1928 a new Finance Minister, the Catholic economist *António de Oliveira Salazar*, was given full powers to put the economy in order. He achieved this by balancing the budget, reducing the national debt, reducing the cost of living and stabilising the currency. The prestige he gained by this success enabled him to outmanoeuvre his rivals for power. Carmona appointed him Prime Minister in 1932, a post which he retained until incapacitated by ill health in 1968. In 1933 a new political constitution was published, converting the military dictatorship into the 'New State', an authoritarian, nationalistic, pro-Catholic and corporate Republican regime. Salazar was made constitutionally responsible to the President and other legislation was passed by the National Assembly, advised by a nominated Corporative Chamber. Only members of the 'National Union'—successor to the coalition of conservative forces who supported the 'National Revolution' of 1926—were ever elected to the National Assembly.

Ostensibly a corporate Republic, the country was effectively ruled by the traditional bureaucracy and the police. The National Union was the political association of the regime. It was allied with a 'youth movement' known as the *Mocidade*, and with the Portuguese Legion, a paramilitary body. Workers were organised into national syndicates but these never had the kind of power achieved by the employers' guilds established in the 1950s. Agricultural workers and fishermen each had their own associations, but these were controlled by their employers. Education was nationalistic and Catholic. (The Church had been rehabilitated by the Concordat of 1940 but was ostensibly kept separate from the State.) The police forces had military commanders and a special secret police force, the *Polícia Internacional e de Defesa do Estado* (PIDE) relied on informers and its own sinister methods to break opposition. Although the armed forces were subject to the civilian regime they never in practice gave up the pretension (assumed in the 19C) of having the final word in national affairs.

Conspiracy was not unusual in the armed forces and old-style Republicans attempted to seize power in 1927, 1931, 1946, 1947, 1958–9, 1961, and 1962. A revolutionary general strike was crushed in 1934; and Anarchists failed to assassinate Salazar in 1937. Salazar supported the Nationalist military rising in Spain in 1936 and cultivated close relations with Franco's dictatorial regime.

Portugal remained neutral during the Second World War but was sympathetic to Britain and gave generous credit. The Allies were able to place bases on the Azores in 1943; but it was not until 1944 that Portugal ceased to sell wolfram to Germany.

From the 1940s the clandestine Communist Party led the opposition, which still included old-style Republicans such as *General Humberto Delgado* (who contested the Presidential election of 1958, and was later assassinated). In the 1960s Social Democrats, Christian Democrats and some Monarchists formed the opposition. The Monarchists had hoped that Salazar would restore *Duarte Nuno*, who aspired to the throne after Dom Manuel's death in exile in 1932.

Limited peaceful dissent was permitted during election campaigns but this was not sufficient to justify politically Portugal's membership in the North Atlantic Treaty Organisation, a membership dictated by geo-strategic factors. Censorship was strictly enforced from 1926 to 1974.

The regime followed colonial traditions inherited from the liberal Monarchy and First Republic, although from the 1930s imperial administration was centralised in Lisbon. In 1951 Portugal's colonies (a term adopted in 1911) were re-styled 'Overseas Provinces', but this did nothing to stem the tide of decolonisation: Goa was occupied by India in 1961; local nationalist elements commenced military operations in Angola in 1961, in Guiné in 1963 and in Mozambique in 1964. Portugal managed to contain these guerrilla movements only at the price of international notoriety, a high level of military expenditure and a continual drain on material and moral resources. In Angola, increasing exploitation of its natural resources contributed to the Portuguese economy. In general the international political cost was excessive.

Social and Economic Change in the 20C. During the 1950s and 1960s Portugal experienced an unprecedented growth rate—almost 9 per cent a year in the industrial sector. But in 1980 it was as low in the European economic league tables as it had been at the end of the Monarchy.

The population rose from five million in 1900 to over nine million in 1980, although emigration to western Europe and elsewhere in the 1960s actually accounted for a decrease for that decade. The proportion of the population working in the agricultural sector fell from 72 per cent in 1864 to 57 per cent in 1911, and to 30 per cent by 1970. The drift to the cities continued throughout this period. The proportion of illiterates had dropped from 69 per cent in 1910 to 25 per cent in 1970.

The greatest economic progress occurred in the 'New State' period. The infrastructure of communications was extended and modernised, and dam construction boosted the production of hydro-electric power. These developments formed the base for Portugal's accelerated growth through the 1950s and 1960s, especially in metallurgical industries. Textiles remained the principal industry, but agriculture stagnated because mechanisation was slow.

As late as 1959 13 per cent of the population still lived in villages inaccessible by road. Widespread subsistence agriculture persisted, largely sustained by remittances from abroad. Tourist receipts, however, helped to make up the chronic deficit in the trade balance. Internal migration continued towards the Braga-Setúbal coastal regions, and Lisbon and Oporto remained poles of attraction.The socio-economic divide between urban and rural areas deepened despite the advent of mass media.

The densely populated Minho remained deeply religious while in the larger cities and the illiterate South religion was a declining social force. In the secular field the present century produced only one literary giant, the poet *Fernando Pessoa* (1888–1935).

Revolution and Democracy. Salazar was succeeded as Prime Minister by *Marcelo Caetano* (1968–74), who sought to reform the New State and find answers to Portugal's overseas problems. He attempted to widen the basis of the regime's political support by introducing liberal measures. More intellectual freedom, however, only led to demands for further democratisation. This was stubbornly opposed by the diehards, including the President, *Américo Tomás* (1958–74). Theories of progressive autonomy for the overseas territories satisfied neither guerrilla leaders nor world opinion, while at home warweariness increased. Rising domestic inflation offset the advantages gained by an improved but rudimentary welfare system. Limited democratisation of trade-union structures enabled the clandestine Communists to obtain further footholds. The necessity to find more officers to carry on the fruitless colonial war only provoked military unrest, and led to the creation of the *Armed Forces Movement* (MFA; *Movimento das Forças Armadas*) in 1973.

There was a premature and unsuccessful rising by the MFA at Caldas da Rainha in March 1974. On 25 April 1974 the junior officers, nominally led by *General Costa Gomes* (the Chief of Staff) and *General António de Spínola* (the former commander in Guiné), achieved a successful and nearly bloodless coup. The rest of the country followed the lead of the capital.

With this revolution there commenced a period of confusion and instability in which the political centre of gravity moved generally to the left until August 1975. General Spínola became provisional President and formed a coalition government comprising Communists, Socialists and Centrists. The authority of the State had largely collapsed, however, and the more radical officers of the MFA remained the real arbiters of the situation.

Economic conditions deteriorated as the political confusion continued, but it was decolonisation which divided Spínola from the Left. The former favoured the creation of a Lusitanian community, including Brazil, while the latter insisted on a speedy withdrawal from the colonies. Spínola consented to the independence of Guiné in 1974 and of Mozambique in 1975, but demurred at handing over Angola to its most leftist local liberation movement. The organisation of a rally in support of Spínola led to a showdown on 28 September 1974, from which MFA radicals and the Left emerged victorious. In 1975 independence was granted to the Cape Verde Islands, São Tomé and Príncipe, and Angola, while East Timor was taken over by Indonesia.

General Costa Gomes became President of the Republic in 1974–76, but power was still effectively exercised by MFA radicals and a coalition government led by *Brigadier Vasco Gonçalves*, himself a MFA radical. There was some uncertainty until 11 March 1975, when an attempted coup by Spínola failed, leaving Gonçalves and the radicals more firmly in power.

Private banks and insurance firms were nationalised, putting about half the economy in the public sector. Elections for a constituent assembly were held on 25 April 1975 and won by the Socialists and Centrists, but Gonçalves remained keen on an alliance with the Communists, who dominated the trade-union movement. Still other MFA officers were in favour of more novel Third World-style revolutionary solutions.

In July a conservative backlash in the north of the country was led by *Mário Soares* and nine key moderate MFA officers, greatly strengthening the Socialist opposition. Opinions became polarised and the MFA disintegrated. Gonçalves was dismissed by Costa Gomes in August and the sixth provisional government of *Admiral Pinheiro de Azevedo* sought a return to normality. Opposition was organised by the Communists and the extreme Left. This period of revolutionary confusion finally ended on 25 November 1975 when the failure of a Leftist revolt against the coalition government permitted democratic and centrist opinion to assert itself.

In 1976 a new constitution, drawn up under MFA influence, attempted to uphold socialism and democracy. It gave considerable potential power to a popularly-elected President. A Prime Minister and cabinet were jointly responsible to the President and to a single-chambered Assembly elected by universal suffrage on a system of proportional representation. The *Council of the Revolution*, a legacy of the now defunct MFA, controlled the armed forces and advised the President. Devolution was granted to the Azores, to Madeira and to Macau, the only remaining overseas possessions. *General António Ramalho Eanes*, leader of the government forces on 25 November 1975, was elected President. Mário Soares, leader of the Socialists, was appointed Prime Minister. Soares' party won the election of 1976 and he was again appointed Prime Minister of a minority government.

Soares at first governed alone, and then in coalition with the Christian-Democrat CDS (Social Democratic Centre). Three attempts in 1978–79 at non-party government by independent Presidential nominees failed to stay the course, the last being led by *Maria de Lurdes Pintassilgo*, the first woman Prime Minister. In the elections of December 1979 the Socialists of Soares were still the largest party, and well ahead of the Communists led by *Álvaro Cunhal*, but both were defeated by the conservative Democratic Alliance (AD; a formation based on the Social Democrats, CDS, and Monarchist parties). The AD's controversial leader, the Social Democrat *Francisco de Sá Carneiro*, became Prime Minister and adopted a right-wing stance until his death in an air crash in December 1980. His successor, the Social Democrat *Francisco Pinto Balsemão*, attempted to steer a moderate course. Under his leadership AD reached agreement with the Socialists to revise the Constitution in 1982, when the Council of the Revolution was abolished. Other changes were minimal. But unrest within the parties of the AD coalition over policies and personalities led to Balsemão's resignation in December 1982. President Eanes (who had been comfortably re-elected in December 1980) vetoed the candidate chosen by Balsemão to succeed him as Prime Minister, and forced Balsemão to stay on in a caretaker capacity until new elections on 25 April 1983. The AD coalition disintegrated meanwhile into its component parties, which gave themselves new leaders. The Socialists emerged from the elections as the largest parliamentary group, but without an overall majority. Their leader, Soares, formed a coalition government with the Social Democrats. This government's policies of economic retrenchment made it unpopular, and a new and more dynamic leader of the Social Democrats, *Aníbal Cavaco Silva*, withdrew his party from it, forcing elections in October 1985. The Social Democrats were victorious, although lacking an overall majority. Cavaco Silva's minority government was the tenth administration since 1976.

Early in 1986 the presidential elections were narrowly won on the second round by Mário Soares, who was installed as the first civilian Head of State for 60 years. Ex-President Eanes took over the leadership of the Democratic Renewal Party, which had obtained almost a fifth of the vote in the election of 1985, the first it had contested.

On 1 January 1986 Portugal became the eleventh member-state of the European Community after negotiations lasting nine years.

Chronological Table

Rulers of Portugal

Some of the more off-quoted nick-names are given: dates in brackets indicate the year of their marriages. Kings are usually referred to by the title *Dom*.

House of Burgundy (or The Afonsin Dynasty)

1128/39-85	Afonso (Henriques) I – Mafalda of Maurienne and Savoy (1146)
1185-1211	Sancho I – Dulce of Barcelona (1174)
1211-23	Afonso II – Urraca (1208), daughter of Alfonso VIII of Castile and Eleanor Plantagenet
1223-48	Sancho II – Mécia López de Haro
1248-79	Afonso III – Matilde, Countess of Boulogne – Beatriz de Guillén (1253), daughter of Alfonso X of Castile
1279-1325	Dinis, 'O Lavrador' ('the husbandman') –Isabel of Aragón (1282)
1325-57	Afonso IV – Beatriz of Castile (1309), daughter of Sancho IV of Castile
1357-67	Pedro I – Blanca of Castile (1328) – Constanza of Castile (1340) – Inês de Castro (1354)?
1367-83	Fernando – Leonor Teles (1372)
1383-85	(Interregnum)

House of Avis

1385-1433	João I (John) – Philippa of Lancaster (1387)
1433-38	Duarte (Edward) – Leonor of Aragón (1428)
1438-81	Afonso V, 'the African' – Isabel of Portugal (1441)

1481-95	João II – Leonor of Portugal (1471)
1495-1521	Manuel I, 'the Fortunate' – Isabel of Castile (1497)
	– Maria of Castile (1500)
	– Leonor of Spain (1518)
1521-57	João III – Catarina of Spain (1525)
1557-78	Sebastião, 'the Regretted'
1578-80	Henrique, the Cardinal-king
1580	António, Prior of Crato

House of Austria (CASTILIAN USURPATION)

1580-98	Philip II of Spain (I of Portugal)
1598-1621	Philip III of Spain (II „)
1621-40	Philip IV of Spain (III „)

House of Braganza

1640-56	João IV – Luisa de Guzmán (1633)
1656-83	Afonso VI – Maria-Francisca-Isabel of Savoy (1666; but unconsummated)
1683-1706	Pedro II (Regent from 1668) – Isabel of Savoy (1668)
	– Maria-Sofia-Isabel of Neuberg (1687)
1706-50	João V, 'the Magnificent' – Maria-Ana of Austria (1708)
1750-77	José – Mariana Victoria of Spain (1729)
1777-1816	Maria (Francisca) I – Pedro III (her uncle; in 1760)
1816-26	João VI (Regent from 1792) – Carlota-Joaquina of Spain (1784)
1826	Pedro IV (who abdicated, leaving the kingdom to his daughter, Maria) – Maria Leopoldina of Austria (1817)
	– Maria Amelia of Leuchtenberg (1829)
1828-34	USURPATION of Dom Miguel – Adelaide-Sofia of Loewenstein-Rosenberg (1851)
1834-53	Maria II, 'da Glória' – August of Leuchtenberg (1834)
	– Ferdinand of Saxe-Coburg-Gotha (1836)
1853-61	Pedro V – Stéphanie of Hohenzollern-Sigmaringen (1858)
1861-89	Luís – Maria-Pia of Savoy (1862)
1889-1908	Carlos – Marie-Amélie of Orléans (1886)
1908-10	Manuel II, 'the Unfortunate' – Augusta-Victoria of Sigmaringen (1913)

Republic

Presidents
(or heads of provisional governments)

1910	Teófilo Braga
1911-15	Manuel de Arriaga
1915	Teófilo Braga
1915-17	Bernardino Machado
1917-18	Sidónio Pais
1918-19	*Adm.* João de Canto e Castro
1919-23	António José de Almeida
1923-25	Manuel Teixeira Gomes
1925-26	Bernardino Machado
1926	*Commander* Mendes Cabeçadas
1926	*Gen.* Gomes da Costa

1926-51	*Gen.* António Oscar de Fragoso Carmona
	(with António de Oliveira Salazar as 'Prime Minister' from 1932 to 1968)
1951-58	*Gen.* Francisco Higino Craveiro Lopes
1958-74	*Adm.* Américo de Deus Rodrigues Tomás
	(with Marcello Caetano as 'Prime Minister' from 1968 to 1974)
1974	*Gen.* António Sebastião Ribeiro de Spínola
1974-76	*Gen.* Francisco da Costa Gomes
1976-86	*Gen.* António dos Santos Ramalho Eanes
1986-	Mário Alberto Nobre Lopes Soares

INTRODUCTION TO THE ART AND ARCHITECTURE OF PORTUGAL

By *J.B. Bury*

General Characteristics. The Portuguese temperament is characterised by a down-to-earth realism generally incompatible with high
flights of imagination or abstract ideas transcending the senses. In
keeping with this uncomplicated, realistic outlook, Robert Smith has
identified a 'pastoral' quality in Portuguese architecture—
recognisable by such features as modest scale, simple constructional
forms, and the neat facing of exterior walls with white plaster, against
which the bare stone of the aperture frames and structural members
provides a clean 'rural' contrast of texture and colour. The national
temperament may also be seen reflected in the architecture of village
churches, which almost invariably convey a welcoming impression.
Inside, the same ingenuous and friendly spirit is maintained—the
images of saints, for example, being always human and approa-
chable, never withdrawn by the tragic intensity or abstraction which
are found in the religious sculpture of some other Catholic nations.
Nor are Portuguese towns completely dominated by huge cathedrals
like those of northern Europe or Spain. In domestic architecture,
equally revealing is the lack of those massive iron grilles or *rejas*
which protect the ground-floor windows of Spanish houses, and
emphatically assert their privacy.

The realistic approach of the Portuguese is also apparent in the very
important status enjoyed by portraiture as a branch of painting, from
Nuno Gonçalves onwards, and, conversely, the relative weakness of
their contributions to more imaginative artistic themes such as those
of mythological, allegorical and history painting. It is worthy of note
that the only Renaissance treatise on the art of portraiture was written
by a Portuguese (*Francisco de Holanda*, 'Do tirar pelo natural'; MS
completed 1549); and perhaps no coincidence that in the distinguished succession of portrait painters of the Spanish House of Austria,
Sánchez Coello (c 1531–88) came from a Portuguese family, and
Diego de Silva Velázquez (1599–1660) was of Portuguese descent on
his father's side.

Similarly in architecture, just as the Portuguese have produced no
great philosopher or mystic, so neither the transcendental aspirations
of Gothic nor the illusionism and theatricality of the Baroque have
strongly appealed to their aesthetic sensibilities—despite superb
examples, some of the finest in Europe, built in their country by
foreign architects, at Alcobaça, for example, and at Mafra. Contrasting with this lack of enthusiasm for Gothic and Baroque, the
Portuguese have positively favoured horizontal rather than vertical
compositions, and they have shown an evident liking for the firmly
based solidity of Roman construction, whether Romanesque or
Renaissance, and even within the latter style have demonstrated a
preference for the two most stable Orders, Tuscan and Doric.

In marked contrast to Spain, domes are rare in Portugal, and even
barrel vaults are not common. This has not been due to lack of good
craftsmen. 'Where shall we meet with such excellent stone cutters as
in Portugal? Perhaps not in Europe', wrote a visiting professional
architect two centuries ago (*James Murphy*, 'Travels in Portugal';
London, 1795). Nor can Portuguese preference for rather low
buildings of simple construction be attributed to seismic risk. It is true

that Portugal has endured numerous earthquakes, and three during the past thousand years have been so severe and widespread in their effects as to be labelled 'great': 24 August 1356, 26 January 1531, and 1 November 1755). But Spain too has suffered considerably from earthquakes, and Sicily and Italy even more so, without any apparent inhibiting effects on the construction of complex systems of vaulting or cupolas, or tall towers.

The truth is that Portuguese builders and architects (as opposed to foreigners working in Portugal such as Terzi, Ludwig, or Nasoni) have seldom shown an interest in spatial composition, and have usually preferred stable rectangular forms to less stable curved shapes, a preference which is especially evident in ground plans. This is already to be seen in the chancels of Romanesque churches in North Portugal, with their usually square as opposed to Carolingian apsidal terminations. In this respect it might be said that the Portuguese resemble the English, among whom Sir Nikolaus Pevsner has detected a 'profound preference for the angular and dislike for full, rich, swelling architectural forms'. Thus the oval plan, a favourite of Italian, Austrian, and German church architects in the 17th and 18Cs, was almost completely rejected, or ignored, by the Portuguese, despite outstanding examples designed by *Guarini* for Lisbon (Divina Providência; never built), and built by *Nasoni* at Oporto (Clérigos; 1731–63).

In compensation, however, for the indifference to, or neglect of, spatial composition in their architecture, the Portuguese have demonstrated a remarkable creative talent for surface ornament—already noticeable in the decorative sculpture of their Romanesque churches; still more manifest in that of Manueline buildings; and visible again in the late Baroque and Rococo architecture of the Minho. The same genius is to be seen in the evolution of church reredoses of gilded wood, culminating at the end of the 17C in what Robert Smith has called the 'national style' of *talha dourada*. This was associated with the appearance of that astonishing, uniquely Portuguese phenomenon, the church interior entirely covered with carved and gilded wood (*a igreja toda de ouro*) of which spectacular examples are still to be seen at Aveiro (Convent of Jesus; before 1725), and Lagos (Santo António), although many of the finest perished in the earthquake of 1755. Further instances of this inventive interest in the treatment of surfaces can be seen in silver and furniture, and to it we may also assign another major Portuguese artistic achievement, the adaptation of blue and white *azulejos* to accommodate very large pictorial designs—an innovation evolved in the 18C after the Dutch and Chinese influences of the late 17C (which superseded earlier styles of Islamic derivation) had been fully absorbed and digested.

Prehistoric and Roman. There is a fascinating example of the adaptation of a neolithic monument to Christian worship at Pavia (Alentejo), where the 16C chapel of São Dinis is constructed from a huge megalithic tomb or dolmen. A good deal is known of Ibero-Celtic Portugal (5–1C BC) from the excavation of hill towns or *citânias*, notably those of *Sabroso* and *Briteiros* in the Minho, which had flagged streets, drainage systems, and numerous habitations, both rectangular and circular, some of the latter of helicoidal construction. (The finds are preserved in the Museu Martins Sarmento, Guimarães.) Our knowledge of Roman Portugal has also been greatly extended by excavations, in particular those of the important town of *Conímbriga* (a few kilometres S of Coimbra), which was already recorded as an *oppidum* in the 1C AD. It was sacked by the Suevi in 468, and eventually abandoned. Here a number of buildings have been unearthed, including baths and houses with elaborate pictorial mosaic floors and hypocausts. A Roman bridge cited in the 'Itinerary' of Antoninus Pius still exists at Vila Formosa, W of Portalegre. At Évora, part of a 2nd or 3C AD Roman temple has survived on the central hill of the city, and the aqueduct completed in 1537 probably follows the course of the ancient Roman one; but most of Roman Évora has been destroyed over the centuries, some even relatively recently (e.g., in 1570 a large structure described as a triple triumphal arch was pulled down to enlarge the main square).

Visigothic and Romanesque. A few examples have survived in Portugal of the small churches built prior to the 8C, when the Visigoths ruled the Iberian peninsula, and others which were built by Christian communities under Moorish domination in the style known as MOZARABIC. To the first belongs the small Latin-type basilica of *São Pedro de Balsemão*, near Lamego in the Beira Alta, dating from the 7C or possibly earlier, which displays carved ornament including serrated and cord motifs, swastikas, rosettes, and lozenge patterns. To the second category belong *São Pedro de Lourosa*, near Oliveira do Hospital, dating from the 10C, and *São Frutuoso*, near Braga, probably of Visigothic origin, but rebuilt in the 11C: both these churches have been much restored and reconstructed in recent years, however. At São Pedro de Lourosa the nave is separated from the side aisles by rows of Tuscan columns supporting horseshoe arches, and there are *ajimeces* above the entrance and chancel arch: in ground plan São Pedro combines rectangle with Latin cross, and has a narthex at the W end. São Frutuoso has a Greek cross plan with apsidal terminations to the arms, a central dome (reconstructed), finely carved capitals and bands of carved ornament.

The independence of Portugal (from the Spanish kingdom of León) was proclaimed in 1143; but it cannot be said that the Romanesque architecture which survives from the formative years of Portuguese nationhood shows any really distinctive national features, except perhaps the aptitude for decorative sculpture. Like Spanish Romanesque, that of Portugal owed much to the inspiration and influence of the Benedictine monks of Cluny, sponsors and patrons of the pilgrimage to the shrine of Santiago de Compostela, some 90km N of the Portuguese frontier. Some of the more important 12C churches, the cathedrals of *Braga, Oporto*, and *Lisbon*, have lost much of their Romanesque identity owing to subsequent alterations and reconstructions. However, two major monuments have fortunately retained their original character, largely unspoilt: the 12C cathedral (*Sé Velha*) of *Coimbra* and the 12–13C cathedral of *Évora*—both continuing the Cluniac style with evident references to the 11C pilgrimage basilica type established at Clermont-Ferrand (N.D. du Port), Toulouse (St. Sernin), and Santiago de Compostela.

Thus Coimbra's old cathedral is cruciform with three apses, a lantern over the crossing, side aisles and characteristic galleried triforia; while externally it presents a fortified appearance, as did Santiago. Subsequent additions in Gothic (cloisters; main reredos) and Renaissance styles (N door, and retable of northern apse) do not detract from the impressive 12C ensemble. Évora cathedral, although already transitional in its pointed arches, continues to follow the Cluniac architectural tradition constructively, and its porch is evidently modelled on the Pórtico de la Gloria at Santiago. The lantern cupola at the crossing, externally a conical dome, or low spire, follows the example of the old cathedral at Salamanca. The many subsequent additions and ornaments, in particular the splendid baroque chancel (*capela-mór*), co-exist harmoniously with the Romanesque body of the church without injuring each other's separate stylistic identity.

Two quite exceptional Portuguese Romanesque buildings of the 12C are the *domus municipalis* at *Branganza*, a very rare example of pre-Gothic civic architecture, and the hexadecagonal *Templar Church* at *Tomar*—perhaps the best-preserved Templar church in Europe.

Literally dozens of small, usually very simple, Romanesque churches survive in N Portugal, many of them decorated with rustic but striking and expressive carvings on their portals and on capitals. Two of the better known are *São Martinho de Cedofeita* at *Oporto* and *São Salvador de Bravães* on the river Lima.

Gothic. Each of the main phases of Gothic architecture is represented in Portugal by examples which are unusually fine even by international European standards. The 'French church' (as W.C. Watson calls it in his 'Portuguese Architecture'; London, 1908) of the abbey of *Alcobaça*, begun in the second half of the 12C, and Pontigny-in-the-meadows in Burgundy, are the two finest surviving specimens of Cistercian architecture in Europe. In the church at Alcobaça is preserved a series of medieval royal tombs including those of Inês de Castro and Pedro I, outstanding masterpieces of Portuguese Gothic sculpture. Cistercian Gothic is also represented at *Coimbra* in the 13C cloister of *Santa Maria de Celas*,, which has the best collection of decorated capitals in the country.

Other fine Gothic churches include *Santa Maria dos Olivais* at *Tomar* (begun second half 13C), which represents the most usual type of church built in the country until the end of the 15C. Also worth visiting is the fortified Templar church at *Leça do Bailio*, N of Oporto (rebuilt early 14C), and in the Alentejo the 14C fortified church of *N.S. da Boa Nova* at *Terena*, which has a Greek cross plan.

The masterpiece of mature Gothic architecture in Portugal is the monastery church of *Santa Maria da Vitória* at *Batalha*, begun in 1388. It is stylistically eclectic, combining French with some English influences, but the result is entirely successful. Over the following century or so there were added to this church a founder's chapel housing royal tombs, a great vaulted chapterhouse, a large cloister with remarkable late Gothic tracery, a second cloister, and at the E end the so-called 'Unfinished Chapels' (*Capelas Imperfeitas*), another example of the very late Gothic which is peculiar to Portugal and called MANUELINE because belonging mainly to the reign of Manuel I (1495–1521), although several important Manueline buildings were completed in the reign of his successor João III (1521–57).

Batalha, built throughout of an ivory coloured limestone, brings to our attention two aspects of Portuguese architecture which visitors should bear in mind. First, Portugal is a country unusually well supplied with building stone of various kinds—from marbles and limestones to granites, each of several different colours and textures. These have been regularly utilised in each locality where they occur, and their diverse appearance contributes to regional variety, adding interest, by contrast, to buildings of similar style in different parts of the country. Secondly, it is essential in order fully to enjoy the architecture and sculpture which Portugal offers in abundance to try to shed any prejudice against the close proximity in a single building of entirely different styles of architecture, decorative sculpture, furniture, and ceramic, woodwork, or other ornament. One's pleasure is appreciably diminished if one is not prepared to adopt a tolerant attitude towards mixtures of heterogeneous if not completely incompatible elements.

A number of fine medieval CASTLES survive in Portugal, although some of them have been rather drastically restored. Among the best known are those of *Guimarães* and of *Lisbon* (the two most historically significant); those of *Monsaraz*, of *Almourol*, on an island in the Tagus between Santarém and Abrantes, and of *Óbidos* (three of the most picturesque); that of *Leiria* (perhaps the most imposing); and the great keeps of *Vila da Feira*, between Oporto and Aveiro, and of *Beja*, and *Estremoz*.

Painting: 1450–1550. There is nothing to suggest that Portugal possessed any flourishing native school of medieval painting; nor does Jan van Eyck's visit in 1428–29 appear to have created one. Apart from a few mural fragments, the earliest works are a series of panels attributed to *Nuno Gonçalves* (active 1450–71), court painter to Afonso V. Of these the most remarkable are six panels in the Lisbon museum portraying the court and various ranks of Portuguese society praying in the presence of a saint usually identified as St. Vincent, patron saint of Lisbon. The style is dry and powerfully realistic. There are similarities to contemporary Flemish painting, especially the work of Dirk Bouts, but also strong indications of Burgundian influence. The portraits, nearly life-sized, are of much historical interest, belonging as they do to the period when the Portuguese were on the threshold of their great overseas adventures. The identification of the portraits and the arrangement of the panels raise questions to which no convincing answers have yet been given.

During the first quarter of the 16C increased wealth resulting in more generous patronage persuaded a number of northern masters to emigrate to Portugal (e.g., the Flemish painter *Frei Carlos*, active 1517–29; and the Dutch miniaturist *Antonio de Holanda*, active in Portugal from c 1515, died c 1557). Pictures were also imported from Antwerp, and under these Netherlandish influences native schools developed. At Lisbon the circle of court painters included *Jorge Afonso* (active 1508–40) and his followers *Cristóvão de Figueiredo* (active 1515–38), *Garcia Fernandes* (active c 1514–65), and *Gregório Lopes* (c 1490–c 1550). With this circle we may also associate the anonymous painter of the charming Arrival of the relics at the Madre de Deus church (c 1520). To the important local school at Viseu belonged *Vasco Fernandes* ('O Grão Vasco', the Great Vasco; active 1506–42), and *Gaspar Vaz* (died c 1568). The prolific output of these so-called 'Portuguese primitives' is to be seen in the museums of Lisbon, Viseu, and Lamego. Their work is characterised by a realism not devoid of sentiment, exceptional skill in portraiture, and a predilection for brilliant colour schemes.

Architecture: the Manueline Style. In architecture, the new wealth and accompanying patronage was demonstrated more strikingly. Late Gothic in the specifically Portuguese variant known as MANUELINE (a term seemingly invented by the engineer Mousinho de Albuquerque in the 1840s) remained the prevailing style throughout the first quarter of the 16C. Certain features of the three-aisled, vaulted Gothic *Church of Jesus* at Setúbal (begun 1494) are generally considered to reveal the first manifestations of the Manueline style—

in particular the dramatic use of twisted forms in the columns, ribs, and corbels. The builder of this church was a certain Master *Boitac* (active 1494–c 1520), probably a Frenchman, who was later employed at the Jeronymite monastery of *Santa Maria de Belém*, near Lisbon (from 1502 to 1517), and at *Coimbra* and *Batalha* (between 1509 and 1519). At Belém, Boitac was succeeded as master of the works by a Spaniard, *João de Castilho* (active in Portugal from c 1510, died 1552), who was responsible for executing the S Portal, the vault in the nave, and transepts of the church, as well as for the completion of the cloister. The work at Belém continued long after the death of Dom Manuel in 1521, so that Renaissance ornament of Lombardic type (introduced to Portugal via Spain and France) makes its appearance both on the pillars of the church and in the cloister. At Batalha the construction of the 'Capelas Imperfeitas' went on so long that Renaissance ornament began to creep in. The master builder in charge there until 1515 was *Mateus Fernandes*, and under his supervision it may be supposed there were executed the great Portal of the Capelas Imperfeitas (1509) and the tracery in the cloister windows, which are among the finest achievements of Manueline architectural decoration.

However, the most spectacular of all Manueline works are the apertures (two in the W wall, one in the S) of the chapter house of the *Convent of Christ* at *Tomar*—famous for their carved stone frames of twisted tree trunks, stumps of branches, artichokes, coral, knots, ropes, and sails. This Manueline masterpiece, begun in 1510, and the *Tower of Belém* (1516–21) on the N shore of the Tagus estuary W of Lisbon, were constructed under the supervision of *Diogo de Arruda* (active 1510–31) and his brother *Francisco* (active 1510–47), respectively. Other important manifestations of the Manueline style are to be seen in the metalwork of the period, notably the gold and enamel Belém monstrance (1506; Lisbon museum), commissioned by Dom Manuel from the goldsmith *Gil Vicente*.

The finest examples of Manueline civil architecture are the extensions made by Dom Manuel to the royal palace at *Sintra*, where some influence of Moorish (*mudéjar*) crafts is visible in the elaborate wooden ceilings (*alfarge*) and glazed tiles (*azulejos*) imported from Seville. In the Alentejo and Algarve a series of curious 'gothic-mudéjar' churches with battlemented parapets and cylindrical cone-capped turrets was built at the end of the 15C— examples being *São Bras* at *Évora* and *Santo André* at *Beja*.

In general, however, *mudéjar* elements in Portuguese 15th and 16C architecture are much less prominent than in Spain and, apart from Sintra, virtually confined to the province of Alentejo—where the *mudéjar* craftsmanship was seemingly dependent upon influence from neighbouring Andalucía—the techniques being brought across the frontier perhaps by itinerant Moorish artisans.

Some more-or-less plausible efforts have been made in the interests of tidy classification by leading art historians, including Reynaldo dos Santos and Robert Smith, to identify common stylistic characteristics between the principal Manueline monuments. But it is probably more realistic to accept Vergílio Correia's conclusion that there were as many different schools of Manueline architecture as there were major monuments. The common factors which make the term Manueline useful are firstly that the buildings so categorised all date from between about 1490 and 1540, and secondly that they are all constructively Gothic and belong to the last phase of that style.

ATTRIBUTIONS. A word of warning should here be interjected on the subject of attributions of the design of buildings and sculpture in Portugal by named artists. Little or nothing is known of Portuguese Gothic or Manueline sculptors. Usually we only have the name of the master builder (*mestre das obras*) who was in overall charge of construction. Sculptors, stonemasons, carpenters and woodcarvers would work under his supervision, but he might or, more likely, might not be responsible for the precise design to which each craftsman worked. There is no evidence for example that Diogo de Arruda designed the sculptural decoration of the chapter house at Tomar—the most striking and original of all Manueline achievements—although the window surrounds were carved while he was master of the works there. For the reign of João III the problem of identifying the designers of buildings becomes if anything even more difficult because the king was a keen amateur architect and from 1541 onwards had at court an artistic adviser, *Francisco de Holanda*, who had spent the years 1538–40 in Italy, sent there by the king himself, to study ancient and modern art and architecture and fortification. In Italy, Holanda was befriended by Michelangelo, Antonio da Sangallo the younger, and Sebastiano Serlio, and he brought back with him to Portugal an impressive collection of drawings (now in the library of the Escorial).

Early Renaissance Architecture and Sculpture. Portugal began slowly to accept Renaissance art and architecture during the 1530s and 1540s. Although (according to Vasari) a leading Italian sculptor-architect, namely *Andrea Sansovino*, had spent some years in Portugal during the 1490s 'leaving behind him one who could complete his unfinished works', the influence of these two forerunners seems to have been negligible. A taste for Renaissance decorative themes was no doubt developed by the importation from Italy of illuminated manuscripts, illustrated books, woodcuts, and small works of art such as medals, ceramics, silver work, and perhaps small paintings. Dom Manuel possessed a magnificent example of Renaissance illumination in the seven-volume 'Jerónimos Bible' (now in the Torre do Tombo National Archive, Lisbon), commissioned by his predecessor João II in 1494 from the Florentine shop of the celebrated miniaturist Attavante.

The first practitioners of the Italian Renaissance style in Portugal were a series of gifted French sculptors who introduced the highly ornate architectural decoration which had originally been developed in Lombardy in the 15C and acclimatised to France early in the 16C. These sculptors—*Nicolas Chanterène* (active in Portugal 1517–c 1540), *Philippe Houdart* (*Filipe Hodart*; active at Toledo 1522–26 and at Coimbra 1530–34), and *Jean de Rouen* (*João de Ruão*; active at Coimbra c 1530–70)—carved statues, portals, tombs, pulpits, retables, and whole chapels, in a style which from the 1530s to 1550s is more or less identical with the Plateresque style which was flourishing contemporaneously in Spain, and similar early Renaissance work elsewhere in Europe, in which great prominence was given to baluster columns, and in which vigorous invention compensates for imperfect knowledge of classical rules and proportions. Chanterène's altarpieces at *São Marcos de Tentúgal* (1522) and *N.S. da Pena, Sintra* (1529–32) exemplify this style. As also in Spain and France, there are only a few exceptional buildings, tombs, and retables prior to the mid century which reveal a more serious knowledge of the Renaissance style. In architecture this may be associated with Sagredo's valuable textbook of the classical rules ('Medidas del Romano'), first published at Toledo in 1526, then twice at Paris in the 1530s, and after that three times at Lisbon in 1541 and 1542. The third and fourth books of

Serlio's 'Architecture', published at Venice in 1537 and 1540, would also no doubt soon have reached the Peninsula (they were translated into Spanish and published at Toledo in 1552).

Among the most elegant and harmonious of early Portuguese Renaissance works are the chapel of São Pedro in the *Old Cathedral* at *Coimbra* (1537), the tomb of Dom Afonso de Portugal at *Évora* (1537), and the very beautiful little church of *N.S. da Conceição* at *Tomar* (dated on good evidence to the 1530s by Professor Rafael Moreira).

Late Renaissance Architecture. For over 150 years from the middle of the 16C Portuguese architecture reacted slowly to the changes of style initiated in Italy—gradually developing a series of individual permutations of late Renaissance or Mannerist designs and resisting the advent of the Baroque until as late as the second decade of the 18C. Nevertheless, despite this *retardataire* aspect, if not because of it, Portuguese architecture during this century and a half offers a number of unusual, interesting, and beautiful buildings.

Among the most important monuments belonging to the third quarter of the 16C are the three new cathedrals constructed after new dioceses had been established in 1545 at *Leiria, Portalegre* and *Miranda do Douro*. These were all rib-vaulted 'hall churches' with side aisles of the same height as the nave. Several fine churches in the Alentejo (e.g., *Santo Antão* at *Évora*, built 1557–63, and the slightly later parish churches of *Estremoz* and *Veiros*) follow a similar pattern. Centralised forms are represented by the octagonal chapel of the Dominican nuns style initiated at *Elvas* (1543–57), the *ermida* of *São Gregório* at *Tomar*, the chapel of *Santo Amaro* at *Lisbon* (1549), and the chapel of *N.S. de Valverde* near *Évora*, a 'crystalline' structure comprising five interlocking octagonal spaces (?c 1550; attributed to *Manuel Pires*). Other complex plans include the palace chapel at *Salvaterra de Magos* (across the river from Santarém), which combines square, rectangular, and hexagonal spaces; and somewhat later the remarkable circular church and cloister (begun 1576) of *N.S. do Pilar* at *Vila Nova de Gaia*. At Belém a vaulted chancel in a severe classical style was added to the Manueline monastery church in 1571–72 (attributed to *Jerónimo de Ruão*). At *Évora* an astonishing sculptural façade was added c 1550 (according to Professor Moreira) to the church of *N.S. da Graça*, and a handsome new church dedicated to the *Espírito Santo*, built for the Jesuits (1567–74) by Manuel Pires and the royal architect *Afonso Álvares* (active third quarter 16C). This latter church, together with *São Roque, Lisbon* (also begun in 1567), provide early examples of Jesuit preaching churches and are important for the history of Jesuit architecture. At *Viana do Castelo* a new façade for the *Misericórdia church* was built by *João Lopes the Younger* (1589) with three storeys of open loggias, a design evidently derived from a Netherlandish or Rhenish architectural engraving.

The most remarkable building of the reign of Dom Sebastião (1557–78), a Palladian masterpiece of European importance, is the main cloister of the *Convent of Christ* at *Tomar*, adjoining the celebrated Manueline chapter house. This cloister was mostly built in 1557–62 by the Spanish master builder *Diogo de Torralva* (1500–66), to whom the design has been doubtfully ascribed: it was finished by the Italian military engineer *Filippo Terzi* (1520–97) in 1587.

Religious Architecture: 1580–1700. During the reign of the Spanish kings, Philip II and his son and grandson, in Portugal from 1580 to

1640, there was current what William Beckford described in 'An Excursion to the monasteries of Alcobaça and Batalha' (London, 1835) as 'the majestic style which prevailed during the Spanish domination of Portugal'. He was specifically referring to *N.S. da Luz* at *Carnide*, in the environs of Lisbon, of 1575–96. The imposing monumental style of this edifice reflects the late Renaissance or Mannerist phase of architectural development which was in fashion in post-Tridentine Italy, and was closely paralleled by the *estilo desornamentado* in Spain. The two finest examples of this style in Portugal, both begun in the 1590s, are the Jesuit church (now *Sé Nova*, or new cathedral) at *Coimbra*, and *São Vicente de Fora* at *Lisbon*. It has been conjectured that *Baltasar Álvares* (active c 1575–1624), nephew of the royal architect Afonso, was responsible for the former. The design of the latter is usually ascribed to Filippo Terzi (see above) who perhaps received some assistance from Baltasar Álvares. It is improbable that any design contribution was made by the Spanish royal housekeeper (*aposentador*) and architect Juan de Herrera, who accompanied Philip II of Spain to Portugal and was with him at Lisbon during Philip's stay there in 1580–83.

Less famous but still impressive churches built in Beckford's 'majestic style' are to be seen throughout the country. The *Dominican church* (early 17C) at *Bemfica* near Lisbon is a good example, and the *Augustinian church* at *Vila Viçosa* (begun 1634) is another: and there are a whole series in and around Oporto, among them several Benedictine monastery churches—the one in the city itself (begun 1602) and those at *Santo Tirso* (first half 17C), and *Tibães* (begun 1628), near Braga; also the churches of the Augustinian monasteries of *Moreira da Maia* (1588–1622), N of Oporto, and of *Grijó* (late 16C), S of the city; and, in addition, the Jesuit church of *São Lourenço* (known as the '*Grilos*'; begun 1614), and the contemporary church of *São João Novo*, which are both in the city and are remarkable for their powerfully monumental façades (which conflate designs by Serlio published in 1551 and 1575).

The considerable number of monastic establishments with fine large vaulted churches which were built during the 60 years of Spanish rule, seem to indicate that this was not a period of economic impoverishment for Portugal. The period of national penury, when art and architecture inevitably suffered from some neglect, was the second half of the 17C. The re-establishment of independence (1640) involved a 28-year war with Spain from which recovery was slow and spending resources therefore severely restricted.

It was not until the beginning of the 18C that the discovery of gold, and later diamonds, in Brazil changed this situation, and patronage of the arts revived. Meanwhile the completion of buildings of religious foundations which had been begun under the Spanish kings was slowly pursued, and a very few new ones started—e.g., the domed church of *N.S. do Carmo* at *Évora* (begun 1670), the church of the *Jesuit College* at *Santarém* (now Seminary; begun 1676), and the convent of *Santa Clara-a-Nova, Coimbra* (1649–96), the design of which is attributed to the mathematician-architect Fr *João Turriano* (1610–79), Portuguese-born son of the Cremonese *Leonardo Torriani* (c 1559–c 1630), who had succeeded Terzi as Chief Engineer (*engenheiro-mór*) of the kingdom in 1598. To the very end of the 17C belongs the impressive convent of the *Congregados do Oratório* at *Estremoz*. The most original building of this period, *Santa Engrácia*, at *Lisbon*, was not completed (and remained unfinished until 1966). This centralised church of Greek cross plan with apsidal terminations to the arms, and towers in the four angles, was begun in 1682 by the architect *João Nunes Tinoco* (1631–90).

W.C. Watson, constrained by the prejudices of his time, described Santa Engracia as 'the real end of architecture in Portugal'. In saying this he ignored almost all the buildings of the 18C which was perhaps the richest and most varied period in the whole history of Portuguese architecture.

Houses: 1400–1800. Although ecclesiastical buildings absorbed the principal architectural skill and resources of the Portuguese up to the end of the 18C, secular architecture was not entirely neglected, being represented, albeit usually rather modestly, by many charming town and country houses. A few late Gothic town houses and town halls survive; e.g., at *Viana do Castelo, Caminhã, Barcelos, Alcáçovas* (Alentejo), and *Évora*, most of them more or less altered by subsequent reconstruction. Houses of the regular and symmetrical kind which were usual in Italy from the 15C were almost unknown in Portugal before the 17C. The old, irregular, royal palaces remained virtually unmodified, indicating a curious indifference to Renaissance ideals of order and balance. Despite Vasari's story, the 'very beautiful palace with four towers' allegedly designed for the king of Portugal by Andrea Sansovino in the 1490s, may, Professor Moreira believes, have furnished the plan for the Castelo novo (Quartel de Cavalaria) begun by Diogo de Arruda (see above) at the southern entrance to the city of Évora. João III received plans from Italy in 1550 for a new royal palace, and construction was begun at *Xabregas*, NE of Lisbon, but the king's death in 1557 interrupted the work and it was never resumed. Small 16C town houses showing Italian influence survive at *Lisbon* (*Casa dos Bicos*, Rua dos Bacalhoeiros) and *Braga* (former *Casa dos Expostos*, Rua de São João); and eventually, towards the end of the century, a large square town house with four towers was built by the waterfront at Lisbon (palace of the marquesses of Castelo Rodrigo, begun 1585, burnt down 1751)—after which regular, symmetrical designs began at last to become more and more generally accepted.

The country house in Portugal developed from the medieval fortified tower, to which, as the land became more peaceful, low wings of one or two storeys were adjoined, in order to provide more commodious living quarters. Fine examples in the Alentejo are the *Torre das Águias* (c 1500) of the Counts of Atalaia, near Mora, and the castle (c 1532) of the Dukes of Braganza at *Évoramonte*, which has vaulted Manueline state rooms on each floor. By the mid 16C the tower, now sometimes duplicated as a concession to Renaissance principles, had become a mere ornamental adjunct; but towers continued commonly to be incorporated in Portuguese country houses, until as late as the 19C.

Two important early country houses near Setúbal which reveal in their design a more than usually strong Renaissance influence are those of the *Quinta da Bacalhôa* (mid 16C), and the *Quinta das Torres* (late 16C). In both the layout includes a garden conceived as an extension of the house. Examples of houses dating originally from the 16C but enlarged and altered subsequently are the enormous *Palace of the Dukes of Braganza* at Vila Viçosa (begun 1501, and preserving its original Manueline arcaded courtyard), the *Casa de Basto* at *Évora*, and the *Casa e Torre de Ribafria*, near *Sintra*: the last two possess loggias, an important 16C innovation, and the Casa de Basto has exceptionally fine state rooms of c 1570, one of them oval, vaulted and ribbed, with lively frescoes signed by *Francisco de Campos* and dated 1578.

Among the architecturally more important 17C noble houses are the *Palace of the Dukes of Aveiro* at *Azeitão*, near Setúbal; the *Palácio da Mitra*, and the *Almada, Galveias, Fronteira*, and *Palhavã* palaces—all in or near *Lisbon*; the *Calhariz* house near *Sesimbra* (Setúbal), the *Vale de Flores* house near *Braga*, and the *Palace of the marquesses of Ponte de Lima* at *Mafra*. Although the five above-mentioned houses in or near Lisbon are now within the boundaries of the city they were originally built (except for the Almada palace) in what used to be open country. The palace of the counts of Galveias and the Calhariz and Vale de Flores houses are built on the French plan (deriving from the Château de Bury, 1511) in which an entrance court formed by lateral wings projecting from the main house is closed in front only by a screen wall. The palace of the marquesses of Fronteira (c 1670) displays two storeys of Palladian loggias in front and at the back it has one of the most beautiful formal gardens in Portugal, integrated architecturally with the house. The Fragosos-Barahonas *solar* at Alcáçovas, SW of Évora, dating from the mid 17C, is square in plan with towers at the corners and a central arcaded courtyard. As the century advanced, the owners' private chapel became an increasingly prominent feature in Portuguese noble houses, especially in the country. In the Vale de Flores house the chapel, dated 1687, occupies the S wing.

The *solar* (that is, the manor house or seat of a noble family) of *Bertiandos*, which lies between Ponte de Lima and Viana do Castelo, admirably demonstrates the development of the Portuguese country house, from the massive medieval square tower (this one reconstructed in 1566) to the sophisticated arrangements of the 18C which here include a monumental approach stairway and first floor verandahs facing SW: the Bertiandos *solar* in fact comprises two separate houses, joined by the tower, and a large private chapel extends outwards at the back. Likewise, in central Portugal, the development of the country house from the 16C to the 18C is admirably displayed in the beautiful house of the *Quinta of Penha Longa* near Sintra, and the *Quinta da Amoreira da Torre* near *Montemor-o-Novo* (the word *quinta* means a country estate, and by association a country house).

There are numerous fine 18C country houses scattered throughout north and central Portugal. In the N the baroque villas built by the Tuscan architect-painter *Niccolò* (or *Nicolau*) *Nasoni* (1691–1773) are especially remarkable: among these are the *Palácio do Freixo* (1750) to the E of Oporto, and the unfinished *Quinta da Prelada* (c 1747), NW of the city. At the latter, Nasoni designed a garden with extraordinary vistas of the type which had been dramatically developed in the 17C at Cetinale, near Siena. The well-known *solar* of *Mateus* near *Vila Real*, and its fine baroque chapel dated 1750, have also been attributed to Nasoni, and they certainly seem to reflect his exuberant, colourful style. At *Braga*, notable examples of domestic architecture include the *Casa dos Biscainhos*, which has a charming formal garden incorporating four rococo fountains and an octagonal gazebo, and several striking town houses including the *Archbishop's Palace* (now Library), the baroque *Town Hall* designed by a local architect *André Soares da Silva* (1720–69), and the exceptionally picturesque *Casa do Raio*, which has been described as 'the most elegant, spontaneous and lyrical rococo exterior in Europe'. Among a number of fine 18C town houses at *Oporto*, the most splendid and imposing is the *Bishop's Palace* (Nasoni; 1734–1877). At *Guimarães*, the baroque town house of the region is paradigmatically represented by the *Casa dos Lobos Machados*, and the country house by the *Palácio de Vila Flor*, with its formal terraced garden, in the southern outskirts of the town. In and around *Ponte de Lima* there are also several fine baroque houses, among which the *Casa Aurora* in the town and the *Casa das Torres*, a few kilometres to the SW, are good examples.

In the small country town of *Lousã*, SE of Coimbra, there is a particularly fine group of 18C town houses, among which that of the *Viscondessa do Espinhal* (c 1780–1818) is especially striking; while about 24km E of Viseu there are two outstanding baroque country houses, namely the *Casa da Insua* (near Penalva do Castelo) and the *Casa Anadia* (near Mangualde), the latter having an notably beautiful interior decorated with azulejos and mural paintings. The towns of the Alentejo nearly all contain fine 17–18C houses, of which the charming *Palacio Amarelo* at Portalegre is a notable example.

In the Lisbon area, among the most architecturally distinguished country houses are that of the architect *J.F.Ludovice (Quinta da Alfarrobeira*, at Bemfica, 1727), the *Galvão Mexia palace* (at Campo Grande, 1746), the *Quinta do Correio-Mór* at *Loures*, Pombal's palace at *Oeiras* (both the last two exemplifying the so-called POMBALINE style of the third quarter of the 18C), and several interesting mansions in the Junqueira district near Belém.

The Neo-classical style of the last years of the 18C is well represented by the *Seteais palace* (c 1790), *Sintra*, and the *Casa do Conde Almeida Araujo* at *Queluz* (after 1795).

The last great *solar* to be built in the 18C tradition was the *Palácio da Brejoeira* (c 1804–34) near Monção on the river Minho.

Unfortunately few Portuguese country houses are regularly opened to the public; but if asked beforehand, preferably in writing, the owner will often allow visitors to see the principal rooms of the house, and the garden.

Gardens, Fountains, and Aqueducts. As we have seen, the concept of the garden as an open air extension of the house, which had been developed in Renaissance Italy, quickly found acceptance in Portugal. Several notable formal gardens have been mentioned above. Others include the *Jardim da Manga* (1528–35) adjoining the monastery of Santa Cruz at *Coimbra*, a remarkable architectural water garden, said to have been designed by João III; the box garden of the Braganza palace at *Vila Viçosa*; the baroque garden of the former bishop's palace, now a museum, at *Castelo Branco*, famous for its statuary; the early 18C gardens of the old convent of *Santa Marinha da Costa*, near Guimarães; and of the quinta of *N.S. do Carmo* at *Estremoz*. To these should be added the garden of the former archiepiscopal *Quinta da Palmeira*, on the river Cávado, N of Braga (first half 18C); and the famous mid-18C gardens of the royal palace at *Queluz*. An especially characteristic and charming feature of Portuguese formal gardens is the large stone-bordered water tank or pool with azulejo wall facings. The level of water in these tanks is sometimes raised several feet above the ground to provide unexpected reflections and shimmering light effects. For botanists there are several remarkable gardens such as the unique forest-park of Busaco—surrounded by a wall 6km long. It was formerly a 'desert' of Carmelite monks, who in 1622 began importing exotic trees, particularly the beautiful 'cedar of Busaco' (*Cupressus glauca* or *lusitanica*) from Mexico. Secondly there are the botanical gardens of Lisbon (1873) and of Belém (Ajuda Palace, 1768). And thirdly, the 19C arboretum-park of the Pena Palace at Sintra.

The visitor to Portugal will soon become accustomed to the ubiquity of FOUNTAINS. Some are ornamental, but the *chafariz* or public fountain was designed for the practical purpose of filling jars. As its importance merited, it was often given monumental form and some-times sculptural ornament—providing one of the most attractive decorative elements in the Portuguese townscape. The *Fonte do Ídolo* at *Braga* may originally have been a prehistoric sacred spring. The *Chafariz dos Canos* at *Torres Vedras* dates from the 14C and despite restoration in 1561 the Gothic arches supporting its roof still remain. There are other such Gothic fountain houses, one for example at *Atouguia da Baleia*, and another at *Santarém*, the latter known as the *Fonte das Figueiras*, being crowned with pointed merlons and decorated with carved coats of arms. There is a superb Manueline fountain in the cloister of the monastery of *Batalha*, a smaller one in the cloister at *Belém*, and a charming triangular one, the *Fonte da Rainha*, at *Montemor-o-Novo*, in the garden of the Amoreira da Torre *quinta*. Fine Renaissance fountains dating from the second half of the 16C are to be seen in the main squares of *Viana do Castelo*, and *Caminha* (both by *João Lopes*) and at *Estremoz* (*Fonte das Bicas*). There are three at *Évora*: one at the *Portas de Moura* (1556), one at the *Porta de Avis* (1573), and the third in the *Praça do Geraldo* (1571), which latter has been described as 'the queen of fountains', and 'deserving to be crowned' (it is in fact surmounted by a crown). Most of the Renaissance fountains follow the design, probably going back to antiquity, which was preserved at Rome in the fountain of Santa Maria in Trastevere, that is a column or stem supporting one or more shallow circular bowls from which the water falls into a polygonal basin at ground level. This design remained popular in the 17C, being used for example at Évora in the cloister of the *Cartuxa* (c 1625), at *Vila Viçosa* (*Fonte do Carrascal*, c 1630); at *Braga* in the *Campo das Hortas*; at *Coimbra* both in the former Bishop's Palace, now museum (c 1677), and in the Claustro do Silencio of the monastery of *Santa Cruz* (c 1637); at *Tomar* in the principal cloister of the Convent of Christ, built by *Pedro Fernandes de Torres*; and at *Barcelos* in the *Largo da Feira* (18C). On the other hand the medieval tradition of fountain houses persisted too in the guise of classical *tempietti*, rectangular but with twin cupolas at *Alter-do-Chão* (1556); also rectangular at *Trancoso*, with a pyramidal roof (*Fonte Nova*, 1589); and circular, with a cupola, at *Elvas* (*Chafariz da Misericórdia*, 1622, designed by *Diogo Marques*).

Some of the monumental fountains mentioned above were spe-cifically installed to make available to townspeople the water brought by newly built AQUEDUCTS. During the 16C aqueducts were built to supply *Elvas* (1498–1622), *Évora* (1534–37), *Coimbra* (1568–70), and *Tomar* (1593–1614). *Lisbon*'s aqueduct of the *Águas Livres* was also under consideration in the 16C, although not eventually built until the second quarter of the 18C.

Among many 18C baroque fountains, the handsome *Fonte Nova* at *Coimbra* (1725) occupies a site on which there has been a public source of water since at least 1137. The fountains designed by the Italian architects *Antonio Canevari* (at *Santo Antão do Tojal*, N of Lisbon, c 1730) and *Niccolò Nasoni* (the *Tortoise Fountain* in the *Quinta da Prelada* near Oporto, c 1750) are notably scenic; and there is an imposing monumental example dated 1789 at *Arruda dos Vinhos*, between Lisbon and Santarém. There is a strikingly elegant Neo-classical fountain at *Borba*, dating from 1781–84.

Among the many fountains of *Lisbon*, several possess artistic merit, including those in the *Largo das Necessidades* (1747), in the *Largo da*

Esperança (designed by *Carlos Mardel*), in the *Largo José Figueir-edo* (1775; with sculpture by *António Machado*), and in the *Largo do Carmo* (1786).

The most impressive and spectacular of all Portuguese fountains are however those which punctuate the stages of the ascent to the great 18C pilgrimage churches of *Bom Jesus do Monte* and of *N.S. dos Remédios*, situated on steep hillsides outside *Braga* and *Lamego* respectively. The fountain in the Court of the Kings below N.S. dos Remédios offers an astonishing dramatic spectacle. At Bom Jesus the central feature of the ascent is a staircase of five stages with late baroque and rococo fountains (completed c 1774) sym-bolising the five senses. This grand design is paralleled on a smaller scale by the early baroque fountain staircase situated a few kilometres away on the other side of Braga in the hillside garden of the monastery of *Tibães*.

The idea of the religious gardens of Bom Jesus and N.S. dos Remédios, in which octagonal and hexagonal domed chapels display life-sized groups of wooden figures, realistically painted, representing scenes from the life of Jesus, seems to derive originally from the sub-Alpine sanctuaries of NW Italy, in particular from the Sacro Monte of Varallo, which was begun in 1486. Likewise the concept of a staircase of fountains in a hillside garden goes back to the 16th and early 17C villas of central Italy at Bagnaia, Tivoli, Frascati, etc. The achievement of the Portuguese designers was to combine these two Italian ideas and from them create a new and original species of scenic garden.

English visitors interested in gardens should not ignore those of the 'Terras de Basto'—the district in and near the river Tâmega above Amarante. Here a score or so of small country house gardens are famous for their architectural and sculptural topiary work and magnificent hedges of box, yew, and other evergreens. This fashion was introduced by two ladies of the locality, Dona Emília and Dona Justina Basto, in the second quarter of the 19C. They learned the art in England where they were educated, and taught it to their gardeners and those of their neighbours, who have passed it down to their successors over several generations.

Bridges. Portugal is intersected by numerous rivers, including three large ones shared with Spain, the Tagus, Douro, and Guadiana. Consequently bridges are an important architectural feature of the country. The Roman bridge near Alter do Chão in the Alentejo has already been mentioned. Not far away there is another, situated in the parish of *Marvão*. In N Portugal a 16-arched Roman bridge crosses the Tâmega at *Chaves*, and the 400m bridge spanning the beautiful river Lima at *Ponte de Lima* is partly of Roman construc-tion. Fine examples of medieval bridges are the four-arched *Ponte de Mucela* crossing the river Alva near *Arganil* (dating from 1298) and the bridges at *Mirandela*, of 17 arches crossing the Tua (14C), at *Barcelos*, spanning the Cávado (15C), and the five-arched *Ribeira de Tera* bridge near *Pavia* in the Alentejo. A long 16C bridge crosses the Lima at *Ponte de Barca*, and there is another fine 12-arched one of similar date, incorporating an earlier structure, crossing the river Vouga at *Lamas*, E of Aveiro. Among numerous fine 18C bridges we may single out for its handsome appearance the Neo-classical one across the Tâmega at *Amarante*, built 1781–90 (replacing an original Roman bridge) and ornamented with obelisks. Portugal's splendid series of 19th and 20C steel bridges are noticed below, in the section on modern architecture.

Painting: 1550–1800. The arts of painting and sculpture in Portugal from the 16th to the early 18C are distinguished by no well-known names. The work of the late 16th and early 17C Mannerists, such as *Francisco Venegas*, a Spaniard settled in Portugal where he was active c 1575–90, and *Simão Rodrigues* (active c 1580–1620), was uniformly undistinguished, as may be seen from the numerous canvases they supplied for retables of the period. *Josefa de Óbidos* (c 1630–84) painted sentimental religious subjects and elaborate still lifes. *Félix da Costa* (1639–1712), a leading painter of the time, wrote a treatise entitled 'The antiquity of the art of painting' (1696) in which he complained of the low esteem into which his art had fallen in Portugal. To judge by engravings from his designs (no certain orginal work of his survives) his artistic talent was very modest: nor does his treatise, which was eventually published in 1967, possess any originality.

From this catalogue of uninspired work it is a relief to turn to portraiture, in which a considerably higher standard of achievement prevailed. To *Cristóvão Lopes* (1516–94), son of the royal painter *Gregório* (died 1550), are attributed the portraits of João III and Dona Catarina in the Madre de Deus convent at Lisbon. Other fine 16C portraits are the Dom Sebastião by *Cristóvão de Moraes* (active 1557–71) and an anonymous Old Lady with a rosary, both in the Museu de Arte Antiga at Lisbon. The leading 17C portraitist was *Domingos Vieira* (c 1600–78), a tenebrist whose *chiaroscuro* technique earned him the nickname *'O Escuro'*. The portrait of Dona Isabel de Moura in the Lisbon museum, which is attributed to him, suggests knowledge of Velázquez—whose influence is still more certainly apparent in a charming youthful portrait of Catherine of Braganza by an anonymous artist (Évora museum).

During the early decades of the 18C the art of painting in Portugal was dominated by Italian masters—notably the Savoyard portraitist *G.D. Duprà* (1689–1770; active in Portugal 1719–30) and the *trompe l' oeil* painters *Vincenzo Baccarelli* (1682–1745; active at Lisbon c 1710–20) and *Niccolò Nasoni* (1691–1773; active as a painter at Oporto and Lamego 1725–c 1740, thereafter working only as architect). Stimulated by the example of these foreigners, and benefiting from new opportunities to study abroad, Portuguese artists were soon able to compete for commissions. Among the most successful were *Francisco Vieira de Matos* (1699–1783), known as *'Vieira Lusitano'*, and *Pedro Alexandrino de Carvalho* (1729–1810), prolific painters of altar pieces, and the former also a skilful engraver. The *Morgado de Setúbal* (c 1750–1809) is best known for his powerfully realistic still lifes. *Fin de siècle* Romanticism had a talented representative in *Francisco Vieira* (1765–1805), known as *'Vieira Portuense'*, who spent 12 years in Italy and England, and painted religious, mythological, and historical subjects as well as portraits (e.g., Angelica Kauffmann painting; Lisbon museum). The work of Vieira's much more famous contemporary *Domingos Antonio Sequeira* is noticed below because it belongs mainly to the 19C.

Sculpture: 1550–1800. As we have seen, during the first part of the 16C the leading Renaissance sculptors in Portugal were immigrant French masters, among whom the most distinguished was *Nicolas Chanterène* (active to c 1540), who was also a herald in the College of Arms and friend of the humanist scholar Clenardus. These sculptors worked mainly in marble and alabaster. During the last decades of the

16C a new type of retable, conceived as an architectural framework showing off a series of paintings, came into fashion, gradually superseding the stone reredos; and stone statuary was increasingly replaced by wood carved and painted figures. The most gifted of the *imaginários* who carved these figures was *Manuel Pereira* (1588–1683) who early in life emigrated to Spain where his most famous work is the St Bruno in the Miraflores monastery near Burgos. Other *imaginários*, whose statues were made of terracotta as well as wood, included Frei *Cipriano da Cruz*, active 1676–1716 at Tibães (near Braga) and at Coimbra, the *Rendufe sculptor*, active c 1720–34, and a certain Brother *Pedro*, active in the last quarter of the 17C at Alcobaça.

From the beginning of the 18C the international Baroque style began to influence Portuguese sculpture thanks largely to the arrival c 1700 of a French sculptor, *Claude de Laprade* (1682–1738), to whom is ascribed the interior decoration of the *University Library, Coimbra*. He was employed at *Mafra* in the 1730s, at which time several dozen large marble statues, commissioned from leading Italian sculptors, were imported and installed in the monastery church where they presented an example to Portuguese artists of the best Italian late baroque work of their day.

The Portuguese sculptor *José de Almeida* (1700–69), who was trained in Italy, also executed commissions for Mafra; and in 1753 the Italian sculptor *Alessandro Giusti* (1715–99) set up a school for sculptors and architects there. The most famous 18C Portuguese sculptor is *Joaquim Machado de Castro* (c 1731–1822), who came from Coimbra (where the principal museum is named after him). He was trained by José de Almeida and worked under Giusti at Mafra (1756–70). His reputation principally derives from the splendid bronze equestrian statue of Dom José, with attendant figures, which he executed for the Praça do Comércio at Lisbon. Good examples of Portuguese Neo-classical sculpture are to be seen at *Queluz* and in the *Ajuda Palace* (Belém). The latter was the main centre of Portuguese artistic, architectural and decorative activity during the first quarter of the 19C.

Carved Woodwork: 1500–1800. From the 15C to the end of the 18C *talha*, or carved woodwork, principally for church interiors, represented one of the most popular and widespread of all forms of artistic expression throughout the Iberian Peninsula. Not only reredoses but also pulpits, organ-cases, frames of apertures, and choir stalls, were elaborately carved; and all this woodwork except such utilitarian elements as the seats of choir stalls was usually painted or gilded. After the discovery of gold in Brazil in the 1690s, the gilding of woodwork (*talha dourada*) became more or less the rule in Portugal.

Late Gothic woodcarving is well represented at *Coimbra* by the reredos in the *Old Cathedral*, which was begun in 1498 by two Flemish craftsmen, and by the choir stalls (c 1513) in the *Santa Cruz* monastery church. Good examples of Mannerist retables dating from the end of the 16C are to be seen in *N.S. do Carmo* at *Coimbra*, the cathedral at *Portalegre*, and *N.S. da Luz, Lisbon*; and somewhat later, the retable of *São Domingos* (c 1632) at *Bemfica* (Lisbon). The reliquary chapel at the monastery of *Alcobaça* exemplifies the early Baroque style. The reredos of the high altar (1698) and the transept reliquary retables in the *Sé Nova* at *Coimbra* are at last fully baroque in spirit, with Solomonic columns, and gilded all over. This Portuguese High Baroque mode of *talha dourada* has been named by

Robert Smith the 'National Style'. Examples are to be seen all over the country. There are 12 retables carved in this style in the Jesuit church of the *Espirito Santo* at *Évora* for example, and 15 at *Santa Clara-a-Nova* (*Coimbra*; c 1696); while the high altar reredoses of *São Bento* at *Oporto* (c 1704) and of *Santo António* at *Lagos* (c 1715) may be cited as exceptionally fine specimens. The last named church exemplifies the peculiarly Portuguese invention of the *igreja toda de ouro*, the interior completely covered with gilded wood-work. Another example is the church of the Dominican *Convent of Jesus* at *Aveiro* (before 1725); while at *São Francisco, Oporto* (c 1720–70) the gilded woodwork displays a sequence of styles from High Baroque through Late Baroque to Rococo. The church of the nunnery of *Santa Clara* at *Oporto* is a late example of a golden church interior, its *talha* carved c 1730 by *Miguel Francisco da Silva* (active 1726–46). Indicative of conservative national taste was the rejection by Portuguese woodcarvers of the *estípite* (inverted obelisk) type of column shaft which achieved so much popularity among late baroque retable-makers in Spain and Spanish America.

The change in style from High to Late Baroque is well demonstrated by the magnificent choir stalls of the nunneries of *Arouca* (1722–25) and *Lorvão* (1745). At the former rosewood has been used for the seats while the rest is *talha dourada*; whereas at Lorvão polished rosewood is used throughout. The Italianate Late Baroque or 'Joanine style' (named after João V, who reigned 1706–50) is represented in *talha dourada* by the chancel of the church of the *Paulistas* at *Lisbon*, and the retables of the high altars of *Oporto* and *Viseu* cathedrals. Splendid examples of late baroque and rococo reredoses are to be seen at *Tibães* (1757–60) and *Falperra* (1763), both near *Braga*; at São *Domingos* (c 1763), *Viana do Castelo*; at the chapel of *Queluz* palace (c 1755) and at *N.S. dos Remédios* (c 1765) at *Évora*. The retable of the church of *Bom Jesus do Monte* near Braga, dating from the beginning of the 19C, is Neo-classical in style.

Among many fine baroque and rococo woodcarved PULPITS we may single out for their high quality those in the *Madre de Deus church, Lisbon*; the monastery church at *Tibães*; and in *São Marcos, Braga*—which belong respectively to the early, mid, and late 18C. Splendid carved and gilded ORGAN-CASES are to be seen in *Oporto* cathedral (1727; design attributed to Nasoni), *Braga* cathedral (two organs, dated 1737 and 1738), *Tibães* (1785), and *São Vicente de Fora* at *Lisbon* (late 18C). The two fine baroque organ-cases (1767–73) in *São Miguel de Refóios*, Cabeceiras de Basto, together with most of the church's *talha*, including choir stalls, retables, and pulpits, were executed by the Benedictine woodcarver Frei *José Vilaça* (1731–1809), a follower of *André Soares*: the work of both of them reveals the influence of Augsburg prints.

Architecture: Baroque, Rococo, and Neo-classical. Polygonal and other regular geometrical ground plans for churches, probably inspired by Serlio's 'Fifth book of architecture' (1st edition Paris, 1547), were employed in Portugal throughout the 17th and 18Cs. The small 18C rustic church of *Janas* near Sintra is circular. Octagonal plans occur at *Figueira da Foz, Belém, Pombal*, Lisbon (*Menino de Deus*, 1711), *Cascais, Braga, Aveiro* (*N.S. das Barrocas*, 1722–32), and *Oporto*; hexagonal ones at *Vila da Feira, Aveiro* (two), and *Caldas da Rainha* (*N.S. da Pedra*, 1740–47; architect *Rodrigo Franco*); and Greek cross plans at *Santarém, Lisbon* (*Santa Engrácia*, 1682), and *Barcelos* (*N.S. da Cruz*, c 1705, attributed to *João Antunes*). These centralised-type plans for churches and chapels were especially popular in the first quarter of the 18C, reflecting Baroque interest in experiments with spatial composition. The most ambitious venture in this direction was the oval church of Bom Jesus do Monte near Braga (1722-25), but it proved unstable and was pulled down and replaced by the present Neo-classical structure (see below). The future for the 'unstable' oval form was to lie not in earthquake-prone Portugal but in Portuguese America.

Meanwhile the new wealth derived from Brazil, and the resulting revival of artistic and architectural aspirations, attracted to Portugal a series of gifted foreigners—among the most prolific and influential of whom were the goldsmith-architect *João Frederico Ludovice* (Johann Friedrich Ludwig, 1670–1752), a German trained in Italy, who arrived in Portugal in 1701 and was responsible for the monastery-palace of *Mafra* (begun 1717) and for the chancel of *Évora* cathedral (1718–c 1728); the French sculptor-decorator *Claude de Laprade* (1682–1738), to whom is attributed the design of the *Coimbra University Library* (1716–28), one of the most colourful and original interiors of 18C Europe; and *Niccolò Nasoni* (1691–1773), a Tuscan painter, sculptor, and architect of remarkable creative genius—still much underestimated—who designed· and rebuilt churches and town and country houses and laid out gardens in the N of Portugal between 1730 and 1770. *Luigi Vanvitelli* (1700–73) designed in 1742 and executed in Italy a complete chapel dedicated to St. John—a masterpiece of neo-Palladianism—which was shipped to Lisbon and installed in 1747 in the church of *São Roque*—thereafter exercising a strong influence on design in the decorative arts of Portugal. Two Italian architects, *Tamossi* and *Azzolini*, were responsible for the *Seminary* (1748–65) at *Coimbra*. Another Italian, *Giovanni Carlo Bibiena* (died 1760) designed the beautiful *Memória* church (begun 1760) at *Belém*; the Hungarian *Carlos Mardel* assisted *Eugénio dos Santos* to rebuild the centre of Lisbon after the 1755 earthquake; the French silversmith and sculptor *J.-B. Robillon* (died 1782) enlarged the royal palace at *Queluz* from 1758 onwards; *John Carr of York* (1723–1807) designed the great hospital of *Santo António* (1770–95) at *Oporto*; and the Italian *F.S. Fabri* (died 1807) designed the *Palacio Foz* (1777) at *Lisbon* and was the principal architect of the *Ajuda Palace* at *Belém* (begun 1802).

These foreign masters together with several talented and original Portuguese architects were responsible for a series of monuments which are representative of almost all the principal European styles of the 18th and early 19Cs. The façade and plan of Mafra recall the great Central European monasteries of the early 18C, e.g., Weingarten and Einsiedeln; and Ludovice also introduced at Mafra various elements derived from his study of High Baroque buildings in Rome, which contribute to the creation of a remarkably successful eclectic composition. The basilica, which has the first fully developed dome, set upon a high drum, in Portugal, inspired several large churches of late baroque style—notably the pilgrimage shrine of *N.S. de Aires* at *Viana do Alentejo* (begun 1743), the church of the monastery of *São Miguel de Refoios* at *Cabeceiras de Basto*, and, most splendid of all, the *Estrela* basilica at *Lisbon* (1779–90), architects *Mateus Vicente de Oliveira* (1706–86) and *Reinaldo Manuel dos Santos* (1740–89). Nasoni's near-oval church of the *Clérigos* at *Oporto*, with its magnificent *campanile* (inspired by the tower of the Palazzo Vecchio at Florence), belongs to a less conventional and more vigorously ornate variant of the baroque style than Mafra, reflecting the freedom of painted *trompe l'oeil* architecture (in which art Nasoni was well versed) and silver work and furniture. An example of the so-called *transparente*, or concealed lighting effect, which was one of the most sophisticated baroque inventions, is to be seen in the north transept chapel of the church of São Francisco at Évora. The fashion for *chinoiserie* is manifest in the University Library at Coimbra.

Rococo is exceptionally well represented in the Minho by a series of fascinating buildings such as the *Falperra* chapel near Braga, designed by *André Ribeiro Soares da Silva* (1720–69), which reveal the ubiquitous influence of Italian and German engravings, here interpreted however in a startlingly original manner. In central Portugal *Mateus Vicente de Oliveira* (see above), who worked with Ludovice at Mafra, introduced important rococo elements into his design for the palace at *Queluz* (1747–52), which are absent in the slightly earlier and almost equally beautiful royal palace of the *Necessidades* (1745–50; architect *Caetano Tomás de Sousa*) in the W end of Lisbon.

The rebuilding of the centre of *Lisbon* on a regular gridiron plan of uniform four or five storey blocks after the 1755 earthquake, following the master plan (1756) of *Eugénio dos Santos* (1711–60), was 'the greatest uniform architectural undertaking of the Age of Enlightenment'. The so-called Pombaline style generally employed by the architects associated with the rebuilding was characterised by an economical simplicity of form relieved by some baroque and rococo decorative details applied with restraint and discretion. The great set piece of Pombaline Lisbon is the Praça do Comércio.

The Neo-classical trend in late 18C architecture is represented in northern Portugal by the Law Courts or *Relação* (1766–96) at *Oporto*, designed by *João de Almada e Mello* (died 1786), under whose influence there were also built the stupendous convent of *Santa Clara* at *Vila do Conde* (begun 1777) and the *Carrancas palace* (c 1790) at *Oporto*. There is also the work of *Carlos da Cruz Amarante* (1748–1815) at *Braga* (notably the church of *Bom Jesus do Monte*, 1784–1811) and at *Oporto* (*University*, begun 1805). English Neo-classicism is represented at Oporto—both by John Carr's hospital already mentioned, and by the *British Factory House* (begun 1785), designed by Consul *John Whitehead* (1726–1802).

At Lisbon the Neo-classical *Theatre of São Carlos* was built in 1792 by the Italianised Portuguese architect *José da Costa e Silva* (1747–1819), who was also one of the architects of the *Ajuda palace* (begun 1802 to the designs of F.S. Fabri). Costa e Silva also completed in 1785 the rebuilding of the Italian church of *N.S. do Loreto* at Lisbon.

To sum up this section, the 18C was a golden period for Portuguese architecture and the decorative arts. Not only were the great monuments at and near Lisbon and Oporto, including the rebuilding of the whole centre of the capital, all admirably successful as sophisticated examples of their various styles, but innumerable smaller buildings in towns and villages throughout the country, and additions made to earlier buildings, as well as their interior decoration and furniture, were no less successful in their more humble way. It would seem as if even local builders, amateur architects, and rustic artisans and craftsmen were inspired, during these years, with instinctive sound judgement and sense of proportion, harmony, colour, and design.

Fortifications: 16–18Cs. The new science of fortification based on polygonal bastions, capable of resisting gunpowder artillery, was invented in Italy at the turn of the 15C, and perfected by French military engineers in the 17C. A most interesting transitional style fortress at *Vila Viçosa*, dating from c 1530 and attributable to the military engineer Benedetto da Ravenna, has the massive round bulwarks recommended by Dürer in his treatise of 1527, and a fine rusticated main entrance. It follows exactly a design by Leonardo da Vinci (MS 'B', c 1490) which was by 1530 already old fashioned. So in 1537, when Francisco de Holanda was sent by João III to Italy, he was particularly instructed to bring back information on the new science. By the end of the 18C nearly all the land and sea approaches to Portugal were defended by powerful fortresses built in conformity with the new principles. Of those which survive, the most interesting coastal forts are the ones guarding the mouths of the river Sado at Setúbal (late 16C and 17C); Tagus (*São Julião da Barra* on the N shore and the circular *Torre do Bugio* on a shoal in the estuary; 16–17Cs); Douro (*Castelo de São João da Foz*, c 1560–1647); Lima (the pentagonal *Forte de S. Tiago da Foz*, 1567–96), and Minho (*Forte da Insua*). On the land frontier during the 17th and 18Cs rings of fortifications were built round several border towns, including *Caminha* and *Valença* defending the N, and *Almeida* (a new fortress town built to a regular hexagonal design enclosing a small 16C square fort with round towers of which only foundations survive), *Campo Maior*, and *Elvas*, defending the eastern approaches. The new fortified perimeter of the latter town was laid out in 1643, and with the construction of two adjacent forts, those of *Santa Luzia* (1641–87) and *N.S. da Graça* (1763–92), Elvas became one of the strongest places in Europe. To the same period belong the new defences of *Estremoz* and *Vila Viçosa*. The city of *Évora*, key to Lisbon, was also re-fortified in the 17C, and six bastions (1651–80) as well as the quadrilateral supporting fort of *Santo António* (1666–70) survive intact. Most of the 17C fortifications of Portugal were surveyed in 1666–68 by the French military engineer Manesson Mallet and are illustrated in his 'Les travaux de Mars' (Paris, 1672).

Architecture: 19th and 20Cs. Portuguese 19th and 20C architecture displays the typical stylistic variety which is characteristic of the period throughout Europe. The styles employed included traditional Italianate (Merchants' Exchange, Oporto, begun 1842; National Theatre, Lisbon, architect *F. Lodi*, 1842–46; Town Hall, Lisbon, architect *Domingos Parente*, 1867–75; Chamber of Deputies, Lisbon, architect *Ventura Terra*, begun 1896; Theatre of São João, Oporto, architect *Marquês da Silva*, 1912–18); Neo-Manueline (Palace Hotel, Busaco, architect *Luigi Manini*, begun 1888; Central railway station, Lisbon, architect *J. L. Monteiro*, opened 1889); cosmopolitan picturesque or eclectic (Pena palace, Sintra, designed by *Baron Von Eschwege*, 1840); Byzantine (Martins Sarmento Institute, Guimarães, architect *Marquês da Silva*, 1881); and functional (house in Rua Honório de Lima, Oporto, architect *Viana de Lima*, 1939; *pousada* near Venda Nova, river Cávado, architect *Januário Goøinho*, 1948; Calouste Gulbenkian museum, Lisbon, architects *Alberto Pessoa, Pedro Cid*, and *Ruy Athouguia*, 1966–69). Other interesting examples of functional architecture at Lisbon built in the second quarter of this century include the cinemas designed by *Raul Lino, Luis Cristino da Silva* and *Cassiano Branco* in the 1920s, the Pavilhão-Radio (*Carlos Ramos*, 1927–33), the Institute Superior Técnico (*Pardal Monteiro*, 1927–35), the Edifício Standar

Electrica (*J.A. Cottinelli Telmo*, 1940), the Lisbon Mint (*J. Segurado*, 1934–50), and the Estoril Estação Telefones (*Adelino Nunes*, 1938).

Portugal also offers one of the finest series of steel bridges to be seen in Europe—notably the bridge over the Tagus at *Santarém* (1876–81); the two over the Douro at *Oporto* designed by *Eiffel* and by *Seyrig*, inaugurated in 1877 and 1886 respectively; the one over the mouth of the *Lima* designed by *Eiffel* (1895); the one across the mouth of the *Douro* (1960–63); and the most recent of all, that across the *Tagus* estuary (1965).

Painting and Sculpture: 19th and 20Cs. During the first quarter of the 19C the Portuguese painter *Domingos António Sequeira* (1768–1837), who enjoyed an international reputation, was working in his native country. He returned to Lisbon in 1795 after a seven year sojourn in Rome, but left again in 1823 for France, thereafter returning to Rome where he spent the last ten years of his life. He painted historical, allegorical, and religious subjects as well as portraits—all adequately represented in the Lisbon museum. He was a brilliant draughtsman and his preparatory studies are often even more impressive than the finished paintings. Among his best-known portraits at Lisbon are: The Viscount of Santarém and his family (1805), The young Count of Farrobo (1813), and The artist's children; but his sketches for these portraits and for those of Beresford (c 1815) and João VI (1826) are more memorable. In his late work he developed an increasingly impressionistic technique with the use of bright, shimmering colours.

Portuguese 19C art after Sequeira can best be studied in the Museum of Contemporary Art at Lisbon, and in the Soares dos Reis Museum at Oporto. The latter is named after *António Soares dos Reis* (1847–89), a sculptor from Oporto whose work was much admired by his contemporaries, and has retained its popularity since (e.g., 'O desterrado', 1872; Oporto museum). Subsequently, the prolific Oporto sculptor *António Teixeira Lopes* (1866–1942) achieved almost as much popular success. Both these sculptors were competent portraitists.

The best portrait painters of the mid 19C were the *Visconde de Meneses* (1820–78) and *Miguel Angelo Lupi* (1826–83)—good examples of their work being the former's Portrait of the artist's wife (1862), and the latter's Marquesa de Belas. The topographical drawings and watercolours of *Carlos Vanzeller* (1811–39) are unusually lively and charming. The most brilliant and promising artist of the second half of the century was *Henrique César de Araujo Pousão*, who died aged 25 in 1884.

The most famous 20C Portuguese painter is *Maria-Helena Vieira da Silva* (born 1908), who has lived and worked most of her life in Paris. Her paintings are to be seen in the principal museums of modern art throughout the world.

Applied Arts. The Portuguese have always excelled in the domestic and practical arts. Wrought-iron balconies, although less striking than Spanish *rejas*, nevertheless distinguish the façades of most town houses in Portugal. The best representative collections of textiles, silver, porcelain, and furniture are those of the Museu de Arte Antiga at Lisbon, and the Machado de Castro museum at Coimbra. Ceramics and furniture are also well represented in the Soares dos Reis museum at Oporto, and there are smaller collections in regional and local museums throughout the country, e.g. those of Évora, Viana do Castelo, Guimarães, Lamego, and Viseu, to mention only a few: and in this context it is worth remarking that the smaller museums in Portugal seldom disappoint the visitor who is interested in the domestic arts, and they are often housed in architecturally important buildings which are worth seeing in their own right. The most famous specialised museum in Portugal is that devoted to ceremonial coaches at Belém, near Lisbon: these masterpieces of cabinet makers' and decorators' art dating from the 16th to the 19C comprise the finest collection of the kind in Europe. Another important collection of carriages may now be seen at Vila Viçosa.

The development in Portugal of the very important Iberian art of painted tiles (*azulejos*) may also be studied in museums throughout the country, notably in Lisbon in the Museu de Arte Antiga and in the Museu do Azulejo (Madre de Deus convent), and at Coimbra in the Machado de Castro museum. The best examples of 16C *azulejos* still *in situ* are those of the palace at Sintra. There are particularly fine displays of 17C *azulejos* at Lisbon in the Fronteira palace, and in the chapel of Santo Amaro, at Santarém (Marvila church), Elvas (Dominican nunnery chapel), Montemór-o-Novo (Convent of N.S. da Saudação), Évora, and Coimbra. 18C painted tiles are to be seen *in situ* all over the country, and nearly always enhance and enliven the interiors and the exterior walls to which they are applied.

Two principal trends should be noted in the development of the *azulejo*. First, colour: up to the end of the 17C a wide range of tints was employed (yellows, blues, and greens predominating); then, from the end of the 17C, the fashion changed to the use of blue and white only; after which, starting in the mid 18C, polychromy returned again to favour, although the blue and white fashion did not by any means die out. Secondly, design: until about the middle of the 17C patterns made up of repeated geometrical and other non-figurative motifs, resembling carpet patterns, were usual; but already by the later 16C tile pictures, often based on engravings, were created, occupying a whole block or panel of *azulejos*; and as the 17C advanced these picorial designs, increasing in size, realism and variety of subject matter, gradually superseded the earlier two-dimensional repetitive patterns, and introduced perspective effects and chiaroscuro, even occasionally achieving effects of *trompe l'oeil*.

Townscape. Few towns in Portugal fail to offer the visitor one or two attractive streets and squares; and sometimes there are whole quarters of exceptional merit. In Lisbon, for instance, the Alfama, the Bairro Alto and the Baixa admirably display the varied types of urbanism they represent—from the natural organic growth of the first to the imposed geometrical plan of the last. Interesting small-scale examples of regular town plans are to be seen at Vila Real de Santo Antonio (1774) in the Algarve and Manique do Intendente (early 19C) SW of Santarém. Among country towns noted for their exceptional architectural charm and urbanistic interest many would put Évora first. Other such towns are Elvas, Vila Viçosa, Portalegre, Óbidos, Tomar, Santarém, Viseu, Guimarães, Valença, Braganza; and less well-known, but at least equally remarkable for their charm and character, are Mirandela, Ponte de Lima, Lamego, and Linares in the N; Castelo de Vide, Borba, and Monsaraz, in the Alentejo; and Tavira and Alcoutim in the Algarve—to cite only a few example.

Glossary

ABÓBADA. Vault.

AJIMECE. Two-light Moorish window divided by a slender column.

ALBARRADA. Floral-patterned *azulejo*.

ALMOFADAS. (Lit. pillows). Rustication.

ALFARGE. *Mudéjar* timber ceiling, usually hipped or domical.

ALPENDRE. Porch.

ARTESONADO. Wooden coffered ceiling.

AZULEJO. Glazed tile, usually painted, and about 13–15cm square.

BARRAGEM. Dam of reservoir.

BILROS. Elaborately turned finials.

CADEIRAL. Choir-stalls.

CÂMARA MUNICIPAL. Town Hall.

CAMARIM. Shrine of an image.

CAPELA-MÓR. Chancel or sanctuary.

CHAFARIZ. Public fountain.

CHAROLA. Ambulatory of centralised church; niche for image of saint.

CIMO. Top or summit.

CITÂNIA. Prehistoric hill-settlement

CLAUSTRO. Cloister.

COLUMNA SALOMÓNICA. Column, usually of Corinthian order, with twisted shaft.

CONTADOR. Counter, desk, or cabinet.

CORO. Choir.

CRUZEIRO. Cross; or crossing of a church.

CUSTÓDIA. Monstrance.

ENTALHADOR. Carver, usually of wood.

ERMIDA. Small church or chapel, often in an isolated situation.

ESMALTE. Enamel.

ESPIGUEIROS. Seen in the Minho, and equivalent to the *hórreos* of Galicia, these small granaries, corn lofts, or storehouses are raised on mushroom-shaped pillars to keep vermin from entering.

GUARITA. Bartizan turret.

IGREJA. Church: IGREJA MATRIZ. Parish church.

IMAGINÂRIO. Carver of images.

JANELA. Window.

JOANINE (*Joanino*). Late baroque style in fashion during the reign of *João V* (1706-50).

JUDIARIA. Jewish enclave, or ghetto.

LACERIA. Islamic geometrical decorative patterning of interlacing polygonal and star shapes.

LARGO. Small square, market place.

MANUELINE (*Manuelino*). Final phase of Gothic in Portugal current during the reign of *Manuel I* (1495–1521) and later.

MARFIM. Ivory.

MÁRMORE. Marble.

MARRANO. A Jew ostensibly converted to Catholicism.

MESTRE DE OBRAS. Clerk of the works.

MIRADOURO. Belvedere, balcony.

MOGNO. Mahogany.

MOSTEIRO. Monastery.

MOZÁRAB (*Moçárabe*). Christian subject to the Moors: a term extended to their architecture.

MUDÉJAR. Moslem subject to the Christians: a term extended to their architecture and decoration.

PAÇO or PAÇOS. Palace or country house.

PAU PRETO. Brazilian rosewood; also *Jacaranda*.

PAU SANTO. Lignum vitae.

PELOURINHO. Stone columns serving the purpose of pillories, seen in numerous towns and villages in the N. half of Portugal, but less frequently S. of the Tagus. They were the emblem of feudal or municipal jurisdiction, and the edicts of town councils were read from their steps. Near the summit of some, iron supports survive, from which were suspended chains, to which criminals were fastened: and it might in addition serve as a gibbet. Many were highly ornamented, while others are quite plain. In view of their ubiquity, only a few examples are specifically mentioned in this Guide.

POMBALINE (*Pombalino*). Architectural style employed in the rebuilding of Lisbon after the 1755 earthquake, while the *Marquês de Pombal* was virtually dictator of Portugal (1750–77).

PRAÇA. Place, square.

PRAIA. Beach.

PRESÉPIO. Christmas crib or manger.

QUARTEL. Barracks.

QUINTA. Country estate, or the main house on such an estate.

RÉS DO CHÃO. Ground floor.

RETÁBULO or RETABLO. Retable, reredos, or altarpiece.

SÉ. Cathedral.

SOLAR. Manor house, or seat of an armigerous family.

TALHA. Carved work, usually in wood. TALHA DOURADA, gilded woodwork.

TORRE DE MENAGEM. Keep of castle.

ZIMBÓRIO. Dome or cupola.

INTRODUCTION TO PORT AND THE WINES OF PORTUGAL

By *David Francis*

Although Portuguese wines are referred to by Chaucer, these came from Lisbon: those of the Upper Douro were first described in the 1460s by a Czech traveller named Rosmital, who found there a strong wine made from over-ripe grapes dried like raisins, which was called '*Vinho da Grécia*'. We find few allusions to a *port* type of wine until 1700, when *Thomas Woodmass*, a young Yorkshireman, left an account of his trip up the Douro to a wild region still the preserve of bandits. By then there was in 'O Porto' a thriving and enterprising *Factory*, or community of British merchants, many of them engaged in importing Newfoundland cod, or cloth from England, who were eager to profit by the sudden growth in demand for Portuguese wines. They had in fact been anticipated by their colleagues in Viana do Castelo, who had found wines of a claret type near the Lima, which with other rivers in the Minho ran through a broad valley; whereas the Douro, although a much larger stream, flowed through a gorge above Oporto, and there was no easy way across the mountains it traversed. An occasional driblet of Upper or Alto Douro wine may have reached Oporto, but in general there was little knowledge of conditions there.

The entry of French wines into Britain had been prohibited from 1679 to 1685. During these years large quantities of wines had passed the British Customs as German, Spanish, or Portuguese, but it is difficult to say exactly where they came from. Portuguese wines averaged 5833 tuns, but in three of these years they fluctuated between 13,000 and 16,000 tuns, incredible if one considers that the figures for 1677 and 1686 were only 427 and 617 *pipes*, of which 407 and 253 pipes respectively came from Oporto, a pipe being a barrel containing 115 gallons, or 320 litres. A start had been made.

After the outbreak of war in 1690, when the prohibition was renewed, the import of Portuguese wines rose rapidly to 8000 pipes, and after a slight recession during the four years of peace, to 10,000 during the War of the Spanish Succession. After c 1713 exports from Oporto gained the lead over those from Lisbon, and the term 'Port Wine' tended to cover all Portuguese wines.

The wines which the British appreciated in particular were the product of vines grown on poor soil on small peasant holdings high up in the mountains, where the schistose terraced slopes produced a crop of red wines of unusual strength, even if scanty. According to legend, *Peter Bearsley* and other adventurous men from Viana and Oporto had visited certain monasteries near the Douro which could sell them wines in quantity. But they were hard to discover, and Woodmass had much ado to avoid a rival party, which threatened to poach on his findings. The British continued to buy from the peasants to their mutual advantage, but the larger landlords, realising that they were on to a good thing, had meanwhile banded together in an endeavour to corner the market.

In the reigns of William and Mary, and of Queen Anne, port and claret were adopted as emblems of the Whig and Tory parties. The Whigs stood for port; the Tories (who favoured an eventual rapprochement with France) supported claret. The Whigs enjoyed claret, burgundy, and champagne as well as anyone else, and while declaiming their political arguements in favour of port, would admit in private that it had its defects: nevertheless it should be drunk as a patriotic duty, if for no other reason.

In 1693 *William Salmon* described port or port-a-port as a strong full-bodied wine with medicinal qualities, although not particularly palatable, for the earlier port wines travelled from their eyries in skins on mule-back, which gave them a strong taste of resin, and much of the wine was bitter or turbid, or, alternatively, syrupy. The so-called 'ambrosia of the north' never really overcame these defects until the close of the 18C, when increased production and competition prompted an improvement, and the art of fortification became better understood. The best port tended to become a rare commodity, and was generally acquired through recommendation. But the demand was growing for ever sweeter and stronger wines, to satisfy which the producers were obliged to lay hands on any liquors they could find, and to use any number of adulterants, and elderberry-juice as a colorant.

The commercial interest in the Anglo-Portuguese trade was such that a Tory attempt to re-introduce French wines on equal terms at the end of the War of Succession was roundly defeated in Parliament. After the war, it grew from strength to strength, and represented over 80 per cent of the total imports from Portugal. By now port wine had ceased to be the emblem of the Whigs only, being regarded by the whole establishment as the only proper wine with which to wash down good English roast beef.

In the early days, the wines of the Upper Douro were a well-kept secret. Even in the 1690s the Portuguese minister *Luís da Cunha* (who had been a district judge in Oporto) could only suggest the Algarve as a possible source of sweet wine to meet the English taste, and made no mention of the Douro. More remarkably, *John Methuen*, author of the famous treaty of 1703 (which limited the duties on Portuguese wines to two-thirds of that paid by French wines, in return for the removal of Portuguese restrictions on British textiles), knew nothing of port wines. He owned a vineyard himself and took a personal interest, but he had lighter wines and Lisbon wines in mind, and was helped to push through the treaty by the fact that several Portuguese statesmen had large vineyards near the capital. Nevertheless, in spite of the supremacy of port at City and Academic dinners, the wines of Lisbon and Madeira, although neglected in the middle of the 18C, still continued to command somewhat higher prices.

Under the shelter of the Methuen Treaty the market in England for port wine spread through the middle classes almost to the proletariate, but more and more colorants, adulterants, and lashings of brandy were being added, producing a concoction which some considered sheer poison. Eventually things got to such a pass that port began to lose its good name, and trade began to fail. It was then, in September 1756, that the future *Marquês de Pombal* intervened, to found the *Company of the Wines of the Upper Douro* (*Companhia Geral da Agricultura dos Vinhos do Alto Douro*). Its aim was to correct abuses, to develop trade with Brazil, and to open up new markets in the Baltic, but it soon attempted to assume control of all wine for export to Britain, and the sale of brandy for fortification.

Not surprisingly, a long battle ensued between the Oporto Factory and the Company, which encroached on the trade in the Portuguese interest, and with considerable success, for they could count on the continuance of the political conditions which prevented the readmission of French wines, and they often inhibited Spanish competition. But it was the Company and the Portuguese middle-men who reaped the benefit rather than the farmers, whom the Company was intended to assist, and they also aspired to penetrate the market inside Britain itself, being in a position to pre-empt the best wines. They might have been able to compete in the quality market, but their connections were not good enough to sustain them very far, and beyond a certain point the Factory was able to hold its own, although such was the growth of counterfeit wines, and of spirit drinking, that the general importation of wine per head into Britain decreased.

Pombal encouraged the Douro trade at the cost of vineyards elsewhere in Portugal, which he considered might be more produc-tive if turned over to corn, and vigilance was necessary to prevent the farmers of the Upper Douro from bringing in wines from outside the demarcated district, but production was increased meanwhile by an extension of the area in which port wine could be grown. An extensive bureaucracy grew up within the Company, but in its first years, at least, it improved the standard of wines and regularised prices. The pure wine alleged to be the Company's aim was not altogether unfortified, for the majority of wines required the addition of some brandy—but not in inordinate quantities—to curb ferment-ation, but the use of elderberries as a colorant, and chemical additives, was diminished.

During this crisis the Oporto Factory was at one time reduced to 30 members, but by the last quarter of the 18C it had recovered, even if constant bickering continued. At one time it was thought that the Factory had become the helot of the Company, forced to take such wines as it was allowed to have, but the steady growth of the British market ensured that there was a living for all, both British and Portuguese.

Wines of a better quality were now being heard of, and in the 1770s 'vintage' wines were first publicly quoted at enhanced prices. In the previous century there had been talk of mature wines, but to what extent such wines, carefully selected and nursed for 20 years in the cellar, really existed, it is hard to tell. Those who had discovered how to produce port wines of quality were naturally jealous of their secret, and sales were restricted to a few favoured customers, but even if not always easy to find, decent wines could still be bought through trustworthy sources. The bulk of the wine, nevertheless, was poor stuff confected with a variety of extraneous additions, and might be anything from a syrupy blackstrap to a violent spiritous compound. The age of gin, which culminated in about 1760, brought about a decline of taste in drinking, even in Oporto, where in 1777 a discriminating British traveller, although impressed by the lavish hospitality of the Factory, considered the port almost undrinkable, and found it hard to comprehend how such stuff could be exported.

In 1786 *William Pitt*'s commercial treaty with France opened the market again to French wines, much to the indignation of Portugal. (Towards the end of his life Pitt, drinking it as a medicine and stimulant rather than as a connoisseur, practically subsisted on port.) Nevertheless, the trade expanded, and suffered remarkably little during the revolutionary and peninsular wars, when duties were again raised, and Portuguese wines did not finally lose their preferential treatment until 1831.

The last decades of the 18C had seen a revival of interest in Lisbon wines, in those of central Portugal, and to some extent in the 'green wines' or *vinhos verdes* of the Minho. *Madeira* had never lost favour, but the small size of the island restricted production to an annual 2000 tuns or so, most of which was exported to America, for as an African offshore island Madeira escaped the prohibitions of the Navigation Act, and could trade with America direct. A good shaking, and the heat of a tropical voyage, helped to mature it, and much Madeira and some port reached England by way of the West and even the East Indies, and then fetched a higher price.

From 1756 to 1801 *John Whitehead* was Consul at Oporto. He was a man of many parts, more of science and learning than of business, although closely connected with the wine trade through his nephew *William Warre, the Elder*. He maintained good relations with both the British and Portuguese, and was personally responsible for the planning and erection of the *Factory House*, which still accommodates the British wine exporters. At the end of the century the Oporto Factory had outstripped in importance that of Lisbon, which had suffered considerably in the 1755 earthquake. It even aspired to be a separate consulate general, but in spite of the recommendations of Robert Walpole, the Minister, these ambitions were thwarted. For a time during the French invasion, the building was in the hands of caretakers, but in 1811 the wine exporters resumed possession, although the Factories had by then ceased to be recognised by Portuguese law as public corporations. A long dispute followed as to its ownership. The wine exporters claimed that as they alone had borne the full burden of paying consulage, the Factory was theirs, while others argued that it belonged to the Consul and the British Community in general. Although the legal arguments rather favoured the latter, the matter was settled in 1834 by an agreement, which left the edifice in the hands of the wine men, the *de facto* occupants. Soon afterwards certain of the more notable members of the opposition, including the founders of the firm of Graham, originally importers of textiles and India merchants, were allowed into the fold.

The early days of the 19C were those of famous vintages, culminating in the Waterloo vintage of 1815. Peninsular victories were celebrated with port, and on Wellington's staff was *General William Warre*, an Oporto man, who could give knowledgeable advice on the subject. Meanwhile, the pure wine school, later led by the famous *Baron Forrester*, engaged in heated controversy with those who preferred the more sophisticated product. Fortified port eventually won the day, but we hear far less of blackstrap and of the various faults which had previously injured the good reputation of port. In 1861 Forrester was drowned in the rapids of the Douro, and his cause foundered. Yet basically the two factions differed less than they appeared to do. Forrester did not object to a reasonable addition of brandy *at the proper time*, and both sides equally condemned adulteration. The best quality port could mature without fortification, but even that was liable to seasonal disturbance and the risk of deterioration. For most ports some fortification was essential to mature the wine for the market without undue delay, and to preserve it by stabilisation.

While expensive and prestigious fortified wines were now the fashion, the bulk of the wine sold was still of the cheaper kind, the grocers' port served by Mr Jawleyford to Mr Sponge, and the universal 'port and lemon' served at every bar. In the same way, in later years, the market was sustained by the Belgian and French demand for aperitif port.

Owing to the number of their Portuguese employees, coopers, artisans, boatmen, etc., and their position *vis à vis* the Portuguese authorities, with no legation to intervene, and being obliged to travel up country in their search for wines, the Oporto Factory was not quite so isolated from the Portuguese as the members of the Lisbon Factory, but their knowledge of the language was as sketchy, and few of them were ever guests in a Portuguese home, although in Whitehead's day there had been some mixing. Later, when the British community backed Dom Pedro during the civil war and siege of Oporto in 1832–34, some of the upper crust occasionally foregathered with the local gentry, and one or two accepted Portuguese titles.

British firms also began to acquire *quintas* or country estates on the Douro. They had seldom done so before, partly owing to the stringency of the Portuguese laws on the subject of foreigners buying land. During the vintage they used them as offices, for they remained essentially export merchants resident in Oporto, and rarely became farmers of vineyards themselves: little has changed in this respect. The Factory has continued on its prosperous course, entrenched in Portugal, yet self-contained and rarely participating in Portuguese society. There has been occasional friction, as in 1899 when Lord Salisbury intervened in Portuguese Africa, and more recently when the British failed to make any effective protest at the Indian occupation of Goa.

Apart from commercial and political problems to contend with, there have been the ruinous diseases of the vine to combat: firstly the *Oidium Tuckeri*; then the dreaded *Phylloxera*. Vintage port has not been quite the same since the outbreak of Phylloxera in the 1870–80s, but it was found that the vines of American stock were resistant to the disease, and by grafting shoots on these the trade won a new lease of life. But even if vintage ports no longer enjoy the prestigious place they occupied in the days of Victoria, when the birth of a son and heir was the signal to lay down a cellar full of port to be ready for his 21st birthday, it has found favour again in recent years, although it represents only about one-fiftieth of the trade in value. This has been caused by an increase in demand for cheaper ports, the export of which to Britain still exceeds that of Portuguese table wines (although they are being imported in large quantities), which have also grown in popularity elsewhere abroad.

Inflation and the general increase in the cost of labour have transformed the industry. Formerly, the bare feet of men trod the grapes during the necessary two or three days' period of fermentation, and the bitterness which would have resulted from the crushing of the pips was thereby avoided. But the old stone troughs or *lagares* are now largely replaced by metal or concrete tanks, with mechanical crushers. The days have passed when the treading of the must was a Dionysian scene, enlivened with music and song and numerous nips of brandy. Formerly, when enough fermentation had taken place, the lagares were unsealed, and the wine poured into great wooden vats or *toneis*. These are now largely superseded, but the quality wines are still pressed from the best black grapes, the basic process of vinification is unchanged, and the quality not impaired. The must is sealed off during fermentation, and not allowed to brim over into the next tank, as with the making of sherry under the *solera* system. Only when fermentation has reduced the sugar content to the right point is the must drained off and dosed with up to 20 per cent of brandy to stabilise it.

There it remains until the spring, when it is taken down the Douro to Oporto. Formerly it was carried in the picturesque sailing craft called *barcos rebelos*; then by the serpentine single-track railway, drawn by vintage British-made engines. A road has replaced the narrow track with its numerous hairpin bends which wound steeply over the Quinhão pass—a generation ago the only land route to the Upper Douro—and the wine is now transported by tanker-lorries.

Once in Oporto—or rather in the *armazens* of transpontine *Vila Nova de Gaia*—it is stored in large wooden vats, made of oak for the best wines, and of chestnut for the others. There it stays for over two years, being carefully watched and nurtured. Tasters test it from time to time, and add blends of other wines and small doses of brandy, up to a further 5 per cent in all, to direct the wine in the way it should go. Aeration and evaporation takes place at a rate of about 2.5 per cent a year, but the casks are regularly topped up.

After about two years the decision is taken as to whether the condition of the best wines justifies the declaration of a vintage year. Each firm decides for itself, but in good years, which occur about once in five, most of their colleagues follow suit. These *vintage ports*, which are not mixed with wines from other vineyards or other years, are then set aside, and bottled. The introduction and general use of the modern straight-sided bottle facilitated the maturing of vintage wines, but until the last decades of the 18C the bottles were bulbous and flat-bottomed like modern decanters, and difficult to store on their sides, although it could be done with a packing of straw. But they had their advantages, for they could not be knocked over so easily, and the long neck could be 'cracked', which left a clean break-off, enabling the wine to be decanted without getting bits of cork into it. In the bottles the wines mature very slowly, and are left undisturbed to mature to perfection, resting on their sides for 15 years or more. By then a deep purple colour, they are considered by many to be the doyen of wines.

Next come the *tawny ports*, so-called because they lose some of their colour and become brown or even straw-coloured. They are kept in the cask for seven years or even longer, and during that period are carefully tended, and helped when necessary by blending with wines from other vineyards and other years.

Ruby port, the commonest ordinary port, made from a blend of lesser wines, is bottled early and drunk comparatively young. It is fuller bodied and sweeter than tawny. Both ruby and tawny are popular in Scandinavia and on the Continent, as is *white port*, port made from white grapes, which may be taken with ice. White port is also making headway in Britain, although in a country where port has always been thought of as essentially red, it has had to fight something of a battle.

Except in Britain, the sale of Portuguese **table wines** (*de mesa*) now vastly exceeds that of port. The best known are the green wines, *vinhos verdes*, so called from their youth and freshness, although they also have a green context, the shady Minho, where the vines grow profusely on high granite trellises (*bardos* or *cruzelas*), and even climb into the branches of adjacent trees (*arjoada*). This last method is an economy of land usage, as crops can grow beneath the trees, but the cost of labour in picking the grapes is now a disadvantage.

In Portugal there are red 'vinhos verdes' as well as white. They both have a slight natural effervescence, but they are somewhat hard to the taste and are less popular abroad. Other white wines are produced in the neighbourhood of Lisbon, and have been for centuries. *Bucelas* and *Carcavelos* (from Oeiras, where Pombal had his estate) were famous, but many vineyards have been swamped by encroaching urban development, and in any case most Portuguese table wines are now blended and are no longer sold under their regional names. The Lisbon area also produces red wines, including that of *Colares* (near Sintra), the vines of which grew in deep sand, and thus survived the Phylloxera. But Colares—even more than Carcavelos and Bucelas— has now been partly built over. *Setúbal* also produces a fortified wine from a blend of black and white grapes known as *moscatel*, and is still a demarcated district, although its production has diminished.

The red *Dão* wine, from an area centred on Viseu, is a full-bodied wine challenging comparison with Burgundy rather than claret, and is usually matured from five to seven years. There are white Dãos as well as red. A similar full-bodied red wine comes from the area of *Pinhel*, further E, between Guarda and the Douro.

An astonishing market success has been obtained by *Mateus Rosé*, a blended wine originating in the Vila Real district, but now drawn from all parts of the country. It is sold in shaped flagons, and may be drunk with anything. Made from black grapes with a white pulp, it is sweet and bubbly, but the bubbles come from carbonated gas and not from natural effervescence as in the vinhos verdes. Connoisseurs are supercilious about it, although Sacheverell Sitwell (who discovered it in 1951 before it was so well known) praised it highly, but then he is a man of eclectic tastes.

Madeira, which was known as a quality wine even before port, retains its good reputation. No longer is it shipped to the tropics to aid its maturing, but undergoes a heat treatment ('*estufado*') in stoves to stimulate the process. Like vinhos verdes, it is grown on trellises. It is a blended wine matured in the cask, and fortified, but the must is not sealed off during fermentation, as is port.

Brandy, which plays so important a part in the fermentation of port, should be made from pure fermented grape juice. It is mainly known for its own sake as French *cognac* or *eau de vie*, but the provenance and nature of the brandy used for port is not much publicised. Much of it comes from the Douro region itself, but brandy can be distilled from common wines anywhere: nine pipes of wine make about one pipe of brandy. In Portugal it is called *aguardente*, but in Spain this term means what in Portugal is known as *bagaceira*, *bagaço* being the product of the pips and skins after the grapes have been pressed. The latter was initially very violent and spiritous, but modern methods have matured and improved it, although it is still very strong compared with some other eaux de vie de marc.

In recent years the wine trade of Portugal has greatly changed in character. It is no longer an Anglo-Portuguese affair concentrated on the British market, but an international business in which twice as much port is exported to France as to Britain, and in value twice as many table wines as port. Even the Portuguese, who in the past had feared—for the sake of their livers—-to drink port, are now taking to aperitif port, but rather as part of the cosmopolitan scene. Nevertheless, port wine is still popular in Britain, and vintage port still plays an important part in that trade. Many scions of the traditional family firms (despite some mergers with larger concerns) continue to work in Oporto, where the visitor will find much of the old flavour still, while in the Factory House vintage port continues to be drunk with the same ceremony and distinction as it always has been.

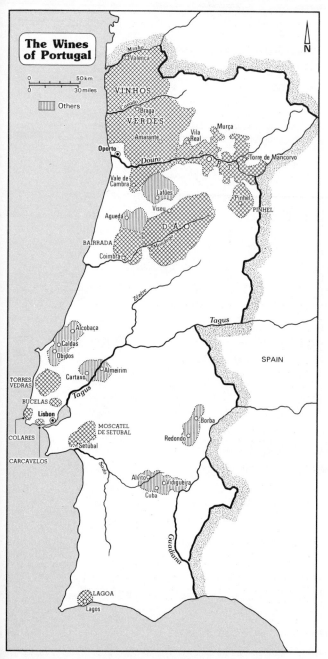

The Wines of Portugal

0   50 km
0   30 miles

Others

N

VINHOS

VERDES

Minho
Valença

Cávado
Braga

Murça

Amarante
Vila
Real

Oporto
Douro
Torre de Mancorvo

Vale de
Cambra
Lafões
Pinhel
PINHEL

Viseu

Agueda
DÃO

BAIRRADA
Mondego

Coimbra

Zêzere

Tagus

Alcobaça

Caldas
Óbidos

SPAIN

TORRES
VEDRAS
Cartaxo
Almeirim

BUCELAS
Tagus

Lisbon
Borba

COLARES
MOSCATEL
DE SETÚBAL
Redondo

CARCAVELOS
Setúbal

Sado

Alvito
Vidigueira

Cuba

Guadiana

LAGOA

Lagos

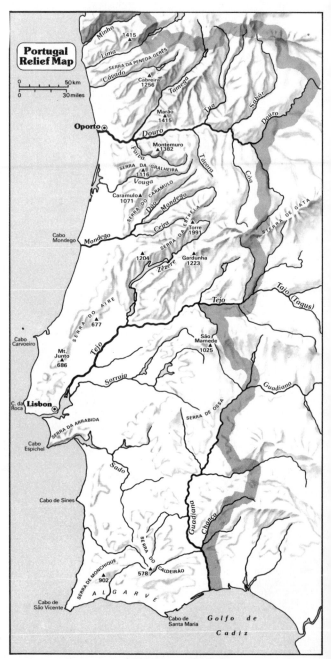

Portugal Relief Map

0 — 50 km
0 — 30 miles

Minho
Lima
1415 ▲
SERRA DA PENEDA-GERÊS
Cávado
Cabreira ▲ 1256
Tâmega
Marão ▲ 1415
Tua
Sabor
Douro
Oporto ⊙
Douro
Paiva
Montemuro ▲ 1382
SERRA DA GRALHEIRA ▲ 1116
Vouga
Caramulo ▲ 1071
SERRA DO CARAMULO
Dão
Mondego
Ceira
Távora
Côa
SERRA DE GATA
SERRA DE ESTRELA
Torre ▲ 1991
Cabo Mondego
Mondego
▲ 1204
Zêzere
Gardunha 1223
SERRA DO AIRE
▲ 677
Tejo
Tejo
Tejo (Tagus)
Cabo Carvoeiro
São Mamede ▲ 1025
Mt. Junto ▲ 686
Tejo
Sorraia
Guadiana
C. da Roca
Lisbon ⊙
SERRA DE OSSA
SERRA DA ARRÁBIDA
Cabo Espichel
Sado
Guadiana
Cabo de Sines
Chança
SERRA DO CALDEIRÃO
SERRA DE MONCHIQUE ▲ 578
▲ 902
A L G A R V E
Cabo de São Vicente
Cabo de Santa Maria
Golfo de Cadiz

GEOGRAPHICAL AND GENERAL INTRODUCTION

Approximately one-fifth of the Iberian Peninsula is occupied by Portugal, which, situated at the SW extremity of Europe, shares to its N and E a land frontier with Spain 1215km long. Its area is 88,550 sq km (34,200 sq. miles), and it is rectangular in shape, 218km (137 miles) at its widest, and 561km (350 miles) from N to S. In 1981 the population of mainland Portugal was 9,294,200, producing a density of approx. 105 inhabitants per square kilometre, but unevenly distributed: see below. The total population of the country, including the Azores and Madeira (251,400, and 257,200 respectively) was 9,803,400.

Many travellers to Portugal will have crossed Spain before reaching its frontiers. Although it may be invidious to make comparisons, it is almost impossible not to do so, for the differences are many and profound, and any tendency to regard Portugal as merely a geographical extension of Spain must be entirely discounted.

Although there are of course similarities, it is the differences which are immediately apparent. Perhaps the most striking of changes is that of vegetation, not merely that far more flowers and bushes are to be seen throughout Portugal, but also far more trees, including extensive areas planted with eucalyptus, which are noticeably absent as one traverses the parched, windswept high-lying Castilian plateau. The roads, more often tree-shaded, are more pleasant to drive along; the landscape in general is softer, greener, and less austere. Portugal is a far more scenically beautiful country than is generally imagined although too often what might otherwise be an attractive village has been spoilt by new houses built in execrable taste, bright with multicoloured azulejos, with their exterior stairs and ornate ironwork. Many have been built with hard-earned money gained in northern Europe. They are at least homes, and considering the conditions in which too many people existed in previous decades under the theocratic dictatorship, although disenchanted one should not protest too much. Too many still live in poverty, particularly in parts of the larger towns, where the non-collection of garbage is also often evident.

In general the people are exceptionally obliging and helpful when their assistance is requested, and even when it is not. Numerous times when travelling in Portugal the Editor has experienced unexpected courtesies increasingly rare in more 'civilised' countries. People will go out of their way to show one the exact whereabouts of a building, for example: the small acts of natural hospitality and kindness, the lack of pretension, an attitude of welcome rather than the negative reaction too often noticeable elsewhere—all these go to make a journey through Portugal memorable. Everywhere, sounds are more subdued than in Spain: the diminution in decibels is quite remarkable. Life is taken at a more moderate speed; indeed, for the traveller in a hurry there may be moments of exasperation. It should also be taken into consideration, particularly when among older folk in rural areas, that a higher proportion than might be expected may not be able to read or write, even if they make every effort to understand a foreigner's broken Portuguese. They do not particularly care to be addressed in Castilian—although they will understand it—unless the visitor makes it obvious that he is a non-Spaniard.

Even the police are usually noticeably more civil when applied to, and are more likely to give the traveller the benefit of the doubt, than elsewhere.

Portugal is a comparatively small and homogeneous country, unlike its neighbour, and there is less emphasis on regionalism: such nationalistic groups as the Basques or Catalans in Spain do not exist; there are, however, some unintegrated Gypsies. The older regions are still referred to as a convenient method of indicating parts of the country, although these were divided for administrative purposes into *districts* in the 1830s, and in 1936 partly sub-divided into *provinces*, but the boundaries between the *províncias* and *distritos* do not always coincide. The mainland divisions are approx. as follows:

Traditional regions	*Províncias*	*Distritos*, named after their capitals
Minho, or Entre Minho e Douro (NW coast)	Minho	Braga, Viana do Castelo
	Douro Litoral	Oporto
Trás-os-Montes (NE)	Trás-os-Montes (Alto Douro)	Braganza, Vila Real
Beira (below the former two)	Beira Alta Beira Litoral	Guarda, Viseu, Aveiro, Coimbra, Leiria
	Beira Baixa	Castelo Branco
Estremadura (Centre W)	Estremadura Ribatejo	Lisbon, Setúbal, Santarém
Alentejo (SE of the former)	Alto Alentejo Baixo Alentejo	Portalegre, Evora Beja
Algarve (S coast)	Algarve	Faro

The province of Douro Litoral is comprised of the lower part of the Minho and the NW part of Beira; that of Ribatejo is partly E Estremadura, and partly NW Alentejo.

As far as the distribution of population is concerned on the mainland, the *distritos* of Lisbon, Setúbal, and Oporto together contain over 40 per cent of the total, inflated since the exodus from Angola and Mozambique, etc. In comparison, the eastern and southern districts (Braganza, Vila Real, Guarda, Viseu, Castelo Branco, Portalegre, Santarém, Évora, Beja, and Faro) contain merely 30 per cent of the population, although they make up over 70 per cent of the area of Portugal.

There are considerable physical variations between some of the provinces. The seaboard province of **Minho**, with a high density of population, originally settled by the barbarian Suevi, is named after the river separating it from Spanish Galicia. The conservative and prolific Minhotos still have much in common with their Gallegan cousins and, like them, provided a high proportion of emigrants— once to Brazil, and now more frequently to northern Europe. The Minho's high rainfall allows intensive cultivation, and the whole province is physically very green. Where it is not cultivated it is covered with woods, except on the bare upper slopes of some

THE OLD PROVINCES

DISTRICTS showing capitals

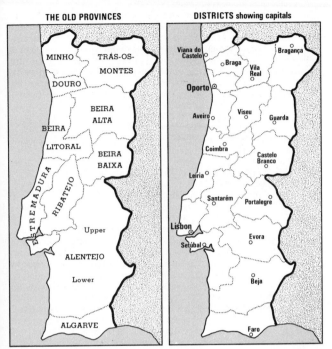

mountain ranges near Spain to the E, among them the Serras do Gerês and da Peneda. It is also divided transversely by the rivers Lima, Cávado, and Ave, whose valleys are dotted by *solares* or manor houses. It is in this early-reconquered area that a high proportion of the Romanesque churches of Portugal may be seen, even if a number of them have been transformed in later centuries, their 18C façades whitewashed between granite outlines. One may still see occasionally the notorious creaking ox-carts, whose heavy wooden axles emit a shrill whine as they are dragged slowly along the narrow lanes by their lyre-horned oxen which are often yoked in pairs by richly ornamented *cangas*. Also to be seen are the *espigueiros*, or small granaries on piles, like the Galician *hórreos*. The Minho is the home of the *vinho verde* (green wine: see p 68), so-called not so much for its colour as for its refreshing and slightly acid taste. The vines are seen trailing over granite props and trellises, even up into adjacent trees, and the fences of its smallholdings (*minifúndios*). Its traditional soup is the *caldo verde*, made from shredded cabbage. Traditional women's costumes are still occasionally seen, together with heavy gold earrings, particularly at the weekly markets held throughout the provinces, and are not donned merely as a tourist attraction. Minhotos are traditionally both superstitious and pious, the ecclesiastical capital long being Braga, a centre of reaction to Republican and Left-wing reforms. The Minho is bounded on the S by the province of DOURO LITORAL, divided by the Douro, and densely populated around Oporto, its capital.

To the E, on the high mountainous uplands, which are an extension of the Castilian plateau, is the backward and empty province of

Trás-os-Montes, literally that area 'across the mountains'. This is divided into the *terra fria* to the N, with its continental climate and long cold winters, and the *terra quente*, a warmer area to the S, where the summer sun is reflected off the schists of the Upper or Alto Douro valley, with its terraces of Port wine vineyards, which provide the Trasmontanos with seasonal employment. It is divided diagonally (from NE to SW) by the rivers Tâmega, Corgo, Tua, and Sabor, all tributaries of the Douro, which, now dammed at numerous points, forms the frontier with Spain between Barco de Alva and Miranda do Douro. Communications with the rest of Portugal are not particularly easy, Trás-os-Montes being divided from the Minho by the Serras de Barroso, da Cabreira, and do Marão. (Just a quarter of a century ago some 13 per cent of the population of Portugal lived in villages inaccessible by road, and even in 1970 one in four could still be described as illiterate, especially in such sequestered districts.)

Some distance S of the Douro, the province is abutted by the **Beira**, the central region of Portugal, comprising three different areas. The E half of BEIRA ALTA is geographically and climatically a westward extension of the Castilian plateau, but less monotonous. Once the descent is made from Guarda into the Mondego valley the difference is considerable. This river bears SW parallel to the great transverse massif of the Serra da Estrela, the highest mountain range in Portugal, rising to 1991m (6530ft) at Torre, and then flows through Coimbra to Figueira da Foz, dividing the lower lying coastal BEIRA LITORAL into two parts. To the N lies Aveiro, with its salt marshes and rice-fields, its lagoon fed by the Vouga, with its high-prowed *moliceiros* or seaweed-gathering craft. To the S are extensive pine forests planted to fix the coastal dunes. Some of the most beautiful countryside in Portugal is to be found in the valleys of the Mondego, the Dão (to the N), famous for its red wine, divided from the coast by the Serra de Busaco; and also in the valley of the Zêzere, flowing parallel to the S side of the Serras da Estrela and de Lousã. On the mountain sides pasture flocks of sheep and goats, whose wool is transformed into blankets at Covilhã, near the ski-slopes of the range. The BEIRA BAIXA, lower as its name implies, is divided from the Alentejo by the Tagus, which, beyond Abrantes, veers S. On both banks of the Tagus extends the province of RIBATEJO, the low-lying *lezírias* on the left bank, a bull-breeding district, being skirted to the NW by hilly country, particularly attractive around Tomar.

Further W is **Estremadura**, comprising the square-ended peninsula W of the Tagus estuary, with Lisbon on its S side, the Sintra range further W, and Nazaré on the coastal strip further N. On the S bank of the estuary, more accessible since the building of the new bridge, it includes Setúbal and the Serra da Arrábida.

The **Alentejo**, once the granary of Portugal, and long in Moorish hands, is another very different yet characteristic part of the country, a vast undulating plain occasionally dotted by *montes* or farms, but largely given over to forests of cork oaks, desert heaths with a maquis of cistus, extensive estates (*herdades* or *latifúndios*). The landowners of these estates—like those of adjacent Spanish Extremadura and Andalucía—have over the centuries exploited the peasantry who are now amongst the most communistically inclined in Portugal. Large flocks of sheep may be seen, guarded by *alentejano* shepherds, who in winter wear curious sheepskin coats (*pelico*) with a square tail and epaulette-like arms. Around Portalegre, to the N, the country is hillier and remarkably attractive, the straight tree-lined roads providing some shade from the torrid summer sun. Throughout the region there are low whitewashed houses surmounted by huge and ornate chimneys. The central half of this large area, the ALTO ALENTEJO, has the river Guadiana forming its E frontier, which further S, in BAIXO ALENTEJO, runs into Portugal between Beja and Serpa, again, in the Algarve, forming the boundary between Mértola and its mouth at Vila Real de Santo António. To the W the Lower Alentejo is irrigated by the Sado and its tributaries.

The **Algarve** (*al-Gharb*; the West, or more specifically the western districts of Moslem al-Andalus) was the last part of Portugal wrested from the Moors; indeed the sovereign was first known, after the conquest, as King of Portugal and the Algarves. It is divided from its neighbouring province by the Serras de Monchique and do Caldeirão, and further E by broken country—similar to the Spanish Sierra Morena—through which the Guadiana flows. The S slopes of these ranges, with a scanty rainfall compensated for by Atlantic humidity, give way to luxuriant semi-tropical landscapes, with carobs, camellias and oleanders, and prickly-pear hedges, and to a rich variety of fruit: figs, almonds and numerous citrus groves.

Sixty years ago a *Blue Guide* remarked that the Algarve was then 'so seldom visited by strangers, that the traveller will find himself an object of the greatest interest, and will probably walk about a town with a tail of 20 or 30 of the inhabitants', but which 'would be an ideal winter resort, superior to Málaga in the absence of parching winds, were it not for the inadequacy of accommodation'. This has been largely rectified since 1945, with the building of colonies of villas and hotels along the coast, with its picturesque cliffs and long beaches, though the Atlantic is colder than the cloacal Mediterranean. The Algarve provides employment for a large population of fishermen, who only in a short season indulge in the sanguinary and much publicised slaughter of tunny. At the far W end projects the Cabo de São Vicente, and that of Sagres, 'where the land ends and the sea begins' in the words of Camoens. It was here that Henry the Navigator planned the exploration of the western ocean.

BIBLIOGRAPHY

The bibliography of books in English on Portugal is extensive. The selection listed here is by no means exhaustive, but many of the books will themselves contain bibliographies for further or more specialised reading. Some will be out of print, but may be obtained through a public library. The *Canning House Library*, 2 Belgrave Square, London SW1X 8PJ (which also produces a Bulletin of Publications on Portugal) and the *British Institute Library* at Rua de Luís Fernandes 1–3, Lisbon 2, should not be overlooked, although the former Anglo-Portuguese Collection is at present housed in the library of the Gulbenkian Foundation (catalogue available).

TOPOGRAPHICAL AND GENERAL, some of which may also cover the rest of the Peninsula: *Sacheverell Sitwell*, Portugal and Madeira (1954); *Roy Campbell*, Portugal (1957); *Rodney Gallop*, Portugal, a book of Folk Ways (1936; reprinted 1961); *Frank Tuohy and Graham Finlayson*, Portugal (1970); *Henry Myhill*, Portugal (1972); *Sarah Bradford*, Portugal (1973); *Ann Bridge (Lady O'Malley)* and *Susan Belloc Lowndes Marques*, The Selective Traveller in Portugal (1949; last revised edition, 1967); *J.B. Trend*, Portugal (1957); *Harold V. Livermore* (ed.), Portugal and Brazil, an Introduction (1953); *Harold and Elizabeth Younger*, Blue Moon in Portugal (1946); *Adolfo Cabral* (ed.), Robert Southey: Journal of a Residence in Portugal 1800–1801, etc. (1960); *Boyd Alexander* (ed.), The Journal of William Beckford in Portugal and Spain 1787–1788 (1954); *Douglas Goldring*, To Portugal (1934); *John Gibbons*, Afoot in Portugal (1931), and I gathered no moss (1939); *Huldine Beamish*, The Hills of Alentejo (1958); *Aubrey Bell*, Portugal of the Portuguese (1915); The Admiralty Geographical Handbooks on Spain and Portugal, particularly volume II (1942).

Also of interest is the folder of reproductions of water-colours by *John Coates* of buildings and other structures in Lisbon associated with Britain, published by the British Historical Society of Portugal.

Those with a sufficient understanding of Portuguese will find À Descoberta de Portugal (published by Reader's Digest, Lisbon, 1982) of some interest; and the Arquitectura Popular em Portugal (2nd ed., 1980), edited by the Association of Portuguese Architects, containing several hundred photographs, and with some English Text.

Among earlier histories and descriptions of Portugal, by no means all of which have been listed in *Rose Macaulay*'s They Went to Portugal (1946; reprinted 1986) are:

James Murphy, Travels in Portugal (1795), and A General View of the State of Portugal (1798); *Richard Twiss*, Travels through Spain and Portugal in 1772 and 1773 (1775); *John Blankett*, Letters from Portugal (?1777); *Henry Frederick Link*, Travels in Portugal (1801); *J. Fr. Bourgoing*, Travels of the Duke de Chatelet in Portugal (1809); *William H. G. Kingston*, Lusitanian Sketches (1845); *Anon.* [prob. the *Rev. Edward Whiteley*], Hints to travellers in Portugal in Search of the Beautiful and the Grand (1852); *Sir Robert Southwell*, Letters (together with the History of the Revolutions of Portugal; 1740); *William Morgan Kinsey*, Portugal illustrated (1828); *Anon. [J.-B.-F. Carrère]*, A Picture of Lisbon, taken on the spot (1809); *'Arthur Costigan'. [Maj. James Ferrier]*; Sketches of Society and Manners in Portugal (1787); *William Beckford*, Italy, with Sketches of Spain and Portugal (1834), and Recollections of an Excursion to the Monasteries of Alcobaça and Batalha (1835; reprinted 1972); *A.P.D.G.*, Sketches of Portuguese Life, Manners, Costume, and Character (1826; with 20 plates); *Robert Southey*, Letters from Spain and Portugal (1797); *Marianne Baillie*, Lisbon in the years 1821, 1822, and 1823 (1825); *William Dalrymple*, Travels through Spain and Portugal in 1774 (1777); *Joseph Baretti*, Journey from London to Genoa (1770; reprinted 1970); *Baron Fagel*, Account of the Campaign in Portugal (1708); *Earl* of Carnarvon, Portugal and Gallicia (1836); *Gén. Dumouriez*, An Account of Portugal as it appeared in 1766 (1797); *John Colbatch*, An Account of the Court under Pedro II (1700); *William Bromley*, Travels through Portugal (etc.; 1702 and later eds.); *John Mason Neale*, Hand-Book for Travellers in Portugal (1855); *W.H. Harrison*, Jenning's Landscape Annual, or, Tourist in Portugal (1839); *Dora Quillinan* (née Wordsworth), Journal of a few Months' Residence in Portugal (1847); *Julia H.S. Pardoe*, Traits and traditions of Portugal (1833); *Lady Charlotte Jackson*, Fair Lusitania (1874); *Oswald Crawfurd*, Travels in Portugal (1875), and (under the pseudonym of *John la Touche*) Portugal Old and New (1880); *S. Inchbold*, Lisbon and Cintra (1907).

Many of these, among others, may be consulted in the Duarte de Sousa library, Palácio Foz, Lisbon.

HISTORY, EARLY AND GENERAL: *Harold V. Livermore*, A History of Portugal (1947), the more compact New History of Portugal (1966; revised ed. 1976), Portugal: a Short History (1973; concentrating more on the evolution of Portuguese society), and The Origins of Spain and Portugal (1971); *H.N. Savory*, Spain and Portugal, the Prehistory of the Iberian Peninsula (1968); *Augustus Harvey*, Journal (1945 ed.); *P.E. Russell*, The English Intervention in Spain and Portugal in the time of Edward III and Richard II (1955); *C.W. David* (ed. and trans.) De Expugnatione Lyxbonensi (1936); *Marcus Cheke*, Dictator of Portugal, a Life of the Marquis of Pombal, 1699–1782 (1938), and Carlota Joaquina, Queen of Portugal (1947); *Sir Thomas Kendrick*, The Lisbon Earthquake (1956); *V.M. Shillington* and *A.B.W. Chapman*, The Commercial Relations of England and Portugal (1907); *Edgar Prestage* (ed.), Chapters in Anglo-Portuguese Relations (1935); *A.H. de Oliveira Marques*, History of Portugal (2nd ed. 1976), and Daily Life in Portugal in the Late Middle Ages (1971); *John D. Symington*, Portugal: the Ancient Alliance (Oporto, 1960); *H.E.S. Fisher*, The Portugal Trade, 1700–70 (1971); *A.R. Walford*, The British Factory in Lisbon (1940); Descriptive List of the State Papers Portugal 1661–1780 in the Public Record Office London (3 volumes; Lisbon, 1979–83); *David Francis*, The Methuens and Portugal, 1691–1708 (1966), The First Peninsular War, 1702–1713 (1975), and Portugal 1715–1808, Joanine, Pombaline and Rococo Portugal as seen by British diplomats and traders (1985); *Sir Richard Lodge* (ed.), The Private Correspondence of Sir Benjamin Keene (1933); *G.F. White*, A Century of Spain and Portugal, 1788–1898 (1909); *George Young*, Portugal Old and Young (1917), and Portugal, an Historical Study (1917); *C.R. Boxer*, The Portuguese Seaborne Empire, 1415–1825 (1969); *Cecil Roth*, A History of the Marranos (1932; reprinted 1974); *Carl A. Hanson*, Economy and Society in Baroque Portugal, 1668–1703 (1981); *Neill Macaulay*, Dom Pedro: the struggle for liberty in Portugal and Brazil, 1798–1834 (1986); *Jorge de Alarcão*, Roman Portugal (1988); *Lopes*, The English in Portugal, 1367–1387 (1988).

PENINSULAR WAR. The standard work is *C.W.C. Oman's* History of the Peninsular War (7 volumes: 1902–30); more compact studies are his Wellington's Army (1913; reprinted); *Jac Weller*, Wellington in the Peninsula (1962); *Arthur Bryant*, The Great Duke (1971); *Michael Glover*, The Peninsular War (1974); *Elisabeth Longford*, Wellington, the Years of the Sword (1969); *Antony Brett-James*, Life in Wellington's Army (1972); *G.L. Chambers*, Bussaco (1910); *S.G.P. Ward*, Wellington's Headquarters (1957); *Michael Glover*, Britannia Sickens, Sir Arthur Wellesley and the Convention of Cintra (1971); *David Gates*, The Spanish Ulcer: a history of the Peninsular War (1986); *Donald D. Horward*, Napoleon and Iberia: the twin sieges of Ciudad Rodrigo and Almeida, 1810 (1984), and The Battle of Bussaco (1965).

Earlier or contemporary works, which are *very numerous*, apart from the general histories of *Southey*, and *Napier*, etc., include: *Andrew Halliday*, The Present State of Portugal and of the Portuguese Army (1812); *Colonel John T. Jones*, Memoranda Relative to the Lines thrown up to cover Lisbon in 1810 (1829); *Lieutenant-General Sir William Warre*, Letters from the Peninsula, 1808–1812 (1909); *Captain W.G. Eliot*, A Treatise on the Defence of Portugal (3rd ed., 1811); *Colonel George Landmann*, Historical, Military and Picturesque Observations of Portugal (1818), for its illustrations only; *Joseph Moyle Sherer*, Recollections of the Peninsula (1823); *J.M. Browne*, An Historical View of the Revolutions in Portugal (1827); *A.L.F. Schaumann*, On the Road with Wellington (1924); *James Wilmot Ormsby*, An Account of the Operations of the British Army (1809); *Lieutenant-Colonel J. Leach*, Rough Sketches of the life of an old soldier (1831); *Major George Simmons*, A British Rifle Man (1899).

Among those concerning the MIGUELITE WARS, or 'War of the Two Brothers': *William Bollaert*, The Wars of the Succession in Portugal and Spain (1870); *Lieutenant-Colonel Lovell Badcock*, Rough Leaves from a Journal kept in Spain and Portugal (1835); *Sir Charles Napier*, Account of the War of Succession in Portugal (1836); *G.Lloyd Hodges*, Narrative of an Expedition to Portugal (1833); *Sir Charles Shaw*, Memoirs (1837); *W.N. Glascock*, Naval Sketch Book (2nd Series; 1834); *Thomas Knight*, The British Battalion at Oporto (1834); *Captain J.E. Alexander*, Sketches in Portugal during the Civil War of 1834 (1835); *[Colonel Hugh Owen]*, The Civil War in Portugal, and the Siege of Oporto (1835).

MODERN HISTORY: *R.A.H. Robinson*, Contemporary Portugal: a History (1979); *Robert Harvey*, Portugal: Birth of a Democracy (1978); *Antonio de Figueiredo*, Portugal: Fifty Years of Dictatorship (1975); *Hugh Kay*, Salazar and Modern Portugal (1970): *P. Fryer* and *P.McG. Pinheiro*, Oldest Ally: a Portrait of Salazar's Portugal (1961); *Mário Soares*, Portugal's Struggle for Liberty (1975); *P.Blanshard*, Freedom and Catholic Power in Spain and Portugal (1962); *Phil Mailer*, Portugal: the Impossible Revolution (1977); *Douglas L. Wheeler*, Republican Portugal: a political history, 1910–1926 (1978); *Rodney J. Morrison*, Portugal; revolutionary change in an open economy (1981); *Lawrence S. Graham* and *Douglas L. Wheeler* (eds.), In Search of Modern Portugal: the Revolution and its Consequences (1982); *Tom Gallagher*, Portugal: a 20C interpretation (1983); *Hugo Gil Ferreira* and *Michael W. Marshall*, Portugal's Revolution: Ten Years On (1986); *Thomas C. Bruneau*, Politics and Nationhood: Post-Revolutionary Portugal (1984); *Walter C. Opello, Jr*, Portugal's Political Developement: a comparative approach (1985); *Gervase Clarence-Smith*, The Third Portuguese Empire, 1825–1975: a study in economic imperialism (1985); *D.L. Raby*, Fascism and resistance in Portugal (1988).

ART AND ARCHITECTURE (but not including works on specific artists or picture books): *Walter Crum Watson*, Portuguese Architecture (1908); *James Murphy*, Plans, elevations, etc....of Batalha (1795): *Robert C. Smith*, The Arts of Portugal, 1500–1800 (1968) and (in Portuguese) Á Talha em Portugal (1962); *George Kubler* and *Martín Soria*, Art and Architecture of Spain and Portugal, etc., 1500–1800 (1959); *G.Kubler*, Portuguese Plain Architecture, 1521–1706 (1972), to be used with caution; *James Lees-Milne*, Baroque in Spain and Portugal (1960); *Carlos de Azevedo*, Baroque organ cases of Portugal (1972). Spanish readers will find a useful reference book in *J.-A. França*, *J.L. Morales y Marín*, and *Wilfredo Rincón*, Arte Portugués (volume XXX in the Summa Artis series, Espasa Calpe, 1986).

PORT AND WINE: *Charles Sellers*, Oporto, Old and New (1899); *David*

Francis, The Wine Trade (1972); *George Robertson*, Port (1978); *Sarah* Bradford, The Englishman's Wine (1969), revised edition entitled The Story of Port (1978); *André Simon*, Port (1934); *H. Warner Allen*, Port and Sherry (1952), and The Wines of Portugal (1963); *Jan Read*, Wines of Spain and Portugal (1973), Wines of Portugal is available separately; *Rupert Croft-Cooke*, Port (1957); *Ernest Cockburn*, Port Wine and Oporto (1949); *Gerald Cobb*, Oporto, Older and Newer (1966); *John Croft*, A Treatise on the Wines of Portugal (Oporto, 1940); *Joseph James Forrester*, A Word or two on Port Wine (1844), and The Oliveira Prize Essay on Portugal (1853); *John Delaforce*, The Factory House at Oporto (1979).

MISCELLANEOUS: *Aubrey F.Bell*, Portuguese Literature (1922, reprinted, with a selective bibliography, 1970); *William Tait*, Birds of Portugal (1924); *José Cutileiro*, Portuguese Rural Society (1971); *William J.Entwistle*, The Spanish language, together with Portuguese, etc. (1936); *R. Peterson, G. Mountfort*, and *P.A.D. Hollom*, A Field Guide to the Birds of Britain and Europe (1965); and *O.Polunin* and *B.E. Smythies*, Flowers of South-West Europe (1973). *Camoens*'s 'Luciad', translated by *Fanshawe*, was reprinted in 1963. Of interest is *W.C. Atkinson*, British Contributions to Portuguese and Brazilian studies (revised ed., 1974).

Maps

For maps of France and Spain see p82. Although general maps of the peninsula cover Portugal, it is advisable to buy in addition one of the following: the new *Michelin* Map of Portugal (No. 437 at 1:400,000); the *Automóvel Club de Portugal*'s Mapa do Estado das Estradas (1:550,000); that published by Kummerly & Frey, or—and the best for contour—the *Instituto Geográfico e Cadastral*'s Carta de Portugal at 1:500,000 (two sheets) or at 1:1,000,000. This last organisation, with offices at the Praça da Estrela, Lisbon 2, publishes a comprehensive range of maps of mainland Portugal, the main series being at 1:50,000 (175 maps); at 1:100,000 (53 maps); and 1:200,000 (eight maps); and they also issue a number of other maps at varying scales.

The Ministry of Defence Series 1404, edition 1–GSGS, sheet Nos 318–C, 347–A and 347–D, virtually covering all Portugal, can also be useful.

The annual *Red Michelin Guide* for Spain and Portugal will be found complementary to this guide. It contains useful town plans for the motorist, indicating the latest points of entry and exit, one-way streets, parking sites, and the position of the main hotels and restaurants.

It is advisable to acquire maps and guides before leaving home, as even the Red Michelin is not easily obtainable in Portugal.

PRACTICAL INFORMATION

Formalities and Currency

Passports are necessary for all British and American travellers entering Portugal.

In general, visitors intending to remain in Portugal for more than 60 days should apply to a Portuguese consulate before their journey, or alternatively by applying to the Foreigners' Registration Service in Lisbon (Av. António Augusto de Aguiar 18) or to District Police Headquarters, seven days before the original period has elapsed.

Consuls, etc. There are *British Consuls* at the British Embassy, Rua S. Domingos à Lapa 35–37, 1296 Lisbon, and at Av. da Boavista 3072, Oporto; and an *Honorary British Consul* at Rua Santa Isabel 21, Portimão.

The *British-Portuguese Chamber of Commerce* (which publishes a monthly magazine) has offices at Rua da Estrela 8, Lisbon (likewise the address of the *Royal British Club*), and at Rua Sá da Bandeira 784, Oporto. The *British Council* (Instituto Britânico em Portugal) is at Rua de Luis Fernandes 3, Lisbon 2; the *British Hospital* is at Rua Saraiva de Carvalho 49, Lisbon. The *British Historical Society of Portugal* is at Rua de Arriaga 13, 1200 Lisbon.

The *US Embassy and Consulate* is at Av. das Forças Armadas, 1600 Lisbon, with a consulate at Rua Júlio Dinis 826, Oporto. The *Canadian* consulate is at Rua Rosa Araujo 2, 1200 Lisbon.

The Portuguese Consulate in London is at 62 Brompton Road, SW3.

Other Anglo-Portuguese organisations *in London* include: the *Anglo-Portuguese Society*, 2 Belgrave Square, SW1X 8PJ (which is also the address of the *Hispanic and Luso-Brazillian Council*, and Canning House Library); the *Anglo-Portuguese Foundation*, 2 Bedford Square, WC1B 3RA; the *Calouste Gulbenkian Foundation*, 98 Portland Place, WN1 4ET; *Portuguese Chamber of Commerce and Industry*, 1–5 New Bond Street, W1Y ONP; and the *Portuguese Embassy*, 11 Belgrave Square, SW1X 8PP.

Customs House. Except for travellers by air, who have to pass the customs (*alfândega*) at the airport of arrival, or those travelling on international expresses, where their luggage is examined in the train, luggage is scrutinised at the frontier or port of disembarkation. Provided that dutiable articles are declared, bona-fide travellers will find the Portuguese customs authorities courteous and reasonable. It is better, unless one has a fluent knowledge of Portuguese, to commence any discussion in English rather than in Spanish (although the latter can later be of assistance).

It is as well to check in advance with the Portuguese Consulate or Tourist Office before starting out as to the latest regulations with regard to the importation of firearms, whether sporting or otherwise, and also with the authorities of the countries through which one may be passing.

Currency Regulations. There are now no restrictions on the amount of sterling the traveller may take *out* of Great Britain. It should be noted however, that no more than 30,000 escudos in Portuguese notes and coins may be taken out of Portugal, although larger amounts of foreign currency may be exported provided that proof is shown that the visitor entered the country with such an amount.

Money. The monetary unit is the *escudo*, written 1$, subdivided into *centavos* (also called *'tostões'*) but these are going out of circulation. Coins are issued by the Banco de Portugal of 1, 2$50, 5, 10, 20, 25, and 50 escudos, and notes of 100, 500, 1000 (also known as a *conto*), and 5000 escudos.

Banks. Branches of Portuguese banks, recently nationalised (and functioning better than the private banks of neighbouring Spain), and foreign banks in Portugal, are found near the centre of most towns. They are normally open from 8.30–11.45, and from 13.00–14.45 from Monday to Friday, and 8.30–11.45 on Saturday. Exchange facilities (Serviço de Câmbio) are also available from 18.00–23.00 in some of the main towns, and there is usually a 24-hour service at the main frontier posts and at airports. It is nevertheless advisable to obtain a small supply of Portuguese currency for incidental expenses before leaving home. Banks provide all the normal facilities in accepting foreign bank cards, traveller's cheques, etc.

Security With a reasonable amount of circumspection, travellers will find their property respected, but it is as well to take out some form of insurance before leaving home, and likewise to take a list of telephone numbers likely to be necessary in an emergency: family, bank (including those for credit-card cancellation), insurance company, etc. Luggage, at airports, railway-stations, and on ferries, should not be left unattended. Cars should always be locked, and it is tempting providence to leave visible in a parked car anything which might be considered of value. Foreign number-plates are obvious. Normally no problems should arise in the countryside, but there has been an increase of robbery in some of the main towns. Women should not display jewellery, and should wear their handbag straps across their body. Valuables should be deposited with the manager of one's hotel against receipt. The police should be applied to in case of any trouble: the Portuguese equivalent of ringing 999 is 115.

Approaches to Portugal and Transport in Portugal

Portugal may be reached directly from Great Britain by a variety of ways, but it is recommended that the traveller intending to tour in the Peninsula should take his own car, or alternatively, Fly-Drive, as it is the only practical way to see large areas of the country.

Travel Agents. General information may be obtained gratis from the Portuguese National Tourist Office at 1–5 New Bond Street, London W1Y ONP, while many of the larger and even smaller towns in Portugal have tourist offices, usually well indicated by sign-posts. They can provide information on accommodation, admission to museums, entertainments, etc.

The Direcção-Geral do Turismo is at Av. António Augusto de Aguiar 86, 1004 Lisbon.

It has branches abroad at: Gran Via 27, *Madrid*; 548 Fifth Av., *New York*; 7 Rue Scribe, *Paris*; and 1801 McGill College Av., Montreal, among others.

The only direct **ferry** between England and the Peninsula at present in operation (1987) is that between Plymouth and Santander (Brittany Ferries, Millbay Dock, Plymouth).

Azulejo panel from São Vicente de Fora, Lisbon

Motorists will save much trouble by joining the *Automobile Association* (Fanum House, Basingstoke, Hants RG21 2EA), the *Royal Automobile Club* (83 Pall Mall, London SW1), the *Royal Scottish Automobile Club* (17 Rutland Sq., Edinburgh), or the *American Automobile Association* (8111 Gatehouse Road, Falls Church, Virginia 22042). These organisations will provide any necessary documents, as well as information about rules of the road abroad, restrictions regarding caravans and trailers, advice on routes, and arrangements regarding delivery of spare parts, insurance, etc. Motorists who are not the owners of their vehicle should possess the owner's permit for its use abroad. The *Automóvel Club de Portugal* has its head office at Rua Rosa Araújo 24, Lisbon, with branches at Oporto, Aveiro, Braga, Coimbra, and Faro. The insurance facilities offered by *Europ Assistance* or similar organisations should used.

Travellers approaching Portugal via France and Spain are advised to obtain the *latest* edition (showing motorways and other improvements) of the *Michelin* Map of France (No. 989) or the Carte Routière of France published by the French *Institut Géographique National*. For Spain, the *Michelin* Map No. 990; or the *Instituto Geografía Nacional* (Madrid) map of the Peninsula Ibérica, both at 1:1,000,000, are recommended, while those requiring more detail may acquire the new series of Michelin maps of Spain at 1:400,000 (although even these do not always give a very correct idea of the contours or windings of every road; but see below). *Blue Guide Spain* will not come amiss. For maps of Portugal see p 79.

Although it is possible that some visitors to Portugal will be touring the country as part of a general exploration of the Iberian Peninsula, this would take a long time. It therefore must be assumed that most travellers driving to Portugal will be taking the shortest route to the Franco-Spanish frontier, and continuing directly SW towards the northern or eastern border of Portugal. Others may wish to take in the Asturias and Galicia (having landed from the ferry at Santander); or even Andalucía en route; or alternatively they may consider passing through those provinces of Spain on the return journey.

The most direct and fastest roads from Irun (at the W end of the Pyrenees), and Santander, converge some 35km NE of Valladolid. From Tordesillas, 30km SW of the latter, there are a number of alternative routes, depending on one's proposed itinerary.

Either (a) turning NW via Benavente to Verín, thence crossing the frontier for *Chaves*: see Rte 32.

(b) Continuing W from Verín via Allariz, Celanova, and Cortegada, to enter at *São Gregório*: see Rte 34B.

(c) Continuing NW from Verín via Orense to cross the Minho at *Valença*: see Rte 34A.

Or (d) driving due E via Toro and Zamora; thence NW to *Braganza*: see Rtes 30 or 31.

One may also drive S and then SW from Salamanca towards Cáceres and Mérida: see below.

Travellers wishing to take in Madrid, or driving from there, will follow the N V to Trujillo, there either continuing due W to Cáceres, or SW to Mérida and Badajoz. From Cáceres there are border crossings to the NW and W: one near Alcántara for Castelo Branco (see Rte 17), and the other near Valencia de Alcántara (see Rte 16).

From Badajoz we cross into Portugal at *Elvas*: see Rtes 5, 14 and 15.

For those making for the Algarve, the route *Elvas—Estremoz—Évora* may be followed (Rtes 5 and 6), thence either Rtes 9 or 10.

Travellers entering Portugal from Andalucía have a number of alternatives. From Seville one may either enter at *Vila Real de Santo António*, W of Huelva, for the Algarve (Rte 13, in reverse, but see above); or take the direct Lisbon road (Rte 8), crossing at *Rosal de la Frontera* for *Serpa* and *Beja*, but the road from Seville, crossing the Sierra de Aracena in Spain, is not the best. Some may prefer crossing further NW between Vilanueva del Fresno and *Mourão* for Évora: see Rte 7. Alternatively, bear NW at Zafra through La Albuera for Badajoz.

Frontier Posts. There are 15 border crossings for vehicles which are regularly in service, and in the majority of cases they are open daily from 7.00 to 24.00, although the less frequented will close at 21.00 in winter. The *ferry* from Ayamonte to Vila Real runs from 8.00 to 23.00 in summer, and until 20.00 in winter.

One of two important new cross-country roads planned, roughly following the route of the present N15 and N16, will improve communications in the N half of the country. The first part of this road has been completed, and it will run SW from *Braganza* to Vila Real, later by-passing Amarante and Penafiel to approach *Oporto*.

The second route, some eastern sections of which have been completed, will run W from *Vila Formoso* (see below), by-passing Guarda and Celorico, and continue W past Mangualde and Viseu. It will later climb parallel to the Vouga valley to meet the A1 motorway just W of Albergaria-a-Velha (see below), to approach *Aveiro*.

The motorway from Lisbon to Oporto is progressing slowly, being completed at the time of writing to a point 52km NE of the capital, and from a point not far SW of Coimbra to Oporto. (Eventually this will be extented N towards Braga, to approach a new international bridge to be constructed over the Minho near Valença to Tui. A second motorway will probably be built running SE from Setúbal to a point midway on the Algave coast. This will be extended E towards another international bridge spanning the Guadiana between Vila Real de Santo António and Ayamonte on the Spanish bank; at present the river can be crossed only by ferry.)

Among other border crossings is that at *Miranda do Douro*, due E of Zamora: see Rtes 28 and 29. The Douro may be crossed further S also, by following the C527 SW from Zamora to *Fermoselle*, to meet the N221 (see Rte 28) some 20km E of *Mogadouro*. (It is possible that C517 leading W from Salamanca will eventually be provided with a bridge over the Agueda at its confluence with the Douro just E of Barca de Alva, further S on the N221.)

At present the main road (N620) from Tordesillas drives SW via Salamanca and Ciudad Rodrigo to reach the frontier at Fuentes de Oñoro for *Vilar Formoso* and *Guarda*: see Rtes 21, 22, 23 and 27, and above.

Driving in Portugal. Continental rules of the road apply, and seat-belts are now compulsory. Speed limits for cars are 90km per hour (55mph), slowing to 60km (37mph) in built-up areas, while the maximum speed on the few motorways is 120km (75mph). Although the Geographical Introduction describes in general the main divisions of the country, it does not attempt to describe the intricacies of the roads in extensive regions. These are not by any means obvious even on the better and recently published road maps. While the N4 (from Badajoz to Lisbon, meeting the A2 at Setúbal) is a reasonably fast road, and while lateral communications will be improved with the completion of the two new roads listed above, it cannot be emphasised too often that the apparently direct road between two points is by no means always the easiest or fastest, particularly off the beaten track. This is especially true in the scenically attractive centre and N of the country, which is remarkably hilly, and numerous apparently major roads, which might appear straight enough on a map, may well wind and climb through broken country for hours.

Communications are frequently easier in the Alentejo, for example, and in the higher-lying but comparatively level *meseta* nearer the frontier with Spain. Some minor roads are in a perfectly satisfactory state (apart from the occasional rash of pot-holes), even if they are narrow and undulating; they may, however, deteriorate unaccountably into rough stoney tracks and continue so for some distance. Even certain highways—such as the N8 between Torres Vedras and Órbidos – were until recently in a lamentable condition.

Unfortunately, few maps give any detailed indication of contour, and most, but not all, roads leading through hilly regions are frequently tortuous. This is almost always the case along the steep sides of the 'valley' of the Douro and its tributaries—such as from Entre-os-Rios to Lamego along its S bank, although some short stretches have been improved. (It is all very well to follow the S bank from Régua to Pinhão, for example, but should one wish to continue E to explore its upper reaches, this will entail a 15km steep climb to Alijó, an 11km steep descent to Tua, followed by another 22km ascent merely to reach Carrazeda de Ansiães, winding all the way.)

Although tourists should plan to reach their destinations in daylight, particularly if travelling off the beaten track, when driving at dusk or after dark, a very sharp look-out should be kept for unlit carts, bicycles, scooters, animals and children.

Petrol. Petrol stations are still comparatively few and far between off the beaten track, and motorists are advised to keep their tank topped up.

While it may be convenient to travel to Portugal **by Rail**, and to use the French Railways (SNCF), Spanish Railways (RENFE), and Portuguese Railways (CP—Companhia dos Caminhos de Ferro Portugueses) for long through journeys, they are not recommended as a means of touring, except by enthusiasts.

Of interest to enthusiasts are the two steam trains maintained by the CP: the 'Historical Train' running on a narrow gauge between Livração, Amarante, and Arco de Baúlhe (Tâmega line), pulled by a German locomotive of 1905 and with contemporary coaches; and the so-called '19C Train', with a British locomotive of 1875, running on a wide gauge between Oporto and Valença do Minho.

For further information on kilometric booklets, tourist tickets, Inter-Rail and Eurorail passes, and special fare rates, apply to tourist agencies or *British Rail, Continental Section,* Victoria Station, London SW1, which provides travel tickets, sleeping berth tickets, seat reservations, etc. on Continental (as well as British) transport services. Make certain that the 'global' price has been offered, including *all* supplements, etc., and check on the validity of return tickets.

Regular **Air Services** between England and Portugal are maintained by *Transportes Aéreos Portugueses* (TAP, or Air Portugal) working in conjunction with *British Airways.* Full information on flights may be obtained from British Airways, 75 Regent Street, London W1, and from TAP, 19 Lower Regent Street, SW1 YLR.

In the USA they have offices in Boston, New York and Washington. There are also offices in Montreal and Toronto, and in most European and non-European capitals, from which there are regular flights.

Flights are also provided by charter companies. Internal or domestic services, including those to Madeira and the Azores, are also maintained by TAP, whose head offices are at Praça Marquês de Pombal 3A, Lisbon. In addition to the Aeroporto de Lisboa (*Portela de Sacavem*), there are airports at Oporto (*Pedras Rubras*) and Faro, to which there are regular flights from London.

From airports there are bus services to the town termini, and in many cases coach connections with other towns or resorts in the area. Taxis will also meet planes, and many car-hire firms have offices at airports. TAP also provide fly/drive facilities, together with fly/rail facilities in conjunction with Portuguese Railways.

There are a number of regular **Bus Services** (*autocarros*) in Portugal between the main towns maintained by the *'Rodoviária Nacional,* apart from additional Tourist Services during the season, details of which may be obtained from travel agents and tourist offices. A bus-stop is known as a *Paragem.*

Taxis, which are still comparatively inexpensive, are numerous in the main towns, and are easily distinguished by their *green roofs.* In smaller towns there are cars which ply for hire, and charge by the kilometre. Surcharges apply for heavy luggage. A tip of 10 per cent is more than sufficient.

Metropolitano (or 'Tube'). There is an underground railway in Lisbon, for which a *caderneta* of ten tickets or a *Passe Turístico* may be obtained.

A Tourist Ticket for a 7-day period may be obtained for travel on public transport in Lisbon (apart from the underground) at most ticket offices marked CARRIS.

Postal and other Services

Post Offices (*Correios*) or C.T.T. are normally open from 9.00–18.00 on Monday to Friday, and the main branches also operate a limited service on Saturday. Correspondence marked 'poste restante' (to be called for) may be addressed to any post office, and is handed to the addressee on proof of identity (passport preferable). Unlike Spain, telephones are also to be found in post offices, apart from a number of public cabins, a few of which will appear familiar to tourists from England, as the Portuguese telephone service was once maintained by a British company. Portugal is in automatic or STD communication with the rest of Europe and elsewhere.

The main *Post Offices* in the principal towns of Portugal are as follows:
Albufeira, Rua 5 de Outubro 8

Aveiro, Praça Marquês de Pombal

Beja, Largo do Correio

Braga, Av. da Liberdade

Bragança, Av. Almirante Reis

Cascais, Rua Manuel Joaquim Avelar

Castelo Branco, Largo da Sé

Coimbra, Rua Olimpio Nicolau Reis Fernandes

Covilhã, Rua Antonio Maria Aguiar

Elvas, Rua da Cadeia

Estoril, Av. de Nice

Estremoz, Rua 5 de Outubro

Évora, Rua de Olivença

Faro, Largo do Carmo

Guarda, Largo João de Deus 24–26

Guimarães, Rua Santo António

Lagos, Rua Porta de Portugal

Lamego, Av. Alfredo de Sousa

Lisboa, Terreiro do Paço, Praça do Comércio,
    Restauradores, Praça dos Restauradores 58,
    Aeroporto

Portalegre, Av. da Liberdade

Portimão, Av. Dom Afonso Henriques

Porto, Município, Praça General Humberto Delgado

Santarém, Teixeira Guedes

Setúbal, Av. Mariano de Carvalho

Sintra, Av. Heliodoro Salgado 53

Tomar, Rua Marquês de Tomar

Viana do Castelo, Av. dos Combatentes Grande Guerra

Viseu, Rua dos Andrades

Press, TV and Radio. Some foreign newspapers and a few magazines are only found, and at an inflated price, at kiosks in the centre of the main towns and in the main tourist areas during the season. The *Anglo-Portuguese News* (Av. São Pedro 25, 2765 Monte Estoril), published bi-monthly since 1937, is of interest to travellers intending to spend any length of time in the country. There is a brief radio programme for tourists in English every morning at 8.30. The ubiquitous TV may be seen in many hotels, and may assist the visitor to gain some knowledge of the language.

Tourist Offices. The main tourist office in Lisbon is at the Palácio Foz, on the W side of the Praça dos Restauradores, with posts elsewhere in the city, and they can provide tourists with information in English by telephone (706341). The Directorate-General of Tourism also has branches in a number of other towns and at the main frontier crossings, passenger docks, Santa Apolónia railway station, and airports. Many towns also have their municipal tourist offices, usually very obliging.

Hotels and Restaurants

Hotels. The standard of comfort, efficiency, and cleanliness of Portuguese hotels is comparatively high, and their sense of hospitality specially so. All have been officially graded by the Directorate-General of Tourism, which produces an annual 'Guide to Hotels', which may be perused at all Tourist Offices.

Hotel accommodation falls into six categories: Hotels, from 1-star to 5-star; Apartment-Hotels (2 to 4-star); *Estalagens* (inns of quality; 4 or 5-star); *Albergarias* (4-star); Boarding-houses and pensions (*pensãos*), 1 to 4-star; and Motels (2 or 3-star). In addition, there are the national *Pousadas*, similar to the Paradores of Spain, a number of them being in buildings of historical interest (for example, at Óbidos, Palmela, Setúbal, Estremoz, and Évora), and most of them are attractively sited.

Every bedroom should display a notice giving details of the maximum price applicable to the room, and this includes a Continental breakfast, all service charges and taxes. The maximum price may be increased by 20 per cent between 1 May and 31 October.

If no single room is available, a double room may be offered, for which the price is that of a double room less the price of a Continental breakfast, but as some hotels choose to assume that single tourists prefer a double room anyhow, this point should be checked. When accommodation is limited, it may be convenient to ask for an extra bed to be fitted into a single room, when an extra charge of 35 per cent may be made to the price of the room; or in apartment-hotels and motels, of an extra 25 per cent per person. The management must inform guests as to any reduced prices available; e.g. for children under the age of eight.

An official *Complaint Book (Livro de Reclamações)* is a requirement of every establishment offering accommodation and in the unlikely case of serious irregularity or indifferent service should be requested without compunction. Complaints may also be made to Tourist Offices, or directly to the Direcção-Geral do Turismo, Av. António Augusto de Aguiar 86, 1 Lisbon.

Up-to-date lists of local hotels are obtainable from any Tourist Office, the staff of which can also advise on extra facilities (e.g. private swimming pools, tennis courts).

Youth Hostels. Information on Portuguese Youth Hostels may be obtained from Tourist Offices or from the *Associação Portuguesa de Pousadas de Juventude*, Rua Andrade Corvo 46, 1000 Lisbon.

Camping. There are some 70 camping-sites throughout the country, details of which, and facilities offered, may be obtained from Tourist Offices.

Pousadas. The following pousadas are at present (1987) open, and new ones are projected. It is advisable to obtain the latest complete list from a tourist office prior to touring, as it is possible that some may be temporarily closed for modernisation. Those marked + are luxury establishments, and priced correspondingly.

They are listed in alphabetical order of the towns in which they are situated, or otherwise the nearest centre or district.

Alijó (16km NE of Pinhão): Barão Forrester
+Almeida (within the fortified town)
Amarante: São Gonçalo, 27km E
Aveiro (in fact over 40km NW, on the far side of the ria): Da Ria.

Batalha: Mestre Afonso Domingues (near the abbey)
Bragança: São Bartolomeu (with a view of the walled upper town)
Caniçada (c 33km NE of Braga, off the N103): São Bento (with plunging views over the Peneda-Gerês National Park)
Caramulo (SW of Viseu): São Jerónimo
Castelo do Bode (between Tomar and Constância, to the SE): São Pedro (overlooking the reservoir)
Elvas: Santa Luzia
+Estremoz: Rainha Santa Isabel (in the castle)
+Évora: Dos Lóios (in the monastery)
Guimarães: N.S. da Oliveira (in the *Largo* adjacent to the *Colegiada*), and +Santa Marinha da Costa (in the former monastery on the hill of Penha, SE of the town)
Manteigas; Hotel de Manteigas. See also Serra da Estrela, below.
Marvão: Santa Maria (with a fine view)
Miranda do Douro: Santa Catarina
Murtosa (in fact over 40km NW of Aveiro; on the far side of the ria): da Ria
+Óbidos: do Castelo (in the castle)
+Palmela: de Palmela (in the restored castle)
Póvoa das Quartas (on the N17, E of Oliveira do Hospital): Santa Bárbara (with an attractive view)
+Sagres (33km W of Lagos): do Infante
Santa Clara-a-Velha (N flank of the Serra de Monchique): Santa Clara
Santiago do Cacem: São Tiago
São Brás de Alportel: São Brás
Serém (on the N1 E of Aveiro): Santo Antonio.
Serpa: São Gens (in the countryside SE of the town)
Serra da Estrela (a short distance N of Manteigas): São Lourenço
+Setúbal: São Filipe (in the castle)
Valença do Minho: São Teotónio (with a view of Tui)
Vale de Gaio (c 25km SE of Alcácer do Sal)
Viana do Castelo; Hotel de Sta Luzia (on a height above the town)
+Vila Nova de Cerveira (15km SW of Valença do Minho): Dom Dinis (within the castle ramparts)

For up-to-date information and advance reservations apply to ENATUR, AV, Sta Joana a Princesa 10A, 1700 Lisbon (telephone 881221; telex 13609/63475 ENATUR P).

Turismo de Habitação. The Portuguese tourist authorities rightly assume that not all travellers wish to spend their holiday, or even part of it, in hotels: some might wish to meet the Portuguese in their own homes. In recent years they have encouraged owners of private houses to accommodate guests, and at the same time defray the cost of the upkeep of their property. The scheme has been developed throughout the country, but predominantly in the interior and N, particularly in the Minho, where there are more suitable characteristic houses or *paços* able to offer such facilities. Some are *quintas* (usually associated with a farm or vineyard) or *solares* (a country seat), and vary from simple but comfortable family home to the more palatial manor or mansion house. Charges vary accordingly. This type of accommodation can offer attractive surroundings unlikely to be found elsewhere.

The owners of such properties in the Minho have formed as association in order to insure standards and to advertise more effectively. Travellers wanting to use such accommodation as a base from which to tour the region should apply in advance to the Delegação de Tourismo de Ponte de Lima, TURIHAB (Associação de Habitação), Praça da República, 4990 Ponte de Lima (telephone 058 942335; telex 32618), who can advise and will endeavour to suit individual requirements.

For more information on Turismo de Habitação elsewhere in Portugal, contact the office of the Direcção-Geral do Turismo at the Rua Alexandre Herculano 51, 1200 Lisbon (telephone 681713).

It should be emphasised that bookings should normally be for a

A typical quinta near Ponte de Lima

minimum of three nights, and that the price includes bed and Continental breakfast. Evening meals at houses some distance from towns and restaurants can be arranged if requested in advance. Some houses can also provide cooking facilities; and some have tennis courts and swimming pools. Almost all have extensive gardens or estates, and there may be opportunities for fishing or riding. There is normally no language problem. If booking in advance from abroad it is preferable to deposit 50 per cent of the cost by sending a cheque in one's own currency directly to the owner.

The prospectus will illustrate each house or mansion and include an outline map showing locations, together with details of facilities at each place, and prices.

Restaurants. While there are comparatively few 'de luxe' restaurants in Portugal, there are numerous less pretentious establishments offering better value than many places of a similar category in some other countries. While some of the larger hotels, particularly in tourist resorts, will also provide a safe 'international' menu, the visitor should not hesitate to savour the numerous local dishes, emulating that 18C traveller to Portugal, Joseph Baretti, who remarked: 'Let it be dinner-time, and I care not a fig for the difference between macaroni and roast-beef, herring and frogs, the olla and the sourcrout; a very cosmopolite in the article of filling one's belly'. Portions are often generous, and a half portion (*uma meia dose*) is often enough, or one *dose* for two, and the differing prices are often so shown on the menu. 'S.P.' (*segundo o peso*) indicates that the food is charged by weight. Service is now included on the bill or *conta*, but one may leave a small gratuity for good service, although this is no longer expected.

Breakfast (*pequeno almoço*), lunch (*almoço*), tea (*chá*: both the beverage and meal), and dinner (*jantar*) are served at normal 'English' hours, particularly lunch: later than in France, but earlier than in Spain.

Tap water (*água da torneira*) is usually perfectly safe, although for

Azulejo panel from the Palácio Marquês da Fronteira

those who prefer bottled waters, there is a considerable variety, and it is not expensive, available with (*com*) or without (*sem*; pron. sin) gás. Portuguese beer (*cerveja*) is very good; while the range of wines available is extensive. Even the ordinary *vinho da casa* is often surprisingly good, and the prices of the quality *vinhos de marca* are in no way prohibitive. Local wines are known as *vinhos da região*, and may be red (*tinto*), white (*branco*), sweet (*doce*) or dry (*seco*); ice is *gelo*. Coffee (*café*) may be ordered *simples*, black; or *com leite*, with milk.

See the Introduction to Port and the Wines of Portugal, particularly p 67.

The MENU (*lista* or *ementa*) which follows contains a number of the more common dishes to be met with:

Acepipes, hors d'oeuvres; also *entrada*

Améndoas, almonds
Azeitonas, olives; *azeite*, olive oil
Pão, bread; *pão de broa*, rye bread
Manteiga,; butter
Pimenta, pepper; *sal*, salt

Sopas, Soups

Caldo verde, the ubiquitous finely-shredded *couve* or Portuguese cabbage soup, with a mashed potato base
Sopa à Alentejana, garlic soup, with egg and coriander
Sopa de marisco, or *de peixes*, seafood bisque
Gaspacho à Alentejana, a refreshing cold soup similar to the Andalucían *gazpacho*, but containing chopped ham or a hard spiced sausage
Caldeirada, a fish soup or chowder, containing onions
Sopa de feijão, bean soup
It will be noted than some people prefer to have their soup at the end of a meal (just to fill up any remaining crevices).

Ovos, Eggs

These may be ordered *cozido*, hard boiled; *mal pasados* or *quentes*, underdone or lightly boiled; *estrelados* or *fritos*, fried; *escalfados*, poached; or *mexidos*, scrambled
Tortilha à Espanhola, Spanish omelette

Peixe e Mariscos, Fish and Shellfish

Ameijoas, clams
Anchovas, anchovies
Arenque, herring
Atum, tuna or tunny
Bacalhau, cod, very often dried salt cod, a staple food served in various appetising ways
Besugo, Dory; also *dourado*
Camarões, shrimps
Caranguejo, crab; *santola*, spider crab; *sapateira*, rock crab
Carapau, mackerel, a variety of which is *cavala*; also *sarda*
Carabineiros, deep-sea prawns; also *gambas*
Cataplana, dish of stuffed clams with bacon and sausage; from the Algarve
Cherne, sea bream
Chocos, cuttlefish
Eirós, or *enguia*, eel
Espadarte, swordfish; *peixe espada*, scabbard fish
Gambas, prawns
Garoupa, similar to but with a whiter flesh than *cherne*
Lampreia, lamprey
Lagosta, spiny lobster or crayfish; *lavagante*, lobster; *lagostim*, crawfish; *lagostino*, langoustine
Linguado, sole
Lota, burbot
Lula, squid or inkfish
Mero, brill
Mexilhões, mussels
Ostras, oysters
Pargo, sea bream
Perceves, goose-barnacles
Pescada, hake
Pescadinha, whiting
Polvo, octopus
Pregado, turbot
Raia, skate
Robalo, sea bass; young ones being *robalinho*
Ruivo, gurnet
Salmão, salmon
Salmonete, red mullet; other mullet are known as *fataca*, or *tainha*
Sarda, mackerel
Sardinhas, sardines
Sável, shad
Solha, plaice
Truta, trout

Carne, Meat (and some cooking terms)

Anho, lamb; also *borrego* or *cordeiro*, baby lamb; *carneiro*, mutton
Bife, steak of beef or cow
Cabrito, kid
Costeleta, chop
Dobrada, tripe; also *tripas*
Fiambre, cooked ham; *presunto*, smoked or spiced ham
Fígado, liver
Língua, tongue
Lombo, fillet
Miolos, brains
Morcela, black pudding; also *mouros*
Perna, leg
Porco, pork; *leitão*, sucking-pig; *paio*, smoked pork fillet
Rims, kidneys
Salsicha, fresh pork sausage; *chouriços*, smoked or spiced sausage
Toucinho entremeado, bacon
Vitela, veal
Assado, roasted; *cozido*, boiled or stewed; *fumado*, smoked; *grelhado*, grilled; *nas brasas*, on a charcoal grill; *no forno*, in the oven; *panado*, fried in breadcrumbs; *passado*, minced; *salteado*, sautéed; *guisado*, stew; *molho*, sauce

Aves domésticas e Caça, Poultry and Game

Coelho, rabbit
Cordorniz, quail
Faisão, pheasant
Frango, chicken; *galinha*, boiling fowl; *capão*, capon
Ganso, goose
Lebre, hare
Pato, duck
Perdiz, partridge
Perú, turkey
Veado, venison

Legumes e Hortaliças, Vegetables (and *especiarias*, spices)

Agriões, watercress
Aipo, celery
Alcachofra, artichoke
Alface, lettuce
Alho-porro, leek
Alho, garlic
Arroz, rice
Batata, potato
Beringela, aubergine
Beterraba, beetroot
Bróculos, broccoli
Cebola, onion; *cebolinha*, spring onion; *chalota*, shallot
Cenoura, carrot
Chu-chú, marrow
Cogumelos, mushrooms
Couve, Portuguese cabbage; *couve-flor*, cauliflower; *repolho*, white cabbage
Ervilhas, peas
Espargos, asparagus
Espinafre, spinach
Favas, broad beans
Feijão, dried beans; *feijão manteiga*, butter beans or haricot beans; *feijão verde*, French beans
Grão, chickpeas
Grelos, turnip tops
Lentilhas, lentils
Nabo, turnip
Pastinaca, parsnip
Pepino, cucumber
Pimento, red or green pepper
Rabanetes, radishes
Salada, salad
Salsa, parsley
Canela, cinnamon; *caril*, curry; *coentros*, coriander; *cominhos*, cummin seeds; *piri-piri*, chilli seasoning

Queijos, Cheeses

Queijo da Serra, a ewe's milk cheese, mostly from the Serra da Estrela, and often served as an hors d'oeuvre, but not available in summer months
Cabreiro, goat's milk cheese
de Tomar, a small white cheese; also *de Castelo Branco*; *de Azeitão*, *de Alentejo*.
Rabaçal, from the region of Pombal.

Sobremesa, Dessert

Açúcar, sugar
Arroz-doce, rice pudding
Bolos, pastries; also *pastéis*; *bolachas*, biscuits
Flan, cream caramel
Gelado, ice cream
Mel, honey
Nata, cream
Pudim, pudding
Marmelada, quince jam or *membrillo*; marmalade is *compota de laranja amarga*
Compotas, jams and preserves

Fruta, Fruit

Alperches, apricots; also *damascos*
Ameixas, plums
Ananás, pineapple
Avelãs, hazel-nuts
Cerejas, cherries; *ginjas*, black cherries
Figos, figs
Framboesas, raspberries
Laranja, orange
Limão, lemon

Maçã, apple; *nêspera*, medlar
Melão, melon; *melancia*, water melon
Morangos, strawberries
Nozes, nuts
Pêssego, peach
Pêra, pear
Tâmaras, dates
Toranja, grapefruit
Uvas, grapes

General Information

Shops are normally open from 9.00–13.00, and from 15.00–19.00, some remaining open during the lunch-hour, the time of which may vary. Many shops close at 13.00 on Saturday during the summer. Supermarkets, which are usually more expensive than local shops and markets, normally close at 20:00.

Public Holidays. The main public· holidays, when museums are closed, are: 1 January; 25 April (commemorating the Revolution of 1974); Shrove Tuesday; Good Friday; 1 May; Corpus Christi; 10 June (death of Luís de Camoens); 15 August; 5 October (Proclamation of the Republic); 1 November; 1 December; 8 December (Independence of Portugal, 1640); and 25 December. The main festivals at Lisbon and Oporto are St. Anthony's day (13 June) and St. John's day (25 June) respectively. Tourist Offices can provide details of other local festivals.

Climate and Season. The climate in general is much milder than that of neighbouring Spain. Except in the Trás-os-Montes and the frontier area near Guarda, and on such heights as the Serra de Estrela, it is rarely cold. The Minho is inclined to be damp in the winter, with a heavy rainfall. In Lisbon this is 69cm (c 27 inches) annually, mostly falling between October and March. The heat in the Alentejo and Algarve is considerable in summer, particularly the inland regions, which are rarely tempered by evening breezes, and are perhaps best avoided—except by salamanders—in high summer. The early spring is perhaps the pleasantest time of year to visit the S, when the almond blossom is out, while areas N of the Tagus are perhaps at their best from May to November.

Language. Although the traveller who knows no language other than English can get along quite comfortably anywhere on the main tourist routes, an attempt should be made to learn a few phrases. French is occasionally understood and, less frequently, German.

While there are similarities with Castilian, both being Romance languages, the pronounciation of Portuguese is very different, being softer in tone and less clear-cut. Consonants are apt to be slurred, and many of the vowels are nasal, so that it may take a foreign ear much longer to become accustomed to the sound.

VOWELS: accented ê and ô are the ordinary long Latin vowels; unaccented they have a short dull sound (the o is often replaced by u: e.g., Manuel rather than Manoel), while the final e is like the French e-mute. Dipthongs are pronounced separately, but the combinations ei, ou, sound almost the same as the ê or ô; the nasal vowels ã, õ (surmounted by a *til*), are pronounced as -an or -on in French; while in the combinations ão, õe, only the second vowel is nasalised (-aon, -oen);

in the last syllable a vowel followed by -m or -ns is nasalised, but its tone is not changed (e.g., 'jardim' is not pronounced as 'jardin' in French, where the final i becomes a nasal e).

CONSONANTS are pronounced more or less as in English except in the following cases: ç (before a, o, and u), as s; ch:, g. and j as in French; gu, qu before e or i = hard g and k, before a, o, u, = gw and kw; lh, nh correspond to the French 'i-mouillé' and gn (Spanish ll and ñ); s before a consonant or in an unstressed final syllable is like sh (e.g., Cascais); between vowels is like z; x is usually like sh, but in certain words of classical derivation it is pronounced like z (e.g, exército).

ACCENTS. Unless otherwise marked by an accent, the stress of words ending in a vowel, -m, -s, or -ns, is on the penultimate syllable (e.g., Leiria, Virgens); in words ending in other consonants it is on the last syllable (e.g., real).

Travellers will soon pick up a number of everyday expressions and words, such as *Sim*, yes, and *Não*, no; *Bom dia*, good morning, *Boa tarde* and *Boa noite*, good afternoon and good evening or night; *Por favor*, please, and *Obrigado*, thank you (note that the latter, when spoken by a female, is obrigada).

Peculiarities which will be noticed, and will require a bit of getting used to, are the days of the week, apart from Saturday (*Sábado*) and Sunday (*Domingo*), which are respectively: Monday, *Segunda-feira*; Tuesday, *Terça-feira*; Wednesday, *Quarta-feira*; Thursday, *Quinta-feira*; and Friday, *Sexta-feira*.

This system, different from other European countries, is probably Suevic in origin: a tombstone in the Minho is carved with the date 28 April, AD 616, SECUNDA FERIA.

Armed with a pocket-dictionary or phrase-book, travellers should not meet with any great difficulty, although there are regional variations in pronunciation, between the Algarve and the Minho, for example.

Visiting Churches, Museums, and Monuments. Most *Museums* are open daily, *except Mondays* and public holidays, from 10.00–17.00, or later in the summer, but some may be closed at lunchtime. The guardians or guides are usually very helpful when their assistance is sought.

Churches are open earlier, but are often closed between 13.00 and 16.00. Unlike so many in neighbouring Spain, whose obtuse sacristans tend to consider the objects committed to their care as merely a source of perquisite, and whose negative attitude is deplorable, the disinterested guardians of Portuguese churches—especially in the centre and south of the country—are proud of any treasures of art or architecture they may contain, are happy to show visitors around, and will even press them to sign the 'Visitor's Book'. In the north of Portugal, where more devotion is shown, the ecclesiastical authorities likewise display more interest: 'where every trifle may be turned into money, money will be expected for every trifle' (to quote Baretti), and this is noticeable particularly in the cathedral of Braga. When churches or other monuments are closed, it is usually possible to find the guardian and his key (*chave*), although in remoter districts it is advisable to make prior enquiries at the tourist post of the nearest town as to his likely whereabouts, or one may be disappointed in one's object. Nor are all monuments yet adequately signposted, and time can be wasted in an endeavour to track down some buildings, let alone obtain admission.

A pocket-torch may be helpful when exploring the darker recesses of some churches, and a small pair of field-glasses will also be found of value.

Entertainment. While most towns of any size have cinemas, fewer have theatres, and concerts are not as frequent as they might be, in spite of the encouragement given to them by the Gulbenkian Foundation.

An entertainment promoted as being as 'typical' of Portugal as *Flamenco* is of Spain, is the **Fado**, which in recent decades has approached the status of an art form when sung by such accomplished performers as Amália Rodrigues, among others artistes.

Its origins are disreputable, it being generally accepted that it derived from the libidinous *lundum*, a dance which came originally from the Congo, and a popular activity among the slave population of Brazil. From Brazil also came the sentimentally lascivious songs known as *Modinhas*, which Beckford considered 'the most seducing, the most voluptuous imaginable, the best calculated to throw saints off their guard and to inspire profane deliriums'. Traditionally, it was taken over by the less than virtuous residents of the port quarter and the Alfama, some of them slaves before their emancipation in 1761, who thus entertained their clients. Among earlier *fadistas* known to polite society were the Brazilian mulatto named Caldas Barbosa, whose compositions were less than delicate, and later (c 1840) Maria Severa, who additionally became the mistress of the bull-fighting Conde de Vimioso. Rarely referred to before the 1830s, *fado* became increasingly popular in the second half of the century, gaining a status similar to the can-can; only comparatively recently has it been considered decent, and probably with respectability and professionalism it has lost much of its earlier spontaneity. Nevertheless, a pleasant late evening may be spent at one of the better *casas de fado*, and local opinion should be sought as to where the best may be heard. They all serve food and drink and, apart from those on the tourist trails, are not overpriced. An interesting introduction is Chapter XI of Rodney Gallop's 'Portugal: a book of Folk Ways'.

Bull-fights. Unlike the sanguinary spectacles of Spain, the Portuguese bullfight is a more civilised form of entertainment, but apart from being promoted in Lisbon at the Praça de Touros do Campo Pequeno during the season (Easter to October) is little seen except in the Ribatejo, the traditional bull-breeding area of the country. Here also, at Vila Franca de Xira in July, the bulls run loose through the streets. In Portuguese bullfights the interest is dependent on the dexterity and horsemanship of the *cavaleiro*, whose mount can in no way be compared with the poor hacks of Spain, who thrusts *banderillas* or *farpas* into the bull's neck muscles. An additional entertainment is the '*pega de cara*', the taking the bull by the horns (sheathed), which is done by the leader of a team known as the *forcado*, who will then pile on behind, the last one grabbing the beast's tail, bringing him down in a heap. The bull is not killed, merely immobilised. He is then enticed from the ring by a herd of gaily caparisoned and tintinnabulating tame bullocks, in whose reassuring company the fighting bull will trot out, probably wondering what on earth it was all about: and the next one will enter.

Sports: *Hunting, Shooting, and Fishing.* Statements claiming that the wild game of Portugal was annihilated within days of the 1974 revolution are exaggerated, but more 'conservative' attitudes now prevail, and the National Parks offer some security to the surviving fauna. Sportsmen should apply to Portuguese National Tourist Offices for the latest information on game and for regulations governing the importation of firearms; similarly concerning sea-fishing and underwater sports.

Tourist Offices can also advise on local conditions in connection with the hiring of equipment, and what facilities are available for *water sports* and *winter sports*. The latter have a short season and are virtually confined to part of the Serra da Estrela. They may also be applied to for a list of *golf courses* and other sports grounds. Most of the larger resorts now have *tennis courts*, particularly in the Algarve and in the Cascais-Estoril areas.

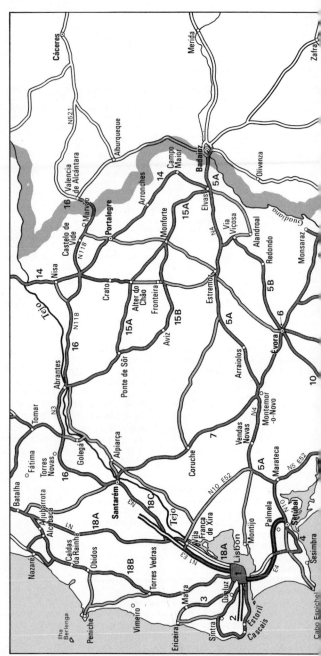

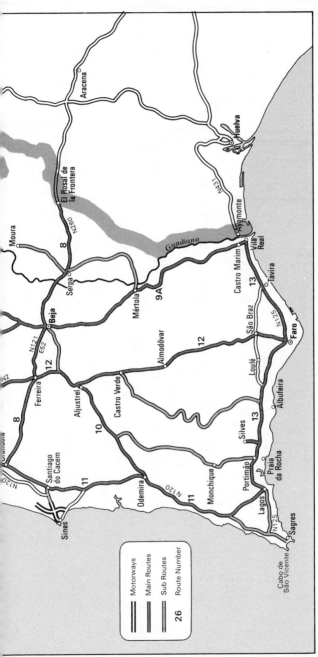

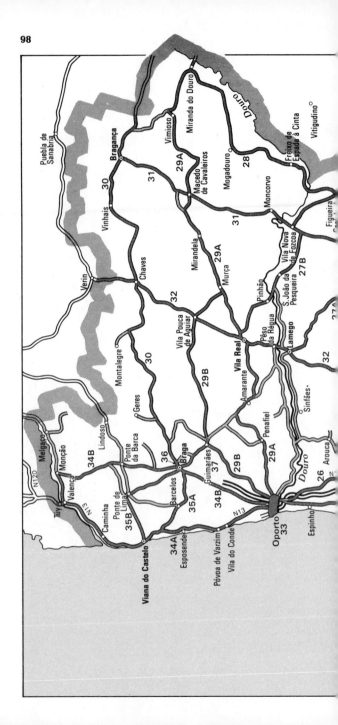

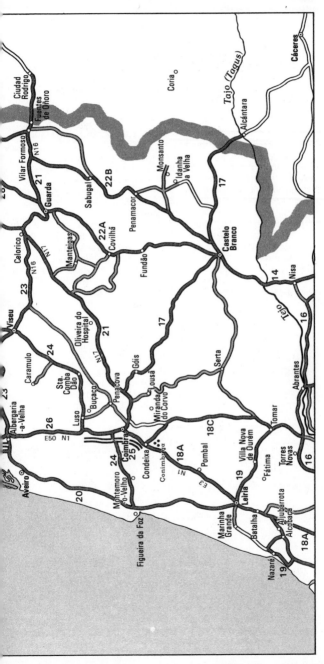

1 Lisbon

LISBON (812,400 inhab.), in Portuguese, **LISBOA**, is the capital and by far the largest city of Portugal. It has been estimated that the present population of greater Lisbon is in the region of 1,900,000. It has long been famous for its magnificent situation on the N bank of the *Tagus* (*Tejo*, in Portuguese), and there is little doubt that since the estuary has been spanned by a bridge, the most impressive approach to the city is from the S bank, as it was previously from the sea. Earlier travellers patronisingly claimed that it was only surpassed in beauty by Naples and Constantinople, but visitors today will find its impact sufficiently strong and its charms enticing enough without any gratuitous comparisons. Certainly most people would agree with Joseph Baretti (an intimate of Dr Johnson's circle), who, when visiting Lisbon in 1760 observed that 'to range about such a wide scene of curiosity as this metropolis and its neighbourhood, gives certainly much satisfaction to an inquisitive pair of eyes'.

The city lies some 15km from the mouth of the Tagus at a point where the river has expanded to form a wide lake-like estuary, referred to as the *Mar da Palha* (Sea of Straw). As at Venice, the water laps the edge of the main square of the old town, the *Praça do Comércio*, still familiarly known to the English as 'Black Horse Square'. Behind this lies the regularly planned lower town (*Cidade Baixa*), laid out after the Great Earthquake of 1755, framed by two of the legendary seven hills on which the city stands. Sightseers will soon find that the irregular and uneven contour of the site is perhaps its most characteristic feature, and a certain amount of stamina is required to clamber about: George Borrow was not the first to notice that 'the streets are in general precipitously steep'. In fact most of the steeper streets are those climbing uphill from the Cidade Baixa towards the *Castelo São Jorge* to the E, and to the *Chiado* and *Bairro Alto* to the W, above the quays stretching towards *Belém*. The wide Avenida da Liberdade ascends a gentler slope to the N and towards more modern quarters on a comparatively flat plateau to the NE.

Late 17.C view of Lisbon

The main roads are rarely congested, but visitors may at first find it preferable to take a green-roofed taxi rather than negotiate a maze of steep one-way streets, some of which—as *travessas* or *becos*—peter out as steps. Along many streets yellow Edwardian-looking (and British- built) trams still run. On certain slopes their place has been taken by funiculars, or inclined rack-railways. The tessellated pavements are largely composed of a white limestone relieved by a variety of designs in black basalt, a feature said to have been invented early last century by the engineer Pinheiro Furtado. Both materials are readily available in the vicinity of Lisbon. These pavements were presumably an improvement, for Twiss, writing half a century before, had complained that the streets were 'very badly paved with small sharp stones, which renders walking almost impracticable'.

Street numbers mount rapidly, as ground-floor windows as well as doors are numbered separately. Still characteristic of the street life of Lisbon are the sellers of lottery-tickets; the boot-blacks; the *varinas* or fishwives, balancing creels of fish on their heads and crying their wares (other goods are also carried on women's heads); and the Gallegan knife-grinders playing their plaintive pan-pipes. A considerable number of refugees from Portuguese ex-colonies in Africa and Asia will also be noticed; likewise gypsies, and occasional beggars.

Some of the older telephone boxes will also remind the Englishman of home, for the telephone system was at one time British-maintained. The shop windows display a variety of exotic fruit, cheese, and fish—which is extraordinarily good here—including the inevitable *bacalhau* or dried cod. There are a remarkable number of shoe-shops, but with those pavements and hills, they presumably find sufficient business. In the Ruas de Santa Paula and da Boavista (to the W of the lower end of the Rua do Alecrim) are ships' chandlers with a bewildering range of tools, machinery, and nautical equipment.

The monastery of the *Jerónimos* at Belém, and *São Roque*, among monuments; and the museums of *Arte Antiga*, of the *Espírito Santo Foundation*, of the *Gulbenkian Foundation*, and the Archaeological museum, are among the more interesting to be seen in a city of very great character.

History, and the English in Lisbon. Ancient chroniclers (being marvellously exact at settling such remote dates—and even now the precise date, not merely the year, is placed on buildings to commemorate their inauguration) attributed the founding of the city to Elishah, grandson of Abraham, in 3259 BC. Others, in seeking a derivation for the name *Olisipo*, claimed Ulysses as its founder, but this is more probably of Phoenician origin (c 1200 BC). The Phoenicians made a permanent settlement on the hill of São Jorge. This the Romans occupied in 205 BC, after the Second Punic War, and in 137 BC Decimus Junius Brutus strengthened the Romans' hold on the place. Julius Caesar raised Olisipo to the rank of *municipium*, with the official title of *Felicitas Julia*, and under the Empire it became, after Mérida (with which it was connected by road) the most important city in Lusitania. It fell to the invading Alans in AD 409, who were followed by the Suevi, and in 457/8 to the Visigoths under Maldras, but it later defected.

In 714 the Moors overran Lusitania and fortified Lisbon, which later (798) was raided by Alfonso II of León. In 1093 it was briefly held by Alfonso VI, but it was not until 1147, after a four-month siege, that Afonso Henriques, son of Henry of Burgundy, aided by a motley force of crusaders including an Anglo-Norman contingent sailing from Dartmouth, that Lisbon was regained. Gilbert of Hastings, an English priest, was consecrated bishop, and he established the Sarum Use, which continued in Lisbon until 1536. In c 1260 Afonso III transferred the court from Coimbra (then the capital) to Lisbon, and the city began to increase in wealth and population. A university founded here in 1290 was twice moved to Coimbra in the following century, but returned to Lisbon in 1377, not being finally re-established at Coimbra until 1537.

Enrique II of Castile besieged Lisbon unsuccessfully in February 1373, but burnt the Rua Nova and Jewish quarter, after which Dom Fernando strengthened its fortifications by erecting new walls possessing 77 towers, 16 gates on the landward side, and 22 towards the Tagus. In 1381 Edmund of Cambridge's fleet, with 3000 troops, entered the estuary as allies of Dom Fernando, before an abortive Anglo-Portuguese campaign against Spain.

Rabbi Eliezer set up a printing-press here in 1489 (the first eleven Portuguese incunables are in Hebrew); but in 1498 the Jews of Portugal were forcibly baptised or deported. A pogrom of 'New Christians' took place in 1506.

The 16C saw many changes, for in 1497 Vasco da Gama had set sail hence on the voyage that opened up the sea route to India, and the subsequent discoveries of Portuguese navigators in Africa, Asia and America brought enormous wealth to the harbour. By the turn of the century the population was 85,000, which by 1527 had been reduced by plague to some 52,000; by 1557 it had risen again to 100,000, leaving the countryside depopulated.

Lisbon experienced a severe earth tremor in 1531, and was again visited by the plague in 1569. The Inquisition was established here in 1536. Between 1580–1640 the city suffered under the domination of Spain, and had Philip II paid heed to his advisors it might have become the capital of the Peninsula. An Irish college was established in Lisbon in 1593, and in 1621 Philip O'Sullivan Beare first published his history of Ireland in Lisbon. In 1628 Simon Fallon of Galway wrote his treatise on mathematics and astronomy here.

After the revolution of 1640 much of Portugal's wealth was spent on its frontier fortresses. It was not until after 1690, with the discovery of

Brazilian gold, that Lisbon achieved perhaps its greatest magnificence. João V lavished this gold on its numerous churches, among other buildings; and Lisbon acquired at some cost the dignity of a patriarchate.

The poet Richard Flecknoe visited Lisbon in 1648, while in the following year Prince Rupert, having landed here with a small squadron, was temporarily blockaded in the Tagus by Admiral Blake. Richard Fanshawe, ambassador here from September 1662—five months after Catherine of Braganza had embarked hence for England—until the following August, described Lisbon: 'with the river is the goodliest situation that I ever saw; the city old and decayed, but they are making new walls of stone which will contain six times their city. Their churches and chapels are the best built, the finest adorned, and the cleanliest kept of any churches in the world. The people delight much in *quintas*, which are a sort of country houses, of which there are abundance within a few leagues of the city, and those that belong to the nobility very fine, both houses and gardens. The nation is generally very civil and obliging ...'. (Fanshawe was also a translator of Camoens, and his version of *Os Lusíadas* was published in London in 1655.) In 1669 Lisbon was visited by Cosimo de Médicis.

With the Cromwellian treaty of 1654 the already long-established British merchants trading and resident in Lisbon—Thomas Daniel had been importing cloth from Bristol as early as 1378—set up what has been described as 'a kind of Chamber of Commerce-cum-Consulate...a Meeting house where the principal Merchants and Factors foregathered to discuss matters of trade, politics, and local interests of the British community'. This was later to develop into a formal corporative body of traders which became known as the *British Factory*, and by the Portuguese as the *Feitoria Inglesa*, whose society a later ambassador—Sir Benjamin Keene—was so much to enjoy, referring to it as the 'jolly free Factory'. They were also at one time to be condemned as a 'nest of Waspes'. Their heyday was probably in the 1730s, at a time when young David Garrick was in Lisbon, working for his uncle, a wine exporter. In 1735 part of Admiral Norris's fleet was based in Lisbon for 21 months, and several of his ships were careened here under the supervision of William Warden, a British subject and João's dock-master and naval architect, who held this important post for several years.

In 1657 the Rev. Zachary Cradock reached Lisbon to take up the post of Chaplain to the British community. He was succeeded by the Rev. Thomas Marsden, and the Rev. Michael Geddes (c 1650–1713; chaplain from 1678 to 1686, when his activities were forbidden by the Inquisition), author of 'Miscellaneous Tracts'. From 1693 to 1700 the Rev. John Colbatch was chaplain, eternally wrangling with the then Envoy, John Methuen (father of Sir Paul Methuen, Minister at Lisbon from 1697–1702, and responsible for the important Commercial Treaty of 1703), whose scandalous relations with Sarah Earle (the Consul-general's young wife) Colbatch could not forgive. Neither could this worthy author of 'An Account of the Court of Portugal in the Reign of Pedro II' much tolerate the laxity of life among the Factory in general: 'such a horrid crew, that he fancied himself in hell, while he was among them'. Colbatch likewise condemned royal morals, writing: 'I never heard that he [Dom Pedro] had any favourite of the sex, unless it were one Frenchwoman....Those he hath his commerce with are said to be of the lowest rank, and very many, and not all of the same colour'. No wonder James O'Hara, Lord Tyrawley, the English

Ambassador from 1728–41, was popular, for Horace Walpole considered him 'singularly licentious, even for the courts of Russia and Portugal'. Not only did João V give him 14 bars of gold on his departure, but Tyrawley returned to England with three 'wives', one Portuguese, Dona Anna, 'with long black hair plaited down to the bottom of her back', and no less than 14 illegitimate children. Another of his children, by Miss Seal, was to become the famous actress George Anne Bellamy.

Tyrawley was certainly no fool, and he had many years of experience of Portuguese affairs and of members of the Factory (some of whom had treated him with 'disrespect and rudeness'), and for his part he condemned the majority of them: 'a parcel of the greatest Jackasses I ever met with, Fops, Beaux, Drunkards, Gamesters, and prodigiously ignorant, even in their own business'. In another of his memoranda he censured their relations with the Customs authorities. When discussing mutual problems with the Provedor d'Alfândega, the latter remarked that the members of the Factory 'were a set of *Casquilhos* (Petits Maîtres) that attended more to their Quintas, Balls, Masquerades & Gaming than to their business; that scarce one of them would give himself the trouble of going to the Custom House to dispatch their own goods, but left it to their Caixeiros (Book-keepers) who were all Portuguese Trapasseiros (Petty-foggers) and the greatest Rogues in the Country, and that there was neither Regularity or Fair dealing scarcely to be met with in our Factory. I did ask some of them (Merchants) why they did not goe to the Custom House to clear out their goods themselves as I had known all their Predecessors in the Trade constantly doe. I was answered that it was so dirty and mobbish a place that no Gentleman could set his foot into it'.

In 1727–28 General James Dormer (1679–1741) visited Lisbon as envoy extraordinary. Insanely jealous of, the consul, Thomas Burnet—more welcome at Court than he was—Dormer ordered his servants to drag Burnet from his carriage and beat him up. The consul was wounded in the fracas, and Dormer was recalled to England in disgrace. In October 1739 the dramatist António José da Silva, born of Portuguese-Jewish parents in Rio de Janeiro, was strangled and burnt in Lisbon at an *auto da fé*.

During Lent in 1754 the Rev. George Whitefield spent some days in Lisbon, methodically in search of 'superstitious pageantry'. In August the ailing Henry Fielding arrived, and here he spent the last two months of his life.

A year later, on the morning of 1 November 1755, Lisbon was shaken to its foundations by the Great Earthquake (whose effects were felt as far afield as Scotland and Jamaica), followed by a series of tremors, by an even more disastrous fire, and by a tidal wave which submerged the quay and overwhelmed the shipping. It has been estimated that 5 per cent of the population of 270,000 perished, among whom were some 78 British dead and about 60 missing 'of the poorer sort'. It has been estimated that there were c 2000 British subjects in Lisbon at the time. Many survivors of the Factory, while awaiting a ship for England, took shelter in the garden of Abraham Castres, the Envoy; and here, in the district known as Buenos Ayres, the Hon. Edward Hay, the Consul, afforded them every assistance. The royal family were likewise camping out in their garden at Belém.

The catastrophic situation was vigorously handled by the Marquês de Pombal, the only able minister, while the Marquês de Alorna announced to the king, Dom José: 'We must bury the dead, and feed the living, and shut the doors', words sometimes attributed to Pombal. Dom José's plan of removing the court to Rio de Janeiro was discouraged; military patrols were posted to check looting, and any damaged houses left standing in the lower town were demolished.

The lower town Pombal later laid out on the regular plan visible today. The British Parliament had immediately voted £100,000 as an earnest of their solicitude, and sent out food, pick-axes, crowbars and spades. The catastrophe served as a text for an attack on the doctrine of a free and benevolent Providence in Voltaire's 'Poème sur le désastre de Lisbonne' (1756), the pessimism of which provoked a letter of protest from Rousseau; the disaster also suggested an episode in Voltaire's 'Candide', published in 1759.

Joseph Baretti, passing through Lisbon in 1760, described the scene, which still left 'a dreadful indelible image' on his mind. In one area 'nothing is to be seen but vast heaps of rubbish, out of which arise in numberless places the miserable remains of shattered walls and broken pillars'. Not much had been saved from the disaster: fine libraries (including the remarkable musical library collected by João IV) and irreplaceable works of art were lost; wardrobes were scattered—many survived only in the clothes they were wearing at the time, some less, for they had not yet dressed for Mass on that All Saints' Day.

'Our poor Factory, from a very opulent one, is totally ruined, at least for the major part...', wrote the Envoy, admitting that they had in previous decades become 'Universal Traders', no longer merely 'respectable, regular & frugal merchants'. Yet Richard Croker, writing 25 years later, suggests that they had to a large extent recovered their fortunes, and again lived 'in a very sociable and pleasant manner', being 'particularly civil and hospitable', confirming Richard Twiss's description, when passing through Lisbon in 1772, who remarked that the Factory assembled once a week during the winter in two long rooms 'to dance and play at cards' (while Mrs May played the harpsichord with 'delicacy and taste'), and that any British stranger was admitted gratis. The Factory, having outlived its usefulness, was eventually disbanded by a treaty signed in 1810, but continued to subsist in a modified form until c 1825.

Mid 17C view of Lisbon

Several British officers, including John Burgoyne (the dramatist and later general, who capitulated at Saratoga in 1777), and Charles O'Hara, Tyrawley's son, were endeavouring to organise Portuguese resistance to the Spanish invasion of 1762. John Hunter, later the celebrated surgeon, was superintending the hospitals at Lisbon, Coimbra, and Santarém.

Among other English travellers of note visiting Lisbon at this period (when conditions had somewhat improved—the street lighting had been undertaken in 1780 by Martinho António Castro) were Nathaniel Wraxall (1772); Major William Dalrymple (1774); William Julius Mickle, the translator of 'The Lusiad' in 1776 (in 1778–79); 'Arthur Costigan' (1779; Major James Ferrier, author of 'Sketches of Society and Manners in Portugal', published in 1789); Richard Cumberland, the dramatist and unsuccessful 'diplomat' (1780); and William Hickey (1782), the diarist. Hickey recorded that the Irish artist Thomas Hickey (no relation) was captured, while en route to India in 1780, by the French and Spanish fleets. After being released at Cádiz, he made his way to Lisbon where he painted numerous English ladies and gentlemen, as well as Portuguese of rank. He eventually reached Calcutta in 1784. Other visitors were William Beckford, England's notorious 'wealthiest son', for the first time (1787), where he was taken up by the Marquês de Marialva but *not* received by the Hon. Robert Walpole, the Envoy, and duly ostracised by the smug Lisbon British; Lady Craven (1791), openly accompanying the Margrave of Anspach; Dr Willis (who had treated George III), summoned to Lisbon in 1792 to attend Queen Maria I, who was suffering from melancholia; and in 1804, Lord and Lady Holland. Many of them would put up at the hotel of Mrs Williams (an Irish widow), or at Mrs Duer's hotel (referred to by Twiss, who visited Lisbon in 1772, as 'an English inn, kept by one De War, on the hill of Buenos Ayres, where there is an ordinary every day, frequented by Englishmen, who reside in Lisbon for their health, and by members of the factory'). Four years later Robert Walpole reported to London that an English tavern-keeper in Lisbon named Dwyer (presumably the same man) had gone to London 'to seduce from England cotton manufacturers for this country'. Other visitors would have stayed at Reeves Hotel in the Rua do Prior (just S of the present British Embassy), although Beckford, who could afford it, and could only survive in a grand style, rented a *quinta*.

In 1786 Robert Southey visited Lisbon for the first time, staying with the Rev. Herbert Hill, his uncle, the then chaplain (from 1782–1807; he had been chaplain at Oporto during the previous four years). The high-minded young poet carped at his jovial congregation, complaining: 'The English here are the most indefatigable dancers and the most inveterate casino players in Europe'. He also disapproved of John Hookham Frere, who in 1800 had succeeded Walpole as Envoy: 'Frere is acting foolishly: he and the consul are slighting the English merchants, and establishing a little aristocracy with the quality-strangers, emigrants, and corps diplomatic'. The Hon. Robert Walpole (1736–1810), a cousin of Horace Walpole, and twice married to daughters of Factory merchants, had been envoy in Lisbon since 1772. He was Beckford's *bête noire*—Beckford called him 'a blundering puppy', and complained of the 'abominable usage' he had received at his hands.

John Adamson, the Portuguese scholar, was living in Lisbon from 1803 to 1807, publishing his study of Camoens in London in 1820. During the same period Byron's 'Hibernian Strangford' (the 6th

Viscount), in spite of his insipid—but popular—translations of Camoens (1803), was also resident here, having been offered the post of Secretary to the Legation. He later became envoy, following the Court to Brazil in 1807. In 1802 Francesco Bartolozzi came to Lisbon from London to direct the National Academy, and here he died in 1815.

In April 1805 Géneral Junot visited the capital in a fruitless attempt to persuade the Portuguese to declare war against Britain. Six months later, the news of Nelson's victory at Trafalgar was celebrated in the Tagus by British ships there firing their guns all night. On 27 November 1807 the royal family (including Maria I, incurably insane since 1792) hurriedly embarked for their long exile in Rio, as Junot again entered Lisbon, this time at the head of a French force of c 1400 men—the only survivors of 14,000 who had set out to march from Bayonne. Additional troops continued to arrive, but did not stay long. The fleet also set sail with members of the government, several thousand other people, half the cash in circulation, and a vast amount of treasure.

After their defeat by Wellington at Vimeiro (21 August 1808), by the disgraceful terms of the Convention of Cintra some 24,000 French troops secured their evacuation in British transports, followed by the execration of the populace.

On 22 April 1809 Wellington disembarked at Lisbon after some months of absence in England. Within 36 hours he was leading the occupying British troops N to evict Soult from Oporto (cf.). That July Lisbon was visited briefly by Lord Byron on his way to Greece.

In October 1810, having halted Masséna at Busaco (cf.), Wellington and his Anglo-Portuguese army retired behind the previously constructed defences known as the Lines of Torres Vedras (cf.), some distance N of the capital. Lisbon remained the main port of supply for the allied forces until the closing stages of the Peninsular War. Here, officers on leave could find the most dissolute distractions. It was also the main base of the army contractors, among them Henrique Teixeira de Sampaio, later Conde da Póvoa (1774–1843).

In March 1817 a liberal conspiracy led by General Gomes Freire de Andrade (who had commanded a Portuguese contingent under Napoleon in Russia) was vigorously suppressed, and Gomes Freire was executed, which did not enhance the waning popularity of General William Carr Beresford, still the British commander-in-chief of the Portuguese army. In March 1821 Lisbon was illuminated to celebrate the passage of a draft constitution: the Papal Nuncio's window, remaining unlit, was forthwith stoned. Although Constitutionalism had come to stay, in May 1823 many of the Lisbon garrison deserted to the reactionary party of the Infante Dom Miguel, and during the subsequent civil war 'of the Two Brothers' Lisbon was frequently the scene of unrest: only with the entry of Marshal Terceira's forces (24 July, 1833) and the defeat of the Miguelites the following year, did the dust of constitutional conflict temporarily settle. Lord Porchester (in 1827), George Borrow (in 1835), and James Holland, the artist (in 1838) passed through Lisbon, while in 1859 it was briefly visited by Francis Palgrave and Lord Tennyson, who drove around the city in 'a blazing heat'. 32 years later, in 1891, it was first visited by Edgar Prestage (1869–1951).

In 1864 Lisbon's population was 163,750, yellow fever and cholera epidemics having killed off over 8000 in 1855–57. In the second half of the century the suburbs extended towards the N and W; railways stations were built, and the port facilities modernised, as they have again been since. By 1900 its population had risen to 356,000, and by 1910 to 435,000. In 1908 Dom Carlos and his eldest son were assassinated in the Praça do Comércio; while on 4 October 1910, with the royal palace under fire from two rebellious warships in the Tagus, the monarchy was finally overthrown. Lisbon experienced a number of incidents during the early years of the Republic, among them the assassination of President Sidónio Pais as he entered the Rossio station in December 1918.

Being the capital, it was the scene of various revolts, among them that of General Gomes da Costa in 1926, precipitating the reaction of General Carmona; and more recently, that of 25 April 1974 (see Introduction to Portuguese History). During the Second World War it had the reputation of being a nest of spies.

Among famous natives of Lisbon (*Lisboetas*) were St. Anthony of Padua (1195–1231); Pope John XXI (Pedro Julião, or Pedro Hispano; died 1277); Fernão Lopes (c 1380–c 1458), chronicler; Francisco de Almeida (c 1450–1510), and João de Castro (1500–48), viceroys of India; Jerónimo Osório (1506–80), historian, and later Bishop of Silves; Francisco de Holanda (c 1518–84), artist and architect; Luis de Camões (Camoens; 1524–80), the poet; António Ferreira (1528–69), poet and playwright; Antonio Vieira (1608–97), writer and preacher; Francisco Manuel de Melo (1608–66), author; Manuel Bernardes (1644–1710), the religious writer; Sebastião José de Carvalho e Melo, Marquês de Pombal (1699–1782); Francisco Vieira do Matos Lusitano (1699–1783), the artist; Nicolau Tolentino (1741–1811), poet and satirist; Marcos Portugal (1762–1830), and Domingos Bontempo (1771–1842), composers; Domingos Antonio de Sequeira (1768–1837), artist; Alexandre Herculano (1810–77), the historian; Camilo Castelo Branco (1825–90), author; Joaquim Pedro Oliveira Martins (1845–94), historian; Fernando Pessoa (1888–1935), poet; José de Almada Negreiros (1893–1970), artist and writer.

Among those who died in Lisbon were Charles Mordaunt, the third Earl of Peterborough (1658–1735; he died only a week after arrival and his body was taken back to England); Henry Fielding (in 1754), author of 'Tom Jones'; Dr Philip Doddridge (1751), the Nonconformist divine; and Francesco Bartolozzi (1815), the engraver: but see p 124.

For some useful addresses in Lisbon see p 80.

Hours of admission to the principal museums, etc. With certain exceptions they are *closed on Mondays* and on national holidays. All are open daily from 10.00–17.00 unless otherwise indicated, but some may close for lunch between 12.30 or 13.00 and 14.00 or 14.30.

The main monuments: *Castle of São Jorge*; *São Vicente de Fora*; the *Monastery of the Jerónimos, Belém*; the *Sé* (cathedral); and *Tower of Belém*, are open daily from c 10.00.

	OPEN	SEE PAGE
Arqueologia e Etnologia Praça do Imperio		142
Arte Antiga Rua das Janelas Verdes 9	and 10.00–19.00 on Sun. and Thurs.	130
Azulejos (Tiles) Madre de Deus Convent	and 12.00–17.00 on Sun.	117
City Museum (da Cidade) Palácio de Pimenta, Campo Grande 245	14.00–18.00	151
Coach Museum (Coches) Praça Afonso de Albuquerque, Belém	to 18.30 in Summer	138
Costume Museum (Trajo) Largo São João Baptista		151
Decorative Art (Espírito Santo) Largo das Portas do Sol	closed Sun.	114
Etnologia Av. Ilha da Madeira		139
Folk Art Praça do Império, Belém		143

	OPEN	SEE PAGE
Gulbenkian Av. De Berna 45	from 16.00-19.30 on Wed. and Sat. in Summer	145
Gulbenkian (Modern Art) Rua Dr Nicolau Bettencourt		150
Marine Museum Praça do Império, Belém	11.00-18.00 on Sun.	142
Musical Instruments Biblioteca Nac., Campo Grande	closed Sat. and Sun; open Mon.	151
São Roque (Religious Art)	the church is open daily	127
Torre do Tombo (Nat. Archives) Largo de São Bento	11.00-16.00, closed Sun.	122

For practical purposes the description of Lisbon has been divided into six sections: **A,** Central Lisbon; **B,** Eastern Lisbon, including the *Castle of São Jorge* and the *Alfama* district; **C,** Western Lisbon, including the *Chiado* and the district of *Rato*; **D,** the *Museu de Arte Antiga*; **E,** *Belém*, further W; and **F,** Northern Lisbon, including the *Gulbenkian museum*. The last two routes are better followed by car.

A.   Central Lisbon

The centre of activity is still to a large extent the **Rossio** (officially the *Praça de Dom Pedro IV*; Pl.10), lying just S of the lower end of the Av. da Liberdade (see below), and N of the Baixa, or planned lower town. Until the 18C this rectangular square was the scene of public executions, autos-da-fé, bull-fights, carnivals, and what not. It was once known to the English as 'Rolling-Motion Square', from the wavy pattern of its white limestone and black basalt pavement, but this has been largely removed in the interest of traffic.

In the centre is a poor bronze statue 'of Pedro IV' (1870; he was crowned king of Brazil as Pedro I), which was in fact cast as a statue of Maximilian of Mexico, and was being shipped out to Mexico when he was assassinated. The boat from Marseille put in at Lisbon, and a deal was made with the authorities, who after making a few slight changes, got a royal statue cheaply.

At the N end of the square is the classical portico of the *Teatro Nacional de Dona Maria II* (1842–46, by Fortunato Lodi, an Italian), restored since its interior was gutted by fire in 1964, and surmounted by a statue of Gil Vicente, Portugal's earliest dramatist.

It stands partly on the site of the Paço dos Estãos, a royal palace built in 1449, which in 1497 was a point of assembly for Portuguese Jews prior to their expulsion from the country. After 1571 it was occupied by the Inquisition, and later, until its destruction by fire in 1836, it was used as government offices.

The W side of the square, lined with crowded cafés, provides a good view of the castle of São Jorge, while from the E side one can see the ruins of the Carmo.

Facing the W side the theatre is one of Lisbon's railway stations (Extação do Rossia; 1891), a mock-Manueline construction by J.L. Monteiro (1849–1942), built on two floors. It immediately abutts the S

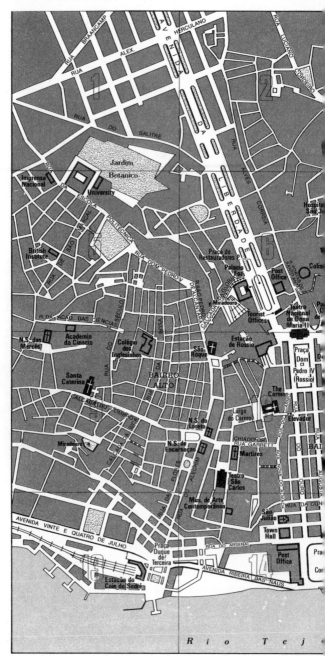

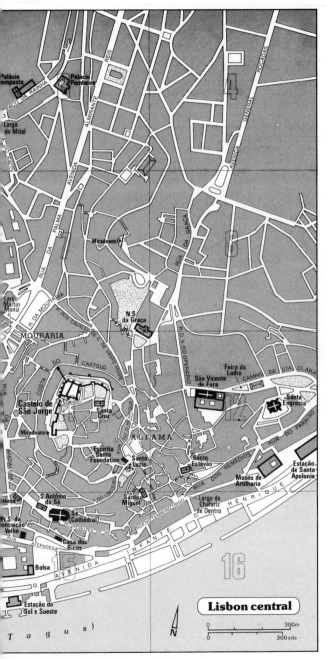

Lisbon central

0 _____ 300m
0 _____ 300yds

end of a long tunnel, the line beyond its N end providing a good view of the Águas Livres aqueduct.

To the E of the theatre is the LARGO DE SÃO DOMINGOS, flanked by the *Paço dos Condes de Almada*, in 1640 the scene of the conspiratorial meetings of the 'Restauradores', who overthrew the Spanish and secured the Independence of Portugal.

At the SE corner of the Largo stands *São Domingos, almost entirely rebuilt by Carlos Mardel after 1755, in which victims of the Inquisition heard their sentences read, and which contains the tomb of the Spanish preacher Fray Luís de Granada (1504–88), whose 'Guia de Pecadores' (sinners) was first published in Lisbon in 1556–57. The church, gutted by fire in 1959 and re-roofed, is most impressive in its partly calcinated state. A few paces to the S of the church is the smaller PRAÇA DA FIGUEIRA, with its statue of D. João I.

Further to the NE is the LARGO MARTIM MONIZ, a somewhat derelict area at the S end of the wide Rua da Palma and its extension NE, the Av. Almirante Reis, which with its continuation NE, leads towards the airport.

From the SW corner of the Rossio, the pedestrian Rua do Carmo climbs steeply up to the *Chiado*: see Rte 1C.

The area immediately S of the Rossio and Praça da Figueira consists of the grid of streets laid out by Pombal, assisted by Manuel da Maia, Eugénio dos Santos de Carvalho (until 1760), and succeeded by Carlos Mardel until 1763. It is generally known as the **Baixa** or lower town (Pl.10, 14). Its three principal thoroughfares are the Rua Augusta (leading off the SE corner of the Rossio towards a triumphal *Arch* only finished in 1873), and to the W and E respectively, the Rua do Ouro (officially Rua Áurea; of the goldsmiths), and the Rua da Prata (silversmiths). The streets were originally allotted to separate trades, but this division is now hardly noticeable.

At the W end of the first transverse street (de Santa Justa) stands the incongruous *Elevador*, a passenger lift (designed by Eiffel), providing a rapid ascent to the *Carmo* (see Rte 1C), and commanding from its summit an extensive panoramic view of the city.

At the E end of the fifth cross street (Rua da Conceição) we may ascend towards the cathedral and castle: see Rte 1B.

The three main streets shortly debouch onto the riverside **Praça do Comércio** (Pl. 14), perhaps more impressive when seen from the Tagus, but much spoilt since used as a parking site. Many would agree with Sitwell who remarked that it 'does not deserve the encomiums that have been lavished upon it'. It is still widely known by its earlier name, TERREIRO DO PAÇO, after the 16C royal palace 'da Ribeira' (of the riverbank) here, destroyed in the convulsion of 1755, but it is even better known—at least to English visitors—as **'Black Horse Square'**, from the effective but somewhat pretentious bronze equestrian statue by Joaquim Machado de Castro, erected in 1775 to commemorate the generosity of Dom José to the victims of the earthquake.

The medallion of Pombal was replaced on the pedestal in 1833, having been previously removed on that minister's dismissal, and hidden by its designer. It will be noted that the horse and the elephant on either side (although done from life) are of equal size.

Three sides of the square are lined with pink-painted 'Pombaline' arcaded façades of government offices, designed by Eugénio dos Santos. At its SE corner stands the *Bolsa* or *Exchange*, adjoining which is the *Alfándega* or *Custom House*, while opposite is the

Estação do Sul e Sueste, or *Fluvial*, providing ferries for passengers and cars to the far bank of the Tagus (6.00–23.00) and *Barreiro*, the terminus for trains to the Algarve.

A few paces to the W, a marble staircase between two columns descends into the river, providing a view of the 'Sea of Straw' or *Mar de Palha*, as this stretch of the estuary is designated, and once familiarly called 'Jackass Bay' by English mariners. Hence, on 23 April 1662, Catherine of Braganza and her suite sailed for England. She reached Portsmouth on 13 May, and married Charles II on the 21st. (She did not return to Lisbon until January 1693.)

From the NE angle of the square we shortly pass, in the Rua Alfándega, the church of **N.S. da Conceição Velha** (of the Conception), built on the site of a synagogue. It is notable for its splendid Manueline *Portal* (c 1520), whose tympanum represents the Virgin sheltering with her mantle Dom Manuel and Dona Leonor (widow of João II, and founder of the church), Pope Leo X, Miguel Contreiras, founder of the brotherhood of the Misericórdia, and other ecclesiastics.

A few paces beyond, on the N side of an open space, stands the so-called **Casa dos Bicos**, once a residence of the Albuquerque family, and adorned with diamond-shaped bosses. In 1982–83 it was gutted, and the restored lower two floors of the 16C building were provided with an additional two floors. The reconstruction faithfully copies the original façade as illustrated in several early engravings (in particular on an early 18C azulejo), which show in some detail the several balustraded upper windows and balconies in the Manueline taste.

For the riverside district further E see Rte 1B.

Leaving the Praça do Comércio at its NW corner, where, by the *Post Office* (*Correio*), Carlos I, penultimate king of Portugal, and his eldest son Luís Filipe, were assassinated on 1 February 1908, we soon reach the small PRAÇA DO MUNICÍPIO, in the centre of which stands a late 18C *pelourinho*, a twisted monolithic column surmounted by an armillary sphere, symbol of municipal authority (see Glossary). The *Town Hall* (*Câmara Municipal*) itself, of 1865–75, from which the Republic was proclaimed on 5 October 1910, stands to the E. Adjoining is *São Julião* (1854), occupying the site of the former cathedral church of W Lisbon.

The Rua Nova do Almada climbs N from beyond the church, providing another approach to the *Chiado*: see Rte 1C.

Along the S side of the square extends the 18C *Arsenal da Marinha*, while the Rua do Arsenal leads W to the PRAÇA DUQUE DA TERCEIRA at the foot of the steep Rua do Alecrim (see Rte 1C), and to the *Estação do Cais do Sodré* (terminal for Estoril and Cascais; Pl.13). From the adjacent quay, Junot and his troops embarked after the Convention of Sintra.

The riverside road continues W to the suburb of *Belém*: see Rte 1E.

B. Eastern Lisbon

This area, only a part of which is known as the **Alfama**, is largely dominated by the Castelo de São Jorge, best approached by the Rua de Santo António da Sé, climbing SE from the Rua da Madalena, two streets E of the Rua da Prata (see Rte 1A).

We first pass (right) the church of *Madalena* (1783), incorporating the Manueline portico of its predecessor, and then (left) *Santo*

António da Sé, by Mateus Vicente, apparently paid for by alms collected in the streets, completed in 1812, and alleged to have been built on the site of the birthplace of St. Anthony of Padua (1195–1231).

A few steps higher, overlooking a small square, stands the **Sé** or ***CATHEDRAL** (Pl.15), its two low battlemented towers rising above a narthex which covers a Romanesque door. The building is still of some interest in spite of the damage caused by earthquakes, fires, and injudicious rebuilding, although its entire restoration is long overdue.

Although legend has it that the cathedral was used as a mosque by the Moors, there is no evidence of it existing before the time of Afonso Henriques. This Romanesque edifice, of which the English crusader-priest Gilbert of Hastings was the first bishop, was largely rebuilt by Afonso IV and his successors after the earthquakes of 1337–47. In 1388, the populace, infuriated by his Spanish sympathies, flung Bp Martinho Anes from the N tower. In 1393 João I raised the see to metropolitan rank.

The short barrel-vaulted INTERIOR, with its low lantern, and plain capitals, and the details of the triforium, is not without merit. Note the rose-windows in the apses, and in the Gothic ambulatory chapels the tombs of Lobo Fernandes Pacheco (14C), together with that of his wife, and of João Anes (died 1440), the first archbishop. The *Capela-Mór*, originally built by Afonso IV, but 'restored' in the late 18C, contains that king's tomb and that of his wife, Dona Brites, two late 18C urns, and Baroque organs of the same period.

Also to be seen is the elaborate *Presépio* by Joaquim Machado de Castro (1766). Housed here are the relics of St. Vincent (brought to Lisbon from Cape St. Vincent in a ship miraculously guided by a pair of ravens, which now figure in the city arms). Three sides of the *Cloisters* (late 13C, but much damaged; the N walk is being restored), entered from the N side of the ambulatory, extend round the apse. A 13C iron screen is notable.

From the S side of the cathedral we may follow the Rua Cruzes de Sé and its continuations to enter the W end of the **Alfama** towards the LARGO DO CHAFARIZ DE DENTRO (Pl.15; see p 118), but it is recommended that the visitor should first continue the ascent along the N side of the cathedral by the Rua do Limoeiro, passing (left) near the slight remains of a 1C *Roman Theatre* (in the Rua São Mamede) and the *Aljube*, once the archbishop's palace, later a women's prison. On the right is the ruinous *Limoeiro*, once a royal palace, later the Mint, and since the late 15C a men's prison, named after a lemon-tree which once stood in its courtyard. It was here that in 1383 João, the Master of Avis, assassinated Andeiro, lover of Leonor Teles, widow of Dom Fernando, and standing at one of the windows, was acclaimed regent by the populace.

Continuing uphill, we pass (right) *Santa Luzia*, adjacent to which one may obtain a good view over the Alfama, into which we may also descend from here. A better view is commanded by the LARGO DAS PORTAS DO SOL, an open promenade.

To our left is the entrance to the ***Espírito Santo Foundation**, established in 1953 by Ricardo Espírito Santo Silva, the banker, with the intention of preserving the traditional skills of Portuguese craftsmanship in the decorative arts, and providing the city with a *Museum of Decorative Art*.

The 21 workshops may be visited during weekdays and orders may be placed for the restoration and fine-quality reproduction of fabrics, furniture, book-bindings (some examples of which are displayed in the museum), and iron-work, etc. The foundation also provides a three-year course in interior decoration.

The *Museum*, accommodated in a 17C palace of the counts of Azurara, preserving some good azulejos and ceilings, contains a remarkably fine collection of Portuguese furniture and silver (some showing English influence), displayed in a series of rooms built round a courtyard. The Directoire furniture in the Oval Room and the Octagon is notable; while a rosewood card-backgammon-and-chess-table is conspicuous. Note the two views of Lisbon by Alexandre Noël (1752–1834) and that of Oporto by Carlos van Zeller; the Indo-Portuguese tapestries; Arraiolos carpets; and embroidery from Castelo Branco, and on an upper floor, the Jacaranda and boxwood cupboard; the doors of sicupira wood; the japanned furniture; the painted ceiling and the silver in the Dining-room; and the model for the 'Black Horse' (see Rte 1A). From the Portaría, with its blue and white azulejos, we enter another suite of furnished rooms, also containing a number of paintings, among them portraits of Pedro II and João V, and of the sieges of Lisbon, and Santarém (17C).

An easy ascent hence to the Castle may be made by retracing our steps downhill and taking the first turning on the right, which leads in a few minutes to the *Porta de São Jorge* (1846), the entrance to the precinct of the **Castelo de São Jorge** (Pl.11), the Moorish citadel occupying the centre of the Phoenician and Roman settlements of Lisbon. Its tree-shaded terraces, rampart walks, and ten old towers, command extensive *Views over the city and its surroundings, but the municipal 'restoration' of the site is suspect, to say the least.

It was long used as a prison, and among its more recent inmates were—in the 1820s—Sir John Milley Doyle, for scheming against Don Miguel; and in 1834 the Miguelite general, Sir John Campbell. On its S side stood the Paço de Alcáçova, the Moorish Kasba, converted into a palace by Dom Dinis, which remained the principal residence of the king until the time of Dom Manuel. João I died here in 1433, and here were born João II (1455) and João III (1502). By the 17C it was a neglected ruin.

At the NW corner a wall descends part of the way down the steep hill to an outlying tower; passing this, we skirt the N flank of the castle to make our exit by the church of *Santa Cruz*.

Continuing downhill, we shortly reach the small LARGO DE RODRIGUES DE FREITAS (Pl.11). Nearby is the church of *Meninos-Deus* (1711–37), attributed to João Antunes. Façade towers were planned but not executed.

Downhill to the left lies the unsavoury *Mouraria*, best avoided after dark, the district relegated to the Moors after the re-occupation of Lisbon, from which one may return to the Rossio.
Almost due N is the Calçada da Graça, with the Baroque church of the Augustinian convent of *N.S. da Graça*, the sacristy of which, with good azulejos, contains the tomb of Mendo de Pereira (died 1708).—From a left turn a short distance beyond, we may climb steeply to reach the *Miradouro de N.S. do Monte*.

By following a lane to the right from the far side of the Largo de Rodrigues de Freitas, after a few minutes' walk we reach the imposing but frigid white limestone church of **São Vicente de Fora** (1582–1627; Pl.12), by Felipe Terzi and Baltasar Alvares, its name a reminder that we are now outside (*fora*) the medieval line of walls. It was later known as the Patriarchal church (of E Lisbon). The square front, in the Italian Renaissance style, is crowned by short twin towers. The dome fell in the 1755 earthquake. The well-proportioned interior is notable for its coffered barrel vault, and its great 18C *Organ*, sited behind the main altar.

The *Cloisters*, entered from the S aisle, contain a wealth of most attractive 18C *Azulejos* depicting La Fontaine's Fables. A passage on the left as we enter leads to the *Pantheon of the House of Braganza* (the refectory being so-transformed in 1855), accommodating the remains—previously displayed in an embalmed state—of the majority of that dynasty from João IV (died 1656) to Manuel II (died 1932, in England), together with his wife (died 1951, at Versailles), and his brother Luís Filipe (assassinated 1908). Catherine of Braganza (died 1705, after 20 years of widowhood, the last 12 spent in Lisbon) also lies there; as do King Carol of Rumania (died 1953) and Mme Lupescu, his morganatic wife.

Of more interest is the *Portaria* to the right of the cloister entrance, with a ceiling by Vincenzo Baccerelli of Florence, dating from 1710 (to be restored), while scenes of the sieges of Lisbon and of Santarém are depicted in azulejos.

It was in São Vicente that the great retable of Nuno Gonçalves was found, and later moved to the Museu de Arte Antiga; and it was here in 1787 that Beckford first met his future protégé, Gregorio Franchi (1770–1828), who was then a choir-boy.

Passing under a bridge on the N side of the church we reach the CAMPO DE SANTA CLARA, occasional scene of a flea-market (*Feira da Ladra*), on the N side of which is an 18C mansion by Manuel da Costa Negreiros, containing some fine azulejos.

A short distance downhill to the S stands the ambitious church of *Santa Engrácia** (Pl.12), begun in 1682 by João Nunes Tinoco, and continued after 1690 by João Antunes to replace an older church apparently demolished in consequence of an act of sacrilege in 1630. The present building, once used as an artillery magazine, was only completed in 1966, with the addition of the balustraded cupola, thus invalidating the expression for never-finished work as being 'obras de Santa Engrácia'. Since its termination it has been proclaimed a 'National Pantheon' (in the manner of dictatorships), and contains the modern cenotaphs of Vasco da Gama, Afonso de Albuquerque, Nun' Álvares Pereira, the Infante Dom Henrique (Henry the Navigator), Pedro Álvares Cabral, and Luis de Camões. The plan is that of a Greek Cross with rounded arms framed by four square towers. On the entrance front four huge Doric columns frame a triad of arches and pedimented niches. The splendid interior with its four ribbed semi-domes of coloured marbles set in contrasting patterns, is spatially one of the handsomest in Portugal.

Descending downhill to the SW, one soon reaches the **Museu de Artilharia** (Pl.12), a so-called *Military Museum* accommodated in the *Arsenal do Exército*, with an imposing Corinthian façade by the French architect Larre. Unfortunately it would seem that the collection, which includes some individually interesting pieces, has hardly been touched since first accumulated here.

To the left of the entrance are some early bronze cannon, some cast in Goa, including the 'Touro' (1518) and 'Tigre' (1549), but the most curious specimens are in the main courtyard, among them the enormous cannon taken at the siege of Diu (1539), cast in 1533.—On the FIRST FLOOR (right) are two rooms (only) devoted to the Peninsular War, specifically the battles of Roliça, Vimeiro, and Busaco, and the Lines of Torres Vedras, including a maquette of the last, showing the position of the lines of fortifications across the peninsula N of Lisbon. Arms, uniforms, and a poor collection of prints and maps are also on show. Other rooms are devoted to Portuguese military operations in the

19–20Cs, including the First World War. To the left of the landing, in a long gallery overlooking the courtyard, are an interminable series of rooms containing an interesting but depressingly displayed collection of uniforms, armour, weapons, and small-arms of all periods, together with daubs of generals, etc., hardly one of which is of any merit.

Just to the E of the museum is the *Estação de Santa Apolónia*, the main station for trains to Spain, France, and Oporto.

A section of the azulejo Panorama of Lisbon

Visitors without cars are advised to take a taxi from here to the suburb of *Xabregas* to visit the secularised *Convent of Madre de Deus, now known as the **Museu do Azulejo**. The convent was founded by Dona Leonor, widow of João II, in 1509, and later enlarged and embellished. The *Church*, to the right of the entrance, is resplendent with gilt Baroque woodwork surrounding paintings of the Life of St. Francis attributed to André Gonçalves (1687–1762), below which are rustic scenes in Dutch tiles (c 1710), and the richly carved pulpit of c 1730–50. The *Sacristy* contains azulejos from the factory of Rato (c 1780). Steps lead down to the lower part of the nave, in fact the floor of the earlier church, from which the main *Cloister* is entered. Off this are rooms displaying other examples of azulejos, among them some from the Lisbon factory (mid 16C), and including caricature *singeries*. Stairs ascend through a patio, and further steps (note the 18C azulejos) lead up to an upper gallery.

The *Chapel of Santo António* retains its azulejos depicting the life of that saint (c 1780), together with a series of canvases. Hence we enter the richly gilt *Coro Alto*, above the stalls of which are numerous reliquaries. Among the paintings here are an *anon.* Portuguese Annunciation (16C), Adoration (15C), and a curious Flemish 'Panorama of Jerusalem' in which are set scenes of the Passion (15C).

Other rooms were recently restored, as was the famous Panorama of Lisbon, a tile picture (c 1730) some 36m long.

Hence we may take a tram or taxi back past the Military Museum to the LARGO DO CHAFARIZ DE DENTRO, the main lower square of the **Alfama**. This is a convenient base from which to explore the characteristic maze of narrow alleys, bright with hanging washing, and the breakneck flights of steps covering the lower slopes of the hill, which have changed little in recent centuries, and recall the Moorish occupation. **Caution** is advised when exploring this area: beware of bag-snatchers.

Regaining the Largo, we follow the Rua do Terreiro do Trigo (corn market), shortly passing (right) the *Chafariz de Dentro*, a 17C fountain, and the *Casa dos Bicos* (see Rte 1A) to regain the PRAÇA DO COMÉRCIO.

The area between the Av. da Liberdade and the Rua da Palma, lying on the hill immediately N of the Rossio, largely devoted to medical and scientific institutions, is of comparatively little interest.

The *Hospital de São José* (Pl.7) contains some fine 18C azulejos in its courtyard and staircase, and retains a sumptuously fitted *Sacristy*, having been until 1769 part of the former Jesuit monastery of Santo Antão o Novo. Camoens is believed to have died in 1579 in a house on the site of Nos 139–141 in the neighbouring Calçada de Sant' Ana.

In the PAÇO DA RAINHA, further N (Pl.3), stands the *Palácio da Bemposta*, since 1851 in military hands, built after 1693 by Catherine of Braganza, the widowed queen of Charles II of England, who lived here on her return to Portugal. Here she entertained the Archduke Charles (the Habsburg claimant to the Spanish throne) in 1704, and died the following year. Over the door are carved the arms of England. Here also resided João VI, and here he died in 1826. The *Chapel* (1794) was designed by Manuel Caetano de Sousa (1742–1802), with a chancel decorated by Pedro Alexandrino de Carvalho (1729–1810).

A short distance beyond is the 18C *Palácio Pombeiro*, now the Italian Embassy.

The **Avenida da Liberdade** (like the Champs Élysées in Paris, with which some have compared it) is not what it was in its heyday, the principal promenade of Lisbon. Extending NW from the PRAÇA DOS RESTAURADORES (Pl.6) to the PRAÇA DO MARQUÊS DE POMBAL or ROTUNDA (see Rte 1F), it was laid out in 1879, and is almost 1.5km long. The thoroughfare itself, some 90m wide, is lined by rather commonplace buildings, many of them now put to commercial use, and few are of any interest in themselves. An exception perhaps is the once-magnificent *Palácio Foz* (1755–77), built for the Marquês de Castelo-Melhor by Francesco Saverio Fabri, on the W side of the Praça dos Restauradores, named in honour of the leaders of the anti-Spanish revolution of 1640. The commemorative obelisk in the centre was only erected in 1886.

The Palácio Foz now accommodates Lisbon's main *Tourist Office*; also the important *Duarte de Sousa Library* (see Bibliography), and a valuable photographic library.

From the NW corner of the square a funicular ascends the steep hillside to the W (the Calçada da Glória) to the *Miradouro de São Pedro de Alcântara*: see Rte 1C.—On the E side of the square is one of the main *Post Offices*.

Parallel to and E of the Avenida, and also approached from the LARGO DE SÃO DOMINGOS, is the entertaining Rua das Portas de Santo Antão, thronged with restaurants and bars. At No. 100 is the *Museu Etnográfico do Ultramar* and the *Sociedade de Geografia*, founded in 1875. It contains an early astrolabe, and a research library; also relics of famous explorers (including David Livingstone's travelling-chair and telescope) and products of Portugal's late colonies. The collections are normally open to view on Wednesdays only. Here also is the huge *Coliseu* of 1890, designed by Cesar Yans, an Italian, and accommodating 8000.

The street leads N, off which a funicular climbs the hill to the E.

C.   Western Lisbon

There are at least four not-so-tiring approaches to this area from the Cidade Baixa: the most rapid is by taking the *Elevador* (Pl.10; see Rte 1A), which deposits you near the entrance to the *Carmo* (see below). The most convenient route for pedestrians is the Rua do Carmo, climbing from the SW corner of the Rossio, which leads into the lower end of the **Chiado**, officially Rua Garrett (Pl.10), long one of the main shopping streets of Lisbon.

Ascending this fashionable promenade, the first turning on the right leads shortly to the LARGO DO CARMO, with its curious fountain. To the right is the ruined church of the **Carmo** (Pl.10), founded by the Constable Nun'Álvares in 1389 in fulfilment of a vow made at Aljubarrota, and shattered by the earthquake of 1755. By 1855 it was harbouring a chemical manufactory. The W front retains its Gothic doorway, and its graceful re-erected nave arches now span a garden. Both this and what remains of the edifice have been laid out as a *Museu Arqueológico*, but its re-arrangement is long overdue.

Among various tombs is the canopied tomb of Rui de Meneses (1528), with a recumbent effigy, while in the N transept is a Manueline window from the Jerónimos at Belém. The first S apse-chapel contains the tombs of Dona Constança, mother of Dom Fernando, and of Fernão Sanches, son of Dom Dinis. The Capela-Mór retains the tomb of Fernando I (died 1383), and a model of that of Nun'Álvares, who took the Carmelite habit in 1423 and died here in 1431, but his remains have been translated to Santa Engrácia (see Rte 1B). A miscellaneous collection of artefacts (some from Vila Nova de São Pedro), Roman epigraphical and other archaeological and architectural remains, four Nottingham alabasters, and various azulejos and ceramics, lie scattered about.—The former dependencies to the N are now occupied by the police.

Regaining the Chiado and turning right, the first left-hand street, the Rua Ivens (commemorating the late 19C African explorer Roberto Ivens), leads to a small square (view) in which, until its removal to the Campo Grande (see Rte 1F) stood the Biblioteca Nacional.

Next (in the Chiado) we pass (left) Bertrand's bookshop, part of a firm established in Lisbon c 1732, and the *Mártires* church (1769–84), dedicated to the English and other Crusaders who fell when retaking Lisbon from the Moors in 1147, but the site of the earlier church of this name was further S. A relief over the portal depicts Afonso Henriques giving thanks to the Virgin for the delivery of the city.

To the left, the Rua Serpa Pinto (commemorating the late 19C African explorer Alexandre Serpa Pinto) leads down past (right) the recently restored **Teatro São Carlos**, the largest theatre in Lisbon. It was built in 1792 by José da Costa e Silva (1747–1819), who had previously spent some years in Rome, on the lines of the San Carlos theatre at Naples, while the rusticated *porte-cochère* and pilastered façade are very similar to Piermarini's La Scala theatre in Milan (1776–78). It replaced the opera house designed by J.C. Bibiena, destroyed seven months after its inauguration in 1755. The oft-repeated story has it that it was outside this theatre that Lord Byron was struck by an angry husband for making advances to his wife.

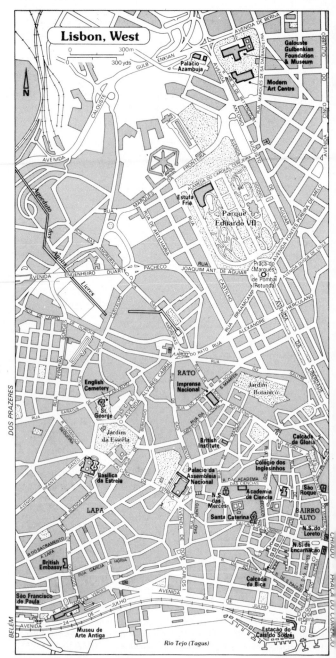

Further downhill on the left is the entrance to the *Museu Nacional de Arte Contemporânea*. Despite its name the majority of its contents date from the late 19C. It is at present in the process of radical re-arrangement, and will probably be moved to another site. It contains representative works by such artists as Anunciação, Lupi, Teixeira Lopes, Prietto, Henrique Pouzão, Silva Porta, Sousa-Cardosa, Almada Negreiros, Pomar, and Vieira da Silva, together with some sculptures by Soares dos Reis, among others.

The Rua Garrett shortly widens into the LARGO DO CHIADO, named after the satirical poet António Ribeiro (c 1520–91; 'O Chiado'), whose statue sits here. On the N side stands the church of *N.S. do Loreto*, that of the Italian colony, rebuilt in 1785 by José da Costa e Silva, and preserving over its main doorway a 17C group by Francesco Borromini. Opposite is the late 18C *N.S. de Encarnação*, by Manuel de Sousa: neither is of great interest, although the W exterior wall of the latter is decorated with blue azulejos.

We now reach the PRAÇA LUIS DE CAMÕES (Pl.10), with a small garden.

Hence the wide Rua do Alecrim (meaning 'rosemary' in Arabic) descends steeply towards the river and the *Estação do Cais do Sodré*, passing (right) a statue by Teixeira Lopes of the novelist Eça de Queirós (1845–1900), tempted by his slightly veiled muse (1903).—In the mansion opposite, the town residence of Géneral Junot, the so-called 'Convention of Cintra' was probably signed.

The British Factory assembly rooms may have been—c 1800—in the Rua do Alecrim, and at an earlier date on a site at the lower end of the Rua das Flores, parallel to the W. They were certainly in this quarter of the town.

From the Praça Luis de Camões a variety of routes may be followed to the W or NW, depending on the visitor's interests and stamina.

A circuit to the W may be made by following the Calçada do Combro. At the third left turn a funicular runs downhill; the next turning leads shortly to the *Miradouro Alto de Santa Catarina*, providing a good view of the *Ponte 25 de Abril*; see Rte 1E.

Further downhill in the Calçada do Combro we pass (right) the church of **Santa Catarina**, or *dos Paulistas*, founded in 1647 and largely rebuilt after the great earthquake. It contains a vault over the chancel decorated c 1730 by António Pimenta Rolim; the plaster ceiling of the nave, attributed to João Grossi (Giovanni Grossi; 1719–c 81), an Italian stuccatore; and decorative sculpture and woodcarving in the apse by Santos Pacheco (active c 1717–55). Note also the Baroque organ.

A recommended short DETOUR may be made by retracing our steps and following the Rua do Século to the N, skirting (right) two semi-circular levels, to reach (left) the *Travessa das Mercês*, in the chapel of which the tomb of Pombal stood neglected from his death until 1923. The house in which he was born in 1699 lies a short distance beyond. Turning here under the *Arco do Jesús* (left) we reach the wide Rua da Academia das Ciências, where, at No. 19 (left) the *Academia das Ciências* (founded 1779), with its important *Library*, has been accommodated since 1934 in the old convent of the Third Order of Penitents. On the floor above is an extensive but old-fashioned *Geological and Anthropological Museum*, including a number of prehistoric and Roman antiquities. By turning left and then right, we shortly reach the LARGO DE SÃO BENTO: see below.

Continuing downhill, we may take the next right-hand turning, ascending towards the façade of *N.S. das Mercês*, a handsome building of c 1760–70 by Joaquim de Oliveira, from which, continuing W (downhill) we soon reach the LARGO DE SÃO BENTO.

This is dominated by the **Palácio da Assembleia da República** (or Houses of Parliament), which since 1834 has occupied the 17C

The organ in Santa Catarina

buildings (much extended after 1876) of the older convent of São Bento da Saúde or dos Negros, where in 1552 the humanist George Buchanan spent four months after his trial by the Inquisition. The official residence of the Prime Minister stands in grounds behind the palace. Its Parliamentary Archives, containing a wealth of information from 1821 on, may be consulted on prior written request. The assembly rooms of the 'Commons' and former Câmara dos Dignos Pares do Reino (Lords) may be visited by appointment.

In the NE wing of this building, entered from the right-hand side of the main portico, is the *Arquivo Nacional*, known as the *Arquivo da Torre do Tombo from the name of the tower in the Castelo de São Jorge where the archives were kept before the earthquake. They were brought here c 1757. A new building to house them is to be constructed.

The visitor (preferably having made an appointment) will be escorted to the strong-room, in which normally is an exhibition of MSS and books. Among the earliest and more interesting (some illuminated) are the following:

Grant founding the Church of Lodosa (882); the Apocalypse of Lorvão (1189); the first document in which Afonso Henriques is mentioned as king (1140); Bull of Alexander III conceding the title 'King' to Afonso Henriques, and recognising the Independence of Portugal (1179); an illuminated Book of Hours from Alcobaça (late 13C?); a Flemish Book of Hours of c 1436; the Hours of Dom Duarte (French; 15C); a missal printed in Naples (1487); a document founding a School at Alcobaça (1269); Treaty ratifying the division of the Atlantic and adjacent territories between Spain and Portugal (Tordesillas, 1494); Testament of the Infante Dom Fernando (1437); *Fernão Lopes*, Crónica de João I (16C), with a view of Lisbon; the 'Livro das Fortalezas' of Duarte Darmas (early 16C); Bulls creating bishops for Baia (1555) and Rio de Janeiro (1676); *João Teixeira*, Plan of the coast of Brazil (1640); Plan of Goa by *Gaspar Correia*, from his 'Lendas da India' (1538); the illuminated Florentine Bible given to the Jerónimos of Belém by Dom Manuel (c 1500; 7 volumes); letters signed by Vasco da Gama, and Magellan; the 'Livro da Nobreza' of *António Godinho* (16C); a copy of the Nuremberg Chronicle (1493); *João de Lisboa*, Livro da Marinharia (16C), showing the coast of Africa; early Views of Portuguese Castles; *Fernão Vaz Dourado*, Atlas (1571); Bull of Clemente VI nominating Frei Diogo da Silva Inquisitor in Portugal (1531); Peace Treaty between João IV and Oliver Cromwell (1654); and a copy of the first Portuguese Constitution (1821).

Bearing round the W side of the building—from which the Av. Dom Carlos I descends to the river—we ascend along the Calçada da Estrela, passing (right) public gardens.

By turning left at the next crossroad (Rua Borges Carneiro) and its continuation (Rua da Lapa: the name *Lapa* serving to describe this secluded diplomatic enclave largely accommodating foreign embassies), after some minutes we reach the Rua São Domingos à Lapa, in which No. 37 (right) has been the *Chancery* of the *British Embassy* since 1940, and previously the Palácio Porto Covo (c 1750). The ambassador's *Residence* since 1875, a short distance further SW (Rua São Francisco de Borja 63), dating in part from the late 17C, was once a convent.—No. 25 in the Rua do Sacramento à Lapa (the first right turn as we bear downhill) is probably the house in which Byron briefly resided in 1809. Southey lived with his uncle in the Rua Buenos Aires, parallel to the N.—By continuing downhill past the embassy we shortly reach a small square off the Rua das Janelas Verdes, opposite which is an entrance to the *Museu de Arte Antiga*: see Rte 1D. This district of Lapa is approximately co-extensive with that previously known as *Buenos Ayres*.

The Calçada da Estrela continues to climb towards the PRAÇA DA ESTRELA, with (right) the Jardim da Estrela, overlooked (left) by the conspicuous **Basílica da Estrela**, built by the devout and melancholy Maria I in 1779–90 in fulfilment of a vow depending on the birth of an heir (cf. Mafra). It was designed by Mateus Vicente de Oliveira, and after his death in 1786 completed by Reinaldo Manuel dos Santos. Although some critics have been fulsome in their approval of the well-proportioned but frigid baroque interior, it is perhaps the decorative appearance of the exterior which is the more effective, with its two tall belfries and imposing dome (from which panoramic views may be obtained). The painting in the retable is by Pompeo Batoni; the tombs of Dona Maria (died 1816, in Rio de Janeiro), and that of her confessor, Fr. Inácio de São Caetano (died 1788), may also be seen. The Estrela Convent was used as a military hospital during the Peninsular War.

Adjacent are the offices of the *Instituto Geográfico e Cadastral*, where a wide variety of maps of Portugal may be obtained.

By bearing round the W side of the gardens, we reach on crossing the street the entrance (ring) to the umbrageous *English Cemetery*, permission for the establishment of which was granted to Consul-general William Poyntz in 1717 on condition that it was called the 'Hospital of the English Factory'. The Dutch Factory acquired an adjoining plot, and the two were united and enclosed by a wall. The plot was first used in 1725. In 1728 Tyrawly, the ambassador, was complaining at the expense to which he was put in maintaining a chapel for some 700 British Protestants 'amongst such a bigoted mob'. The avenue of cypresses (which caused the Portuguese to call the *Cemitério dos Ingleses* that *'Os Ciprestes'*) leads to the church of *St. George* (1885, replacing one of 1815 which had burnt down), off which (left) is the tomb (1830, replacing one erected by the Factory) of Henry Fielding (1707–54)—'on a spot selected by *guess'*, according to Mrs Quillinan (Wordsworth's daughter), who visited the site in 1846. Fielding, the celebrated 47-year-old author of 'Joseph Andrews', 'Jonathan Wild', and 'Tom Jones', had made an unavailing voyage to Lisbon to recover his health, and died only two months after his arrival; the 'Journal of a Voyage to Lisbon' was published post-humously.

Henry Fielding's grave: a watercolour by John Coates

Among the many other burials here are: Dr Philip Doddridge (1702–51), the eminent Non-conformist divine and hymn-writer, who survived only 13 days in Lisbon; Abraham Castres (died 1757; see p 104); Thomas Barclay, born in Strabane (Ireland) in 1728, and killed in a duel in Lisbon in 1793, whom Washington had made American consul in Morocco in 1791 at the request of Jefferson; Daniel Gildemeester *père* (see *Seteais*); Prince Christian August von Waldeck (1754–98), who was to command the Portuguese army in 1797, but did not long survive; Thomas Horne (1722–92), Beckford's agent and banker in Lisbon; Admiral Nicholas Horthy (1868–1957), Regent of Hungary (1920–44), who died in exile at Estoril; and a number of Dutch and Scandinavian Protestants, apart from members of the Anglo-Portuguese community who have died here during the last 250 years, and other non-Catholics.

A building of c 1730 bearing the name of the Hospital, and used as such until c 1843, which is now the adjacent *Parsonage*, was rebuilt in 1793 by Gerard de Visme (c 1725–98), a wealthy merchant. The present *Hospital* (1910) lies to the N of the cemetery, above the old Jewish graveyard.

The *Cemitério dos Prazeres* (pleasures!; further W), likewise shaded by fine cypresses, deserves a visit.

A few minutes' walk to the NE along the Av. Pedro Álvares Cabral is the LARGO DO RATO, a busy road junction, from which nine streets radiate.

It was in this district that the *Royal Factory of the Rato* operated until 1835. It had been created by Pombal in 1767 (in emulation of the porcelain factory of Buen Retiro, established in Madrid in 1759), with Tomás Bruneto of Turin as its first director, but the production of porcelain in Portugal was not firmly established until José Ferreira Pinto Basto founded the factory of Vista Alegre, near Aveiro, in 1824.

Part of the Águas Livres aqueduct, as seen a few years ago

A few paces to the N is the *Casa das Águas Livres*, or *Mãe* (mother) *d'Agua*, the old reservoir of the aqueduct of *Águas Livres* (Free Waters), with a capacity of 1.25 million gallons, and the starting-point for the various channels feeding the city's fountains. The *Aqueduct das Águas Livres* itself, of which the most conspicuous part—the

Passeio dos Arcos, of 14 pointed arches—strides across the Alcântara valley to the NW, is borne on a total of 109 arches of *pedra lioz*. It was constructed in 1729–48 by the engineer Manuel de Maia and the architect Custódio Vieira to bring water from Caneças, some 18.5km N. Still one of the 'lions' of Lisbon, it was visited by most travellers in the past, even if some of them suffered a 'lapidation' from the denizens of the district, as did Baretti in 1760.

The Rua Alexandre Herculano leads E from the Rato to the upper part of the Av. da Liberdade, off which the Rua Braamcamp forks left direct to the PRAÇA MARQUÊS DE POMBAL, while the Rua do Salitre bears SE downhill to the centre of the Avenida.

Our route turns S down the Rua da Escola Politécnica, passing (right) the *Imprensa Nacional*, the successor of the royal printing-press founded in 1768, and (left) some *University* faculty buildings in the old *Colégio dos Nobres*, an aristocratic foundation dissolved in 1837. Adjacent is the entrance to the JARDIM BOTÂNICO, a luxuriant sub-tropical garden founded in 1874, and temporarily closed after a recent fire. It contains a *Meteorological Observatory* of 1863.

Opposite, the Rua São Marçal leads downhill to the buildings of the **British Institute**, the first of its kind established abroad by the British Council (1938), which moved to its present address—Rua Luís Fernandes 1–3—in 1943. Branches had been opened at Coimbra and Oporto in 1939 and 1941 respectively. Previously it had been known as the *Palácio do Menino de Oiro* ('the Golden Boy'), after its builder Luis Fernandes (1859–1922), who devoted his fortune largely to the acquisition of works of art: his ceramic collections may be seen at the Museu Nacional de Arte Antiga.
On his death the mansion was bought by Francisco Alves dos Reis, who gained considerable notoriety as 'the man from Lisbon' in the financial scandal known as the 'Portuguese Bank-note Case' (1925), in which Waterlow, the printers, were involved. When raided by the police, cases full of crisp 500-escudo notes were found in the basement (now enlarged and accommodating the Institute's Language Laboratory). The building also contains a general library (including films and records), but the important Anglo-Portuguese Collection—built up over the years by Dr Carlos Estorninho under the enlightened auspices of George West—is at present housed in the library of the Gulbenkian Foundation (see Rte 1F). A compilation rather than a selective catalogue of 536 pages was issued in 1984. The British Institute has extended its premises and its English-language-teaching programme in recent years, now having some 10,000 students in Portugal.

We next pass (right) the PRAÇA DO PRÍNCIPE REAL, in the gardens of which is a remarkable cedar with branches trained to form a huge arbour. On its SW side are the offices of the *Instituto de Cultura Portuguesa*.
We now skirt the N end of the BAIRRO ALTO proper, a network of narrow streets of some character, little affected by the earthquake of 1755—although parts are now little less than tenements—and containing a number of restaurants.
An alley half-way down the Rua da Rosa, which bisects this district, leads up (right) to the often restored buildings of the **'Colégio dos Inglesinhos'**, founded in 1628, during penal times, for the education of English seminarists, and until recently for students from the English dioceses.

In May 1671 Consul Maynard, reporting to Lord Arlington in London, refers to the 'implacable malice of the English Seminary to our Religion'. Among its professors was Richard Russel, who partly negotiated Catherine of Braganza's marriage with Charles II, taught her English, and accompanied her as almoner; he later became Bishop of Portalegre, and then of Viseu. Dr Godden, President of the College, became her chaplain and preceptor. Fr Edmund Winstanley offered his services to Wellington as chaplain to the military hospitals around Lisbon during the Peninsular War. It was visited out of curiosity by George Borrow, who had to admit that the view from its roof was 'very grand and noble'.

From 1634 there had also been an Irish Dominican community in Lisbon, that of Corpo Santo, one of whom, the devious Fr Daniel O'Daly, was the queen's confessor. More popular were the English Brigittine nuns, whose convent, rebuilt in 1760 after its destruction in 1755, stood at the corner of the Rua das Francesinhas and the Travessa do Pasteleiro (a short distance SW of São Bento). They had moved to Lisbon in 1594, and remained there until 1861. They were referred to by many travellers, among them by Baretti, who remarked that visitors were 'used by them with such endearing kindness, that their parlatory is in a manner never empty from morning till night. The poor things are liberal to every body of chocolate, cakes, and sweet-meats...'.

A certain Thomas Robinson, who had been 'secretary' there some 150 years earlier, chose to abuse them in 'The Anatomie of the English Nunnerie at Lisbon in Portugall' (London, 1622).

The Rua Dom Pedro V, which we now follow, is continued by the Rua São Pedro de Alcântara, on the E side of which is an extensive terrace and *Miradouro*, immediately beyond which a funicular descends to the Praça dos Restauradores; while just opposite, at No. 45, in a palace of 1747 by Ludovice, are the offices of the Lisbon branch of the *Port Wine Institute*, with a bar in which every variety of port may be sampled, at a price, in comfort.

A few paces beyond brings us to the outwardly unpretentious Jesuit church of *São Roque (Pl.10), begun by Afonso Álvares in 1567, followed after his death in 1575 by his nephew Baltasar Álvares, while Felipe Terzi was active there from 1582. Its interior is more impressive, and surprisingly well kept. Notable are the azulejos by Fr de Matos (1584) in the third right-hand chapel. To the right of the altar is the Baroque *Chapel of the Assumption*; to the left is the sumptuous *Chapel dedicated to *St. John the Baptist*, commissioned by João V in 1742, and designed and erected in Rome by Luigi Vanvitelli (1700–73), the celebrated architect, and Niccolo Salvi. After being blessed by Benedict XIV, it was dismantled and shipped to Lisbon, where it was installed in 1747 under the supervision of the Italian sculptor Alessandro Giusti (1715–99).

It is an opulent confection of lapis lazuli, agate, porphyry, and ormulu, etc., but is also notable for the mosaic picture of the Baptism in imitation of oil-painting, while the hanging lustres are also excellent examples of Italian craftsmanship of the period. The effect caused a sensation, even if the cost was crippling, and its artistic value is still much exaggerated by the Portuguese.—Adjacent is another chapel rich in inlaid marbles, while nearer the entrance is a long inscription in memory of Sir Francis Trejean (died 1608), a Cornish recusant, who is buried upright near the pulpit. Father Henry Floyd, SJ (also known as Fludd), a zealous converter of souls, and chief visitor of the Inquisition for the English, resided here at the turn of the 17C. Above the chapels is a series of paintings of the Life of St. Roche, while the flat wooden ceiling is painted to give the impression of a vault, a form of *trompe l'oeil* noticeable elsewhere in the church. Note also the 18C German organ. The *Sacristy*, with its blue and yellow azulejos, should also be visited. It contains a number of paintings of the Lives of St. Francis Xavier by Andrés Reinoso, and of St. Ignatius Loyola.

Just to the right of the entrance of the church is the *Museu de São Roque*, containing an impressive collection of vestments, frontal hangings, etc., many of gold and silver filigree-work, and in a remarkable state of preservation. Also a collection of silver-gilt altar-furniture, etc., mostly Italian, including two paschal candlesticks. In a vestibule are portraits of João III and his wife Catarina, by Cristóvão Lopes.

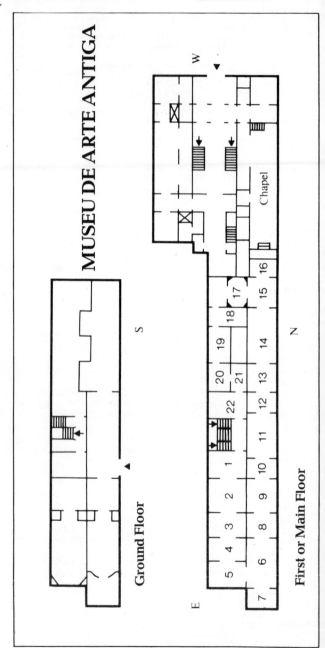

MUSEU DE ARTE ANTIGA

Ground Floor

First or Main Floor

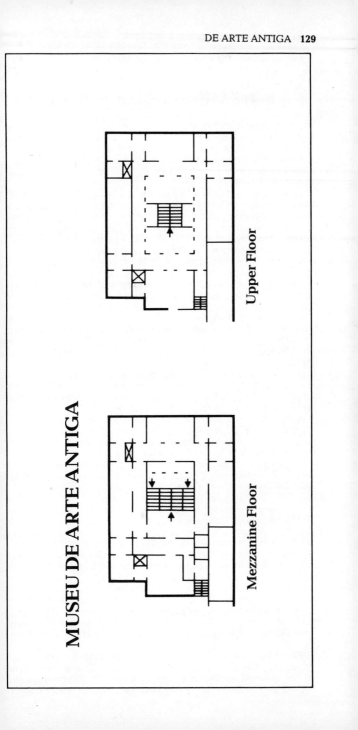

MUSEU DE ARTE ANTIGA

Upper Floor

Mezzanine Floor

Continuing down the street, we shortly regain the *Chiado*.

D. The Museu Nacional de Arte Antiga

This important *MUSEUM, a visit to which is essential for an understanding of Portuguese art, is perhaps best approached by car or taxi from the Praça do Comércio, or alternatively by bus or tram travelling along the Rua das Janelas Verdes ('Green Windows'), the street skirting the N of the building, after which the museum was for some time named.

It is partly housed in the 17C palace of the Counts of Alvor, in which two mutilated ceilings by Vincenzo Baccerelli survive, and later a residence of Pombal. This is extended to the W by a chapel, part of the Carmelite convent of *Santo Alberto*, on the site of which a new building was erected in 1937–39. This was the object of radical internal reconstruction in 1982–83, and a mezzanine floor was incorporated, which provided it with 50 per cent more display space. The main entrance to the museum is now at this W end, from where the description starts, although it is almost certain that the present distribution will be slightly changed during the life of this edition of the guide.

The collection itself, based on material accumulated after the suppression of the monasteries in 1838, and which has grown considerably since, further enriched by donations by Luís Fernandes and Calouste Gulbenkian, among others, was first opened to the public in 1883.

Steps, and a ramp, ascend from the Jardim 9 de Abril to the main entrance hall. To the left a gallery overlooks the *Chapel*, to which steps descend. It remains largely intact, retaining its richly carved and gilded woodwork, paintings, and azulejos, recently cleaned and restored. Note the huge *Presépio* or Christmas crib.

Adjacent are a collection of copes, etc., two anonymous 16C paintings of St. Vincent and St. John the Evangelist, and a polychrome statue of St. Michael weighing souls.

To the right of the entrance a series of rooms displays a good collection of **Portuguese furniture**, tapestries, Arraiolos carpets. brocades, and metal-work, etc.

A broad flight of stairs ascends to the MEZZANINE FLOOR. Ahead is the *Treasury*, containing collections displaying the art of the **Goldsmith**, among them numerous reliquaries, chalices (including a 16C English example), salvers, processional crosses, croziers, and other cult objects. Note also the rock-crystal crosses. Remarkable are the Monstrance of Belém (1506), made by Gil Vicente from gold sent back from the Indies by Vasco da Gama; the so-called Cross of Sancho I (1412); and the Cross of Alcobaca (14–15C). The collection—enriched in 1981 by the donation of numerous pieces by Francisco de Barros e Sá—extends into adjoining rooms, containing 17–18C silver, including a monstrance said to have been designed by Ludovice; a sumptuously chased late 16C silver-gilt salver; and 18–19C silver from Oporto, showing English influence in the tankards and tea-services.

The following open-plan rooms contain an extensive collection of Portuguese **Glass** (largely from the Marinha Grande, and Vista Alegre factories) and **Ceramics**, including some of Oriental origin, the Portuguese being the first Europeans both to import and copy in faïence the porcelains of the East, much of it imported from Goa, and therefore known as 'porcelana da India'; from Japan between c 1550–1640; and Macau.

The main Portuguese factories were those of *Rato* (established 1767) and *Bico do Sapato* (1796), both in Lisbon; that of *Miragaia* in Oporto (founded 1775), and *Massarelos* (1783; although operating from c 1730); and *Santo António do Vale da Piedade* (1785), and *Cavaquinho* (1789), both at Vila Nova de Gaia; at *Darque* (Viana do Castelo; 1774); at *Rocio de Santa Clara* (Coimbra; 1784); apart from others at *Caldas da Rainha*; *Brioso* and *Vandelli* (Coimbra; 1784); and *Vista Alegre* (near Aveiro; 1824), *Estremoz*, etc.

In the N wing are collections of furniture from Portugal's former overseas possessions, particularly Goa, and including several fine examples in ebony with bone or ivory inlay; also a remarkable Indo-Portuguese hunting-scene in cotton and raw silk (16–17C); and full-length Indo-Portuguese portraits of Francisco d'Almeida (1505–9), and Afonso de Albuquerque (1509–15). Adjacent are several carved ivory boxes, Virgins, and the Infant Christ (Bom Pastor).

Japanese screen (late 16C)

Adjacent sections display a very remarkable collection of Japanese *Biombos Namban screens depicting the arrival and disembarkation of the Portuguese at Nagasaki, where they were known as the Namban-jin (barbarians from the south). The first one of a pair of these large six-fold screens (*honken* in Japanese) was made in Kyoto, and is attributed to Kano Domi (1593–1600); the second pair—in which the Portuguese are shown setting sail from Goa (?) to Japan, and their landing—is by Kano Naizen (c 1603–10). A third screen (or *sho-byobu*), of which the musem has only one of a pair, is later in date, perhaps between 20 and 30 years after the Portuguese were forced to leave Japan (1639). The detail is not so well characterised, for the artist had probably not seen the Namban-jin in person, nor their ships.

(An informative and well-illustrated catalogue is available.)

Adjacent is a large 7C bronze statue of Bothisava.

Stairs ascend to the UPPER FLOOR, its landing devoted to a remarkable collection of polychrome wood or stone **Sculpture**. Notable among the former are a Santiago, St. Jerome with his lion, and a Virgin and Child (reading); and among the latter, Virgin and Child with St. Anne, St. Lucia, St. Caterina, John the Baptist, and a Pietà.

A section at the W end of this floor displays several works by *Frei Carlos* (active 1517–40) or from his studio, including Christ appearing to the Virgin, Annunciation, Assumption, Ascension, and (notably) a Resurrection; also a Descent from the Cross by the *Master of the Tabulo da Capela-Mór,* and a copy of a *Flemish* Apparition of an angel to SS. Coleta, Ines, and Clara.

Other rooms on this floor will probably contain more masterpieces of the **Portuguese School** (see p 135), at present displayed on the Ground Floor to the right of the Janelas Verdes entrance to the museum—also reached by descending the stairs adjacent to R22 (see plan), and then turning left. At the time of writing the placing of the paintings has not been decided, nor the rooms numbered.

Descending to the Mezzanine, continue ahead, passing a book stall, to reach **R18** (possibly to be renumbered) of the older building. This contains several portraits: *Romney*, Sir John Orde; *Reynolds*, General William Keppel, and of Dr Duheny; *John Russel*, pastel of Sir Richard Clode d'Orpington; *Largillière*, M. de Noirmont (?); *Rigaud*, Cardinal de Polignac; and *Hoppner*, Country woman.

R19 contains a resplendent collection of **French Silver**, including the so-called Duke of Aveiro's Banquet Service, made by *François Thomas Germain* of Paris and his assistants; a remarkable epergne by *Thomas Germain*; silver-gilt figures; and an equestrian Portrait of Louis XIV *attributed to A.-F. van der Meulen*, offered to the king by the Portuguese ambassador, the Conde de Atalaia.

R20 French Furniture, and *Hubert Robert*, The Mill; a Portrait of the Marquis d'Argenson, *attributed to Largillière*, and his Portrait of Mme Largillière.

R21 contains more French furniture, and porcelain, and a carved wooden font *attributed to Grindling Gibbons*.

R22 has panelling of 1769 from a palace in Vienna, and furniture by *Louis Charles Carpentier* (active 1752–88) covered with Beauvais tapestry.

Crossing a landing, **R1** is entered, displaying a Greek male torso of Parian marble (4C BC), and a grey basalt Lion, a Graeco-Egyptian work of the Ptolemaic period.

R2 *Hans Memling*, Virgin and Child; *Bernardo Martorell*, Triptych of the Descent from the Cross; *anon. 15C Dutch* Mystic Marriage of St. Catherine; *Bartolomé Bermejo*, St. Damian; *attributed to Ramón Destorrents*, St. Anne and the Virgin; *Piero della Francesca*, St. Augustine; and an *anon. 15C Italian* Battle of Darius.

R3 *anon. (School of Cologne)* Triptych of the Calvary (c 1500); *Raphael*, St. Eusebius bringing three men back to life; *anon. 16C Flemish* Virgin and Child; *Jan Provost*, Triptych; *Jan Gossart (Mabuse)*, *The Holy Family, with SS Barbara and Catherine; *Gerard David*, Rest on the Flight into Egypt.

R4 *Hieronymus Bosch*, *The Temptation of St. Anthony; *Dürer*, *St. Jerome (1521; offered to Rui Fernandes de Almada, then living in Antwerp, but later it was seen hanging in the library of the convent of the Jerónimos at Belém); *Cranach the Elder*, *Salome, and St.

Bosch, The Temptation of St. Anthony

Catherine (*attributed to Cranach*); *Patinir*, Landscape with St. Jerome in adoration.

R5 *Master of the Morrison Triptych*, Virgin and Child, with SS. John the Evangelist and John the Baptist; *Isenbrandt*, St. Jerome; *Cornelius van Cleve*, The Virgin; *Quentin Metsys*, The Virgin of Sorrows, The Presentation, Jesus disputing with the doctors, and a Calvary; *anon. 16C Flemish* St. Luke painting the Virgin; *attributed to Eduardo, o Portuguese* (a disciple of Metsys), Virgin and Child; *Hans Holbein, the Elder*, Virgin and Child with saints (presented by Christina of Sweden to João IV, who in turn gave it to his daughter Catherine of Braganza).

Hence we turn into **R6**, displaying among others, *Morales*, Virgin and Child, off which is **R7** (closed at present), accommodating a number of Italian polychrome faience panels of the *Della Robbia workshop*, and *Bronzino*, Holy Family.

R8 *Brueghel the Younger*, Beggars; *H.-C. Vromm*, Naval Battle; *David Vinckeboons*, Kermes; *Antiveduto Grammatica*, St. Cecilia and two angels; and *attributed to P. Snayers*, Sack of a town.

R9 *Jacob-Adriaensz Backer*, Courtesan; *Van Dyck*, Portrait of Lucas Vosterman, the Elder; *Andrea del Sarto*, Self-portrait; *Velázquez*, Portrait of Mariana de Austria, wife of Philip IV of Spain; *anon.* Portrait of João I; *António Moro* (Anton van Dashorst Mor), Male Portrait; *anon. 16C Flemish* Portrait of Jean de Luxembourg, a knight of the Golden Fleece.

RR10–12 at present contain Spanish, Delft, and Italian ceramics, and furniture, including a *bargaño*, and *reliquario*, and an *anon.* (sour-faced) Portrait of the Infante Don Carlos (1607–32).

R13 *Zurbarán*, a group of Twelve Apostles (1633; requiring cleaning), commissioned for the patriachal palace of São Vicente de Fora.

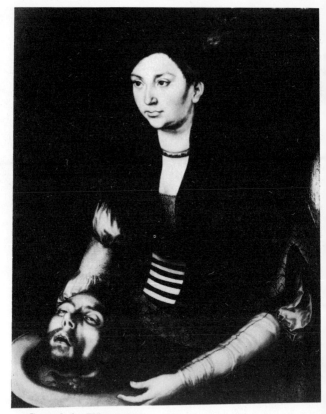

Cranach the Elder, Salome

R14 *Ribera*, Martyrdom of St. Bartholomew, St. Peter's Denial, and *attributed to Ribera*, Vision of St. Francis of Assisi; another painting of the same subject by *Luca Giordano; Pieter Fransz de Grebber*, Family Group.

R15 *Pannini*, Ruins of ancient Rome; *anon. French* Portrait of the sculptor Jacques Buirette (1631–99); *Wouwerman*, two Landscapes with figures.

R16 *David Teniers, the Younger*, Weapons' store; *Pieter de Hooch*, Conversation piece; *Murillo*, Mystic marriage of St. Catherine.

R17 *Hubert Robert*, Ruined Temple; and examples of the work of *G.-B. Tiepolo*, and *Vernet*.

From here we regain the passage-way between the two buildings, and may turn left to stairs descending to the ground floor of the old palace.

The main collection of Portuguese paintings is at present displayed here.

Among the more notable are the masterpiece of *Nuno Gonçalves*, an artist worthy of comparison with the foremost figures of his age, who died before 1492, the polyptych or *Retable of the Infante, painted c 1467–70 for the altarpiece of the chapel of St. Vincent in the Sé. It consists of six panels representing the youthful St. Vincent, patron of Lisbon, receiving the homage of the king, court, and various national communities, and many of the 60 faces have been variously identified.

The panel on the extreme left depicts Cistercian monks from Alcobaça, possibly including Vasco Tinoco, the king's Grand Almoner; beside it are a group of fishermen. On the extreme right is a rabbi, representing the important Sephardic community, which, before its forcible conversion by Dom Manuel, made a considerable contribution to the prosperity and culture of Portugal, together with a beggar or pilgrim, and clerics. The lower figure is displaying the saint's relics (part of his skull). Adjacent are armed nobles, who have been identified as Fernando, 2nd Duke of Braganza (brother of Afonso V), with behind him, (left) João, his youngest son, and (right) Fernando, his eldest; and above them, an unidentified Moorish nobleman, wearing a helmet of Oriental design.

Of the two principal panels, that on the right is known as the Bishop's panel, because of the presence there of a bishop identified as Jorge da Costa, archbishop of Lisbon from 1464 to 1500. The figure in the upper right-hand corner is probably Gomes Eanes de Azurara, the chronicler; while the half-kneeling figure before the saint, surrounded by knights, is assumed to be Prince Fernando. To the left is the Infante's panel, with the moustached figure said to be Prince Henry the Navigator, Infante of the House of Avis; the young Prince João, later João II; and in the foreground, Afonso V (1438–81). To the left is a figure thought to be Queen Leonor (died 1455), and behind her is probably the widowed Duchess of Braganza; while in the upper left-hand corner is what is possibly a self-portrait of Nuno Gonçalves.

A statue of the saint probably once separated the two central panels, and it is likely that the whole was a votive picture offered by Afonso V, 'the African', in gratitude for his victories in Morocco, in particularly that at Alcaçer in 1463.

Also remarkable are an Adoration of the Magi from the *studio of the Master of Sardoal* (early 16C); an *anon.* early 16C painting of the Apostles; a Martyrdom of the eleven thousand virgins, by the *Master of the retable of St. Auta* (early 16C), and an *anon.* Portrait of a Knight; *Francisco Henriques* (fl. 1500–18; Master of the Retable of São Francisco at Évora), Christ appearing to Mary Magdalen; SS. Cosmas, Thomas, and Damian, and eight other panels; also Our Lady of the Snows, a new acquisition.

Gregório Lopes (active 1513–c 50), Martyrdom of St. Sebastian; *Cristóvão de Figueiredo* (active 1515–43), Entombment; *Cristóvão Lopes* (1615–94), Portraits of João III and his wife Catherine of Austria; *Cristóvão de Morais* (active 1557–71), Portrait of the ill-fated king, Dom Sebastião; panels by the *Master of the Retable of S. Tiago* (St. James); the *Master of the Paradise*, Retable of the Life of the Virgin; *Master of the Arches*, Presentation in the Temple (1538), and a St. Jerome; *Master of the Retable of São Bento*, Adoration of the Magi, and Presentation in the Temple; and six panels by the *Master of the Retable of Santos-o-Novo*.

Among several *anon.* paintings are a lurid Vision of Hell (16C); St. Anthony preaching to the fishes; Martyrdoms of St. Hippolytus, and of St. Andrew; Virgin and Child with angels (probably from Tomar, and showing German influence); Birth of the Virgin; Portrait of a Nun with a rosary; and a Portrait (c 1524), perhaps of Vasco da Gama.

Other sections contain later 17C and 18C canvases of the Portuguese School, among them a selection of paintings by a master of European significance, *Domingos António de Sequeira* (1767–1837). The museum possesses hundreds of his drawings. It was Sequeira who in 1813–16 was commissioned to design the silver service offered to the Duke of Wellington, now in Apsley House, London. His paintings include one of Mariana, his daughter, playing the piano, and one of the family of the 1st Viscount of Santarem. Other artists of the period whose works are displayed here are *Josefa de Ayala* (or *de Óbidos*; (1634–84), *Francisco Vieira, Portuense* (1765–1805), *Francisco Vieira de Matos* (*Vieira Lusitano*; 1699–1783); and *José António Benedito de Barros* (c 1750–1809; better-known as the *Morgado de Setúbal*), a Male portrait by whom is a recent acquisition. Other paintings here include an *anon.* View of Goa, of c 1600; *Domingos Vieira* (c 1600–78), Portrait of Isabel de Moura; and *Felipe Lobo* (1650–73), View of Belém.

Here also is the *Library*, and the *Department of Prints and Drawings* (seen preferably by appointment). Among the drawings are many by the Bibiena family (fl. 1665–c 1780); *João* (Giovanni) *Carlos Bibiena*, son of Francisco, who died in Lisbon in 1760. Also several by *Jean Pillement* (1728–1808), who visited Portugal on three occasions, the longest in 1780–86.

We may make our exit into the Rua das Janelas Verdes.

Continuing E, at No. 32 in the street, the long-established hotel of '*York House*' is passed, installed in a 16C convent (with an extension almost opposite). No. 46 was the residence of the British consul in 1811. Hence one may return towards the centre.

E.   Belém

Driving W from the Museu de Arte Antiga (see Rte 1D, above) by the upper road (Rua Presidente Arriaga; the continuation of the Rua das Janelas Verdes) we shortly pass (right) *São Francisco de Paula* (founded 1719), with a ceiling by Inácio de Oliveira Bernardes (1695–1781). We then cross the Av. Infante Santo, with a good view of the *Ponte 25 de Abril* over the Tagus (see below), the *Doca de Alcântara*, and *Gare Marítima*. We may turn towards the riverside Av. da Índia from the PRAÇA DA ARMADA, which is soon reached.

Up to the right, standing in its gardens (the '*Tapada*') is the pink **Palácio das Necessidades** (no adm.), a royal palace of 1745–50, designed by Caetano Tomás de Sousa, and built on the site of a chapel dedicated to N.S. das Necessidades. It was the regular Lisbon residence of the royal family from the time of Maria II, who died here in 1853, until October 1910, when Manuel II was driven out by shells from rebel warships in the Tagus. In 1916 the building was transferred to the *Foreign Office*, and its valuable contents were largely dispersed among museums, among them the Museu de Arte Antiga.

The main riverside thoroughfare now leads below the huge **Ponte 25 de Abril*, the longest suspension bridge in Europe, commenced in 1962 and inaugurated as the 'Salazar Bridge' in August 1966, and now commemorating the Revolution of April 1974. The central span is 1013m long, and some 70m above water-level. The total length of the structure above the river is 2300m, extended on the N bank by a viaduct some 950m long.

Beyond, we pass (right) *International Trade Fair Grounds*, replacing old rope-walks. Uphill to the right stands the unusual chapel of *Santo Amaro* (1549), with a circular domed nave, round

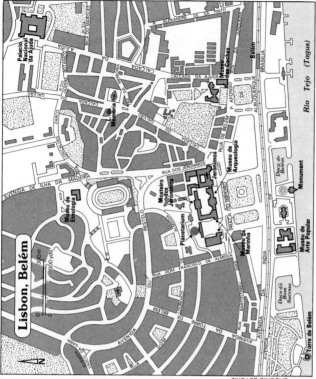

part of which is a vaulted porch of seven bays, and containing azulejos from the Rato factory.

After some little distance we reach (right) the PRAÇA AFONSO DE ALBUQUERQUE, immediately to the N of which is the *Museu dos Coches**, accommodated in the *Picadeiro* or riding-school (by Giacomo Azzolino) of the *Palácio de Belém*, or *Quinta de Baixo*, bought by João V from the Conde de Aveiras in 1726, and under the monarchy used mainly for the reception of royal guests. It was also known as the *Quinta 'dos Bichos'* (beasts), as at one time Moroccan lions were mewed up in cages in one of its courtyards. Beckford once considered renting the place. The palace is now the offical residence of the President of the Republic.

The collection of extravagantly carved and gilt coaches, and the actual quantity still preserved, is impressive, and certain of them, such as the plain travelling-coach (No. 1; 1619) of Philip III of Spain (II of Portugal), are of historical interest, but few will want to give them more than a cursory inspection. Other notable examples are that of João V (No. 3), and the elaborately carved ambassadorial coaches of the Marquês de Fontes, envoy to the Vatican in 1716; and in the adjoining room, an 18C *sege* (No. 50); a carriage constructed in London in 1825 (No. 51); and in the entrance hall, one of 1824 made for João VI. A collection of livery and harnesses is also on view, together with bull-fighting costumes, etc.
Another extensive collection of carriages may be seen at *Vila Viçosa* (Rte 5B).

A steep street to the E of the museum entrance climbs up to the **Palácio da Ajuda** (right). A vast and pretentious edifice, it was begun in 1802 by João VI on the site of a wooden palace built to shelter the royal family after the 1755 earthquake; this even had an opera-house, damaged by fire in 1787, and the rest was burnt down in 1795. The plans for its replacement were by José da Costa e Silva, collaborating with Francisco Saverio Fabri. It was continued by António Francisco da Rosa, but never completed. The N wing of the building now houses the offices of the *Instituto Português do Património Cultural* (IPPC).

The interior, usually entered from the E, may be visited by those curious to see the sumptuous furniture and decoration, but decadent taste, of the time of Maria II and her second husband, Ferdinand of Saxe-Coburg-Gotha (a cousin of Prince Albert), of Pedro V, married to Stéphanie of Hohenzollern-Sigmaringen, and of Dom Luís, married to Maria-Pia (daughter of Victor Emmanuel II of Italy), who, as Queen-Dowager, lived here until her death in 1911.

The important *Library*, of which Herculano was once librarian, is on the ground floor and may be visited by appointment. It includes scores by João de Sousa Carvalho (died 1778).

Visitors are escorted in small groups through a series of rooms, some of which, such as the *'Jardin d'Hiver'*, faced with light brown marble, are of interest; likewise the *Private Dining-room*, with tapestries after Goya, and the silver service by Thomire; the *Chinese Salon*; the set of Naval chairs, etc. Impressive are the *Oval Room*, and the *State Dining-room*, still occasionally used, with its three huge lustres, and the silver by François Thomas Germain (1757–64). Most of the rest is an ostentatious collection of inferior objects selfishly acquired at the expense of the Portuguese people in an epoch that could ill afford such extravagance. But, as that discriminating 19C traveller Richard Ford remarked of its finer equivalent at Madrid: 'Nothing is more tiresome than a palace, a house of velvet, tapestry, gold and bore...'.

Just SE of its W end are *Gardens* laid out on two levels, where Beckford was entranced by a blue-eyed Irish girl, and admired the

balustrades. The Rua do Jardim Botânico leads W to the church of the **Memória**, founded in 1760 in thanksgiving for the escape of Dom José from an attempted assassination on this spot in 1758, and designed by João Carlos Bibiena.

The alleged conspirators, the Duke of Aveiro, the Marquês of Távora and his wife, the Count of Atouguia, among others, were executed at Belém in 1759 (where a rusticated Pelhourinho is almost hidden from sight). Pombal, himself suspected of instigation, took advantage of the outrage to accuse the Jesuits of complicity, and had them driven from the country that same year. In 1923 Pombal's remains were transferred here from the Mercês.

The Calçada do Galvão descends to the main road and the monastery of Belém, passing (left) the entrance to the *Jardim e Museu do Ultramar*. At one time linked with the Institute of Hygiene and Tropical Medicine, the gardens contain plants mostly gathered from Portugal's former colonies, and also an *Agricultural Museum* and *Herbarium*.

The next main street to the W, ascending steeply past the square apse of the *Jerónimos*, is the Rua dos Jerónimos; it later skirts (left) a stadium and is extended by the Ave Ilha da Madeira. To the W stands the new building of the ***Museu de Etnologia**, containing the extensive collections of the Instituto de Investigação Científica Tropical. Although there is no permanent exhibition, it is the site of regular important temporary exhibitions from Portugal and from its former empire and colonies, including Brazil, Mozambique, Angola, Goa, Macao, and from other areas. The complex comprises four exhibition galleries, a library and archive, and study rooms for the professional.

A few minutes' walk to the W from the Museu dos Coches brings one to the ***MOSTEIRO DOS JERÓNIMOS**, or of *Santa Maria*, at Belém, one of the most beautiful and accessible of Lisbon's monuments. An excellent example of the exuberant Manueline style

Mosteiro dos Jerónimos

of architecture, it has impressed Baretti, Borrow, and all other travellers to the monastery.

The site, occupied in the 15C by the *Ermida de Restelo*, a mariners' chapel founded by Henry the Navigator and served by the Order of Christ, was chosen by Dom Manuel in 1496 for the foundation of a monastery of Hieronymites. The name was changed to Belém (Bethlehem), and the Order of Christ was compensated with the Conceição Velha.

The departure from Belém of Vasco da Gama's fleet in 1497 and his successful return in 1499 inspired the king to expend every effort to make the new monastery a splendid memorial of Portugal's thanksgiving, and the first stone was probably laid in 1502. The first master of the works was Diogo Boitac, succeeded c 1517 by João de Castilho. Nicolas Chanterène, a French sculptor, was also working here. Suspended for a while in 1551, the work was later continued by Diogo de Torralva and Jerónimo de Ruão (from 1571), son of the better-known Jean de Rouen. The 1755 earthquake caused only slight damage, but extensive 'restorations' were undertaken in the 19C, when a dome was added to the SW tower. The W extension of the building, in a pseudo-Manueline style (largely reconstructed since its partial collapse in 1878), dates from 1850.

EXTERIOR. The magnificent *S Portal*, constructed by João de Castilho, consists of two doors enclosed within a deep round archway between buttresses, and is surmounted by a statue of N.S. de Belém. A figure on the central pillar is said to represent Henry the Navigator. Over all is a canopy with a hierarchy of statues in niches, crowned by a top-heavy niche above which is the cross of the Order

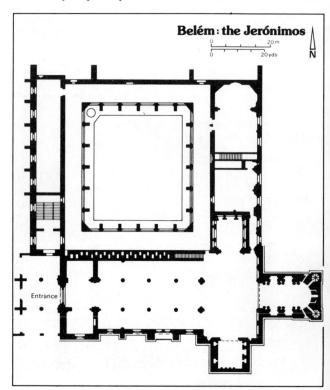

Belém : the Jerónimos

N

Entrance

of Christ. The two large windows on either side and the elaborate roof balustrade harmonise with the design. The Mannerist chancel was built by Jerónimo de Ruão.

The *W Portal* has suffered by being at various times overshadowed by bridges built to connect the monastery with its more modern extensions, but, in spite of mutilations, preserves the portrait statues of Dom Manuel and Maria, his second wife (daughter of Fernando and Isabel of Spain), with their patrons SS. Jerome and John the Baptist, by Chanterène (1517); above are the Annunciation, Nativity, and Adoration of the Magi.

INTERIOR (91m long; 25m wide; 25m high). The general effect of the church, with its soaring columns and bold vault, is both delicate and imposing. The nave has six lofty columns, with Renaissance decoration in low relief, but with empty niches, supporting a vault of uniform

Jerónimos: interior

height extending over the aisles. Beneath the *Coro Alto*, with fine stalls of c 1550, above which are 17C panels, are two dark chapels, one used as a baptistry. In the N wall of the nave are confessionals, alternating with others facing the S walk of the cloister. On the NW pier of the crossing (completed 1522) is a medallion with the alleged portrait of Boitac or João de Castilho. Note the ornate pulpits built into the E shafts.

The Renaissance *Capela-Mór*, completed by Jerónimo de Ruão in 1572, contains the tombs of Manuel I and Dona Maria (N) and João III and Dona Catarina (S), plain sarcophagi borne by elephants, as is that of Dom Sebastião in the S Transept, while in the N Transept is the tomb of Henrique, the Cardinal-king. Hence we may enter the *Sacristy*, a Renaissance room vaulted from a single central pier.

Making our exit from the W Portal (see above) we turn right to visit the **Cloisters*, with a lion-fed fountain at its NW corner, surrounding its garth. The lower storey, contemporary with the church, is elaborately decorated by João de Castilho and his assistants, each bay being divided by three columns supporting traceried arches. Note also the unusual corner canopies. The upper storey, each bay of which contains a single supporting column, was not finished until 1544.

On the E side is the *Chapter House*, not completed until the 19C, containing the tomb of Alexandre Herculano (died 1877), the anticlerical historian. Opposite is the *Refectory*, a long hall with a good depressed vault with 18C azulejos illustrating the story of Joseph.

To the N of the monastery are the Manueline chapels of *Santo Cristo* and *São Jerónimo*; the latter, commenced c 1514, with a portal possibly designed by Boitac, and probably completed by Rodrigo Afonso.

To the W is the entrance to the **Museu Nacional de Arqueologia e Etnologia**, installed here in 1903, an extensive and interesting collection of objects illustrating prehistoric and primitive Portugal.

It is presently being modernised, and some sections are likely to be opened to the public in 1988. Under these circumstances no detailed description of the archaeological collections can be given; in general, however, they comprise excavated material ranging from the Chalcolithic to the early 8C in Portugal. Bronze Age objects include bracelets, collars, and other artefacts from sites such as Vale de Viegas (Serpa), Arnozela (Fafe), Cabeceiras de Basto, Sobreira (near Castelo Branco), and Herdade do Álamo (Moura); Iron Age artefacts include the remarkable gold bracelet from Torre Vã (Grândola); the Roman collections include sculptures, mosaics, cameos, bronzes, coins, inscriptions, weapons, jewellery, and a stone statue of a Lusitanian warrior. There is also a small collection of Egyptian antiquities.

Since its thorough reorganisation in 1980 the museum has become the principal institution for Portuguese archaeological research, and includes interdisciplinary units concentrating on paleoecology and underwater archaeology. A series of archaeological guides, with English summaries, is being published.

At the far end of the long 19C façade of the western extension to the monastery is the entrance to the **Museu da Marinha**, containing collections describing the seafaring exploits of the Portuguese over the centuries, accommodated on two floors. It is particularly rich in ship's models.

It is convenient to visit first the FIRST FLOOR (stairs to the right), passing on a landing a room devoted to the Far East, containing Oriental furniture, a 17C screen showing a plan of Nagasaki (Japan); a painting depicting the Action of Bocca Tigris against Chinese pirates (1810), and mid 19C Chinese views of Macao, etc. On the upper landing are seen some 18C Indo-Portuguese sculptures of St. Francis Xavier; St. Philip Neri; Luis Frois, a Jesuit missionary who died at Nagasaki in 1597; and of Santa Isabel (1271–1336), queen of Dom

Dinis, all from the Oratory at Goa founded in 1682.—A large room on the right displays numerous models and half-models; ship's furniture; paintings; models of slipways; guns, and decorations, and photographs of the Lisnave and Setenave shipyards, etc.

On the GROUND FLOOR (note the display cases decorated with rope-work) are larger models; uniforms; navigating instruments; and among the miscellaneous paintings, one of Admiral Sir Charles Napier at the Battle of Cape St. Vincent (5 July 1833, against Dom Miguel), by Morel Fatio (1842). The N wing contains further models (19–20C), models of river-craft, and furniture from the royal yacht 'Dona Amélia' (1900; dismantled 1938), in which Manuel II set sail from Ericeira in 1910.

A modern extension to the museum has been built on the far side of the adjacent square, its N side flanked by the *Calouste Gulbenkian Planetarium* (1965).

In the entrance-hall of this extension, in the form of a large hangar, is an interesting collection of charts and maps, mostly in facsimile, but including José da Costa Miranda's map of the Atlantic, of 1681. Also here is the Fairey 17 sea-plane 'Santa Cruz', which, with Gago Coutinho and Sacadura Cabral as pilots, was the first plane to cross the Atlantic, in 1922 (from Lisbon to Rio); also a Schrenck F.B.A. hydroplane of 1917. Also protected here are two ceremonial oared Royal Barges or *galliotes*, that of Maria I dating from 1785, and embellished by Pillement; and some Merryweather fire-engines.

Turning S towards the Tagus, we may descend into a pedestrian tunnel below the main road to reach the **Museu de Arte Popular**, opened in 1948, illustrating the folk art of the provinces of Portugal, with a representative range of ceramics; metal, wood, and leather-work; costumes; fabrics; carpets; domestic utensils, and farm implements; toys; musical instruments; basketry; and jewellery. Although some sections have been re-arranged recently, the display is old-fashioned, and the objects deserve the more sophisticated presentation projected.

To the E stands an ill-conceived and supererogatory *Monument* erected under Salazar in 1960 to commemorate the quincentenary of the death of Henry the Navigator. On its N side is carved a huge sword, the hilt of which is in the form of the Cross of Avis.

The Torre de Belém from the SW

Some distance further W, partially hidden beyond trees, and adjacent to the coastal *Fort of Bom Sucesso*, is the famous ***TORRE DE BELÉM**, its bold silhouette familiar as the much-illustrated classic example of Muslim decoration applied to Manueline architecture. In 1983, as part of the 17th Exhibition of the Council of Europe, its tower contained a fine display of 15–16C Portuguese arms and armour, which will probably remain a permanent feature.

As the Bulwark of Restelo, this defensive tower was originally designed for João II by Garcia de Resende, the historian, but was constructed of *pedra lioz* on another plan by Francisco de Arruda between 1515 and 1520, and dedicated to St. Vincent. At the time it was entirely surrounded by water, until stranded on a sandy beach. Some idea of its original state is provided by the recently erected retaining wall, connecting it to both banks, which is covered at high tide. It served as a state prison from 1580 until 1828, when opponents of Dom Miguel were mewed up in its water-lapped dungeons. It was restored in 1846 and again in 1983.

Its main external features are the square tower adorned with *ajimece* windows and Moorish balconies, and the advanced platform whose battlements bear the shield of the Order of Christ. At each corner of its landward side and on the summit of the tower itself are circular casemates or sentry-boxes topped by segmented or melon-shaped domes; others line the platform. Between and below these are rope-mouldings.

A cat-walk leads to the main entrance. The ground floor contains a series of gun-emplacements approached by a wide vaulted passage lit by an interior patio, while below were the magazines and store-rooms. Steps to the right of the entrance ascend to a terrace. On the seaward side of the interior balustrade is a richly carved niche protecting a statue of the Virgin holding the Child and a bunch of grapes. On either side are columns topped by armillary spheres, the device of Dom Manuel. Note also the delicacy of the carving of the balustrade of the long gallery on the side of the tower, which we now enter, the first level of which provides entry to the corner casemates. A spiral stair ascends to the second level, with a corner fireplace, and balconies, and up again to another room with window seats set into the thickness of the wall. Above is the Oratory, a well-vaulted room (note the face carved on a corbel), off which is a wall-walk. Hence the stairs lead to the flat roof, providing a fine panoramic view of Lisbon and the river-mouth.

For the coast road, the Avenida Marginal, to *Estoril* and *Cascais*, see the latter part of Rte 2, in reverse.

F.   Northern Lisbon

At the N end of the wide AVENIDA DA LIBERDADE (see p 118) is the **Rotunda**, or **Praça do Marquês de Pombal**, dominated by a statue of that dynamic but dictatorial statesman, unveiled in 1934 in the centre of a busy roundabout.

A wide street (at first called the Rua Joaquim António de Aguiar) leads steeply uphill almost due W from the Rotunda, and is later continued by the Auto-estrada do Oeste, bearing W towards Sintra (see Rte 2), off which forks the Av. da Ponte, the most direct approach to the *Ponte 25 de Abril*.

N of the Rotunda extends the large **Parque de Eduardo VII**, laid out in honour of Edward VII of England's visit to Lisbon in 1903 (he had also visited Lisbon in 1876, when Prince of Wales), and now over-looked from the W by the *Ritz Hotel*. Near its NW corner is the **Estufa Fria** (or 'cool' greenhouse) built into a quarry in 1910, later enlarged, and opened to the public in 1930. Supported by columns of rusticated masonry is a roof constructed of bamboo slats through which the sunlight filters. At a higher level is the *Estufa Quente* (or 'hot' glasshouse), with a glass roof. Together they protect an extensive and varied collection of tropical and sub-tropical plants, those in the Estufa Fria being comprehensively labelled. Both the botanist and casual visitor will find this curious garden—almost a jungle—with its rivulets, flamingo-pool, ferns, banana-trees, and cacti, etc., a place of pleasure and interest.

Further N is a *Prison* (Penitenciária) of 1874, and conveniently near, the new block of the *Palace of Justice* (1970). A new congress centre is to be built here. A good view down the Avenida towards the Tagus is commanded from a central point on the N side of the park.

The Av. Fontes Pereira de Melo leads NE from the Rotunda to the PRAÇA DUQUE DE SALDANHA, passing near (left) the small *Casa-Museu Dr Anastácio Gonçalves* (8 Av. 5 de Outubro), with collections of furniture, ceramics, and 19–20C paintings, etc. For this district see below.

The Av. António Augusto de Aguiar, the first thoroughfare forking left from the Av. Fontes Pereira de Melo, climbs for some distance before descending to the PRAÇA DE ESPANHA.

On the SW corner of this junction stands the *Palácio Azambuja* or *Palácio dos Meninos de Palhavã*, dating from 1660, and in which Maria-Francesca of Savoy died in 1683. It was later the gloomy residence of João V's bastards (see p 216), and since 1918 that of the Spanish Embassy. It has been restored since being severely damaged by fire in anti-Spanish demonstrations on 26 September 1975.

To the SE, in part of the gardens of the palace, stands the **CALOUSTE GULBENKIAN FOUNDATION**. Its Museum, inaugurated in 1969, comprises one of the more important collections of art in the world, considering its size, and that it constitutes the lifetime's accumulation of one man, whose varied tastes it reflects.

Calouste Sarkis Gulbenkian (1869–1955) was born at Scutari, Turkey, into an already wealthy Armenian family, and later studied at King's College, London. Although he acquired British nationality by naturalisation in 1902, he later resided for some years in Paris, but spent most of the last 13 years of his life in Portugal. Here the *Gulbenkian Foundation* has its headquarters, with an important branch in London (at 98 Portland Place). To the foundation he left his collections of art, and substantially the whole of his very considerable estate, largely based on his 5 per cent interest in the Iraq Petroleum group of companies. The offices of the Foundation, established in 1956, stand adjacent to the Museum: its purpose is to further work of a charitable, artistic, educational, and scientific nature.

The main building, of four storeys above ground, stands in land-scaped gardens, and comprises an administrative block; three audito-riums, one seating 1400, where numerous concerts take place (the Gulbenkian Orchestra was created in 1962); lecture-rooms, and a Library; adjacent is an open-air theatre. (See below for the *Centre of Modern Art.*)

The *MUSEUM* itself is located to the E of the main block, with the entrance to the *Library*, and a bookstall for the sale of the Foundation's publications, on the floor below.

The museum is laid out as a series of open-plan sections built around two interior patios, and divided into two main groups: Oriental Art and Classical Art; and European Art. The whole is well planned and tastefully decorated, and the exhibits well labelled although some deserve better lighting (such as the Japanese boxes). Explanatory notes are at hand in each section. A complete illustrated catalogue is now available.

A. Egyptian Art: 14, Statuette of the Lady Henut Taoui, of polychromed wood and gold (18th Dyn.); 23, Bronze statue of the Lady Chepes; 24–26, Bronze cats; 28, Silver-gilt mask for a mummy (30th Dyn.); 29, Sun-boat of Djedher (bronze; 30th Dyn.); 32, Bas-relief study for a portrait of a pharaoh (early Ptolomaic period); 35, Head of a priest (?; green shist; middle Ptolomaic period).

B. Graeco-Roman Art; largely devoted to Greek coins, for which Calouste Gulbenkian had a passion; jewellery, and Roman glass; notable are a gold Winged Victory (51), and 50, a silver two-handled bucket.

C. Middle Eastern and Islamic Art; 85, Urn with two handles from Mesopotamia or Persia (2–3C BC), and 86, Alabaster bas-relief (Assyrian; 9C BC).—We now enter a long room containing an extensive display of ceramics, azulejos or tiles, glass, rugs and carpets, costumes and brocades, lacquered doors, illuminated Armenian MSS, Persian book-bindings, and Syrian mosque lamps; notable among a remarkable collection are 282, a pale green jade Jar (15C Persian), and the miniatures on six 17C Persian screens (284).

D. Oriental Art: an extremely fine collection of Chinese porcelains; carved jade and rock crystal objects; and a 12-panel Chinese screen (411; ? 18C). A collection of carved and gilt Japanese lacquer boxes, etc.; *inros* and *netsukes*; and Japanese prints (displayed in rotation), by such artists as Utamaro (1735–1806), Hokusai (1760–1849), Hiroshige (1797–1858), et al.

A series of rooms devoted to **European Arts** is now entered.

E A collection of French ivories (14C), notably 630 and 632, Scenes from the Life of the Virgin, and from the Life of Christ. Also several illuminated MSS, including (497) the Book of Hours of Margaret of Cleves (early 15C), and a late 13C English Apocalypse (498).

F. Paintings and Sculpture: 899, *anon.* Portrait of a young couple (16C); 892, *Lochner*, Presentation in the Temple; 894, *anon.* Virgin and Child (Flemish; 15C); 896, *Van der Weyden*, St. Catherine; 895, *Dirk Bouts*, Annunciation; 981, *Cima da Conegliano*, Holy Conversation; 980, *Carpaccio*, Virgin and Child, with donors; 979, *Ghirlandaio*, Portrait of a young girl; 898, *Gossaert (Mabuse)*, Virgin and Child; 983, *G.-B. Moroni*, Portrait of Marco Antonio Savelli; 984, *Giuliano Bugiardini*, Portrait of a young woman; 964, *Hals*, Portrait of Sara Andriesdr. Hessix; 900, *Van Dyck*, Portrait of a Man; 904, *Paul de Vos*, Cock-fight; 969, *Ruysdael*, Landscape, 968, View of the coast of Norway, and 970, View near Haarlem; 965, *Jan van der Heyden*, Dutch landscape; 905, *Sébastien Bourdon*, Portrait of Colbert; 603, *Coysevox*, Bust of Maréchal de Turenne (bronze); 903, *Rubens*, Portrait of Helen Fourment; 966, *Rembrandt*, Pallas Athene, or Alexander, and 967, Figure of an old man; 921, *Hubert Robert*, 'Le Tapis Vert', and 922, 'Le Bosquet des Bains d'Apollon'; 910, *Fragonard*, Fête at Rambouillet; 914, *Lépicié*, The Astronomer, and 915, Self-portrait; 916, *Nattier*, Portraits of a noble, and 918, of Louis

Tocqué; 911, *Lancret*, Fête galante; 604, *Caffieri*, Bust of Molière (terracotta); 606, *Lemoyne*, Bust of Robbé de Beauveset (terracotta); 912, *Maurice-Quentin Delatour*, pastel Portraits of Mlle Sallé, and 913, of Duval de L'Épinoy; 924, *François-André Vincent*, Portrait of Mlle Duplant; 609, *Houdon*, Statue of Diana (marble). (See below for other paintings.)

Portrait of Mlle Duplant, by F.-A. Vincent

G. Furniture and furnishings (together with some paintings, etc.): most of the furniture is by French *ébénistes*, including *Nicholas Blanchard, Charles Cressent, Jean Desforges, Jacques Dubois, George Jacob, Jean-François Oeben, Jean-Henri Riesener, J.-B.-C. Sené, M.G. Cramer*, and *Martin Carlin*. Also 909, *Fragonard*, The Regatta; 626, *attrib. to Antonio Rossellino*, marble bas-relief of the Virgin and Child; 627, *Luca della Robbia*, Ceramic plaque of Faith; 601, *anon.* St. Martin dividing his cloak (French; 1531); 701, an eight-panel lacquer screen (18C); 1004, Brussels tapestry (mid 16C); and 1005, three Italian tapestries, probably after cartoons by *Giulio Romano* (Ferrara, c 1540); 1015, a 15C Venetian velvet parasol.

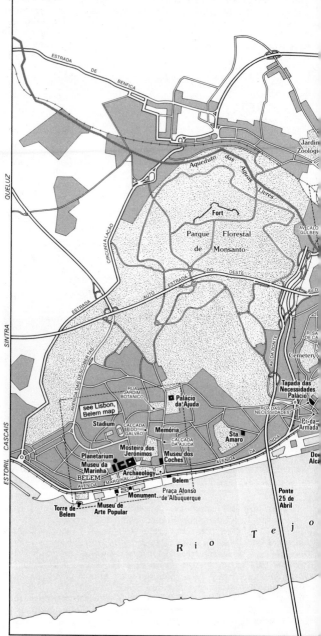

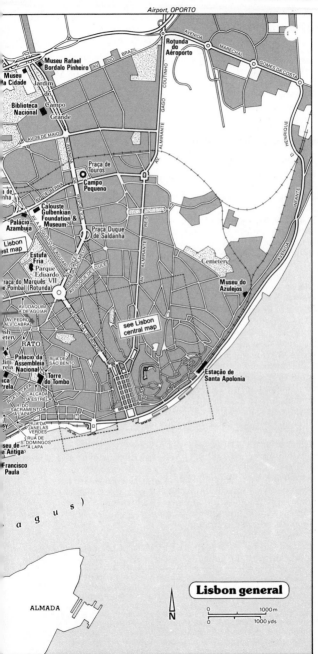

Lisbon general

0   1000 m
0   1000 yds

N

A collection of Italian bronze **Medals** (15–16Cs), some designed by *Pisanello* (648–54).

A collection of 18C **French Bindings**, several attributed to binders such as *Derôme* and *Padeloup*.

607, *Clodion*, terracotta Nymph and Satyr; 917, *Nattier*, Portrait of Madame de la Porte; 906, *Largillière*, Portrait of M. et Mme Thomas Germain; 1012, Beauvais tapestry, *after Boucher* (1755); and 1008–11, four Aubusson Chinoiserie tapestries, *after Pillement*.

A collection of French snuff-boxes, and **Silver** and silver-gilt, elaborate and massive, by *orfèvres* such as *Auguste, Biennais, Durand, F.-T. Germain, Lehendrick, Mongenot, Roettiers,* and *Spire*. The following section contains paintings of the English School among others: 971, *Gainsborough*, portrait of Mrs Lowndes-Stone; 973, *Romney*, Miss Constable; 972, *Hoppner*, Miss Frances Beresford; 974, *Lawrence*, Lady Elizabeth Conyngham; 976, *Turner*, Quillebeuf, and 975, Shipwreck; 941, *Diaz de la Peña*, Forest of Fontainebleau; and representative works by *Daubigny* (936–40), and *Lepine* (947–50); also a collection of 19 paintings by *Guardi* (985–1103); several works by *Corot* (929–35); 954, *Millet*, Winter; 951, *Manet*, Boy with cherries, and 952, Blowing bubbles; *Fantin-Latour*, Still-lifes (942–45); 893, *Mary Cassat*, Maternal attention; 960, *Monet*, Boats, 961, Still Life, and 962, The Thaw; 963, *Renoir*, Portrait of Mme Claude Monet; 958, *Degas*, Man and puppet, and 959, Self-portrait; 977–8, *Burne-Jones*, The Mirror and Bath of Venus; and (unnumbered), *Boldoni*, The painter Brown and family.

Several **Bronzes** by *Barye, Rodin, Carpeaux,* and *Dalou*.

The visit ends with a large and varied collection (742–849) of the exotic art of **René Lalique** (1860–1945) displayed in a suitably designed *art nouveau* room. On making our exit, a bronze statue of Apollo, by *Houdon* (610), is passed to the left.

An extension of the Gulbenkian Foundation's activities is the *Modern Art Centre, inaugurated in 1983, entered from the Rua Dr Nicolau Bettencourt immediately to the W. Partially screened by gardens, it is an attractive stepped structure sustained by reinforced concrete ribs. Its overall design was entrusted to Sir Leslie Martin. It has a roomy, well-lit interior with a main exhibition room on three levels.

The larger area (1800 sq m) is devoted to temporary exhibitions of Portuguese art (from 1911), selected from its extensive reserves; an upper gallery displays contemporary foreign art, and below this is a section for exhibiting prints and drawings. In the vestibule there are two triptychs by Almada Negreiros (1893–1970), a forerunner of Portuguese modernism. The building also contains other temporary exhibition rooms, experimental studios, and a documentation and research department.

A small Children's Pavilion, reached from the Rua Marquês Sá da Bandeira, to the E, was opened in 1984 to promote an interest in the arts amongst the young.

Approximately 1km NW of the museum lies the *Jardim Zoológico* of Lisbon; while further W, in the Largo São Domingos of the suburb of **Benfica** is the church and convent of *São Domingos*, containing the tomb of João das Regras (died 1404), who secured the election of João I. In the cloister is a chapel with the tomb of João de Castro (died 1548; Viceroy of Portuguese India).

Nearby is the quinta built by Gerard de Visme; and a short distance beyond are the attractive gardens of the *Quinta* or *Palácio do Marquês de Fronteira*, containing curious 17C azulejos, including an equestrian group.

From the PRAÇA DUQUE DE SALDANHA (see above) the wide Avenida da República leads due N, passing (right) the CAMPO PEQUENO, off the centre of which is the *Praça de Touros* (Bull Ring; 1892), on the site of which Baretti attended a bull-fight in 1760.

At the far end of the avenue extends the elongated JARDIM DO CAMPO GRANDE. Beyond its W side are the buildings of the *Cidade Universitária* and the unimaginative block of the **Biblioteca Nacional**.

Inaugurated in 1969, it looks more like the mammoth Hospital further W than a library, but no doubt it is more practical than its predecessor. The Biblioteca Nacional was founded in 1796 and these functional new premises with all their modern facilities now preserve as 'Reservados' its chief treasures, among which are numerous incunables and MSS, none of which is at present exhibited, which is a pity.

The important *Collection of musical instruments** (including a double virginal by Ruckers of 1620 among c 500 other instruments of considerable interest and quality) is at present housed here, while the *Museu Instrumental do Conservatório Nacional* awaits a more suitable home. It may be inspected on application.

At the NW end of the Campo Grande stands the *Palácio Pimenta*, an attractive building attributed to Carlos Mardel, and traditionally built as a residence for Madre Paula (see Odivelas). Since 1979 it has housed the municipal *MUSEU DA CIDADE**, a visit to which is essential to a proper historical perspective of Lisbon. When last visited by the Editor, the museum was closed for another re-distribution of its contents, its archaeological collections being displayed on the GROUND FLOOR. Its Ceramic collections include numerous examples from the Fabrica do Rato, among other rare pieces (boar's head, and Negro heads). Another room contains a set of 17C bronze weights.

Several rooms are devoted to an extensive collection of interesting **Views of Lisbon**, including engravings by *Dirk Stoop* (1610–80) depicting the Embarkation of Catherine of Braganza from 'Black Horse Square' (then with a fountain in the centre), escorted by Lord Ambassador Montagu.—Views of Lisbon before 1755, including some of the Aqueduct, and designs for fountains.—A copy of a Panorama of 1763, and a vista by *G. Lemprière* (1756); watercolour plans for the reconstruction of the city after the great earthquake; an *anon*. Portrait of Pombal; Views by *J.P. Lebas* (1757); a View painted on glass of the Praça do Comércio; Views by *Henri L'Evêque* (1816), *Alexandre Noël, J.C. Stadler* and *Albert Dufourcq; Delarive*. The Feira da Ladra; *J. Pedroso* (1825–90), The Tobacco Factory; *Robert Batty* (c 1830), sepia wash Views; and watercolours by *George Atkinson* (1838); Maps of Lisbon of 1837 and 1884; *Isaias Newton* (1838–1922; who was born in Lisbon and died there), Views of the Ajuda Palace; also a vista of the city; and *James Holland* (1800–70), The church of N.S. da Conceição Velha.

At the NE corner of the Campo Grande is a small *Museum* devoted to the curious ceramic art (much of it carried out at Caldas da Rainha) of Rafael Bordalo Pinheiro (1846–1905), together with examples of his caricatures.

The right turn at the end of the Campo Grande leads shortly to the *Airport*.

Approximately 2km N, in the suburb of *Lumiar*, perhaps best approached by the Av. Padre Cruz, is the *Museu do Trajo** (Costume), inaugurated in 1977, and installed in the *Quinta Palmela*, off the Largo de São João Batista. It retains most of its original decoration and azulejos. It was here that Mrs Norton (Sheridan's daughter) met Almeida Garrett.

The extensive collections of costumes (over 5000 items, and being continually extended by donations) are displayed in rotation, not only for reasons of space, but in the interest of the preservation of the many fragile fabrics. It is therefore impossible to describe in detail any specific section. Nevertheless, the museum is of considerable importance for an understanding of Portuguese dress, and a visit is recommended to all interested in the history of costume. There is a small restaurant, and the gardens are most attractive. In out-houses (once a cow-shed) are looms, dyeing baths, etc., where the processes of hand-blocking, etc. may be seen.

Near by, at Estrada do Lumiar 12, the restored *Quinta do Monteiro-Mór* ('Master of the Hounds') accommodates the **Museu National de Teatro**, containing extensive archives, and exhibitions of material illustrating the history of the Portuguese stage from the early 19C to the present.

At *Carnide*, c 2km SW of Lumiar, is the monumental church of *N.S. da Luz* (1575–96).

For *Odivelas*, further to the NE, see Rte 18B.

2   Sintra: Cascais: Estoril

This circuit from Lisbon, of approx. 90km, is a convenient form in which to describe the main sights en route, but may of course be followed in the reverse direction. Rte 3 may also be considered a pendant. Queluz may also be visited on the way, while Mafra may be visited directly from Sintra. It was the excursion to Sintra and Mafra which almost all past travellers to Lisbon would make, even if they got no further afield, and this excursion is still recommended.

From the *Rotunda* in Lisbon we bear uphill to the W onto the auto-estrada (N7), with a good view to the right of the *Aguas Livres* aqueduct (see Rte 1C) as we cross a viaduct over the Alcântara valley. The road traverses the thickly wooded *Monsanto Park*, and on making the descent on the far side we bear right onto the N117.

3.5km. **Queluz**: see Rte 3.

The main road (now the N249) continues NW through rolling country, with a view ahead of the hills of Sintra. We first reach the village of *Ramalhão*, with the 18C quinta occupied by Beckford from July–October 1787, where he would trifle away the whole morning 'surrounded by fidalgos in flowered bed-gowns and musicians in violet coloured accoutrements, with broad straw hats...'.

In 1794 the quinta was acquired by the intriguing Carlota Joaquina. She retired here in 1822 on having refused to take the oath to the Constitution, and who would have been expelled from the country had not ten doctors declared that she was unfit to travel! Nevertheless she survived for another eight years, continuing to plot meanwhile. From here, in 1833, Don Carlos of Spain, her reactionary brother, proclaimed against his niece Isabel II, thereby precipitating the start of the First Carlist War.

The right-hand fork here leads to Mafra, first skirting the E side of Sintra to the main crossroads, where we turn left towards the centre.

FROM SINTRA TO MAFRA (22km). Turning right at this junction, after c 3km we fork right again for (5km) *Pero-Pinheiro*, noted for its quarries of pink marble, which adorns so many Portuguese churches. The road traverses some desolate country studded with windmills, with a view ahead of the hilly district to the NE of Mafra, the towers of which may be discerned in the distance. At Pero-Pinheiro we meet the main road from Lisbon and turn left. For the remainder of the route see Rte 3; likewise for the alternative road back via *Ericeira*.

SINTRA (equally well known to the English as **Cintra**), beautifully sited on the N slope of the SERRA DE SINTRA, has had its praises sung over the centuries, often being described both in poetry and prose. While its main attractions may be seen in a day, the proper exploration on foot of its bosky heights and many quintas requires, and deserves, more time. Unfortunately, although delightfully cool in summer, the views are often obscured by sea-mists, which cling to the higher summits of the range. Of its monuments, the most interesting is the ancient palace, with its two curious conical oast-house-like chimneys dominating the main square.

The **Palácio Nacional*, not surprisingly, had long been a royal summer residence.

João I set about enlarging the palace which already existed on this site at some time before 1415. The central block dates from this period, although its *ajimece* windows and arabesque balustrading are of c 1500–20, when the right wing was added; the buildings on the left are 18–19C additions. It was here that João I decided on the Ceuta expedition (1415), and received the Burgundian envoy in whose train came Jan van Eyck (1429). Afonso V was born and died in the palace (1432–81); Dom Sebastião, who was proclaimed king here when three years old (1557), held his last audience here before starting on his disastrous African expedition of 1578; and the irresponsible Afonso VI spent his last impotent years here, a virtual prisoner (1674–83). The palace was damaged in the earthquake of 1755, according to Baretti, who visited it five years later. The entrance courtyard has been cleared of miscellaneous accretions during the last century.

Steps ascend to the entrance vestibule below a plain Gothic arcade, where we await a guided tour: tickets to the left. Passing through the *Sala dos Archeiros*, from which we are shown the *Kitchens*, with their pale grey tiles and two huge chimneys, we ascend to the *Sala dos Árabes*, attractively tiled with green, blue, and white azulejos (15C), and with a marble fountain. The adjacent *Chapel*, with an artesonado roof and a late 15C azulejo pavement, has been redecorated in the last century in a repellent style. Afonso VI died of apoplexy in the gallery while hearing mass, terminating his imprisonment in the so-called *Sala de Afonso VI*, whose azulejo floor he is said to have worn away by his incessant pacing. The *Chinese Room* contains an ivory pagoda presented to Carlota Joaquina in 1806 by the Chinese emperor, Chippendale chairs, and attractive black, pink, and white azulejos.

A clumsy Manueline doorway admits to the *Sala dos Brasões*, named from the 74 blazons of the noble Portuguese families of the years 1515–18 which decorate its magnificent artesonado dome. One blank space is incorrectly pointed out as being that from which the arms of the Aveiros were erased after their participation in a plot against Dom José in 1758: in fact it once held the arms of the Coelhos. The shields are hung from stags' heads, while blue and white azulejos below depict hunting scenes.—Descending, we pass a charming patio, and other rooms including *Dom Sebastião's Bedroom* (with 16C vine-leaf azulejos) to reach the *Sala das Sereias* (sirens or mermaids, playing musical instruments), containing Indo-Portuguese furniture.

We next enter the *Sala das Pêgas*, much restored, named after the numerous painted magpies inhabiting its compartmented ceiling. Each bears in its beak the device 'Por Bem', that of João I, a decoration suggested by him to satirise the chattering gossip of the court after he had been surprised by Queen Philippa surreptitiously embracing one of her ladies-in-waiting while presenting her with a rose: so goes the story. Note also the 16C Hispano-arab azulejos, the marble chimney-

The aretesonado dome of the Sala dos Brasões

piece (from Almeirim, near Santarém), and the *contadores* or *bargaños*. Hence we pass through the central patio overlooked by *ajimece* windows, to enter the Manueline *Sala dos Cisnes*, with its fine doors and shutters, green and white azulejos, and magnificent polychrome roof panelled in octagons and adorned with the 27 gold-collared swans which gave the room its name.—Also shown is the private study of Manuel I, with its azulejos, and a tapestry displaying the armillary sphere, that king's device. Hence we make our exit. The *Gardens* of the palace may also be visited.

Travellers pressed for time are recommended to continue the circuit of the range by car via the palace of Seteais and the Quinta of Monserrate, although on a clear day the excursion up to the Pena Palace may be made, if only for its gardens and for the extensive views it commands, but these are often obscured by sea mists.

THE EXCURSION TO THE PENA PALACE. From the upper end of the main street of Sintra, we continue uphill, passing (right) the old *Hotel Lawrence*, where Byron put up in 1809 and is said to have conceived 'Childe Harold', and perhaps that referred to some 50 years earlier as 'an English inn kept up by a society of English merchants'. Turning sharp left, we zig-zag steeply up through the thickly-planted hillside, with its moss-covered rocks, to a ridge separating the Pena from the *Castelo dos Mouros*, which rises boldly to the left.

The castle stands at 450m, an imposing ruin of undoubtedly Moorish foundation, although its battlements were restored in the mid 19C. The remains of Moors and Christians slain in 1147 when the fortress was taken by Afonso Henriques were unearthed during restorations, and reburied. The castle also commands fine views.—Hence a steep path descends direct to the town via the *Trinidad Convent* and Gothic *Santa Maria*.

The road continues the ascent towards the main entrance to the **Castelo da Pena**, built on the site of an Hieronymite monastery founded by Manuel I in 1509, which was certainly superbly placed. Unfortunately the picturesque position of this eyrie prompted Ferdinand of Saxe-Coburg-Gotha (consort of Maria II and a cousin of Prince Albert) to commission a certain Baron von Eschwege (1777–1855) to design a suitably 'Romantic' or 'Gothick' baronial castle amongst its dank and horrid crags. This was begun c 1840. The result is certainly among the most extraordinary architectural confections imaginable. It should—having got this far—be seen to be believed.

The castle is approached by passing over a drawbridge and through a tunnel. One may first visit the small *Cloister* of the original monastery, and the *Chapel*, with an alabaster altarpiece carved by Chanterène for João III in 1532, next to which is a Nottingham alabaster of the Crucifixion. The azulejos date from c 1620, and the vaulting is Manueline. Hence one is escorted through a series of rooms whose only interest is that they are preserved in almost the exact condition in which they were left by the royal family on 4 October 1910, before their flight to Ericeira, and thus remain a monument to their taste. The *Views*, however, to a great extent make amends for the distractions of the edifice.

To the SW is a peak crowned with a statue of Von Eschwege in armour, to the left of which is the *Cruz Alta*, the highest point in the SERRA DE SINTRA (529m). Further to the W is the *Feiteira da Condessa*, a fern garden above which is a rustic cottage surrounded by rhododendrons, erected by Ferdinand for the Condessa d'Edla (a German singer named Haensler, who was his mistress after the death of Maria II in 1853). Perhaps the best way to get an idea of the surprising mixture of temperate and sub-tropical vegetation characteristic of the *Park* and of Sintra itself, is to descend through the *Jardim das Camélias* to the *Fonte dos Passarinhos*, a tiled Moorish pavilion surrounded by fine trees, whence walkers may climb down to regain the main road.

Motorists descending from the Pena palace may follow a number of routes:
A. The first right turn leads down steeply to the village of *São Pedro* towards *Ramalhão* (see above) there forking right for *Linhó*, on the direct road to *Estoril*, 11km S, or Cascais, to the SW (passing a monument to the Arab poet Ibn Muqana, born at Alcabideche c 1042).—At Linhó an attractive road leads to *Malveira* (see below), skirting the lower slopes of the range, shortly passing (left) the Hieronymite monastery of *Penha Longa*, founded by João I in 1355, but rebuilt in the mid 16C, with a charming cloister and garden-chapel.
B. The first left turn as we descend from the Pena leads round the S side of the higher slopes of the massif, dominated by the peak of *Peninha* (490m), after 4km passing a turning (right) to the *Convento dos Capuchos*, long known to the English, many of whom visited the hermits (according to Baretti, who did so in 1760), as the **Cork Convent**, from the slabs of cork which line the damp walls of the

rock-cut atrium; the 12 cells are merely some cavities cut into the rock. It was founded in 1560 by Álvaro de Castro. Lower down is the cavern in which the 95-year-old hermit Honorius died in 1596 after 36 years as a recluse. The road meets the Colares road (see below) 4km further W.

C. Just as we regain the village of Sintra, at the Hotel Lawrence, we turn left onto the Estrada Velha de Colares, skirting the N flank of the range, passing various quintas, and (after 1km) the grandiose entrance arch (c 1802) of the palace of *Seteais (seven sighs), virtually completed by 1787 for Daniel Gildemeester *père*, the Dutch Consul in Lisbon, and a diamond merchant. His son, also consul, sold it a decade later to the 5th Marquês de Marialva, Beckford's friend, who had previously resided in what is now the *Quinta do Marquês de Valada*, nearer Ramalhão. At a party here Beckford sat opposite the codfish merchant Mr Burn and his mistress, Mrs Hake. It was long supposed to have been the scene of the signature of the reprehensible 'Convention of Cintra' (30 August 1808; see p 121), by which General Hew Dalrymple allowed Géneral Junot and the weakened French forces to evacuate Portugal unmolested, carrying off most of their spoil. The document, although despatched from Sintra, was actually signed in Lisbon, but the name has been thus associated with this disgrace to British arms since the publication of Byron's vitriolic lines in 'Childe Harold' (I, 24—26). The building is now a luxurious hotel.

Further along on the same side is the quinta of *Penha Verde*, where João de Castro (1500–48), viceroy of India, retired in 1542 and died in comparative poverty. In the garden here he planted the first orange-trees in Europe. Sir Benjamin Keene spent two months here during the summer of 1748.

After c 2km we reach the **Quinta de Monserrate**, built by James Knowles in 1856 for Sir Francis Cook, first Visconde de Monserrate, and long associated with the English. It is famous for its *Gardens, covering 30 hectares, laid out in the 1850s by William Stockdale, the artist, with the advice of William Nevill from Kew. The head gardener, until 1924, was an Englishman. The collection of exotic plants, trees, and shrubs, is still very fine.

The fine tree-ferns and the sub-tropical garden at the foot of the hill are noteworthy, and the eucalyptus trees are the descendants of the first of their kind brought to Portugal, where they are now ubiquitous. There are some 25 species of palm and some huge conifers, among a variety of other trees, and a *Bog Garden*, most of which can be seen by following the signs, but the rose-garden is of slight interest.

The Quinta itself takes its name from the vanished chapel of N.S. de Montserrat, and once belonged to Gerard de Visme, a wealthy English merchant. William Hickey, who visited it in 1782, was entertained by de Visme 'in a manner never surpassed and seldom equalled'. It was described by Beckford, who rented it in 1794, as 'a beautiful Claude-like place, surrounded by a most enchanting country', as confirmed by Lady Craven, who three years previously had remarked on its glorious situation, even if it was 'a Vile Planned house', for De Visme was 'Gothicizing' it, and Beckford may well have continued to dabble in 'improving' the villa, and landscaping. Nevertheless, to quote Rose Macaulay: 'Both at least are absolved from the barbarous orientalism of the Monserrate of today, constructed in a Moorish delirium by the Visconde Cook of 1856'. The contents of the house were auctioned off in 1948, and the property sold to the State, but the structure is in a sorry state of abandon.

The road goes on through the village of **Colares**, famous for its red wine: 'a sort of half-way excellence between port and claret' to Southey's taste. The valley here was already (in 1760) being compared to the Garden of Eden, according to Baretti.

Both here and in the nearby hamlet of *Penedo* the parish churches contain interesting azulejos.

From Colares a road leads NW to the coast at *Praia das Maçãs*, with a sandy beach, and further N, the fishing-village of *Azenhas do Mar*. Inland from here, at *Janas*, is the curious circular 16C church of *São Mamede*.

3.5km beyond this turning we meet the road from the *Cork Convent* (see above), and turn again towards the Atlantic after another 3km, reaching a road leading to the precipitous *Cabo da Roca*, the W extremity of continental Europe—Ireland is further W—a tall slender mass of granite, often misnamed the 'Rock of Lisbon' by English sailors. The main road now descends to *Malveira*, where we may either drive direct to *Cascais*, 7km S, or, by turning right prior to the village, follow the coastal road (12km) via the beach of *Guincho* and the so-called *Bôca do Inferno* (where the sea roars at high tide when entering a cavern in the cliff), passing (left) as we enter the town the *Castro Guimarães museum* and (right) the old *Citadel*, where Dom Luís died in 1889.

CASCAIS (12,500 inhab.), attractively sited among pines and eucalyptus woods, has grown considerably since 1870, when it was first patronised by the Court. It is now both a fashionable dormitory suburb of Lisbon and a summer resort, but it has few attractions in itself, apart from the Baroque church of *N.S. da Assunção*, which contains a series of paintings by Josefa de Óbidos. Cascais is the terminus of the railway from the Cais do Sodré station, Lisbon.

An old seaport, Cascais was the birthplace of Afonso Sanches, the pilot who in 1486 was driven westwards by a tempest to an unknown land, and contriving to return to Madeira, was there entertained by Columbus, who is believed to have had his hopes of a westward route to India reinforced. The town was sacked in 1580 by the Duke of Alba, when advancing on Lisbon to enforce the Spanish claim to the throne of Portugal; and again, in 1589, by a retaliatory expedition from England after the Spanish Armada's failure (1588).

FROM CASCAIS TO LISBON (31km). Cascais now merges with *Monte Estoril* and **ESTORIL** itself, both with luxurious villas and the residence in recent decades of miscellaneous monarchs and pretenders in exile, including Carol of Rumania (died 1953), Umberto of Savoy (died 1983), and Juan de Borbon (father of Juan Carlos of Spain).

Estoril has a casino. The area has long been popular with British valetudinarians, who have sensibly congregated on this Portuguese 'Costa do Sol', with an equability of climate unrivalled in Europe, and colourful with a luxuriant sub-tropical vegetation. Aubrey Fitz Gerald Bell (1881–1950) first settled here in 1911.

The coast road (N6), running parallel to the railway, skirts a number of minor resorts, later passing the dismantled 16C *Fort of São Julião da Barra*, a political prison during the Miguelite wars, opposite which is that of the *Torre do Bugio*, marking the sand bar at the mouth of the Tagus.

Carcavelos, on the inland road, is noted for its wine; while at *Oeiras*, a village of ancient origin further E, is a Baroque *church* (1744) and the *Quinta* built for Pombal by Carlos Mardel, its gardens decorated with sculpture by Silvestre de Faria Lobo and Joaquim Machado de Castro, and preserving a charming fishing pavilion. Until recently the palace housed the Gulbenkian collections: see Rte 1F.

Before reaching the present approach to the auto-estrada (N7; avoiding the built-up W riverside suburbs of Lisbon), we pass *Caxias*, with a former royal country residence with pleasant 18C gardens; and c 1km inland, the buildings of one of the two Carthusian monasteries in Portugal, founded in 1595 by Simoa Godinho, a negress. It was here that the artist Domingos António de Sequeira (1768–1837) was a novice during the years 1798–1802.

In the suburb of *Dáfundo*, which we next traverse, is the *Vasco da Gama Aquarium* (founded 1898).

A short distance inland is the well-designed stone-built *National Sports Stadium* (1944).

Shortly beyond, we get a distant view of the *Ponte 25 de Abril*, spanning the Tagus, and soon pass (right) the *Tôrre de Belêm*: see Rte 1E.

3   Lisbon to Queluz and Mafra

Total distance, 40km (25 miles). For an alternative direct road to *Mafra*, see Rte 18B.

We follow Rte 2 as far as (13km) **QUELUZ** (41,100 inhab.), now a dormitory of Lisbon, where we fork right for the palace.

The *****Royal Palace**, one of the most notable monuments of Rococo architecture in the vicinity of the capital—indeed, in Portugal—was built for the Infante Dom Pedro in 1747–52 by Mateus Vicente de Oliveira (1706–86). It is an irregularly planned two-storey edifice of *pedra lioz* and rose stucco, entered from a courtyard (emulating in miniature that at Versailles) in which stands a Neo-classical *Statue of Maria I* (1797) surrounded by Four Continents, by F.S. Fabri and João José de Aguiar (1769–1841).

Single storey extensions to the building were started in 1758 by Jean-Baptiste Robillon (died 1782)—who also laid out the Gardens—just prior to Dom Pedro's marriage to his niece, the future Maria I. Géneral Junot lived here briefly in 1809.

In the N wing are the old palace *Kitchens*, of interest in themselves, now accommodating the luxury restaurant known as the *Cozinha Velha*.

The interior of the palace (guided tour) contains some imposing rooms, many preserving furniture showing English influence, among them the *Sala do Trono*, decorated by Antoine Collin and Silvestre de Faria Lobo (died 1769); a richly gilt oval *Hall of Mirrors*; the *Music Room*, containing an *anon.* Portrait of Maria I; the *Sala dos Azulejos*, containing a Mafra-like bird-cage, red lacquer screens from Macao, and childrens' furniture; the *Sala dos Embaixadores* (1757–62), seriously damaged by fire in 1934; the *Council-room*, with a fine hardwood floor; the mirrored *Queen's Dressing-room* (1774–86); the circular *King's bedroom*, in which Pedro IV was born and died (1798–1834), with a series of scenes by Manuel da Costa depicting the exploits of 'Don Quixote'; and the coffered *Sala das Merendas*, or breakfast-room, with pleasant 'Goyaesque' picnic scenes.

The heavily-swagged W front overlooks the *****Gardens**, with their formal parterres, in which Beckford ran a race with one of the maids of honour to Carlota Joaquina in 1796. They are particularly attractive, with box hedges, urns and topiary, cypress avenue, fountains, colonnades and steps, lead statuary (regrettably 'cleaned'), and azulejos, some of maritime scenes.

Opposite the palace is the *Royal Chapel* (open for mass on Sundays), also decorated by Silvestre de Faria Lobo (1750–60), which may be visited.

We follow the N17 to the N, turning right and then left just N of the palace, passing through *Belas*, and traversing undulating country, after 17.5km meeting the N9 from Sintra, a view of which we have to the W.

After descending to *Cheleiros*, in a deep valley with a small bridge (restored) probably of Roman origin, the road makes a detour to the E, and after skirting part of the stone wall of the park, turns right, with the immense bulk of the convent-palace rearing up immediately to the right

The small town of **Mafra**, entirely dwarfed by its convent, but which once surrounded the vanished castle, is of little interest except for the *Casa de Brasão*, and the church of *Santo André* (c 1400), containing the tomb of Diogo de Sousa and his wife. Pedro Julião, better known as Pedro Hispano, was priest here before his election to the papacy in 1276 as John XXI. A small local museum may be visited.

The main façade of the Convent of Mafra

The **CONVENT DE MAFRA*, impressive by its sheer size, in plan has little similarity with the Escorial (near Madrid), with which it has been occasionally compared. Its main W Front, 220m long, is some 12m longer than the Escorial, but the whole is slightly smaller in area. Each end of the main façade is terminated by square corner pavilions (which Beckford described as 'pagodas') crowned by squat onion-domes, each lit by a series of oval windows.

The pavilions have certain similarities with the towers of the royal palace in Lisbon destroyed in 1755. The long flat, indeed ponderous, façade beneath the two pavilions is relieved by tall twin steeples (68m high) and an Italianate portico. Over the crossing is the imposing Baroque dome. The church, lateral pavilions, and aperture frames, are of the local limestone, which, exposed to Atlantic storms, has been darkened by lichen. The rest of the building is mainly built of bricks, plastered over.

The present convent was erected by João V (married to Maria-Ana of Austria in 1708) in fulfilment of a vow that on the birth of an heir to the throne he would found a monastery there. In 1711 their first child, Maria Barbara, was born, later to become queen of Spain. Three years elapsed before their first son, Pedro, was born (who only survived two years), and in the event João chose to rebuild the Capuchin friary of Mafra as the votive church and convent. (His actual successor, Dom José, was born in 1714.)

Work began in 1717, and the design entrusted to Johann Friedrich Ludwig (Ludovice; 1670–1752), a German trained in Augsburg and Rome, who had come to work for the Jesuits in Lisbon, assisted by an Italian, Carlo Battista Garbo (a Milanese settled in Portugal since c 1698, who died in 1724). Senior to Garbo were the architect-engineers who worked immediately under Ludovice, namely his son J.P. Ludovice, Custodio Vieira, and Manuel da Maia. The original scheme was gradually enlarged, and absolutely regardless of the expense, some 15 to 20,000 craftsmen being employed on the erection and decoration of the edifice, rising in the peak years 1729 and 1730 to 45,000, while a special hospital for their care, and a military force of c 7000 for their control, apart from assisting with the actual construction, were organised.

The church was consecrated in 1730, and by 1735 the building was completed—large enough to house not 13 (as had originally been intended), but 280 friars and half as many novices as well. The cost has been variously estimated: it was certainly sufficient to hasten the financial ruin of the country in spite of the riches of Brazil.

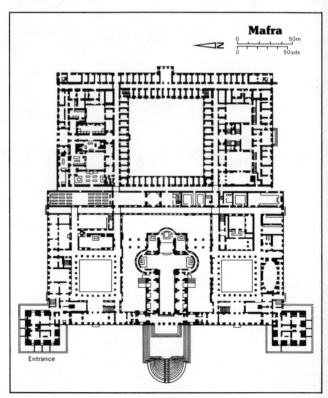

Mafra

0 _____ 50m
0 _____ 50yds

Entrance

Within 73 years Géneral Junot was in occupation; to be followed soon after by seven British regiments (all at once), and here in November 1810 Wellington gave a dinner for 200 and a dance on the occasion of Marshal Beresford being invested as a Knight of the Bath. In 1827 Lord Porchester found Sir Edward Blakeney and a British expeditionary force quartered here; by 1835 Borrow found it 'abandoned to two or three menials'. Since the dissolution of the monasteries it has been intermittently used as a military school: indeed half the building is again in military hands. Manuel II and his suite passed their last night in Portugal here: see *Ericeira*, below.

The **Church* is remarkable for its excellent proportions and comparatively sober ornament, the main decorative scheme consisting in the skilful use of red, black, blue, and yellow marbles, among which the rose coloured Pero-Pinheiro (see p 152) is easily identified. Only the statues of saints in the vestibule, the imported work of Italian sculptors, are of Carrara marble. Among sculptors working in the church were Cláudio de Laprada (Claude de Laprade, of Avignon; 1682–1738) and, later, the Italian Alessandro Giusti (1715–99), who in 1753 commenced the replacement of the painted altarpieces, which had deteriorated in the damp coastal climate. Beckford was impressed by the carving of the capitals and overdoor decorations. Note the cases of the six organs (completed c 1807), in construction when visited by Baretti in 1760, who refers to the fact that Eugene Nicholas Egan, a diminutive Irishman, was working on them.

The guided tour of the monastery-palace takes the visitor along an interminable series of galleries with their well-polished hardwood floors, and up numerous flights of steps. The circuit includes the **Hospital*, infirmary, and hospital kitchens; collections of models for the sculptures, and relics; the *Audience Room*, with its *trompe l'oeil* panelling; the principal corridor along the W Front, providing a good view of the church from the royal oratory; and a collection of incunables and illuminated books of hours. The 'palatial' apartments are of slighter interest.

One of the finest rooms is the **Library*, a magnificent Baroque hall, 88m long, well lit, and preserving some 40,000 volumes. Southey reported that the friar who accompanied him suggested that 'it would be an excellent room, to eat and drink in'; while when Byron was visiting the monastery in 1809 (an example of 'magnificence without elegance' in his opinion), the monks asked him 'if the *English* had any *books* in their country?'.

A visit may also be paid to the towers and dome, the former containing over 50 bells each, including carillons cast at Malines, near Brussels, in 1730. It is said that when the Flemish bell-founders expressed a doubt as to Dom João's ability to pay their price, the king retorted by sending double the required amount in advance. One is shown the clock mechanism, tools and machines used in the construction of the building, together with a fine Balance of 1697.

The original kitchens and refectory are unfortunately in military hands at present, and cannot be visited.

Those wishing to drive N from Mafra may follow the N9 to (31.5km) *Torres Vedras*: see Rte 18B.

Driving NW, after 12km we descend to **Ericeira**, a pleasant fishing village, with one or two churches of slight interest, including the hexagonal hermitage of *São Sebastião*. It was from this small port that in October 1910 the king and queen-mother embarked on the royal yacht 'Dona Amélia' on their flight from Portugal, first to Gibraltar, later being escorted to England. Dom Manuel II, the 'Unfortunate', settled at Twickenham, devoting himself to his library (see Vila Viçosa), and died in 1932.

From Ericeira we may drive S direct to (22km) *Sintra*, the first part of the road providing a good distant view of Mafra to the E. For **Sintra**, see Rte 2. The road passes through *Odrinhas*, where remains of a Roman villa may be visited adjacent to an archaeological museum. Several menhirs are visible from the road.

4 Lisbon to Setúbal: the Serra da Arrábida

From Lisbon on the E4 motorway to **Setúbal** is 46km. Hence the upper road along the Arrábida ridge to *Vila Nogueira de Azeitão*, 25km. From the junction just W of Vila Nogueira to *Cabo Espichel*, c 20km.

The S bank of the Tagus estuary, known as the *Outra Banda*, is not now of great beauty (and since 1959 dominated by an offensive monument), but it commands magnificent *Views of Lisbon and the coast to the W of the capital. For the *Ponte 25 do Abril*, see Rte 1E.

On the cliff to the W are the buildings of the *Lazareto*, or quarantine station, where until a century ago many passengers arriving by ship were first obliged to spend some days.—*Trafaria*, some 5km W of the *Ponte 25 de Abril*, at that time a small fishing village of rush-roofed huts, was burnt to the ground in January 1777 on Pombal's orders, for resisting press-gangs, an unnecessarily Draconian act which was later held against him. Even decades later when officers of the law visited the spot, which they seldom did, but perhaps in search of some delinquent, they were accompanied by a military force.—To the SW is the *Costa da Caparica*, its long beaches now the playground of the Lisbon populace. The rebuilt mid 16C *Capuchin friary* is conspicuous.

To the E of the motorway lies the industrial area of **Almada** (41,500 inhab.), with the *Convent of São Paulo*, founded in 1568. Further E are the *Lisnave* shipyards, etc. on the many-armed S bank of the estuary, beyond which is **Barreiro** (50,700 inhab.), with its railway terminus adjoining the quay, from which ferries ply to the Terreiro do Paço Station in Lisbon.

We now traverse pine forests, with intermittent views ahead of the castle-crowned hill of Palmela, which it is convenient to approach by turning off at c 35km.

The town of **Palmela** (*Pousada de Palmela*), with the exception of the 18C azulejos in *São Pedro*, is of little interest apart from its position. The views S from the esplanade, and from the commanding height of the castle itself, are very fine. The prospect was described by impressionable young Southey, who visited it in 1796, as the most beautiful he had ever beheld. The *Castle* was taken from the Moors in the mid 12C, and from 1288 it was the headquarters of the Portuguese Order of São Tiago, but it was considerably damaged in the 1755 earthquake, and abandoned. In recent years it has been extensively restored to accommodate a luxurious *Pousada*, and is a pleasant centre from which to explore the area. One church, on the site of a mosque, was destroyed in the earthquake; the other (1443–82) contains the tomb of Jorge de Lencastre (died 1551), the last Grand Master of the Order, and son of João II.—A megalithic necropolis was discovered 3km to the W about a century ago.

From Palmela we may descend directly by the N252 to (c 8km) Setúbal.

SETÚBAL (76,800 inhab.; *Pousada de São Filipe*) is an important commercial and fishing port and industrial centre, although no longer quite the 'terrestial Paradise' described by Hans Andersen, who visited it in 1834. Nevertheless its animated older streets retain one or two buildings of interest, and its museum an important series of paintings. Long famous for the export of salt obtained from the marshes of the Rio Sado, on the wide estuary of which it stands, and reputed for its sardines, rice, oranges, and muscatel grapes, it was once familiarly known to British sailors as 'St. Ubes'. The extensive *Setenave* shipyards are close by.

Setúbal inherits the name but not the site of Roman *Cetobriga*, which it is believed occupied the site of *Tróia*, on the far side of the estuary (see below), for the present town was founded in the 12C. João II, who here married Leonor de

The interior of the Igreja de Jesus

Lencastre (1471), often favoured it with his presence. Its medieval walls, of which little remains, were in the 17C superseded by a second line of defences, part of which is preserved to the W of the town. Setúbal suffered severely in the 'Lisbon' earthquake of 1755. Its most famous natives were the opera-singer Luisa Todi (1754–1833), and Manuel Maria de Barbosa du Bocage (1765–1805), the poet, a 'pale, limber, odd-looking young man' whose compositions apparently 'thrilled and agitated' Beckford in 1787.

From a central point in the wide AV. DE LUISA TODI, between the old centre and the river, a few minutes' walk to the N brings one to the *Igreja de Jesus and its adjacent museum. The hall-church, with its six thick spiralling cable-like breccia columns, and rope-like ribs of the apse, all to become symbols of the Manueline style, was begun in 1494 by Diogo Boitac. A better view of the interior may be obtained from the shuttered grille of the *coro alto* (also containing a good Flemish primitive), entered from the *Museum*, installed around the monastic cloister. Outstanding in the Sala dos Primitivos is the series of eight 16C paintings by the *Master of Setúbal*, among them the large Annunciation and the Calvary; and the Saints of Morocco; also notable are the *anon.* 15–16C Flemish paintings of Santa Clara, Santa Inês and Santa Coleta, and an Ascension. The museum also contains a good numismatic collection.

A short walk to the SE is the PRAÇA DO BOCAGE, at the SE corner of which is the *Igreja de São Julião*, with a Manueline N Portal of 1513, and 18C azulejos inside depicting the life of the saint. Hence we may traverse some of the narrow streets of the old town, before regaining the Av. de Luisa Todi further E.

Here (at No. 181) is the small *Museu Oceanográfico e de Pesca* and, adjacent, an *Ethnographical Museum*, largely devoted to the fishing industry, with ship models (including working models of dredgers, etc., which the guardian enjoys setting whirring), and also collections of agricultural implements and a section concerned with lace-making, spinning, etc.; and some naïve ex-voto paintings.

A street almost opposite leads to the riverbank and to the point of embarkation for the regular Tróia ferry (approx. every 20 minutes) and hovercraft (when functioning).

Tróia, on the far side of the estuary, is believed to occupy the site of Roman *Cetobriga*, probably of Phoenician foundation, and said to have been overwhelmed by a tidal wave in the 5C. The ruins, opposite the Marina, may be visited, including tanks for fish salting. Some important finds have been made since excavations began in 1850, but the area described half a century ago as 'now a wilderness of sand, gay with flowers in spring' is unfortunately again overwhelmed, this time by tall blocks of flats described as a 'Tourist Complex'.

Immediately to the W of Setúbal rises the *Castelo de São Filipe*, attributed to Filippo Terzi (1590), and built by Philip II of Spain (I of Portugal) to cow the local inhabitants and as a defence against projected English attempts to make a landing in the vicinity. Recently converted to accommodate a *Pousada*, it commands a good view over the town, estuary, and Tróia peninsula.

For the excursion along the Arrábida ridge to *Vila Nogueira de Azeitão* see below.

Vila Nogueira may also be approached directly by the N10 from Setúbal, climbing up the N flank of the Serra da Arrábida, descending past (right; hidden behind a thick hedge just prior to meeting the N379 from Palmela), the *Quinta da Bacalhôa (admission by arrangement with the caretaker during normal working hours).

This small palace was built in 1480 for the Infanta Brites (Beatriz), possibly—as suggested by Sitwell—by Sansovino, who spent six years in Portugal at about this time. The *Gardens* were begun after 1528, when the property was acquired by the son of Afonso de Albuquerque (first viceroy of India). He built the pavilion with its three towers, where the azulejo depicting Susanna and the Elders (1565) is the earliest dated tile picture in Portugal. The palace was much neglected from 1650 until 1890, when it was inherited by the Conde de Mesquitella, and again from 1910 until 1936, when it was bought by a Mrs Herbert Scoville (née Zabriskie) from Connecticut, who brought some order to the garden, with its topiary hedges, water-tank, orchard, melon-domed towers, etc.; it is hoped that it will not be allowed to deteriorate again.

At adjacent *Vila Fresca de Azeitão*, just to the W, is the 16C *Quinta das Torres*, with a small formal garden, with azulejo panels. The quinta has been transformed into a hotel and restaurant. The church here contains some early azulejos.

Vila Nogueira de Azeitão, some 2km further W, is an attractive village, containing the *Távora Palace*, its coat of arms erased by Pombal after the arrest here of the then Duque de Aveiro for his alleged complicity in a plot against Dom José.

For the road hence to *Cabo Espichel*, and/or back to *Setúbal* over the Arrábida range, see below. Those returning to *Lisbon* may continue N on the N10, after 14km joining the motorway.

FROM SETÚBAL TO VILA NOGUEIRA VIA THE SERRA DA ARRÁBIDA (25km). There are two alternative routes, the lower road skirting the coast via *Portinho da Arrábida* being slightly shorter, but not so impressive. It first passes the old fort of *Albarquel*, and the 14C tower of *Outão*. The stalactite cave of *Lapa de Santa Margarida* may be visited.

The upper road turns right after 4.5km past a cement works, and climbs steeply towards the summit of the limestone ridge (which rises to 500m at the *Formosinho*), on which a number of belvederes have been built, providing a distant panorama of Lisbon. The road descends past (left) the *Convent of Arrábida* (founded 1542), a beautifully sited group of buildings, with little hermitages and chapels scattered over the steep seaward slope (*Views*).

We descend, bearing away to the N, and c 5km after meeting the lower road, reach a junction 2km W of *Vila Nogueira*: see above.

The excursion may be continued to *Cabo Espichel*, c 20km SW. We turn left onto the N379. After 5km a left turn leads to *Calhariz*, with the 17C palace of the Palmela family. —2.5km *Santana*, whence the N378 leads 21km N to meet the motorway to Lisbon.

The left-hand turn descends steeply to (3km) **Sesimbra**, a fishing port and resort, defended by the 17C fort of *São Teodósio*. The 15C *Misericórdia* contains a painting of N.S. da Misericórdia attributed to Gregório Lopes (1531/40); the *Igreja Matriz* is 16C.

A minor road leads SW just beyond Santana to the restored *Castle of Sesimbra*, of Moorish origin, providing good plunging views, and preserving a church rebuilt in 1721. Here also is a small archaeological collection.

Regaining the main road and continuing W we eventually reach the pilgrimage church of *N.S. do Cabo* (1701), in a semi-derelict condition, at the end of a long forecourt flanked by ranges of equally derelict pilgrim accommodation built over arcades. Beyond lies **Cabo Espichel**, the Roman *Promontorium Barbaricum*, with its lighthouse, from the summit of which we have a plunging view to the Atlantic far below; of the coast below the Serra de Sintra to the NW; and towards Sines to the SE.

5 (Badajoz) Elvas to Lisbon

A. Via Estremoz

Total distance, 251km (156 miles). 7km to the frontier. N4. 12km
Elvas—43km **Estremoz**—42km *Arraiolos*—25km
Montemor-o-Novo—23km *Vendas Novas*—13km *Pegões*
crossroads—N10.14km *Marateca* crossroads—21km **Setúbal**—E4
auto-estrada—51km **Lisbon**.

For *Badajoz* see *Blue Guide Spain*. Shortly after crossing the
Guadiana we reach the frontier (Customs), marked by its tributary,
the Caia, beyond which we traverse open country, with a good view
ahead of Elvas and its hill-top forts on our approach.

ELVAS (12,700 inhab.; *Pousada de Santa Luzia*), strategically sited,
was once one of the strongest fortresses in Portugal, and still retains its
walls. It is a lively and characteristic frontier town, commanding a
distant view of modern Badajoz across the border, and providing a
pleasant introduction to visitors to Portugal. It is noted for its olive oil,
plums and striped blankets.

Elvas was finally recaptured from the Moors in 1230, when a band of Portuguese
knights found it suddenly abandoned. A bishopric was founded here in 1570 but
was abolished in 1882. In June 1580 Elvas gave way to the invading Spanish
troops after the death of Henrique, the Cardinal-king, but in 1644, under the
Count of Alegrete, it successfully resisted a retaliatory Spanish attack. Numerous travellers passed this way on the road between Lisbon and Madrid. Here in
1760 Joseph Baretti was kept awake until three in the morning by extempore
dancing at the inn; while in January 1836 Borrow spent his last night in Portugal
here before carrying his Testaments into Spain, but he was unable to obtain
permission to view the adjacent forts. It was an important base of operations, and
hospital, during the Peninsular War, particularly before the sieges of Badajoz in
1811 and 1812. Manuel Cardoso (c 1569–1650), the composer, was born here.

A convenient entrance to the town from almost opposite the *Pousada*
is the *Porta de Olivença* (1685), in its Vaubanesque fortifications, from
which a street leads directly to the Praça da República.

Olivenza lies c 25km S as the crow flies, beyond the Spanish bank of the
Guadiana (no bridge). Once strongly fortified, it was occupied by the Spanish in
1801. Despite provision in the 1814 Treaty of Paris for its return to Portugal, this
was never implemented.

Halfway along this Rua de Olivença (known to have been so-called
since 1435) a right turn leads shortly to the conventual church of *São
Salvador* (17C), adjacent to which, its entrance beneath a characteristic porch covered by a cupola of azulejos (1715), are the *Library* and
Museum. Both are in a sad state of disorganisation, but improvements
are promised, even if few of the individual items displayed in this
curiously miscellaneous collection are of any great interest. The
library contains an important musical section. —An alley runs
downhill hence to *São Domingos* (13C), with a good Gothic apse.

At the upper end of the PRAÇA DA REPÚBLICA, with the *Town Hall*
(Câmara Municipal), and *Tourist Office*, stands the former *Cathedral*
(1517–37), by Francisco de Arruda, but much altered since, preserving part of a 13C tower. The nave and sacristy contain early 17C
azulejos, and the organ dates from 1762.

Behind, to the right, is the curious octagonal church of the *Freiras de São Domingos (or N.S. da Consolação; 1543–57), built on the plan of a Templars' church on this site destroyed in 1540, its vaulted lantern supported by elegant marble pillars, with gilt and polychrome carving, and with beautiful mid 17C azulejos.

Uphill to the right is a *pelourinho*, and ancient archway, beyond which, adjacent to the Moorish *Castle*, with a Torre de Menagem added in 1488, and commanding an extensive view, is the oldest part of the town. By following alleys skirting the walls we may descend to the SE to *São Francisco* (1761) and *São Pedro* (1227, but much altered), to make our way back to the centre. The arcaded Rua da Cadeia, below the central square, overlooked by a medieval tower, leads down towards the *Porta de São Vicente* and the marble *Misericórdia Fountain* (by Diogo Marques; 1622).

A section of the Aqueduto da Amoreira

The most imposing individual monument of Elvas is the *Aqueduto da Amoreira (1498–1622), strengthened by cylindrical buttresses, which lies just W of the town, a good prospect of which is gained from the main Lisbon road. It brings water here from a distance of c 7km.

It is worth while to drive round the N side of Elvas, by following the road leading through the aqueduct, for a view of the fortifications. Also to the N is the outlying *Forte N.S. da Graça* (1763–92), or *de Lippe* (from its designer, Count William of Schaumburg Lippe-Bückeburg, an English-born German, called the 'Grão Conde', reorganiser of the Portuguese army in the early 1760s), its terrace commanding a wide view. —To the E, Elvas is overlooked by the older *Forte de Santa Luzia* (1641–87).

For the roads from Elvas to *Portalegre* and *Castelo Branco*, and to *Abrantes*, see Rtes 14 and 15 respectively; and for *Vila Viçosa* and *Évora*, Rte 5B.

THE EXCURSION FROM ELVAS TO (34km) ALANDROAL AND BACK VIA VILA VIÇOSA. The N373 leads SW to (18km) the village of *Juromenha*, once an important frontier station, and probably of Roman foundation, on a height overlooking the sluggish Guadiana. It was captured briefly from the Moors by Geraldo Sem-Pavor in 1166, but not definitively until 1230. It capitulated to Don

Juan of Austria after a short siege in 1662. The river here was crossed by Beresford in April 1812, prior to the siege of Badajoz. The deserted ruins of its *Castle* (rebuilt 1312), severely damaged by an explosion in 1659, provide a good *View* across towards *Olivenza*, see above. —The road continues SW to (16km) *Alandroal*, with the extensive remains of a late 13C *Castle*. —Hence the N255 leads S via (10km) *Terena*, with a castle and fortified church (14C) to (27km) *Reguengos de Monsara*: see Rte 7. *Redondo, on* the road to Évora, lies 12km SW; see Rte 5B.—Turning N from Alandroal, after 12km we reach *Vila Viçosa* (see Rte 5B), 5km beyond which, at *Borba*, we regain the N4 30km W of Elvas.

Driving W from Elvas, after c 10km we obtain good retrospective views before by-passing *Vila Boim*, in attractive rolling country, later passing (right) a lake, and skirting (left) the *'Tapada'* of *Vila Viçosa*, for which, and for *Borba*, see Rte 5B.

We shortly see white *Estremoz* ahead, which we enter after c 11km.

ESTREMOZ (*Pousada da Rainha Isabel*), an attractive, well-sited, and important garrison town, noted for its earthenware and its white marble, was granted a *foral* in 1258. It is commanded by the fortified upper town.

The main feature of the lower town is the *Rossio* or PRAÇA MARQUÊS DO POMBAL, the large central square.

Here, in the local *estalagem*, Joseph Baretti put up in 1760 during a masquerade in honour of the Princess of Brazil's marriage to her uncle. He visited 'the two principal convents of the town, but saw nothing worth noting in either', and next morning, after sleeping on a straw-bag placed over the chinks of his floor-boards, was awoken at five by the drummers and pipers of the garrison. Beckford, when passing through in 1787, took the precaution of spreading round his bed the Arraiolos carpets he had acquired en route. In January 1836 George Borrow passed a night in the same inn. By the time T.M. Hughes passed that way in 1846 things had improved, and he had sheets, even if they were damp, which next morning, when his bed was transformed into a table, passed as breakfast tablecloths!

Facing the Rossio are the convents referred to above, one of 1698, now the *Town Hall*; the other, once that of the Order of Malta, with two cloisters and a church of c 1540, has since 1880 been the *Misericórdia*, preserving azulejos, adjacent to which is a small regional handicraft museum. Close by is the Largo General Graça, with *São Francisco* (founded in the 13C, and now in military occupation), where one may enter the Chapel of the Senhor dos Passos, with a Manueline window. Near is the 17C *Tocha Palace*, preserving 17C azulejos.

Hence we may ascend to the upper town clustering within the walls of Afonso VI, to the 13C *Torre de Menagem* (27m high, and similar to that at Beja), abutted by part of the *Palace*, much damaged by an explosion in 1698, but rebuilt by João V. It now accommodates the luxuriously appointed *Pousada*. Adjacent is the stark façade of *Santa Maria do Castelo* (commenced 1559, by Afonso Álvares), replacing part of a Gothic church built on the site of a mosque. Beside it is a relic of the earlier palace, with its Gothic arcade, in which Isabel, the 'Rainha Santa', wife of Dom Dinis, died in 1336, and where his grandson died in 1367.

Opposite, in the old *Hospício de Caridade*, is the recently installed *Municipal Museum* of Archaeology and Ethnography, containing a good collection of popular painted ceramic figures (*bonecos de Estremoz*), stelae, furniture, carved and gilt woodwork, a reconstructed kitchen, firearms, a plan of the town in 1758, etc.

For routes from Estremoz to *Portalegre*, and to *Crato*, see those on p 201, in reverse.

FROM ESTREMOZ TO ÉVORA (46km SW). We fork left off the N4 onto the N18 some 7km W of Estremoz, shortly starting the climb into the wooded SERRA DE OSSA and to (11km) **Évora Monte**, a village retaining a *Castle* of 1306 damaged in the earthquake of 1531, with a 16C keep preserving Manueline piers, and providing extensive views. Its name is famous for the Convention signed here in May 1834 by which Dom Miguel ostensibly abandoned all claim to the throne. Although he sailed from the country, on reaching Genoa he denounced the agreement as being signed under compulsion, but after settling in Austria he no longer played any active part in peninsular politics. —The road descends into the plain of the Alentejo and after 28km enters **Évora**: see Rte 6.

Quitting Estremoz, we continue W, after 24km by-passing (right) *Vimieiro*.

Hence the N251 diverges NW to (18km) *Pavia*, said to have been colonised after its reconquest in the 13C by Italians under Roberto de Pavia. It has a church with cylindrical buttresses similar to that of São Bras at Évora, and the minute chapel of *São Dinis* (16C) which in part envelopes a megalithic tomb. —*Mora* lies 16km beyond, to the S of which, 3km from *Brotas*, is the imposing *Torre das Aguias*.

18km. High-lying **Arraiolos**, by-passed, is a very ancient town dominated by a ruined *Castle* (early 14C; Views). It was once famous for its flourishing carpet-weaving industry, many late 18C products of which may be seen hanging on the walls of museums in Portugal. It is also reputed for its sausages. The 16C *Convent* (or now *Quinta) dos Lóios*), with its cloister, beautifully sited in a valley to the NE, is doubtless that which refused Baretti lodging in 1760, as the friar 'did not chuse to have an Heritick under his roof'.

About 3km SE, some distance to the left off the Évora road, is the *Solar da Sempre Noiva* (c 1500), the former country-house of Abp Afonso de Portugal, preserving relics of Manueline *ajimece* windows, but much deteriorated.

25km. **Mòntemór-o-Novo**, the old centre of which is by-passed, a market town which George Borrow thought exceedingly picturesque, retains a ruined Moorish *Castle* (rebuilt late 13C). It was the birthplace of St. John of God (Juan de Díos, or de Robles; 1495–1550), of Jewish lineage, and the founder of the Order of Charity. He devoted his life to the care of captives, foundlings and the sick; he died at Granada. The Inquisition was active here in 1623.

For the road hence to *Santarém* see Rte 7. *Alcácer do Sal* (see Rte 11) is 46km SW of Montemór on the N253.

We cross the lonely undulating plain of the Alentejo, with plantations of cork-trees and evergreen oaks extending on either side, with an occasional isolated '*monte*' or farmstead of the region, before entering (23km) **Vendas Novas**, an agricultural centre which grew up round a palace built in 1728 by João V in one of his many fits of extravagance, merely to house the bridal cortège of the Infanta of Spain, Mariana Victoria, wife of Dom José. The kitchens impressed Borrow, when he passed that way.

We now traverse a sandy region, after 13km reaching the crossroads of *Pegões*, where we turn left.

An alternative route hence to Lisbon is that via *Vila Franca de Xira*, 45km NW on the N10, where we cross the Tagus: see Rte 18C. This was the main motor road from 1951, when the Maréchal Carmona bridge was inaugurated, until the Ponte 25 de Abril, spanning the Tagus at Lisbon, was opened in 1966.

An older route was that continuing due W to (31km) *Montijo*, until 1930 known as *Aldeia Galega*, whence ferries used to ply to the capital. It is reputed for its oysters. The *Igreja Matriz* (15 and 17C) contains azulejo panels.—At *Alcochete*, 6km N of Montijo, is a much restored church preserving a Gothic rose-window; some paintings by Diogo Teixeira of 1586/88 may be seen in the church of the

Misericórdia, also said to contain a Virgin and Child attributed to Lucas de Leyden.

Bearing SW through scattered pine woods, after 14km we reach a road junction just N of *Marateca,* on the main road from Lisbon to the Algarve: see Rtes 11 and 12.

We shortly pass (left) an arm of the Sado estuary, and approach (21km) **Setúbal** (see Rte 4), with the Arrábida range to the W, and dominated by the hill and castle of *Palmela* to the NW.

Those driving directly to Lisbon are advised to turn right onto the auto-estrada just E of the port. The auto-estrada bears N and then NW round *Palmela* (see Rte 4), traversing a thickly wooded area, and by-passing the industrial and ship-building districts on the S side of the Tagus estuary.

On reaching the *Ponte 25 de Abril* we have an impressive *View of Lisbon ahead, and although vehicles are prohibited from stopping on the bridge, it is worth while to make the crossing slowly for the sake of the panorama, having first studied the map (pp 148–9) in order to make an exit on the far bank.

For **Lisbon,** see Rte 1.

B.   Via Vila Viçosa and Évora

Total distance, 258km (160 miles). 7km to the frontier. N4. 12km **Elvas**—28km *Borba*—N255. 5km **Vila Viçosa**—N254. 54km **Évora**—N114. 30km *Montemór-o-Novo*—23km *Vendas Novas*—13km *Pegões* crossroad—N10. 14km *Marateca* crossroad—21km **Setúbal**—E4 auto-estrada—51km **Lisbon**.

For the road to *Borba* see Rte 5A.

Borba, a pleasant little white town, twice occupied by the Spaniards in 1662/3, is noted for its white marble and its wine. It preserves an imposing *Fountain* of 1781, and slight remains of its walls and 13C castle, while the only church of any interest is that of *São Bartolomeu* (late 16C).

In spite of statements to the contrary in every recent English guide the Editor has perused, the large Renaissance cloister of the *Convento das Servas* no longer has its walls and central fountain covered with 17C azulejos. The arcades have been bricked in, the fountain removed to embellish some quinta, and there is not a tile to be seen in the ruinous relic of a cloister, long put to commercial use: and all this happened, so confirmed the local priest, over 40 years ago.

A monument c 4km SW commemorates the battle of *Montes Claros* (June 1665), in which Schomberg finally defeated the Spaniards under the Marquês de Carracena. Colonel Sheldon, a commander of the British contingent, which had a principal share in the battle, was killed.

Bearing SE through marble quarries, we shortly enter **VILA VIÇOSA**, an attractive town dominated by its bastioned *Castle,* built by Dom Dinis, and the original *solar* of the ducal family of Braganza. It was briefly Edmund of Cambridge's HQ in the Anglo-Portuguese campaign of 1382. The marquisate was bestowed on Fernando, the second duke (beheaded at Évora; see p 179) in 1470. Adjacent to the Castle (in which it is planned to install an archaeological museum) is the church of the *Conceição,* lined with 17–18C azulejos. To the S is the long PRAÇA DA REPÚBLICA, at its far end *São Bartolomeu* (1636–98). Off the N side of the square, the main street leads shortly to the TERREIRO DO PAÇO, flanked by the huge and monotonous classical façade of the *Paço Ducal*, the *Chagas Convent* of 1530 (in which lie the tombs of the Braganza wives), and *Santo Agostinho*, founded in 1267 and rebuilt in 1634 as a ducal pantheon. The high-arcaded cloister is in the Tuscan style, with later additions.

Note, before visiting the palace, the *Gate of Knots* (*Porto dos Nós*) on the left side of the main road leading N from the square.

The **Ducal Palace**, mainly 17C, was begun in 1501, and its façade was faced with Monte Claros marble in 1601–02. It now contains the Braganza archives and collections.

Here, in 1512, the duke stabbed to death his wife and her page, with whom he assumed she was having illicit relations. It was a residence of the kings of Portugal of the House of Braganza after 1640; here the future João IV (more interested in music and the chase than politics) received the first overtures of the nationalist party, which brought about his accession. Among composers of music for the chapel have been Gines de Morata and António Pinheiro. Catherine of Braganza was born here in 1638.

Joseph Baretti, who visited the place in 1760, was not impressed, remarking: 'The furniture is rather mean than old, and there are a hundred houses in Genoa incomparably better'. Dom Pedro (who later married Maria I) occasionally visited the palace, but preferred to lodge in a small house adjoining, which, Baretti was assured, was 'elegantly fitted up'. Here Carlos I (an amateur artist) and his eldest son passed their last night before their assassination in Lisbon in 1908.

The *Kitchens* (glittering with copper pans), and an important part of the establishment, if one is to judge from Dom Carlos's appearance, are first visited (guided tour); then the important **Library* of Early Portuguese Books, accumulated by Manuel II during his long exile at Fulwell Park, Twickenham, the catalogue of which was published by *Maggs Bros* in 1929–35.

The 414 items are described in c 2500 pages in three handsome volumes, containing over 1000 facsimiles. Limited to an edition of 698 copies altogether, the catalogue has itself been described as 'one of the few really great books ever prepared by a monarch'.

We are later shown the *Chapel*, in Pompeian style; the *Music Room*; the *Sala de Hércules*; and *Sala dos Duques*, etc. Apart from a painting attributed to Cristóvão de Figueiredo, and a portrait of Dom Manuel by Laszlo, some tapestries after Rubens, one or two items of furniture and porcelain, and some 16C Dutch tiles, the palace and its contents are disappointing. Perhaps of more interest are the rooms in the older palace, and the *Gardens*.

A propitiatory ***Collection of Carriages**, some 70 in all, complementing those in the *Museu dos Coches* at Belém (see Rte 1E), may be visited in the three adjacent ranges of stables. Notable are one made for the Conde das Galveias (No. 18; London, c 1820); No. 29, the square landau in which Carlos I and his son were riding when assassinated (see above); No. 31, belonging to the Távora family; No. 51, a charabanc (by Thrupp of London); and No. 70, the mail-coach, made in England in the second quarter of the 19C. Almost all are in perfect condition.

The *Tapada*, a walled hunting chase of considerable extent (some 18km in circumference) is near, and it was while on a hunting expedition here that in 1861 Pedro V, and a younger brother, Fernando, were taken fatally ill with typhoid fever.

Turning SW, we traverse the wooded SERRA DE OSSA, passing near a series of dolmens, to (19km) *Redondo*, an old hill-top town, preserving some of its fortifications, but its churches are of no great interest. Here we veer due W through attractive undulating country, towards (35km) **Évora**: see Rte 6, below.

From Évora we continue W, shortly bearing NW to regain the main Lisbon road (N4) at (30km) *Montemór-o-Novo*, for which, and the road beyond, see Rte 5A.

6   Évora

ÉVORA (34,100 inhab.; *Pousada dos Loios*), the ancient walled capital of the Alentejo, and one of the most picturesque and interesting towns in Portugal, stands on a low hill among rolling plains, for which it is an important market. Remains of every age from Roman times onwards survive, and the windings of its narrow streets preserve more of a medieval aspect than in many other towns, while much also recalls its long Moorish occupation.

Celtic *Ebora* may have been a headquarters of Quintus Sertorius (c 80 BC); it was later awarded the title of *Liberalitas Julia* by Julius Caesar. A bishop of Évora attended the Council of Elvira (near Granada) in 300. It was in Moorish hands from c 715 until 1166, largely controlled by the Ibn Wazir family, when it was taken by surprise by the outlaw knight, Geraldo Sem-Pavor (Gerald the Fearless), who thus regained the favour of Afonso Henriques, and it remained a Christian bastion in the Alentejo until 1211. With the accession of the House of Avis in 1385, following its capture by João I in 1382, Évora became a frequent residence of the kings, and here the Cortes were often summoned. By the end of the 15C its population had grown to some 25,000. A Jesuit university was established here in 1559, to be suppressed by Pombal 200 years later. The Card.-king Henrique was archbishop of Évora before his accession in 1578; it had been an archbishopric since 1540.

At Évora occurred the first serious outbreak (1637–38) against the Spanish domination; and in 1663 the town was briefly occupied by the besieging army of Don Juan of Austria until relieved by the victory of Ameixial (8 June). It suffered a worse fate in July 1808, when brutally sacked by Géneral Loison after its defending forces had been massacred. Here, in 1828, Lord Porchester, when travelling through, was imprisoned for his own safety during fanatical Miguelite rioting. Among other earlier visitors was George Borrow, who spent the 8–17 December 1835 in Évora, putting up at a hostelry opposite the convent in the Largo de São Francisco. Borrow remarked that it then contained only 5000 inhabitants, but he could not find a bookshop in the town; nevertheless, he circulated Testaments, and attempted to convert the peasants near a stone fountain 'about half a mile from the southern wall'.

On 9 September 1973 the Roman temple was the rendezvous of disillusioned junior officers, who were to precipitate the Revolution of 25 April 1974.

Évora was the birthplace of Ibn 'Abdūn (1100–66), the Arab poet; Garcia de Resende (1470–1536), poet and architect; André de Resende (1498–1573), the antiquary; the 15C mathematician Abraão Zacuto (also claimed by Salamanca); Pedro Fernandes de Queirós (1563–1615), discoverer of Australasia; the 15C miniaturist, Álvaro Pires; António Ribeiro (called 'Chiado'; c 1520–91); Duarte Nunes de Leão (c 1530–1608), the historian; João dos Santos (c 1550–c 1625), missionary; and the Arruda family of architects (16C).

Luis António Verney (1713–92), known as 'El Barbadiño', author of the influential 'Verdadeiro Método de Estudar' (1746), was Archdeacon of Évora. Gil Vicente, the dramatist, died here c 1540.

Perhaps the most convenient entry into the upper town is that from the NE (Rua Cordovil), which after a short climb brings us to a high wall (left), immediately beyond which turn left to gain the highest point, dominated by the remains of the *****Roman Temple**. It is arbitrarily known as that 'of Diana', and dates from the 2nd or 3C AD. The best preserved of its type in the Peninsula, it was apparently hexastyle and peripteral, although the S colonnade has vanished. Most of the podium remains, and the existing granite Corinthian columns have only 12 rather than the normal 24 flutes; they are crowned with white Estremoz marble capitals. The building was once 'fortified', and long used as shambles; indeed it was not cleared of its centuries of accretions until 1870.

Opposite its E side is the former **Monastery dos Lóios**, the buildings of which have since 1965 accommodated the comfortable *Pousada*. The Gothic *Cloister* (with a Renaissance gallery above) preserves the beautiful Luso-Moorish doorway of the Chapterhouse of two granite horseshoe arches supported by delicate twisted marble columns with curious capitals. Beneath the crowning ogee of the doorway is a representation of the stockade either of Arzila in Morocco, captured by Rodrigo Afonso de Melo in 1470, or of Azammur, where the 1st Earl of Tentugal was wounded.

Tombs of the family may be seen in the adjacent church of *São João Evangelista* (1485), generally known as *Os Lóios*, after the order of Canons Regular founded by St. Eloi, who served it. It is notable for its Flamboyant entrance portal and the azulejos of 1711 by António de Oliveira Bernardes (1684–1732) depicting the Life of St. Laurence Giustiniani, patriarch of Venice. Note also the *trompe l'oeil* azulejo window.

A few paces downhill stands the old *Palace of the Melos*, also known as that *of the Cadavals*, with two tall towers. The terrace of the palace is built above a massive stretch of Roman wall, parts of which can be discerned between this point and the PRAÇA DO GIRALDO. A small 'museum', to the left inside the entrance, contains an equestrian portrait of the 3rd Duque de Cadaval, by Pierre Antoine Quillard (1701–33), and two Flemish brasses, etc.

Returning past the Pousada, we skirt the *Library* (established 1805), now containing the important collection of some 33,500 volumes donated by its founder, Abp Manuel do Cenáculo Vilas-Boas (1724–1814), among others. A copy, by Isaias Newton (1872), of his portrait, hangs in the main reading-room. The collections—increased by those of conventual libraries after 1834—include some 250,000 volumes; 500,000 MSS and 660 incunables.

Facing the S side of the temple stands the former *Archbishop's Palace* (late 16C–early 18C), bearing the arms of Abp Luís da Silva (1691–1703), and now housing the *****Museum** which, under the aegis of Mário Tavares Chicó (director from 1943–66), grew to become one of the most important in Portugal. But the basis of the collection was formed by Abp Vilas-Boas.

Vilas-Boas, son of a Lisbon blacksmith, was described by young Southey who met him in Beja (in 1801, where he was then bishop), as 'a little, cheerful, large-eyed man'. He was apparently the only person who bought a book in Beja, so the bookseller complained to Southey, to whom the bishop also hospitably gave 'cheese and incomparable wine' for his journey on. In July 1809 he entertained Lord and Lady Holland in his palace at Évora, 'which is very large, and contains some handsome, lofty, well-furnished rooms'. A year previously Géneral Loison, having given his word 'of honour' to the archbishop that his palace would be respected, thereupon broke into a cabinet of medals and antiquities, and 'plundered the collection of all the gold and silver medals, of which he had a very valuable series, leaving the copper and bronze untouched' ... 'heaps of MSS were destroyed'; while Lord Holland was assured by a priest that 'Loison *himself* stole from a table whilst the Archbishop was sleeping his episcopal ring', and pocketed it. By the time Borrow visited the building, in 1835,

Évora

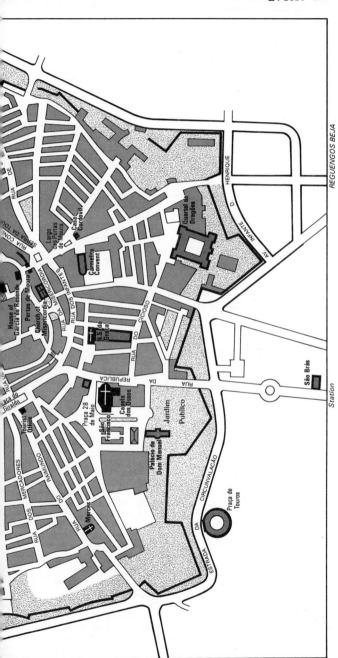

House of
Garcia de Resende

Portas de Moura
Church of
Misericórdia

Casa
Cordovil

Largo
das Portas
de Moura

Carmelite
Convent

Quartel de
Dragões

RUA CONDE DA SERRA DA TOUR

RUA DE

RUA DA INSERICORDIA

RUA DOS INFANTES

N.S. da
Graça

RUA DO CICIOSO

RUA DA GRAÇA

Tourist
Office

aça do
Giraldo

RUA DA REPUBLICA

Praça 28
de Maio

São
Francisco

Capela
dos Ossos

RUA DA REPUBLICA

Jardim
Público

São Brás

Station

AV. INFANTE D. HENRIQUE

REGUENGOS BEJA

Palácio de
Dom Manuel

RUA DOS MERCADORES

RUA DO RAIMUNDO

Mercês

Praça de
Touros

ESTRADA DA CIRCUNVALAÇÃO

and saw its 'superb library' and 'a collection of pictures by Portuguese artists, chiefly portraits', it was the residence of the Governor of Évora.

The archaeological collections ranged around the central cloister contain a number of examples of Roman sculpture and stelae excavated in the neighbourhood, but also include a Female head from Tavira. Notable are a frieze from a Roman temple; the lower half of a bas-relief of a Vestal Virgin; a barrel-shaped tombstone; and the sepulchres of Fernão Gonçalves Cogominho (1364), a hero of the battle of Salado; the cenotaph of Rui Pires Alfageme (14C); a marble relief of the Annunciation (1382); and the monument to Bp Fernando Martins (mid 14C).

Adjacent is the escutcheon of Évora, and an *ajimece* window from the old town hall (1516), destroyed in 1895 to be replaced by the new (at the S end of the Praça do Giraldo); the Tomb of Álvaro da Costa (1535), by Nicolau Chanterène, who worked in Évora between 1533 and 1540; two marble pilasters from the Monastery of Paraíso (1533), likewise attributed to Chanterène, and also the Cenotaph of Bp Afonso of Portugal (1537); and a basalt Allegory of the Portuguese Discoveries (16C; from the Palace of the Earls of Unhão). The azulejos displayed on this floor should not be overlooked.

Stairs ascend to the FIRST FLOOR. **R1** *Master of Sardoal*, Portraits of two bishops; turn right into **R2** *Master of the Retablo of Évora Cathedral*, Life of the Virgin, a series of 13 paintings (Flemish; late 15C): the central panel of the Virgin surrounded by angels playing musical instruments is attributed to *Gerard David*; and six smaller paintings of the Life of Christ (Flemish; early 16C).—**R3** *Frei Carlos*, Nativity; in the centre, a Triptych of the Calvary in Limoges enamel (early 16C); *anon.* Portraits of Joana de Bragança, and Catherine of Braganza in her youth; and several portrait miniatures.—**R4** Furniture, most of which originated in this building, when it was the archbishop's palace, much of it of fine quality and including an *Escrivaninha*, or desk.—**R5** Attributed to *Josefa de Óbidos*, Lamb of God.—**R6** *Hendrick Avercamp*, Skating scene; and *A. de Vris*, Male portrait (1631).—Other rooms contain 18–19C furniture; several Still Lifes, attributed to *Josefa de Óbidos* and to *Sanchez Cotan*; and a collection of ecclesiastical silver, including a fine silver and gilt chalice, and silver mitre (17C).

An archaeological collection is being formed in the Basement.— The church of *Mercês* serves as an annex to the museum, where other ecclesiastical treasures are displayed; see p 179.

The granite ***Cathedral** or Sé, abutting the museum, one of the largest and finest churches in the S of Portugal, is believed to have been begun in 1186, possibly on the site of an earlier mosque. It was consecrated in 1204 and virtually finished by c 1250. The chancel was rebuilt in the 18C but the rest remains almost in its original state.

EXTERIOR. The *W Front* consists of a deeply recessed ogival porch protecting a series of sculpted Apostles of local workmanship (14C), built between two dissimilar towers, and approached by a flight of steps. The *N Tower*, containing a number of irregularly placed windows, is surmounted by a conical cap covered with azulejos; the buttressed *S Clock Tower* and Belfry is topped by a series of turrets surrounding a cone, somewhat resembling the central octagonal lantern or *Zimbório*, which with its scale-like tiles and eight subsidiary turrets, is of the Salmantine type (i.e. like the lanterns of the *Old* Cathedral at Salamanca, and at Plasencia, etc.).

One of the series of early 16C Flemish paintings of the Life of Christ

INTERIOR (70m by 22.5m). The eye is immediately drawn to the disconcerting accentuation of the mortar-joints, a peculiarity of Évora: see São Francisco, below. Note the curious 'rosary-like' chains supporting the chandeliers. The *Nave*, with seven rectangular bays, lower lateral aisles, and a triforium, is lit by a curious W Window and by fine rose windows in the transepts. At the end of the N Transept is a Renaissance *Portal* ascribed to Chanterène. The incongruous *Capela-Mór*, previously—until 1717—embellished by the retable now in the museum, was entirely rebuilt in vari-coloured marbles by J.F. Ludovice, the architect of Mafra, in 1718–46. In the S Transept is the tomb of André de Resende (died 1573). The *Treasury*, reached by steps in the S tower, contains an unusual ivory figure-triptych of the Virgin (13C) with a later wooden head; a silver-gilt monstrance (16C); an early 16C Bishop's crook; a Reliquary of the True Cross; several copes, and a collection of ecclesiastical plate. Adjacent stairs ascend to the flat roof, which is worth the climb for the panorama and for a closer view of the lantern.

Request entry to the Gothic *Cloister*, which the S transept abuts, and to which two flights of steps descend. It dates from c 1325. Figures of the Evangelists stand at the corners, while in the SE corner is a chapel containing the tomb of the founder, Bp Pedro. Some of the openings pierced above the main arcade are markedly Moresque in pattern, and might indicate Mudéjar influence.

Facing the cathedral, on the NW side of the LARGO DO MARQUÊS DE MARIALVA, stood the Court and Palace of the Inquisition, the first branch of the Holy Office to be established in Portugal (1536), occupying part of the earlier house in which Vasco da Gama lived before his appointment as Viceroy of India in 1524.

Returning towards the *Library*, we may pass below the archway connecting it to the old archbishop's palace, and turning left shortly reach a tower, next to which is the entrance to the *Palace of the Condes de Bastos*, originally a Moorish palace on the Roman walls adjacent to the so-called *Torre de Sertório*, which later became a royal residence. Much of its exterior decoration is of c 1500; admission to the interior may be granted on application.

On regaining the cathedral apse and bearing left, we descend towards a block of buildings consisting of the old *University* (see History), retaining a *Refectory* vaulted from a central line of columns, a restored *Sala dos Actos*, with good azulejos, and an imposing arcaded courtyard, seen through a gateway at a lower level than the porch of the severe church of *Espírito Santo* (by Afonso Álvares and Manuel Pires; 1567–74); the latter preserves a tomb intended for the Card.-king Henrique, who founded the University, but which in fact contains the remains of an infante, Duarte, Duke of Guimarães (died 1576).

Turning SW along the Rua Conde de Serra da Tourega, overlooked by a belvedere, we shortly reach the LARGO DAS PORTAS DE MOURA, with another belvedere on the right, just S of which is a spherical fountain (1556), beyond which is the 16C *Casa Cordovil*, with a delicately columned belvedere. Steps descend nearby to the former *Carmelite Convent*, with a strange 17C portal, a Baroque version of the Manueline style.—Further S is the large *Quartel de Dragões* (Dragoon Barracks; 1736–1803), built on the site of the early 16C castle erected by Diogo de Arruda.

Just within the Portas de Moura is the Manueline *House of Garcia de Resende* (see History), a few paces beyond which steps ascend to regain the cathedral.

By following the Rua da Misericórdia to the W, we shortly pass (right) the *Church of the Misericórdia* (1554, with a portal of c 1767), the interior of which is in the Baroque style.

By crossing to the left at the next road junction, and turning down an alley, we approach the monastery of **N.S. da Graça**, of 1524–29. Its church, attributed to Diogo de Torralva, has a striking but ill-designed Renaissance façade, added c 1550, on which are displayed two enormous 'rosettes'. It is crowned by four colossal figures appearing to support globe-like grenades. The interior is of little interest, and the nave has collapsed three times in the past. The rest of the building, with a small cloister, now accommodates an officers' club.

Continuing W, we cross the Rua da República, and turn left and then right, passing (right) a vaulted building once a royal *grain-store*, and now a display centre for handicrafts, etc., to reach the PRAÇA 28 DE MAIO.

This is dominated by the church of **São Francisco**, of 1480–1500, a large aisleless Gothic edifice crowned with battlements and pinnacles. The narthex combines semi-circular, horseshoe, and pointed arches in one arcade. The interior is remarkable for the scarcity of windows and for the accentuation of the lines of mortar (as with the cathedral). Off the S side is a gruesome 17C charnel-house (*Capela dos Ossos*; which young Southey found 'really shocking'), lined with human bones, and with the much-quoted inscription over its entrance: 'Nós, ossos, que aqui estamos, Pelos vossos esperamos' ('The bones here are waiting for yours'). Additional curiosities are the numerous recent photographs left on an adjacent altar as ex-votos.

In the nearby gardens overlooking the mid 17C **Town Walls** (designed by Nicolas de Langres) stand the disfigured relics of the so-called *Palácio de Dom Manuel*. Don Manuel in fact enlarged it, adding a brick arcade on granite piers, but it was begun earlier, in the 15C.

From this point we can see the strange battlemented hermitage of *São Brás*, with 14 cylindrical buttresses crowned by conical caps, but otherwise of little moment, and except as an architectural curiosity it hardly merits the detour.

Ascending the Rua da República, we shortly reach the S end of the central **Praça do Giraldo**, the main centre of activity in the town, with a low arcade over the pavement on its E side, from which the Rua 5 de Outubro ascends towards the cathedral. Here João II watched the beheading of his over-mighty brother-in-law, the Duke of Braganza, in 1484; and here some 17 victims of the Inquisition were burnt alive in an auto-da-fé in 1573, in the presence of Dom Sebastião. At the N end of the square, beyond a fountain of 1571, stands *Santo Antão*, a hall-church of 1557 with large drum pillars supporting its lofty vaulting, but otherwise of no great interest except for the wooden tomb-covers in the nave.

On the W side of the square is the *Tourist Office*, besides which the Rua do Raimundo descends towards the late 17C church of **Mercês**, containing subsidiary collections of ecclesiastical art not housed in the Museum, and azulejos of 1773, etc.

Between this street and the Rua de Serpa Pinto (leading NW from the square) was the *Judiaria* of Évora, in which a number of old houses are preserved. In the latter street stands the church and convent of *Santa Clara*, founded in 1452, later enlarged, and a cloister added. Juana, La Beltraneja (daughter of Enrique IV of Castile and Joana of Portugal), who had professed at Coimbra in 1480, may have resided here for some time. The derelict interior is now of slight interest.

From the E side of Santo Antão, we may continue N along the arcaded street to the LARGO LUIS DE CAMÕES (or *Porta Nova*) to reach the gardens (left) of the PRAÇA J.-L. DE AGUIAR, by the near corner of which is the little church of the *Hermandad, Santa Marta* (1698). Adjacent to the *Theatre* at the far end of the square is a garage built into part of the old convent of *São Domingos*.

Continuing down the main street (Rua de Cândido dos Reis), after a few minutes we reach (left) the *Calvário Convent* of 1570, with a small cloister, where Juliana de Sousa Coutinho retired after refusing to marry Pedro de Carvalho e Melo, Pombal's son.

Just beyond this point is a good stretch of the 14C outer ***Town Wall** (left), while to the right we get a view of the fine 9km-long ***Aqueduct**, known as that of 'Agua de Prata', executed in the 1530s by Francisco de Arruda, most probably on the site of a Roman one.

On regaining the *Porta Nova*, bear left to pass below two low arches of the aqueduct, then to the right along the Rua Salvador, on the left of which is the *Igreja do Salvador* (1605; its interior covered with azulejos), to gain the PRAÇA DE SERTÓRIO. By taking the right-hand lane at the far end of this small square we pass on the next right-hand corner a cistern (*caixa*) of 1536.

Turning left here, we next pass (left) *São Tiago* (15C, but modernised in the late 17C), containing Dutch tiles of 1700. Bearing round the church, we continue uphill to regain the Roman temple.

São Mamede (c 1566), with a classical porch, also with Dutch tiles of contemporary date and with a profusely decorated ceiling to its vaulted nave, stands a short distance to the NE.

Three convents may be conveniently visited from Évora. The *Cartuxa* lies to the right of the Arraiolos road, c 3km NW, beyond a stretch of the *Aqueduct* crossing the road. This, one of two Carthusian monasteries in Portugal, with a 17C church, is unfortunately somewhat derelict, although retaining an imposing classical façade attributed to Terzi. The cloister of c 1615 is *in clausura*.

A short distance beyond, to the left, is the Benedictine *Convent of São Bento de Cástris*, founded in 1274, with an attractive 16C cloister showing Mudéjar influence, a 14C Chapterhouse, and Refectory, etc. The nearby hill commands a good view of Évora.

The *Convent of N.S. d'Espinheiro*, c 4km N of Évora, dates from 1458, although later altered. It contains a contemporary cloister and a number of interesting tombs, among them, in a small chapel, that of Garcia de Resende (1520; see History). Frei Carlos, the painter of Flemish origin, professed here in 1517.

Some 12km W of Évora is the cromlech of *Almendres*, SW of the hill of Herdade dos Almendres. There are several other megalithic remains in the vicinity, but they are hard to find.

7 (Jerez de los Caballeros) Mourão to Évora and Santarém

Total distance, 232km (144 miles). C4311. 19km *Oliva de la Frontera*—28km *Villanueva del Fresno* (Spanish Customs)—9km *São Leonardo* (Portuguese Customs)—7km **Mourão**—N256. 18km *Reguengos-de-Monsaráz*—36km **Évora**—N114. 30km *Montemór-o-Novo*—46km *Coruche*—33km *Almeirim*—6km **Santarém.**

For *Jerez de los Caballeros* see *Blue Guide Spain*. Hence we follow a slow winding road W and then SW to *Oliva*, there turning NW along a new road which undulates through more open country to the Spanish frontier-post beyond *Villanueva del Fresno* (Customs).

16km. *Mourão*, a characteristic Portuguese village and old frontier fortress, with its early 14C *Castle* abutted by its *Igreja Matriz*, overlooks the Guadiana, which we shortly cross.

From the W bank the DETOUR should be made to (7km) *Monsaraz, approached by turning right. (The road passes near the cromlech of *Xeres*, a square of stones in the centre of which is a 4m-high menhir.—There are two other menhirs below the fortress-hill of Monsaraz: that of *Bulhoa*, engraved with symbols; and the 5.6m example of *Outeiro*.) The picturesque ridge-top village of Monsaraz, largely unspoilt, was reconquered by Geraldo Sem-Pavor in 1167, given to the Templars, and later passed to the Order of Christ. It is said to have been sacked by the unpaid English archers of Edmund of Cambridge in 1381. It preserves its extensive fortifications, commanding wide views, including Vaubanesque outworks added in the 17C. Cars should be left in the parking-place near the entrance gate. In the narrow cobbled Rua Direita a Gothic house contains a 15C fresco. The 16C *Igreja Matriz* preserves the marble tomb of Gomes Martins (late 13C).—*Reguengos* lies 17km to the W.

Regaining the main road, we continue W through rolling country to *Reguengos-de-Monsaraz*, lying among its vineyards .

After 20km we reach the turning (left) from Évora to *Beja* via *Portel* (see Rte 9B), and after 16km enter **Évora** itself: see Rte 6.

Hence we bear NW to (30km) *Montemór-o-Novo* (see p 169).

The N114 continues NW across somewhat uninteresting country to (46km) *Coruche*, a large agricultural town on the Rio Sorraia, here crossed by several bridges. It was rebuilt in 1181 after its destruction by the Almohads. A small *Misericórdia* preserves curious azulejos, some suggesting Oriental influence.

32km. *Almeirim*, once a favourite residence of the Avis dynasty, of whose palace nothing remains, although it was the scene of several Cortes. The Card.-king Henriques was born and died here (1512–80).—*Alpiarça* (p 202) lies 7km NE.

We approach and cross the Tagus by the *Ponte de Dom Luís* (1876–81), its steep N bank overlooked by **Santarém**, to which we shortly climb: see the latter part of Rte 16.

8 Rosal de la Frontera to Lisbon via Serpa and Beja

Total distance, 256km (159 miles). 2km Portuguese Customs. N260. 36km **Serpa**—28km **Beja**—N121. 25km *Ferreira do Alentejo*—N259. 44km *Grândola*—N120. 23km **Alcácer do Sal**—31km *Marateca* crossroads—N10.21km **Setúbal**—E4 auto-estrada. 46km **Lisbon**.

For the road from *Seville* climbing through the Sierra de Aracena to *Rosal de la Frontera* (Spanish Customs) see *Blue Guide Spain*. The first town of any consequence we reach after traversing ancient olive-groves is (36km) *Serpa*.

Serpa (*Pousada de São Gens*, 2km S, with an extensive view), known to the Romans by the same name, was conquered by Geraldo Sem-Pavor in 1166, retaken by the Moors, and finally regained c 1232; but in view of Castilian claims, the frontier here (including Moura) was not settled until 1297, and was again briefly occupied by the Spaniards in 1707–8.

It is now an agricultural centre, with a reputation for its cheeses. The old town, on the slope of a spur of the SERRA ABELHEIRA, preserves stretches of walls, a ruined *Castle* and, among medieval gateways, the *Porta de Beja*, abutted by remains of a huge *nora* or chain-pump and aqueduct. The only ecclesiastical buildings of interest are the *Convent of Santo António* (1463; rebuilt 1502), with a church similar to São Brás at Évora, and a small cloister; and Gothic *Santa Maria*, containing mid 17C azulejos.

FROM SERPA TO MOURA (29km). Following the N255 NE through olive-groves, we approach **Moura**, famous for its olive-oil. Its history is very similar to Serpa's, but the romantic legend of its capture is without foundation. It was the birthplace of Afonso Mendes (1579–1656), Patriarch of Ethiopia in 1623. Its *Castle*, rebuilt by Dom Dinis, again in 1510, and partly restored in 1920, commands an extensive view. The Manueline doorway of the *Igreja Matriz* and the restored *Convent of N.S. do Carmo*, the first Carmelite house in Portugal (c 1251), with a classical cloister, are of interest.

Minor roads continue NE to *Mourão* (see Rte 7), but those wishing to explore the remotest recesses of the Alentejo may make a long DETOUR to *Barrancos*, c 50km E, and the abandoned village and castle (1308) of *Noudar*, some 10km beyond to the NW, overlooking the Rio Ardila, here the frontier with Spain. From Barrancos we may drive 49km NW to *Mourão*.

For the road from Serpa to *Mértola* see p 185.

A rough road leads directly S from Serpa via *São Brás* to (c 18km) the *Pulo do Lobo* ('Wolf's leap'), a waterfall almost 60m high.

We cross the Guadiana some 6km beyond Serpa, and approach (22km) **Beja**, the tall keep of its castle prominent: see Rte 9A.

Hence we proceed W across undulating cornlands to (25km) *Ferreira do Alentejo*, an agricultural centre of slight interest, and descend into the valley of the Sado. Some 22km after crossing the river, *Grândola*, with cork factories, is entered. The town played a small part in history on 24/25 April 1974, as the broadcasting of the old popular song entitled 'Grândola vila morena' was the pre-arranged signal confirming that the military coup was *on*.—Here we turn N to meet the improved N120, bearing through pine woods to (23km) *Alcácer do Sal*: see Rte 10.

At *Marateca*, 31km NW, we join the N10, turning left for **Lisbon**: see Rte 5A.

9 Évora to Beja, Mértola, and Vila Real de Santo António

A. Via Viana do Alentejo

Total distance, 199km (124 miles). N18. 2km then turning right onto N254. 29km **Viana do Alentejo**—11km **Alvito**—16km *Cuba*—19km **Beja**—N122. 51km **Mértola**—67km *Castro Marim*—4km *Vila Real de Santo António*.

Viana do Alentejo, on the N slope of a small range of hills, preserves the walls of its *Castle* (rebuilt 1482), with pepper-pot corner towers, and a wall-walk providing attractive views. Within the enceinte stands the well-buttressed granite **Igreja Matriz* (16C), with a notable Manueline portal, and surmounted by a wealth of conical pinnacles and crenellations. The interior contains a number of interesting details.—1km E of the town stands the large pilgrimage church of *N.S. de Aires*, rebuilt between 1743–90, with twin belfries and an octagonal cupola. Its interior is plastered with ex-votos.

Some 5km beyond is the *Solar de Águas de Peixes*, a mansion of the Dukes of Cadaval, with a Renaissance courtyard.

Climbing through the hills to the S, in 11km we reach **Alvito**, with a curious half-Moorish late 15C *Castle* begun by Diogo Lobo, baron of Alvito, with moulded brick horseshoe arches typical of the district. Rooms off the courtyard have recently served to house a supermarket! The 16C *Igreja Matriz*, higher in the town, contains good mid 17C azulejos.

Bearing SE, in 6km we reach *Vila Ruiva*, with a Roman *Bridge* over the Odivelas, where we may turn S through (10km) *Cuba* to approach the N18 7km beyond; or, alternatively, continue E to reach the main road at (13km) *Vidigueira* via *Vila de Frades* with its Roman villa: see Rte 9B.

The country becomes more open as we approach *Beja*.

BEJA (19,700 inhab.), capital of its district, and an ancient episcopal city, dominating the rich rolling wheat-belt of the Lower (*Baixo*) Alentejo, has long been an important centre of communication, on the direct road between Seville and Lisbon, and between Évora or Lisbon and Faro.

Founded by Julius Caesar, *Pax Julia* (whose name refers to its pacification), later corrupted by the Moors into Beja, was the capital of one of three Roman *conventus* in Lusitania, the others being Santarém and Mérida. The Muslims walled the town, and it remained in their hands until 1162. In 1252 it was re-fortified. Its history since—apart from its sack by Colonel Maransin during the French occupation (June 1808)—has been comparatively uneventful, but in recent years it has had a reputation as a stronghold of Communism, while still a thriving agricultural centre, this largely in reaction to centuries of exploitation by the large landowners of the Alentejo. A NATO air base was constructed to the NW in the 1960s. An abortive revolt against the Salazar regime, planned by General Humberto Delgado, took place at Beja on 1 January 1962. Delgado was assassinated near Badajoz three years later by secret police.

Beja was the birthplace of Jacinto Freire de Andrade (1597–1657), author of a famous 'Life of João de Castro' (1651); and Agostinho de Macedo (1761–1831), the writer and pamphleteer.

From the main road junction to the W of the town, we may enter with ease towards the castle, first passing (left) the 15C *Ermida de Santo André*, with cylindrical buttresses similar in outline to those of São Brás at Évora.

The **Castle**, whose 40m-high limestone *Torre de Menagem dominates the area, abuts a short stretch of *Town Wall*. It was built in 1272–1310 by Dom Dinis on foundations probably Roman, and was restored in 1940. Some 200 steps ascend to its three floors, each with a vaulted room, and providing progressively wider views, the panorama from the summit being bounded on the NW by the Serra de Sintra, by Évora to the N, and to the E by the Spanish sierras. A small military museum has been installed off the courtyard.

The Torre de Menagem

A short distance downhill to the NW stands the pre-Romanesque but now disaffected church of *Santo Amaro, preserving a number of Visigothic columns and capitals, etc., and in which it is intended to install a *Lapidary Museum*.

Immediately E of the castle stands Renaissance *São Tiago* (1590).

Turning SW from the castle, we shortly pass (right) a *Hospital*, in which the relics of two cloisters may be seen, beyond which is a small square, in which stands the small chapel of *N.S. dos Prazeres*, of 1672.

Turning left uphill we soon reach the hall-church of the *Misericórdia* (1550), with a rusticated porch, said to have been built as a covered meat-market, which faces the PRAÇA DA REPÚBLICA. By following a lane beyond the far end of this long square (off which, in another street to the right, a fine Manueline window is preserved) we approach the entrance to the former *Convent of N.S. da Conceição, founded in 1467, and once amongst the richest in Portugal. It now contains the *Regional Museum*.

It was from this convent, it has been assumed, that Mariana Alcoforado (?1640–1723) may have written the five reproachful letters to the Chevalier de Chamilly (Colonel Noël Bouton, Comte de Saint-Léger, later Marquis) who had made her his lover during the latter part of the Portuguese war with Spain of 1661–68, and then deserted her. The letters were published in a French version in 1669 and in an English translation nine years later, which gave the reputed 'Portuguese Nun' some notoriety. Spurious letters were added to later editions.

The exterior copings are crowned by balustrades influenced by Batalha, and above the W door is a charming *ajimece* window brought from the palace of the Dukes of Beja (once the title held by the king's second son), destroyed in 1895, which stood further to the E, joined to the convent by a brick gallery. The Baroque *Chapel* is richly gilt, while the whole interior is remarkable for the azulejos with which the Cloister and Chapterhouse are covered (16C and earlier; some Mudéjar). The contents of the museum are somewhat miscellaneous, and include archaeological collections; costumes; and, among paintings, a Flemish Virgin and Child, and three saints attributed to *Ribera*, an *anon*. Martyrdom of St. Vincent, a Decapitation of St. Barbara, and a portrait of the bibliophile bishop, Manuel do Cenáculo Vilas-Boas (see Évora).

To the NE, at a lower level, is *Santa Maria*, with a 15C narthex and apse, but largely rebuilt.

Downhill to the SE, beyond a junction of streets (that bearing right leads to the *Tourist Office*), steps descend to the sad remains of the 13C *Convent of São Francisco*, with relics of a chapel and cloister. After 1834 it served as barracks, but it deserves a happier fate.

Some 7km SW, approached by a rough track leading to the right off the Aljustrel–Faro road, lie the extensive remains of the Roman ruins of **Pisões**, preserving a villa, pool, baths, mosaic pavements, etc., dating from the 1–4C, but much excavation still remains to be done. The interested visitor is advised to contact the Tourist Office in Beja before making the excursion.

Travellers intending to drive direct from Beja to *Lagos* or *Faro* will follow the N18 to the SW, meeting the N2 at (21km) *Ervidel*, there turning left for (13km) *Aljustrel*, where the two roads diverge: see Rtes 10 and 12.

The road between Beja and Mértola, 51km SE, is somewhat monotonous.

An interesting ALTERNATIVE but longer and slower route is that via *Serpa*, 28km SE: see Rte 8, and from thence to Mértola, 53km S on the N265. This lonely twisting road first leads SE to (36km) the *Minas de São Domingos*, whose copper mines, known to the Romans, and an extension of those at Tharsis and Rio Tinto beyond the Spanish frontier (which here follows the course of the Chança), were re-discovered in 1857, and worked by a British company. A mineral railway leads down to *Pomarão*, on the Guadiana. We pass a lake among eucalyptus woods, and bear W before descending steeply (views) to cross the Guadiana at (17km) *Mértola*, the highest point to which the river is navigable.

Mértola, (*Pousada* under construction) lies at the confluence of the Guadiana with the Oeiras, and is impressively sited beneath its Moorish castle.

Founded in remote antiquity, it was known to the Romans as *Myrtilis*, and was one of the four *municipia* in Lusitania. By 440 it was in Suevic hands (who here seized Censorius, the Roman legate), until occupied by the Moors in 712. It was later captured by Ibn Qasi, when rebelling against the Almoravids in 1143/4. He in turn was ousted in the Almohad invasion of 1146 (whose forces wintered here before marching on Seville), but it was eventually lost by them in 1238.

On the riverbank—the Guadiana was the Roman *Anas*, later arabic *Wadi-Anas*— is a curious pier-like structure, built of Roman materials, but dating perhaps not earlier than the Moorish occupation. Below the castle is the battlemented *Igreja Matriz*, where the discovery of a *mihrab* confirms that it was a converted mosque, as once suggested by its square plan. Its fine vault is probably contemporary with the castle keep (1292). A tombstone from Mértola (now in the Ethnological Museum at Belém), of AD 525, displays the horseshoe 'Moorish' arch, confirming that it was used in the Peninsula before the Moslem invasion of 711. The crumbling *Castle* itself is in a poor state, and deserves slight restoration. A few archaeological relics have been stored in its keep, which commands interesting views.

Climbing out of the Guadiana valley, we obtain some impressive retrospective views of Mértola before reaching higher and deserted cistus-covered tracts and traverse broken country on entering the hills of the eastern Algarve (an extension of the Spanish Sierra Morena), which here run parallel to the coast, threaded by a number of tributaries of the Guadiana.

34km.—6km E is *Alcoutim*, an ancient river-port preserving a ruined castle and a Renaissance church, facing the Spanish town of *Sanlúcar del Guadiana*.

The right-hand turn here leads W via (25km) *Martim Longo*, to meet the N2 35km further SW, some 13km N of *São Brás de Alportel*, the road providing several fine views.

The main road continues to wind S, descending steeply into the valley of the Ribeira da Foupana, and climbing again before reaching lower land on approaching (35km) **Castro Marim** (*Pousada* projected), Roman *Baesuris*. It was also the first headquarters of the Order of Christ (1319), before its transfer to Tomar. The huge *Castle*, built by Afonso III, but damaged by the earthquake of 1755, contains the ruins of the 14C church of *São Tiago*.

Traversing the flooded estuary of the Guadiana, we soon enter (4km) *Vila Real de Santo António*, the easternmost town of the Algarve: see last paragraphs of Rte 13.

B.   Via Portel

Total distance, 202km (126 miles). N18. 16km, there turning right for (21km) **Portel**—16km *Vidigueira*—25km **Beja**—N122. 51km **Mértola**—67km *Castro Marim*—4km *Vila Real de Santo António*.

The rather dull road reaches more attractive wooded country on approaching (37km) **Portel**. It is dominated by its *Castle* (late 13C) of the Dukes of Braganza, reconstructed by Manuel I. The town itself is of slight interest.

There is a well-preserved *Castle* of c 1350 at *Amieira*, 14km due E; and at *Vera Cruz*, 6km S, a 13C church once belonging to the Order of Malta, on earlier foundations.

16km. *Vidigueira*, where in the neighbouring Carmelite church the remains of Vasco da Gama, Conde de Vidigueira, lay from 1539 until transferred to Belém in 1898 (since when they have been moved to the pantheon of Santa Engrácia). Baruch Spinoza's family may have lived here before the expulsion of the Jewish community from Portugal.

Some 4km to the W, and 1km beyond the village of *Vila de Frades*, on the Alvito road, a signposted lane to the right leads to the imposing remains of the Roman villa of *São Cucufate*, later used as a monastery, and in idyllic surroundings. Work is being carried out on the consolidation of the structure, and excavation of the extensive site is progressing.

From Vidigueira we continue S to (25km) **Beja**, see Rte 9A, and for the remainder of the route.

10 Évora to Odemira via Ferreira do Alentejo, for Lagos

Total distance, 156km (97 miles). N380. 32.5km *Alcáçovas*—N2. 12.5km *Torrão*—30km *Ferreira do Alentejo*—23km *Aljustrel*—N263. 58km *Odemira*.

We follow the N380 SW from Évora.

After 11km a right turn leads shortly to the *Quinta de Valverde*, or *Mitra*, once a country seat of the archbishops of Évora, where the church of the Capuchin monastery founded in 1544, known as that of *Bom Jesus*, is of considerable architectural interest, in spite of its diminutive size, its longest dimension being merely 6.5m. It has been ascribed to both Manuel Pires and Diogo de Torralva, the latter being more likely.

Its plan consists of five domed octagons separated by four squares, with eight free-standing marble columns supporting the central dome, with its clerestory, and 24 others abutting the walls. Admission should be requested at the adjacent house.
Beyond the village of Valverde is the chapel of *São Brissos*, abutting a megalithic tomb (cf. Pavia).

On regaining the main tree-lined road, we continue SW.—Beyond the second railway crossing a road leads 12km SE to *Viana do Alentejo*: see Rte 9A.

6km. *Alcáçovas*, an ancient town, which gave its name to the peace treaty with Spain of 1479, preserving the palace of its counts, and that of the Barahonas, with curious towers, and a Manueline hall-church.—3km to the W is the 16C chapel of *N.S. da Esperança*, a relic of a Dominican monastery, with azulejos of interest.

12.5km. *Torrão*, near the head of the Xarrama reservoir, the birthplace of the poet Bernardim Ribeiro (1482–1552), preserves slight Roman remains, and a small Manueline church containing 16C azulejos.

Hence we turn S past (17km) *Odivelas*, near the dam of another reservoir, to approach (13km) *Ferreira do Alentejo*; see Rte 12. Continuing S, after 23km we reach **Aljustrel**, a very ancient town, whose copper-mines were known at least as early as Roman times, but which—apart from its small *Museu da Mina*, with archaeological collections—is of slight interest.

The N2 bears S to *Faro*: see Rte 12.

We continue SW on the N263, beyond *Messejana* descending into the upper valley of the Sado, and rising again, reach (35km) cross-roads 3km beyond *Santa Luzia*.

FROM SANTA LUZIA TO PORTIMÃO VIA THE SERRA DE MONCHIQUE (84km). The left-hand turn leads S to (8km) *São Martinho das Amoreiras*, whence bearing SW, after c 20km we reach *Santa Clara-a-Velha* and a bridge over the Rio Mira. Immediately beyond, a road to the left leads to the huge reservoir—Barragem de Santa Clara—overlooked by the *Pousada de Santa Clara*. The main road shortly commences to climb into the thickly wooded Serra to the high-lying village of (32km) **Monchique**, the *Igreja Matriz* of which has a Manueline portal. To the SE rises the peak of *Picota* (774m; view); and to the W a road ascends to the summit of *Fóia* (902m), the highest of the range, climbed by young Southey in 1801, and providing extensive panoramic *Views*.—Another road turns right off the main road a few kms S, skirting the upper slopes of the Serra to *Marmelete*.—We descend past *Caldas de Monchique*, the waters of which—known to the Romans and Moors—João II took in 1495 in a vain attempt to relieve his dropsy, soon after which he died. The road continues to descend the S slope of the Serra (views) to (11km) *Porto do Lagos* (some 11km E of which is *Silves*); *Portimão* is 7km beyond that: see Rte 13.

From this road junction we proceed SW over a bare ridge providing distant views to the W towards the Atlantic, and gently descend to (23km) *Odemira*, on the Rio Mira, where we meet the N120 from Lisbon to *Lagos*: see Rte 11, below.

11   Lisbon to Lagos via Santiago do Cacém

Total distance, 275km (171 miles). E4 auto-estrada to (51km) **Setúbal**—N10. 21km *Marateca* crossroads, there bearing right onto the N5 for (31km) **Alcácer do Sal**—N120. 48km **Santiago do Cacém**—52.5km *Odemira*—48km *Alfambras*—23.5km **Lagos**.

For the first 72km see the latter part of Rte 5A in reverse.

From the *Marateca* crossroads, the road to Alcácer is of slight interest, traversing low-lying sandy tracts and pine woods in the neighbourhood of the Sado estuary.

Alcácer do Sal lies on the N bank of the Rio Sado, with its rice-fields and salt-marshes. Once of considerable importance, it is no longer so.

Known to the Romans as *Urbs Imperatoria Salacia*, Alcácer was later a strong Moorish fortress (Qasr Abi Dānis), and Afonso Henriques was here wounded in an unsuccessful attempt to capture it soon after the fall of Lisbon. After repeated assaults it was taken in 1158, but fell into Almohad hands in 1191. It was eventually retaken after a long siege in 1217, with the help of a contingent of crusaders who had anchored off the estuary, and was handed over to the Order of São Tiago. It was the birthplace of the mathematician Pedro Nunes (c 1492–c 1577).

The ruined Moorish *Castle* in the upper town encloses a Romanesque church *(Santa Maria)*, near which are the gypsy-infested ruins of the *Convent of Aracoeli* (founded 1573). Below the castle lies the Renaissance church of *Santo António* (1524), while in the former church of *Espírito Santo*, in which Manuel I married his second wife in 1500, a small archaeological collection has been installed.—About 1km to the W is the Gothic church of *Senhor dos Mártires*, with an octagonal chapel of 1333, near which is a pre-Roman burial-ground.

For the road hence to *Faro* see Rte 12.

The straight and monotonous road proceeds due S through undulating pine forests. Bearing right 5km prior to *Grândola* (see Rte 8), we follow a new road built to approach *Sines* (see below), which avoids the SERRA DE GRÂNDOLA. We regain the old road some 11km N of Santiago do Cacém.

Santiago do Cacém (*Pousada de São Tiago*) is pleasantly sited on a hill slope dominated by its ruined Moorish *Castle*, rebuilt by the Templars, the walls of which now enclose a cemetery (views). On an adjacent hill to the N, a turning (right) off the Lisbon road not far from the *Pousada* leads shortly to the extensive ruins of Roman *Merobriga* (or *Miróbriga*), only partly excavated, commanding a fine view E towards Beja, the castle keep of which may be discerned in clear weather.

23km SW of Santiago do Cacém is **Sines**, some 50 years ago described as 'a remote little town', with a sheltered fishing harbour, its only claims to fame being as the birthplace of Vasco da Gama (1469–1524) and the port from which Dom Miguel sailed to exile after the Convention of Évora Monte in 1834. It has recently been transformed into a tanker terminus, the flourishing centre of vast new oil refineries (Petrosul), the whole area being wreathed with pipelines and new roads, making it a sinister tubular jungle into which only the most intrepid traveller will want to penetrate.

From Santiago we continue S to (22.5km) *Tanganheira*, some 13km to the W of which is the small fishing harbour of *Porto Covo*, off which is the islet of *Pessegueira*, with the ruins of a fort and old church.

7km. *Cercal*.

Hence the N390 bears SW to (15km) *Vila Nova de Milfontes*, at the mouth of the Rio Mira, once an important harbour on this coast, with a striking *Castle*, which was once sacked by Algerian pirates and 'half converted into a poor dwelling house' in Southey's day; and when the poet broke a drinking glass at the estalagem here, he was told that they would have to send to Lisbon for another! Hence we can now cross the estuary of the Mira to regain the main road 23km SE.

23km. **Odemira**, re-peopled by Afonso III in 1252. A Count of Odemira (died 1661) was tutor to the ungovernable young Afonso VI. The town is pleasantly sited on the Rio Mira, but of slight interest in itself. Here we cross the river and ascend steeply up the S side of the valley, later reaching a ridge providing views, which we follow to (23km) *Odeceixe*, the first village in the Algarve. The river here separating it from the Alentejo could only be crossed 'in a square boat pulled by a rope', when Southey passed this way in 1801. We cross by the bridge and climb through a district of wild geraniums, with views to the E towards the SERRA DE MONCHIQUE, before descending to low-lying (18.5km) *Aljezur*, conquered in 1246. The ruins of a Moorish castle crown the hill. When Francisco Gomes de Avelar, Bishop of Algarve (1739–1816) began to build a church on higher and healthier ground to the E, the locals weren't interested, and at his death the project was abandoned.

6.5km. *Alfambras*, where we bear left across a shoulder of the SERRA DE MONCHIQUE to (23.5km SE) **Lagos**: see Rte 13.

FROM ALFAMBRAS TO LAGOS VIA SAGRES (70km). The right-hand fork (N268) leads through lonely country broken up by humpy hills to *Carrapateira*, protected by a ruined fort, close to the sea, and on to (27km) *Vila do Bispo*, before 1515 known as *Santa Maria do Cabo*, once of importance, but severely damaged in the 1755 earthquake. Its church (rarely open) is said to contain good 18C azulejos. Hence the road continues SW to *Sagres*.

Sagres (*Pousada do Infante*), a windswept resort among rocks and dunes, lies to the left of a T-junction, ahead of which stands an old fort and more modern 'rosa do ventos' (wind-compass). It preserves a house claiming to have been occupied by Prince Henry the Navigator, but this was more certainly at Cape St. Vincent, 5km to the W. This, known as *Vila do Infante*, was sacked by Drake in 1597 and further damaged in the earthquake of 1755. Here Henry founded a school of navigation and set up an observatory, and here he died in 1460, after which the place decayed, with the centre of maritime studies moving to Lisbon.

There remain on ***Cape St. Vincent** (Cabo São Vicente) a ruined 16C monastery and a lighthouse. This barren SW extremity of mainland Europe is certainly majestic in its desolation. On three sides of its high rocky promontory the Atlantic heaves.

This *Promontorium Sacrum* of the Romans takes its present name from the legend that the relics of the martyred St. Vincent were brought here in the 8C, whence, guarded by ravens, they were in 1173 miraculously translated to Lisbon. Several naval engagements have been fought off this cape, among others the defeat of Sir George Rooke by Admiral Tourville (1693). Here Rodney attacked a Spanish fleet in 1780; while on 14 February 1797 Admiral Jervis (later Lord St. Vincent) and Nelson with 15 vessels defeated 27 Spanish men-of-war; Sir Charles Napier defeated a small Miguelite squadron here in 1833 during the War of the Two Brothers.

Returning to *Vila do Bispo*, we fork E onto the N125 through *Raposeira*, where the 'Infante de Sagres' (Henry the Navigator) resided before setting up his headquarters at Vila do Infante, 'being remote from the tumult of people and propitious for the contemplation of study'. The hermitage of *N.S. de Guadalupe*, with interesting capitals, dates from the 13C. The dull road, which runs parallel to the coast, off which a number of resorts such as *Praia da Luz* may be approached, leads E to (23km) *Lagos*, a good view of which we obtain from crossroads overlooking the town from the W.—For **Lagos** itself, see Rte 13.

12 Lisbon to Faro via Ferreira do Alentejo

Total distance, 310km (192 miles). E4 auto-estrada to (51km) **Setúbal**—N10. 21km *Marateca* crossroads, there bearing right onto the N5 for (31km) **Alcácer do Sal**—34km *Torrão*—N2. 30km *Ferreira do Alentejo*—23km *Aljustrel*—23km *Castro Verde*—21km *Almodôvar*—44km *Barranco do Velho*—13.5km *São Brás de Alportel*—18.5km **Faro**.

An alternative to the road from Alcácer to Ferreira via Torrão is that via *Grândola*, described in reverse in Rte 8.

For the first 72km of this route see the latter part of Rte 5A, in reverse; and from the *Marateca* crossroad to *Alcácer*, Rte 11.

At *Alcácer do Sal* we turn E parallel to the N bank of the Sado, after some 20km bearing away to the NE past the Xarrama reservoir, to *Torrão*, for which, and for the road hence via *Ferreira* to *Aljustrel*, see Rte 10. Those wishing to drive direct to the E end of the Algarve can turn E at *Ferreira* to (25km) *Beja*, there following Rte 9A SE to *Vila Real de Santo António*.

From *Aljustrel* we continue due S to (23km) **Castro Verde**, a well-sited agricultural centre of ancient origin, where the *Igreja Matriz* contains azulejos of 1713 depicting the Battle of Ourique, while the *Igreja das Chagas* preserves some 17C azulejos of Dutch inspiration.

The battle of the **Campo de Ourique** may have taken place near, but its site is in dispute; the present consensus of informed opinion is that it was fought at *Chão de Ourique*, near Santarém. Here on 25 July 1139 Afonso Henriques defeated no less than five Moorish 'kings', afterwards adopting as his coat of arms their five shields ('as cinco quinas'), each charged with the five wounds of Christ, in memory of a vision of the Crucifixion which he had the night before the engagement, which was probably little more than a successful raid into enemy-occupied territory.

FROM CASTRO VERDE TO ABUFEIRA (117km). This alternative road to the central Algarve is followed by turning SW to (14km) the village of *Ourique*. Some 6.5km beyond, on the N264, a track leads c 4km right to the Luso-Roman camp of *Castro dos Palheiros* or *da Cola*, now on the bank of the Santa Clara reservoir, and surrounded by a rectangular walled enclosure.—Regaining the main road, we soon start to ascend between the E foothills of the SERRA DE MONCHIQUE and the SERRA DO CALDEIRÃO to (40km) *São Marcos de Serra*, and then SE to (15km) *São Bartolomeu de Messines*. This village, 1km W of the road, has a late 14C church containing spiral columns and a carved marble pulpit.—After 4km a left-hand turn leads 6km to *Alte*, where the 16C church preserves interesting early azulejos.—There are some bat-haunted stalactite caves in the neighbourhood known as the *Buraco dos Mouros* and the *Igrejinha dos Soudos*.—Continuing S on the N270, we by-pass (left) *Paderne*, with a ruined Moorish *Castle* captured in 1248, before reaching the N125 crossroads (see Rte 13) 22km S of São Bartolomeu.—5km beyond lies *Albufeira*; see p 193.

Our route continues due S from Castro Verde to (21km) *Almodôvar*, where the church in the main square has an interesting Manueline window, and commences to climb over the round-backed SERRA DO CALDEIRÃO, providing extensive views, before reaching (57.5km) **São Brás de Alportel**, passing (right) the *Pousada de São Brás*, with a good seaward view, before descending to the town.

For the cross road from the N125 via *Loulé* to *Tavira* see p 193.

The only monument of note between São Brás and the coast is at (7km) *Estoi*, where just SE of the crossroads a turning (left) leads immediately to the ruins of *Milreu, Roman *Ossonoba*, apparently destroyed after the 8C. It was visited by Southey in 1801, but most of the 2–6C ruins were not excavated until 1876; these include a temple converted into a Paleo-Christian basilica, and 3C baths ornamented with mosaics. Some of the latter, and other finds from this site may be seen in the gardens of the neighbouring *Palace of the Condes de Carvalhal*, Viscondes de Estoi (18C, with 19C additions; but private property); see also the Museum at Faro.

Continuing S we shortly reach the sprawling outer suburbs of **Faro**: see Rte 13.

13 Lagos to Faro and Vila Real de Santo António: the Algarve

Total distance, 133km (83 miles). N125. 18km **Portimão**—8km **Silves** lies 6.5km N.—21km **Albufeira** lies 5km S.

8km. The N270 (inland road) forks left via (13km) **Loulé** and (13.5km) *São Brás de Alportel* to (22km) **Tavira**.

4km after this turning, *Vilamoura* lies 5km SE.—21km **Faro**—8km *Olhão*—22.5km **Tavira**—22.5km *Vila Real de Santo António*.

LAGOS (10,000 inhab.), the most westerly town of any consequence on the Algarve, and once its capital (from 1578 to 1755), lies on the W bank of an estuary sheltered from the SW by the promontory of *Ponta da Piedade*. It has a fishing port and sardine-canning factories, and in recent years has been developed as a holiday resort.

The successor of Roman *Lacobriga* was by-passed by the Crusaders in 1189, who rather than attacking the Moorish capital at Silves, proceeded to sack the adjacent stronghold of Alvor. Lagos itself was not captured from the Moors until 1241. It later became a favourite residence of Prince Henry the Navigator (see Sagres), who here formed a company for trading with the newly discovered African territories; while in 1574 and 1578 it was one of the main ports of assembly for the ill-fated expeditions of Dom Sebastião.

A decline set in after it was laid in ruins during the 1755 earthquake. It was off the coast here that in 1759 Admiral Boscawen defeated a French squadron commanded by De La Clue, who lost five ships. It was visited by Southey in 1801, who was arrested for not having 'waited on' the Corregedor on his arrival. Here he bought a work-bag of aloe-fibre for his wife as a curiosity: one of the first tourists to patronise the local handicraft industry!

Stretches of the old *Walls* are preserved close to the Av. dos Descobrimentos, skirting the waterfront, more so at the seaward end, where they are set off by gardens, its defensive towers on its landward side well seen from the main road climbing to the S of the town. Near here is the *Aqueduct* of 1490–1521, and a fort. Overlooking the harbour is the *Fort of Pau da Bandeira*.

In the PRAÇA DA REPÚBLICA, half-way along the promenade, is the old *Custom House*, below the arches of which African slaves were once auctioned, and the church of *Santa Maria*, with its Manueline windows, from which it is said Dom Sebastião harangued his troops in June 1578 before embarking on the disastrous Moroccan campaign.

Beyond (left) is the *Chapel of Santo António of c 1710–20, richly embellished with carved and gilt woodwork above *albarrada* azulejos. The painted vault was added after the 1755 earthquake, probably replacing a ceiling of framed paintings. Here too is the grave of Hugh Beatty (died 1789), a colonel of the Irish Regiment.

Adjacent is the local *Museum*, containing very miscellaneous collections, the most interesting of which are those of ethnography and archaeology, deserving more scholarly attention.

Turning right along the Rua de Silva Lopes—less narrow than many of the lanes leading off it—we reach the Largo de Marquês de Pombal, and just beyond, the Praça Gil Eanes, in the town centre.

There are some curious rock formations S of the town, beyond the *Ponta da Piedade*. For the longer excursion to Sagres and Cape St. Vincent see the last section of Rte 11, in reverse.

Leaving Lagos, after 5.5km we traverse *Odeáxere*, some 8km NW of which is the attractively sited Odeáxere reservoir.

9km. Some 4km to the SW is *Alvor*, an ancient port assumed to be the Carthaginian *Portus Hannibalis*, sacked and plundered by a crusading fleet in 1189, when some few thousand Moors who had taken refuge there were massacred. Here died João II in 1495, after taking the waters at Caldas de Monchique in a futile attempt to obtain relief for his dropsy. It has a good Manueline church. There are slight remains of Roman origin at *Abidaca*, on a slope to the E.—Hence a minor road leads directly E to (5km) *Praia da Rocha*, see below.

3.5km. **PORTIMÃO** (previously *Vila Nova de Portimão*; 19,600 inhab.), a fishing port with canning factories, and a growing resort, lies on the estuary of the Arade, where in July 1189 another force of crusaders (including some English), led by Sancho I, landed to besiege Silves (see below). Most of its older buildings were destroyed in the 1755 earthquake. The river mouth is defended by two old forts.

On the W side lies the popular resort of **Praia da Rocha**, well-known for the strangely shaped rocks and caves of this indented coast, and for its sandy beaches.

4km. *Estombar*, birthplace in 1031 of the poet Ibn 'Ammār, with a Manueline church containing a curiously carved column, 4km beyond which, at *Lagoa*, a left turn leads 6.5km N to Silves.

SILVES, once, as *Shalb*, the capital of the kingdom of Algarve, lies on the N bank of the river Arade, crossed by a new bridge parallel to the old. We get the best view from the S bank, but the town retains little but its walls, the ruined red sandstone castle, and the cathedral, to remind one of its illustrious past.

The Arab chronicler Idrisi reported that it was protected by a strong wall, possessed a port and shipyards, and was 'of fine appearance, with attractive buildings and well-furnished bazaars. Its inhabitants are Yemenite Arabs and others, who speak pure Arabic, compose poetry, and are eloquent in speech and elegant in manners, both the upper and the lower classes'. In the mid 12C it was the centre of Ibn Qasi's revolt against the Almoravids.

In 1189, after a terrible three-month siege by Sancho I, assisted by Crusaders, some of them English, the starving citizens opened their gates to the Christians, who proceeded to sack the place, but by 1191 it was again in Moorish hands, who were not finally driven out until c 1249.

A decline set in with the silting up of the river-port, and in 1755 what remained of the then depopulated city was severely damaged in the earthquake, so much so that it was described a century later as 'one of the most desolate and deserted places in Portugal'.

We approach the upper town through a *Moorish Gate* in the *Walls*, which themselves deserve inspection, to reach the **Cathedral** of dark sandstone. Until 1579 the city was a bishopric, then transferred to Faro. In 1596 the building was apparently sacked by Essex, and it has been largely spoilt by restorations since the earthquake. Its W Portal, flanked by two towers, the plain octagonal piers, and vaulted chancel are its main architectural features of any interest. It was probably erected on the site of a mosque. —Above stands the Moorish *Castle*, 'the colour of congealed blood' as clinically described by Sarah Bradford. Its interior, now laid out with gardens, contains little of interest apart from the huge vaulted cisterns, but its parapet walk commands pleasant views of the orange and almond orchards in the vicinity.

11km. *Alcantarilha*, reputed for its tangerines.—3km S lies *Armação de Pera*, a small resort near more denticulated rocks; on the E bank of its estuary is an 18C fort.—From adjacent *Pera* one may follow a minor road directly to (9km) *Albufeira*, the main road to which turns right 10km E of Alcantarilha. The left-hand turn leads 23km N to *São Bartolomeu de Messines*: see p 191.

Albufeira, now a popular resort, preserves the remains of a Moorish *Castle*; while from the lower town the beach is reached by a tunnel pierced in 1935. There are some curious rock outcrops and caves in the vicinity.

8km. *Boliqueime* lies to the left of the road. It is said that Henry the Navigator made his first plantations of sugar-canes here, which he had introduced from Cyprus; they were later transplanted to Madeira, and Brazil.

The INLAND ROAD (N270) to (48.5km) *Tavira* forks left here, climbing up to (13km) *Loulé*, a well-sited and thriving town, preserving some remains of its Moorish ramparts, and an interesting 13C *Igreja Matriz* (behind the large market), recently restored. The old open-work chimneys of Loulé are curious, but are perhaps better seen in some of the smaller towns and villages of the Algarve.—The busy road, providing occasional sea views, continues E to

(13.5km) *São Brás de Alportel* (see p 191), later descending to the coast at (22km) *Tavira*: see below.

4km beyond this turning, a road to the right leads to the coast at **Vilamoura,** where adjacent to the extensively developed resort of *Quarteira* the important excavations of a large **Roman villa* may be seen: work in the area is continuing. Hence one may follow a maze of lanes flanked by modern villas among the trees to regain the main road to the NE.

10km beyond the village of *Almansil* we pass (left) the church of **São Lourenço*, the interior of which, including the dome, is entirely covered with blue azulejos of 1730, attributed to Policarpo de Oliveira Bernardes.

10km. **FARO** (28,200 inhab.; airport), the most southerly town in Portugal, and prosperous capital of the Algarve, while long famous for its figs and almonds, cannot on any account be considered a city of much architectural attraction, preserving few relics of antiquity and no modern buildings of any consequence.

Probably of Moorish origin, for the Roman city of *Ossonoba* lies some 8km to the N, Faro (also known as *Santa Maria de Harune*) was taken by Afonso III in 1249, and increased in prosperity, having a large Jewish colony, who in the 15C established a printing-press here. In 1596, when under Spanish domination, an English force under the Earl of Essex, finding Loulé and Faro deserted, sacked and burnt the latter, but he had the forethought to carry off the well-bound theological library of some 200 volumes (already mutilated by the Inquisition) belonging to Bp Osorio (known as the 'Portuguese Cicero'), and later gave the indigestible tomes to the Bodleian Library, which was considered a generous gesture from a Cambridge man. The city again suffered severely in the earthquakes of 1722 and 1755, and its rebuilding was largely due to its energetic bishop, Francisco Gomes de Avelar (1739–1816).

The only area of interest in the straggling modern town is the walled enceinte (*'Vila-a-Dentro'*), just SE of the harbour (*doca*) and yacht basin, with a *Maritime museum* to the N. It is not the easiest part to approach, owing to a confusing system of one-way streets.

Ferries to the resort of *Praia de Faro*, on a sand-spit to the SW, leave from a terminus just S of the harbour. This beach is one of a number of such sand bars S of Faro, the *Cabo de Santa Maria*, with a lighthouse, being the southernmost extremity of Portugal.

The old town is entered from the adjacent *Jardim Manuel Bivar* by the 18C *Arco da Vila*, with a statue of St. Thomas Aquinas, beyond which we shortly reach the **Cathedral** or *Sé*, a Renaissance building damaged in earthquakes, preserving a squat 13C tower of an older church. The interior, embellished with azulejos, contains the 18C tomb of Bp Pereira da Silva, supported by two lions, a 17C altar in the Sacristy, and a red and gilt Chinoiserie organ painted in 1751 by Francisco Cordeiro.—The old *Episcopal palace* lies to the W.

Facing a small square just S of the cathedral apse is the *Convent of N.S. da Assunção* (1539), recently well restored and transformed into a **Museum**, most of the rooms of which surround its attractive two-storeyed cloister by Afonso Pires. Notice the roof (cf. Tavira).

The archaeological collections are important, including Roman remains from *Ossonoba*, a mosaic being prominent. The church contains a 14C Nottingham alabaster. The paintings, among them Four Doctors of the Church by Vieira Portuense, are of less interest. Note also the 16C chest (? from Goa) of mother of pearl (*madrepérola*), and some Mudéjar azulejos.

Turning to the right on making our exit, we pass through the old *Arco de Repouso* and bear diagonally across a deserted square to reach, adjacent to barracks, the 17C church of *São Francisco*, preserving azulejos of 1762 and a richly gilt Capela-Mór.

Hence, bearing due N, we approach the PRAÇA ALEXANDRE HER-CULANO and, just beyond, the Rua de Santo António (a continuation of one of the main thoroughfares). Immediately to the right is the *Ethnographical Museum*, with interesting displays of models of chimneys, costumes, old photographs, and a room devoted to the fishing industry, and basketwork, etc.

The street is continued by the tree-lined AV. 5 DE OUTUBRO, beyond the far end of which is the high-lying chapel of *Santo António do Alto,* commanding the best view of Faro and its lagoon.

Some minutes' walk to the NW of the latter museum, via the Ruas Vasco da Gama and José Estêvão, brings us to *São Pedro* (16C; rebuilt), which escaped the fire of 1596, containing a well-painted polychromed and gilt Last Supper.—Behind the church is the LARGO DO CARMO, dominated by the two belfries of its early 18C church, with an attractive 18C organ, and a macabre ossuary.

For *Estoi*, 8km N, see the latter part of Rte 12.

Continuing E, at 8km we pass (right) **Olhão** (19,800 inhab.), the older cubist quarters of the fishing port being engulfed by recent development. It was one of the first towns in the Algarve to rise against the French in 1808, and it is said that fishermen from here conveyed the news of their expulsion to João VI in Brazil.

16km. *Luz*, where the church preserves a good Manueline portal, shortly beyond which we enter the W outskirts of *Tavira*.

TAVIRA, although damaged during the 1755 earthquake, remains one of the pleasantest towns on the Algarve, and was so described by J.M. Neale in the 1850s. It lies in well-cultivated country on the river Gilão, spanned by a 17C bridge in the town centre, and lined by 18C houses with unusual Oriental-looking triple-gabled tiled roofs. It is an important tunny-fishing port, but the *copejo*, or sanguinary slaugh-tering of the tunny shoals in the estuary during the summer is one of its less pleasant aspects. It has a reputation for its figs and almonds, and its mullet are particularly succulent.

Although a 1C Greek inscription has been found in the vicinity, Tavira's early history is vague. It may have been Roman *Balsa*. It was captured from the Moors in 1239 by Paio Peres Correa, and raised to the rank of a city in 1520. With the silting up of the port (dredged in 1932), and visitations of plague, a decline set in, but it was briefly reputed for its tapestries in the late 18C.

From the arcaded central PRAÇA DA REPÚBLICA (whose medieval arches have been replaced by modern copies) adjacent to riverside gardens, we may ascend into the old walled town, shortly passing the church of the *Misericórdia*, with a fine portal of 1541 and well-carved altar-mór. Beyond (left), adjacent to the ruins of the *Castle*, is the church of *Santa Maria do Castelo*, traditionally on the site of a mosque, rebuilt after 1755, with a 13C Gothic doorway. In its chancel are the tombs of Correa (died 1275; see History), and an inscription recording the 'Sete Caçadores', seven Christian knights treacher-ously slain by the Moors during a truce, while they were out hunting. Their deaths precipitated the final successful assault on the town.

Hence we continue E, after (5km) *Conceição*, whose church preserves its Gothic portal, obtaining intermittent sea views as we proceed parallel to the coast, shortly by-passing *Cacela*, whose church has a fine Renaissance door, a decayed port of ancient origin where the

Duque da Terceira disembarked in June 1833 with 2500 men before his march on Lisbon, which was abandoned by the Miguelites on 24 July.

We also pass a road leading right to *Monte Gordo*, a recently developed resort, before reaching (17.5km) *Vila Real*.

Vila Real de Santo António at the mouth of the Guadiana facing *Ayamonte* (see *Blue Guide Spain*), to and from which plys a regular car and passenger ferry (Customs). There is a project to build an international *Bridge* across the Guadiana here, which will improve communications. *Seville* is 163km due E of Ayamonte.

The place was run up in some five months in 1774 by Pombal near the site of *Santo António de Arenilha*, an ancient town, possibly a Phoenician settlement, which had been engulfed by the sea c 1600. The 'new' town is laid out on the rectangular grid plan he had chosen for the rebuilding of the Baixa quarter in Lisbon, and apparently all the ashlar used in its construction was brought here from Lisbon at a ruinous expense, *after* which some stone quarries were 'discovered' only a few miles distant!

Apart from a small museum devoted to printing, there is little to see in Vila Real, which is important as a tunny-canning centre, and for the export of the copper ore of *São Domingos* (see p 185).

For *Castro Marim*, and roads hence to *Mértola*, *Beja* and *Serpa*, see Rte 9A and B, in reverse.

14   Elvas to Portalegre and Castelo Branco

Total distance, 150km (93 miles). 19km *Campo Maior*—N371. 27km *Arronches*—N246. 23km **Portalegre**—N18. *Alpalhão*—12km *Nisa*—17.5km *Ródão*—28.5km **Castelo Branco**.

Although the direct road (N426) from Elvas N to *Arronches* is 14km shorter, the more interesting route is that via *Campo Maior* to the NE, which, an old frontier town, was the centre of Wellington's defensive position in 1811-12 facing Badajoz. The left flank was at *Ouguelo*, some 8km beyond, with a ruined castle of 1310 (Views); while there is an Iron Age site at *Castro de Segóvia*, 5km S.

Campo Maior, of Roman origin, was taken from the Moors in 1219. In 1310 it was fortified, but the *Castle* was enlarged at a later date, and provided with Vaubanesque outworks under the direction of Nicolas de Langres.

In 1732 its powder magazine was struck by lightning, the explosion not only destroying most of the citadel, but also numerous houses, and killing 1500 people. Nevertheless, during the Peninsular War it successfully withstood minor attacks. The position was strong but unpleasant, according to commissary Schaumann, who was stationed here, for 'All day long we were infested by snakes, blowflies, and other vermin, while our water came from a dirty stream known as the River Caya, in which the whole army bathed, the cattle went to drink, and dirty clothes were washed. At night we were plagued with scorpions, mosquitoes, and a piercingly cold wind'.

Its two churches are of slight interest; and the river Caia has now been dammed to form a reservoir to the W of the town.

We bear NW, with views to the E, to approach (27km) *Arronches*, the Roman *Plagiaria*, which (like *Assumar*, 9km W, Roman *Ad Septem Aras*), with ruined walls, lay on the Roman road from Mérida to Lisbon, and the area was then perhaps more populous.—*Alegrete*, c

12km N of Arronches, preserves the ruins of an early 14C castle on the site of an earlier fortress.

We continue NW, parallel to the Serra de São Mamede, to approach (23km) **PORTALEGRE** (14,800 inhab.), capital of the Alto Alentejo, and since 1545 an episcopal city, standing at the foot of the SERRA DE SÃO MAMEDE, the highest range in Portugal S of the Tagus. The district was well described by Huldine Beamish in her study, 'The Hills of Alentejo' (1958).

Although of Roman foundation and known as *Amoea*, its long history has been unexceptional. It was besieged for five months in 1299 by Dom Dinis during the dynastic feuds of the period, and suffered a shorter Spanish siege in 1704, when Stanhope's regiment was captured. During the Peninsular War it was often the winter quarters of British troops: military bands would play in the outer courts of nunneries to entertain their inmates; races were organised; and occasional hunts took place between here and Castelo de Vide.

The walled city, retaining a few old mansions, stands on a height to the SW, dominated by its **Cathedral**, with its twin pinnacled towers, commenced in 1556, but mainly of the 18C. It is a plain building, with massive pilasters. Its architectural retables (c 1590) are by Gaspar and Domingos Coelho, with paintings possibly by Simão Rodrigues. Also notable are the azulejos in the *Sacristy*, and the pediment to its *Cloister*.

Adjacent to the cathedral is the *Municipal Museum*, pleasantly installed in one of the few remaining 18C mansions of Portalegre, containing small collections of furniture, ceramics, fans, silver snuff-boxes, a Chinese silver tea service, worn Arraiolos carpets, and paintings and sketches by Abel Santos.—To the N is the yellow *Palace of the Abrancalhas* (*Palácio Amarelo*), in a poor state of repair, but preserving ornate 17C ironwork.

There is a good small museum in the house of the poet José Régio, a short distance SE of the old town centre, with collections of folk art, crucifixes, ironwork, etc.

Perhaps the most impressive monument surviving is to be seen in the *Convent of N.S. da Conceição**, some minutes' walk to the E of the LARGO A.J. LOURINHA, the main square of the lower town to the N. The convent (also known as that of *São Bernardo*), now in the hands of a training school for military police (who on application at the gate will courteously escort visitors round), was founded in 1518 by Jorge de Melo, Bp of Guarda, whose *Tomb* (c 1540), attributed to Chanterène or a pupil, is seen in the church. The building itself, with a good portal of 1538 in its porch, is decorated with very fine *azulejos* of 1739; it preserves two cloisters, not improved by the military presence.

The town contains cork factories, among them that developed by George Wheelhouse Robinson in the late 19C; and once with a reputation for its textiles, it retains in an abandoned Jesuit convent of 1695 a much-publicised Tapestry factory, but it is of slight interest.

Crato, see Rte 15A, lies 21km due W of Portalegre.

FROM PORTALEGRE TO MARVÃO (22km). The direct road (N359) forks to the right off the N246 just N of Portalegre, shortly climbing over the SERRA DE SÃO MAMEDE, off which, some 12km N, at *Aramenha*, is the site of Roman *Medobriga*, but most of its scanty remains have been removed to Lisbon. We descend to meet the main road from the Spanish frontier some 7.5km SE of *Castelo de Vide*, and 6km S of *Marvão*, crowning its mountain: for both see Rte 16.

A slightly longer road (29km) climbs due E from Portalegre, off which a track to the right leads up to the summit of the range (1025m), commanding extensive

Views.—Castelo de Vide can also be approached by continuing N on the N246
(off which a minor road crosses the Serra) after 18km reaching the main road
3.5km W of the town.

We follow the N18 NW through (23km) *Alpalhão* to (12km) **Nisa**, with
remains of fortifications and gates; and 3km away, relics of the older
town, beyond which we traverse hillier country, before descending
steeply (Views) into the Tagus valley.

The river is crossed just E of the *Portas de Ródão*, where it forces its
way through a narrow gorge between high perpendicular cliffs, of
which the bridge commands a good view. The river crossing here was
of great importance during the Peninsular War, and provided with a
bridge of boats by Wellington. The Passage of the Tagus at this point
was reproduced in a number of contemporary drawings and
lithographs.

Vila Velha de Ródão, with remains of a castle, lies on the far bank.
It has a small *Museum* in the Largo do Pelourinho, partly devoted to
the important archaeological remains of the area, including copies of
Palaeolithic engravings from now-submerged sites on the banks of
the Tagus.

The road turns NE through the rolling country of the Beira Baixa,
with occasional distant views of the SERRA DA ESTRELA to the N
beyond the nearer SERRA DA GARDUNHA, to approach (28.5km)
Castelo Branco: see Rte 17.

15   Elvas to Abrantes

A.   Via Monforte, Alter do Chão, and
Ponte de Sor

Total distance, 130km (81 miles). 16km *Barbacena*—17km
Monforte—N369. 28km **Alter do Chão**—N369 and N119. 35km
Ponte de Sor—N2. 34km **Abrantes**.

Passing under the aqueduct, we follow the N246 briefly before
forking left for (16km) *Barbacena*, with remains of a 16C fortress,
beyond which we traverse rolling country to (17km) **Monforte**, with a
ruined *Castle* of 1309. It was the birthplace of Manuel Barradas
(1572–?), the Jesuit missionary.

We descend into a small valley dotted with chapels, and cross a
medieval bridge.

After c 4km from Monforte a left turn leads 1km to the well-sited
Quinta da Torre de Palma. A muddy track leads SW from its main
gate, and we approach the extensive remains of a *Roman Villa*,
Paleo-Christian basilica (c 4C), and burial-ground.

Regaining the main road, continue NW to (15km) *Cabeça de Vide*,
with ruins of a *Castle*, and, 9km beyond, **Alter do Chão**, of Roman
foundation, just N of crossroads. In the central square rises the
restored *Castle* of 1359; here also is seen the 18C *Solar de Vasconcelos*, and a Renaissance fountain.—Some 4km E, at *Alter Pedroso* is
another ruined fortress (Views); while 3km NW is the *Estação*

Zootécnica, replacing a stud farm established here in 1748 by João V.—For *Crato*, 11.5km N, see p 201.

We now turn due W.

At 9km the left-hand fork leads to (16km) *Avis* (see Rte 15B) via *Seda*, with relics of walls, later skirting the picturesque Ribeiro de Seda, now part of a reservoir.

The right-hand fork descends into the valley of the Seda, which after 3km we cross on the imposing six-arched *Roman Bridge of Vila Formosa*, beyond which we follow the Roman road to (23km) **Ponte de Sor**, now an important cork centre, and then bear NW to (34km) *Abrantes*: see Rte 16.

B.   Via Monforte and Avis

Total distance, 141km (87 miles). 33km **Monforte**—N18, which we follow to the SW for 4km, there turning right (no sign) onto the N243—16km *Fronteira* lies 1.5km N.—23km **Avis**—N224. 31km *Ponte de Sor*—N2. 34km **Abrantes**.

For the road to *Monforte*, see Rte 15A, above.

Turning SW hence, we follow an attractive road parallel to the S bank of the Ribeira Grande to (20km) *Fronteira*, founded in 1226 by the Master of the Order of Avis, Fernão Rodrigues Monteiro. Near here took place the battle of *Atoleiros* (1384), in which Nun' Álvares defeated a superior Spanish force (traditionally 'without loss'), the first engagement in the campaign terminating at Aljubarrota.

23km. **Avis**, a village attractively situated on a height above the confluence of the swollen Ribeiras de Avis and de Seda.

It was granted to the Spanish military order of Calatrava, known in Portugal as the Knights of Évora, in 1220, who built here a *Castle*, and settled in the area, becoming soon known as the Knights of Avis (or Aviz), and later as the Order of São Bento. João I (son of Pedro I and Teresa Lourenço) was Grand Master of the Order before he acceeded to the Portuguese throne in 1385 and married Philippa of Lancaster in 1387: the Avis dynasty survived until 1580.

The *Monastery of São Bento* was frequently transformed, the last time in 1711, but the church preserves a good Baroque retable, and a large 16C Sacristy; while three imposing towers remain of the original fortress.

The road bears NW to (31km) *Ponte de Sor* (see Rte 15A) and *Abrantes* (see Rte 16), 34km beyond.

16   (Cáceres) Valencia de Alcántara to Abrantes and Santarém, for Lisbon

Total distance, 178km (110 miles). 12km to the frontier at *Galegos* (Customs)—10km the Marvão crossroads: **Marvão** lies 6km to the N and *Portalegre* 16km to the SW.—7.5km **Castelo de Vide**—N246. 15.5km *Alpalhão*—N18. 33km *Gavião*—27km **Abrantes**—N3. 25km *Entroncamento* crossroads: **Tomar** lies 18.5km N, and *Goleaã* 7km S.—48km **Santarém**.

The start of the E3 auto-estrada for (52km) **Lisbon** is 26km SW of Santarém, approached by forking right at *Cartaxo*.

The main road (N521) from *Cáceres* to (96km) *Valencia de Alcántara* becomes slow and winding after (32km) *Aliseda*, and it is recommended to make a detour—11km longer—by turning off here onto the C521 for *Alburquerque*, 40km SW, there bearing NW on the C530 to (35km) *Valencia de Alcántara*: see *Blue Guide Spain*.

From Valencia we turn SW to the frontier at (12km) *Puerto Roque/Galegos* (Spanish and Portuguese Customs), situated in a narrow wooded valley between a serrated ridge of the SERRA DE SÃO MAMEDE and the SERRA DE MARVÃO (SW).

10km. The Marvão crossroads, on the approach to which we see the fortress of Marvão itself crowning a commanding height to the NW, which more than merits the ascent, unless visibility is bad.

A view of Marvão, drawn in the early 19C

Turning right at the crossroads, we climb steeply to (6km) ***Marvão** (*Pousada de Santa Maria*), a village of considerable attraction. The Marvão range was known to the Romans as *Herminius minor*, and this outcrop has been fortified from remote antiquity. Its 13C *Walls* remain practically intact, but outworks were added in the 17C. The *Castle* commands very extensive *Views (From the Tôrre of the Serra da Estrela to the NW, to Cáceres to the E). The church of the *Convent of N.S. da Estrela*, on the left as we approach the summit, founded in 1448, is of comparatively slight interest.

FROM MARVÃO TO ESTREMOZ VIA PORTALEGRE (77km). For roads from the Marvão crossroads to (16km) **Portalegre**, see p 197, in reverse. Hence we follow the N18 to (27.5km) **Monforte** (see Rte 15A), and (14km) *Veiros*, by-passed, with a church of 1559, and *Castle* of 1308, partly destroyed in 1662, 2km S of which is an Iron Age fortification. For **Estremoz**, 14km beyond, see Rte 5A.

7.5km. Castelo de Vide, an attractive and beautifully situated old spa on the slope of a spur of the SERRA DE SÃO MAMEDE, was possibly the birthplace of Garcia da Orta (1500–c 1570), the natural philosopher, physician, and traveller. The central PRAÇA DE DOM PEDRO V is flanked by the 17C *Torre Palace*, birthplace of José Xavier Mousinho da Silveira (1780–1849), the Liberal statesman (now a hospital), and the Baroque church of *Santa Maria*. Numerous smaller chapels, mansions (including the *Town Hall* of 1721), and fountains are to be found throughout the place, which also preserves its medieval *Judiaria*. The large *Castle*, successfully defended by an Anglo-Portuguese force against a Spanish incursion in June 1704, was seriously damaged by an explosion the following year. The chapel of *N.S. da Alegria* here is lined with 17C azulejos, more of which may be seen in *São Tiago*.

Dotted over an area to the N, between Castelo de Vide and Castelo Branco, are a number of circular stone edifices or 'beehive' huts, similar to those at the Citânia de Briteiros, known as *chafurdoēs*.

FROM CASTELO DE VIDE TO ESTREMOZ. There are two alternative routes, that turning left after 3.5km to (18km) **Portalegre**, see Rte 14, whence we follow the sub-route outlined above to (55km) **Estremoz**; or that via *Alpalhão*, 12km further W on the main route. Hence the N245 leads due S to (72km) Estremoz via *Crato*. We first reach (14km) the village of *Flor da Rosa*, with (right) the ruins of a large fortified *Convent founded by the prior Álvaro Gonçalves Pereira (father of Nun' Álvares) in 1356; the church, cloister, and chapter-house are being restored.—2km. **Crato**, an ancient little town, one of the headquarters or *Grão Priorado* of the Order of Crato, a branch of the Knights Hospitallers, transferred here from Leça do Bailio in 1350. The last of the Grand Priors was Dom António, in 1580 a rival to Philip II in his claim to the Portuguese throne. António (1531–95; died in Paris) was the bastard son of the Infante Luíz and Violante Gomes, known as 'the Pelican'. Little remains of the once powerful 13C *Castle*, destroyed in 1662 by Don Juan de Austria, but the *Igreja Matriz* (rebuilt in 1456, and later altered) contains some pleasant 18C azulejos, and good altars.—Hence the road climbs S, later passing (right) a tumulus, to enter (11.5km) *Alter do Chão* (see Rte 15A) and, 17km beyond, *Fronteira* (see Rte 15B).

We continue S past (11.5km) *Sousel* and (right) *Ameixial*, where in May 1663 Don Juan de Austria was decisively defeated by the Conde de Vilar Flor and Schomberg, with English troops under the command of Thomas Hood. It is said that Afonso VI, on hearing of the gallantry of the British troops, sent each company a present of snuff, which they threw away in disgust; while Charles II of England ordered 4000 crowns to be distributed among them.—16km. **Estremoz**; see Rte 5A.

15.5km. *Alpalhão*. For the road hence to *Nisa* and *Castelo Branco* see Rte 14.

We veer NW, and after 21km pass some 6km S of *Amieira*, with a 14C *Castle*, to approach the Tagus at (12km) *Gavião*.

6km to the N, on the far bank of the river, stand the ruins of the late 12C *Castle of Belver, restored in 1390, surrounded by round towers.—There are Roman bridges near *Mação*, 13km NW of Belver, and near *Envendos*, c 12km E of Mação.

11km. *Alvega*, an ancient village near which stood Roman *Aritium Vetus*, beyond which we reach *Rossio*, on the S bank of the Tagus opposite *Abrantes*, which we approach by a long bridge. There are some curious medieval towers and walls on the S side of the river near Rossio.

ABRANTES (5700 inhab.), well sited above the Tagus, is not a town of any great attraction, although always of strategic importance.

It resisted an Almohad attack in 1179; was a headquarters of João de Avis in 1385, prior to the battle of Aljubarrota; was captured by Gén Junot in 1807 in his advance on Lisbon (for which Napoleon created him Duc d'Abrantes); and was briefly Wellington's HQ before his march on Talavera in 1809, and remained an important base throughout the war, even passing into proverb: 'Tudo como dantes, Quartel General em Abrantes' ('Headquarters at Abrantes, Everything as before').

Near the hill top stands *Santa Maria do Castelo* (1215, but rebuilt in the mid 15C), now housing the *Museu Lopo de Almeida*, and containing the tombs of the Almeidas, counts of Abrantes, notably that of João de Almeida (died 1512), mid 16C paintings, 15C sculptures, and early Sevillian tiles, etc. The *Castle Keep* (1303) commands a wide view. Other churches which may be visited are *São Vicente*, a spacious 16–17C edifice; *São João Baptista*, founded in 1300 by Santa Isabel, but rebuilt in the 16C with a coffered ceiling; and that of the *Misericórdia* (16C).

At *Sardoal*, 10km NE of Abrantes, seven paintings by the 16C Master of Sardoal are said to be preserved in the church of *São Tiago e São Mateus*.

FROM ABRANTES TO SANTARÉM ALONG THE SOUTH BANK OF THE TAGUS, VIA ALPIARÇA (63km). We follow the N18 to the W, roughly parallel to the river, after some 15km passing near the picturesque *Castle of Almourol* (see below).—10.5km. A right turn leads across the river—here forded by a force under João de Avis in 1385 in the expectation of an invasion from the SE—to (5km) *Golegã*, its *Igreja Matriz* preserving a very fine *Manueline portal* with all the characteristic ornament of the period (1510–20), surmounted by a bull's eye window decorated with two armillary spheres, etc. The *Galeria Carlos Relvas* (a collection of early photographs), and a museum devoted to the sculptor Martins Correia may be visited. It is also the site of an important horse fair in mid November.—Regaining the S bank, after 4km we reach the market-town of *Chamusca* and, 17km beyond, **Alpiarça**.

The **Casa dos Patudos**, just S of the village, was the home of the politician and collector José Relvas (1858–1929), and is now a museum. Normally only open from 14.00–18.00 on Thursday, Sunday, and holidays, but if closed, apply to the Secretary of the Old Peoples' Home across the road, which Relvas also founded. One is guided round the very miscellaneous collection, which contains some items of interest, although some attributions are doubtful. Apart from numerous Arraiolos carpets (including a silk embroidered example of 1761); English grandfather clocks; objects concerned with Portuguese bull-fighting; Ceramics, and what not, among the paintings displayed throughout the house are: *Van Dyck* (?), Portrait of Anne of Austria; *anon*. Portrait of Domenico Scarlatti (said to be the only one known of the composer); *anon*. Portrait of Henriette of France; *dessus des portes* by *Vieira Portuense*; four panels by *Francisco Henriques* (fl. 1500–18); *anon*. Flemish Virgin; Portrait of a Young Man, *attributed* to *Reynolds*; works by *Silva Pôrto* (1850–93), and a painting of Silva Pôrto in his studio, by *Columbano* (1857–1929); representative works by *Carlos Reis* (1863–1940), *António Ramalho* (1859–1916), *Marquês d'Oliveira* (1852–1927), and *Alberto de Sousa* (died 1961); three Still lifes by *Josefa de Óbidos* (and also in the dining-room, some interesting azulejos); *School of Sanchez Coelho*, Portrait of Juana of Castile; Virgin and Child *attrib*. to *Perugino*; *Columbano*, Portrait of Carlos Relvas; *anon*. Tobias and the Fish; *anon*. Portrait of Pope Clement XIII; and examples of the art of *Constantino Fernandes* (1878–1920); and also in the Library, a collection of enamelled watch-cases.

Hence we cross the Tagus below *Santarém*, some 10km SW; see below.

The road continuing on the E bank of the river, following the N118 through (7km) *Almeirim* (see Rte 7) and (13.5km) *Muge*, where numerous Palaeolithic artefacts have been discovered, is of small interest.—12km. *Salvaterra de Magos*, a town damaged in an earthquake earlier this century, preserves the slight remains of the royal palace of the Avis dynasty. We cross the Rio Sorraia at (6km) *Benavente*, and reach the N10 9km beyond, there turning right for (9km; see Rte 18A) *Vila Franca de Xira*, on the far bank of the Tagus, 31km from **Lisbon** on the E3 auto-estrada.

From Abrantes we follow the high N bank of the Tagus to (13km) *Constância*, Roman *Pugni Tagi* (whence the name *Punhete*, by which it was known until 1836), at the confluence of the Zêzere and Tagus.

A right turn here ascends the left bank of the Zêzere to (8km) *Castelo de Bode*, and the *Pousada de São Pedro*, overlooking the huge reservoir here.—7km beyond the dam we meet the N110, and turn right for (7km) **Tomar**: see later part of Rte 18C.

Crossing the Zêzere, we shortly reach the important military and air base of *Tancos*, which played its part in the 1974 Revolution.

A lane to the left here leads shortly to a viewpoint overlooking the ***Castle of Almourol** on its picturesque island site, rebuilt in 1171 by Gualdim Pâis on the foundations of an earlier fortress. The tall central Torre de Menagem is surrounded by a rampart with nine other towers, including the square gate-tower on the S. A boat (*abrangel*) may be hired to circle the island.

It is referred to in the 16C romance of 'Palmeirim de Inglaterra', by Francisco de Moraes Cabral, which as translated by Southey, correcting Anthony Munday's Elizabethan version, was called 'Palmerin of England' (1807). An edition of the Portuguese original, edited by Agostinho José de Costa Macedo (1745–1822) had been published in 1786.

12km (from Constância) we reach the crossroads at *Entroncamento*. *Golegã* (see above) lies 7km to the SW.—**Tomar** (Rte 18C) is 17.5km to the N, approached via (2km) *Atalaia*, with a 16C church, its façade widened by buttresses. The rich Renaissance portal dates from c 1545, possibly by Chanterène, while the interior preserves some interesting azulejos, particularly those of angels playing contemporary musical instruments.

8km. We pass (right) **Torres Novas** (10,000 inhab.), a small industrial and agricultural town commanded by a ruined late 14C *Castle*, and with a *Misericórdia* preserving a Renaissance portal and azulejos of 1674. In the vicinity are the remains of the Roman villa of *Cardílio*. It was the birthplace of Carlos Reis (1863–1940), the artist.

Some 3km beyond, we reach a road junction. The right fork (N243) leads NW across the SERRA DE AIRE, providing extensive views beyond (8.5km) *Moitas*, to (31.5km) **Batalha**, via *Porto de Mós*: see p 227. The road later passes near the stalactite caves of *Santo Antonio* and *Alvados*.

The main road, bearing left, which we follow, after 16km traverses *Pernes*, once fortified, and 21km beyond, enters Santarém.

An attractive alternative road is that turning W via (10km) *Alcanena* (near which is the Bronze Age site of *Marmota*) to *Alcanede*, 19 km SW; see p 227

SANTARÉM (15,300 inhab.), on a commanding height overlooking the Tagus, and once one of the strongest fortresses in Portugal, is interesting more for its historical associations than for the majority of its surviving monuments. It is the capital of a rich agricultural district, site of the Ribatejo Fair in June, and the centre of Portuguese bull-fighting.

Roman *Scallabis*, dignified by Julius Caesar with the title of *Praesidium Julium*, and one of three *conventus* in Lusitania (the others being Mérida, and Beja), derives its present name from Santa Iria (Irene), a nun of Tomar, who, accused of unchastity, suffered martyrdom in 653. Her body (some say in its marble coffin) was flung into the Nabão, and after floating down the Tagus was here washed ashore, her innocence being then indisputably established by miraculous apparitions. They were a credulous lot, and were singled out in the proverb: 'Quem burro vai a Santarém, Burro vai e burro vem' (The ass who goes to Santarém, Ass he goes and ass returns). Others have suggested that this referred more specifically to the seminarists.

Santarém was a Moorish stronghold (*Shantariya*) from 715 to 1093, when it was taken by Alfonso VI of León, whose son-in-law (in 1095) called himself 'Lord of Galicia and Santarém'. But the Moors recaptured the place. It was not finally regained until 1147, by Afonso Henriques (who founded the Abbey of Alcobaça in gratitude), in a night attack. Sancho I held the place against a desperate attempt by the Almohads to reconquer it in 1181. In 1223 Afonso II died here, a leper, and excommunicate. Dom Dinis died at Santarém in 1325; and here were executed the murderers of Inês de Castro in 1357.

It was the scene of many gatherings of the Cortes in the 14–15Cs, being conveniently near *Almeirim*, a favourite summer residence of the Avis dynasty. In 1491 the Infante Dom Afonso, only son of João II, falling from his horse, was drowned in the Tagus here. In 1811 Masséna briefly held a line between Santarém and Rio Maior during his retreat from Torres Vedras, when it was sacked: '11 Convents and 8 Churches fell a Victim to the French, who have been guilty of the most wanton Mischief', recorded Captain William Bragge.

In 1833 it was the last stronghold of the reactionary Miguelites.

Among eminent *Scalebitanos* may be listed the poet Ibn Sāra (fl. 1095–1123); Fernão Lopes de Castanheda (c 1500–59), the historian; Frei Luís de Sousa (1555–1632), the chronicler; and the Marquês de Sá da Bandeira (1795–1876), the radical leader.

Alexandre Herculano spent the last ten years of his life on his estate of Vale de Lobos, in the vicinity.

The principal square of the old town, the LARGO SÁ DA BANDEIRA, just S of the main junction of roads, is dominated by the many-windowed façade of the *Seminário*, built for the Jesuits in 1676 by João Nunes Tinoco.

To the NE of the Seminary is the church of *São Francisco* (c 1240), degraded to stable cavalry; and beyond the road descending steeply to the Tagus, *Santa Clara* (c 1258, but much altered since).

Following the Rua Serpa Pinto from the SE corner of the Largo, we reach after a few minutes' walk the early 16C church of *Marvila*, with diamond-patterned azulejos of 1617/20, and coffin-lid wooden roof.

By taking the next right turn beyond the church we shortly reach that of *Graça*, with a portal imitating Batalha and perhaps the finest *Rose-window* in Portugal. Steps descend into the restored nave. Here are the tombs of Pedro de Meneses (c 1437), governor of Ceuta, and his wife; and the tombstone of Pedro Álvares Cabral (died c 1526), the discoverer of Brazil.

Regaining the main street and turning right we reach (right) opposite the 15C *Torre das Cabaças* (or *Cabaceiro*), the 13C church of *São João de Alporão*, perhaps on the site of a mosque, but now containing a lapidary museum, in which the over-restored *Tomb of Duarte de Meneses* (died 1464), governor of Alcácer-Ceguer, is outstanding. Crum Watson considered it the finest 15C tomb in Portugal. It is said to contain only a relic of the governor, killed in Africa: one tooth!—The area behind the church was once the *Judiaria*.

The walk may be continued along a promontory towards the gardens of the *Portas do Sol*, laid out within the walls of the Moorish citadel (Alcáçova), which commands an extensive panorama over the

Tagus valley and plain of the Alentejo, but hardly deserving Pal-grave's ecstatic eulogy.

At *Almoster*, 10km due W of Santarém on the N365, is the restored Bernardine convent of *Santa Maria*, founded in 1289, with remains of a later cloister. The church preserves good Baroque woodwork, and a 14C carved crucifix.

For **Alpiarça**, 10km NE, on the far bank of the Tagus, see p 202.

For the road from Santarém to **Lisbon** see Rte 18C, in reverse. The E3 auto-estrada may be gained some 26km SW of Santarém, approached by forking right at *Cartaxo*.

17 Alcántara to Coimbra via Castelo Branco

Total distance, 232km (144 miles). C523. 11km *Piedras Albas* (Spanish Customs)—8km *Segura* (Portuguese Customs)—N355. 7km. Turn left onto the N240. 49km **Castelo Branco**—N112. 67km *Pampilhosa da Serra*—23km. Turn right onto N 20km *Góis*—20km. Turn left onto N17. 27km **Coimbra**.

The second half of the route traverses attractive but mountainous country, and the going may be slow.

For *Alcántara*, 62km NW of *Cáceres*, see *Blue Guide Spain*.

19km. We cross to *Segura* on a bridge of Roman foundation over the Rio Erges (a tributary of the Tagus), which here forms the frontier. Slight remains of a fortress may be seen.—After 7km we reach a T-junction.

The right turn leads to (21km) the isolated spa of *Termes de Monfortinho*, passing after 6km a right turn for *Salvaterra do Extremo*, with ruins of an old frontier *Castle*.—From Monfortinho the road bears W to (23km) **Monsanto**: see Rte 22B.

The main road turns left at the junction.

After 12km the N353 leads 14km NW to **Idanha-a-Nova**, a small agricultural centre, founded in 1187 by Gualdim Páis, preserving ruins of a *Castle* erected by the Templars, and one or two 18C mansions.

31km. We meet the N233 (see Rte 22B), and turn left for (6km) **CASTELO BRANCO** (21,300 inhab.), the administrative and commercial capital of the Beira Baixa.

Of ancient origin, it was refounded by the Templars in the early 13C, and a century later passed into the hands of the military Order of Christ, and remains of its walls and castle are still evident. The area is said to have had a large crypto-Jewish community in the 16C; gypsies are now more obvious.

Being no great distance from the Spanish frontier, it has often been subject to attack, both in 1704 and 1762. The French under Junot, briefly quartered here in November 1807, proceeded to sack the place; while in April 1809 Géneral Marmont held it briefly, retreating after the fall of Badajoz. Wellington passed through on 1 July 1809 when advancing on Talavera.

Since the late 18C it has been known for its embroidered *colchas* or bed-spreads, a fine range of which may be seen in the museum.

Its few monuments of interest lie some short distance to the N of the central ALAMEDA DA LIBERDADE. We pass (right) the church of *São Miguel*, which served as a cathedral from 1771 to 1881, when the diocese became extinct.

Beyond arcaded steps bridging the street is the entrance to the elaborate formal *Gardens* of the old Bishop's Palace, laid out in the mid 18C, with a multitude of ornamental Baroque statuary, including balustraded steps surmounted by naïve statues of Portuguese kings; a water-tank, lined with azulejos, and surrounded by urns and obelisks; the whole green with a parterre of box arabesques, and an abundance of topiary.

Adjacent is the enterprisingly directed *Museu Francisco Tavares Proença Júnior, accommodated in the old *Bishop's Palace*, containing important archaeological, ethnographical, and ceramic collections; some representative Portuguese 16C paintings; 16C Flemish tapestries; and an extensive series of *Colchas de Castelo Branco*, some showing Persian, Indian, or Oriental influences. The building also houses a school of embroidery to carry on the strong tradition, and work can be commissioned here.

For the N18 for *Covilhã* see Rte 22A, in reverse.

FROM CASTELO BRANCO TO TOMAR (125km). We follow the N233 through undulating country for 46km, traversing few villages, before turning onto the N241 for (4km) *Proença-a-Nova*, some 15km SW of which, at *Cardigos*, is a Roman bridge.—22km. **Sertã**, with a Gothic church on the site of an earlier edifice.—Hence the N2 leads 18km N, first descending steeply to cross the Zêzere next to the *Barragem do Cabril*, and ascending its far bank to *Pedrógão Grande*, well sited on a height. It is an old town, probably of Roman origin, with a 12C church rebuilt in 1537.—For the cross-country road hence to *Lousã*, see below.

From Sertã we follow the N238 to (9km) the high-lying village of *Sernache do Bomjardim*, birthplace in 1360 of the Constable Nun' Álvares Pereira, the victor of Aljubarrota.—We climb down steeply to cross the Zêzere. Some 2km to the right on the far bank, on a meander of the river, is the picturesquely-sited village of *Dornes*, with a medieval tower and 14C church with a pulpit of 1544.—23km. *Águas Belas*, just SE of which is *Ferreira do Zêzere*.—The road winds down (views) to meet the N110 leading S to (21km) **Tomar**: see Rte 18C.

From Castelo Branco, the N112 leads NW towards and over foothills of the SERRA DA GARDUNHA, at 48km crossing the Zêzere at *Cambas*, and then traverses the wild broken country of the SERRA DA LOUSÃ, passing through (19km) *Pampilhosa da Serra*, and after another 37km of winding road reaches a junction.

In the valley 5km to the right is **Góis**, a small agricultural centre, beautifully situated, with a Manueline bridge over the Rio Ceira, and in the church the Renaissance tomb of Luis da Silveira by Diogo de Torralva (1531).

The road then climbs over two ridges and descends to meet the N17 after 24km.—*Penacova* (see Rte 23) lies 13km N.—We turn left to follow the winding valley of the Rio Ceira, a tributary of the Mondego, to (27km) **Coimbra**: see Rte 25.

The left-hand turning at this junction climbs over a ridge to (16km) **Lousã**, a pleasant town with old paper factories, beneath the Serra named after it, which rises to 1202m, forming the SW extremity of the SERRA DA ESTRELA. It has a *Castle*, 18C mansions, and a *Misericórdia* with a Renaissance portal of 1568. Hence we descend via *Foz de Arouce* (see p 240) onto the N17 7km NW, there turning left for (20km) **Coimbra**: see Rte 25.

An alternative approach to Coimbra from Lousã may be made by continuing W on the N342 via *Miranda do Corvo* (see Rte 18C), and then climbing over a ridge to *Vila Sêca*, to meet the N1 at (26km) *Conímbriga* (see p 213), 15km SW of Coimbra.

18 Lisbon to Coimbra

A. Via Rio Maior, Batalha, Leiria and Conímbriga

Total distance, 201km (125 miles). E3 auto-estrada for 52km, there making our exit onto the N366 for (11km) *Alcoentre*—15km *Rio Maior*—11km The left-hand fork here leads 18km N to **Alcobaça**—30km **Batalha**—11km **Leiria**—27.5km **Pombal**—29km *Condeixa*, for **Conímbriga**—14.5km **Coimbra**.

We follow the motorway past (left) the *Airport*, and bear NE parallel to and above the W bank of the Tagus through a scruffy industrial area, after 22km passing an exit for *Bucelas* (8km to the W), well-known for its wine, and 9km beyond, the exit for *Vila Franca* (see below).—At *Arruda dos Vinhos*, 15km N of Bucelas, the church preserves a good Manueline portal of c 1530. To the NW, between the two exits, took place the internecine battle of *Alfarrobeira* (1449), in which Pedro, Duke of Coimbra was killed, his nephew Afonso V being victorious.—We also by-pass (right) *Alhandra*, birthplace of Afonso de Albuquerque (1453–1515), viceroy of India; it marked the E end of the *Lines of Torres Vedras*: see Rte 18B.

Vila Franca de Xira (17,600 inhab.) is said to have been founded by French followers of Afonso Henriques c 1200. Here took place the military *pronunciamento* (or 'Vilafrancada') of 27 May 1823 of the reactionary absolutists against the liberal government of the time. The British-built *Maréchal Carmona Bridge* (1300m long) spanning the Tagus here, was inaugurated in 1951.

At 8km an exit is provided for **Alenquer**, 6km NW, an old town once famed for its paper manufactories, but sacked by the French during Masséna's occupation in 1810–11. It is said to derive its name from its foundation by the Alans (*Alanokerkae*), claiming to occupy the site of Roman *Jerabrica*, but the origin of its name may as easily be Arabic. *São Francisco*, founded c 1222 by Dona Sancha, daughter of Sancho I, retains a 13C portal and Manueline cloister. Close by is the ruined *Castle* (13C), while in the lower town rebuilt *Santa Maria da Várzea* contains the tomb of Damião de Góis (1501–74), the humanist, a friend of Erasmus, and a victim of the Inquisition. He was probably also born here, as was Pêro de Alenquer, a pilot with both Bartolomeu Dias in 1488 and Vasco da Gama in 1497.

In the neighbourhood is the prehistoric *Castro da Pedra de Ouro*.
Aldeia Galega da Merceana, c 14km NW, contains two churches of some interest.

From Alenquer, the N1 ascends N over the SERRA DE MONTEJUNTO, passing (left) a TV station, to reach a junction. The left-hand fork here leads 29km NW to *Óbidos* and on to *Caldas da Rainha*: see Rte 18B. —We bear right to cross the N366 near *Alcoentre* (2km right).

After 14km we leave the motorway, which it is proposed to extend NE; meanwhile see Rte 18C for the road on to *Santarem*. Our route bears NW on the N366 to (11km) *Alcoentre*, to enter the N1 a short distance beyond.

At *Manique do Intendente*, some 6km E of Alcoentre, approached by a road turning right just N of the latter, stands the huge derelict palace of great

pretension erected by Diogo Ignácio de Pina Manique (1733–1805), the intend-
ant of police during the reign of Maria I, whose family originated here. The key
to this architectural curiosity may be found at the adjoining *venda*.

15km. *Rio Maior*, an agricultural centre of very remote origin.
Numerous prehistoric artefacts have been found in the district.—
Speleologists will be rewarded by a visit to the *Cave of Alcobertas*,
9km N.—The road via *Alcanede* (see p 227), 16km NE, is a pleasanter,
if longer, alternative to the main road.

We follow the wide valley parallel to the bald SERRA DOS
CANDIEIROS, off which after 18km a road forks left along a ridge
(views) direct to (18km) **Alcobaça** (see Rte 18B) via *Évora de
Alcobaça*, whose *Igreja Matriz* preserves above a side door a bas-
relief of an armoured knight.

After c 25km we cross the battlefield of **Aljubarrota** (see Rte 18B)
and descend gently towards *Batalha*, passing (right) a turning for
Porto de Mós; see p 227.

Batalha (*Pousada Mestre Afonso Domingues*), a small town in a
fruitful vale, is famous for its magnificent 'Battle-Abbey', *Santa Maria
da Vitória*, its surroundings not improved by the high ramp of the
nearby main road, or by the erection of 'model' houses in its
immediate vicinity, largely devoted to selling souvenirs.

The *ABBEY OF BATALHA, once served by Dominicans, lacks the
austere grace of Cistercian Alcobaça, but is undoubtedly one of the
masterpieces of Portuguese architecture, although some details recall
the English Perpendicular style. The nave reminded Beckford 'of
Winchester in form of arches and mouldings, and of Amiens in
loftiness'.

It has recently become the site of several cultural activities during summer
months, exhibitions of Nottingham alabasters, sculpture, concerts, etc.

Its construction dates from 1388, in consequence of a vow made by João I, Master
of Avis, prior to the Battle of Aljubarrota (15 August 1385), fought not far away, if
he should gain a victory over the Spaniards. Dom João's building comprised the
church, the founder's chapel, the first cloister, and the chapter-house, and its
masters of works were Afonso Domingues (1388–1402), and Huguet (or Ougete;
1402–38). Dom Duarte (the eldest son of João I) in 1437 commissioned the
erection of an octagonal chapel behind the apse, while Afonso V commissioned
the construction of the second cloister (1438–77), built by the Alentejans Martim
Vasques and Fernão de Évora. Work on the pantheon was resumed during the
reign of Dom Manuel, executed by Mateus Fernandes the Elder (1480–1515),
who also is buried here; and intermittently by Diogo Boitac, from 1509–19. But
this was finally abandoned when Dom Manuel (died 1521) turned his attention
to his own mausoleum at Belém.

An additional cloister, destroyed in 1811, was built by João III c 1550. The
whole was only comparatively slightly damaged during the earthquake of 1755
and the Peninsular War, although General Picton's Division was briefly quartered here in October 1810. Since 1839 the care of its fabric has been in the hands
of the State, who chose to place here the Tomb of Portugal's Unknown Soldiers,
apart from gutting the building almost as drastically as they have done at
Alcobaça. In the 1850s J.M. Neale, who was also a Puseyite clergyman, and as
such biased, described some of the fittings as being 'in the most wretched
modern taste', while the glass had been outrageously 'restored' by a Frenchman
in 'so abominable a character that they would be scouted in any gin-palace in
England'. Parts of the cornice of the Capelas Imperfeitas (see below) were added
in the late 19C.

In 'Plans, elevations, sections and views of the church of Batalha' (including an
imaginative reconstruction of the projected Capelas Imperfeitas), and in his
'Travels in Portugal' (both published 1795), James Kavanaugh Murphy—
condemned by Beckford as 'that dull draftsman'—who had resided there for
some months, describes the building in detail.

The EXTERIOR lacks major vertical accents in its composition, and
there is no important tower or central feature to hold the eye. The

Detail of the W Doorway, Batalha

details of the many-pinnacled WEST FRONT are extremely interesting, especially the statues of the Evangelists in the tympanum. In the centre is Christ in Majesty, surrounded by numerous saints, etc. The apostles on the splay are modern copies. The traceried limestone above the portal, weathered to a honey tint, is surmounted by a fine Flamboyant window. To the right rises the octagonal lantern of the founder's chapel, once capped by an openwork spire, which fell in 1755. The plainer S Doorway is likewise of interest.

INTERIOR. Like Alcobaça, the church is long and high in proportion to its width (80m by 22m, and 32m high). The nave consists of eight bays separated from the aisles by plain piers, while the small apsidal choir is flanked by two chapels on either side. The transepts are 32m across. A few steps inside the W Door is the tomb-slab of Mateus Fernandes, the master of works (see History).

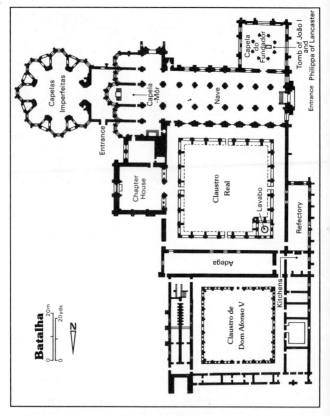

From the S Aisle we enter the **Capela do Fundador** (1426–34), a chapel 20m square, covered by an octagonal *Lantern* 12m in diameter; the delicate clustered columns and arches and the elaborate star vault with its central rosace are all remarkable. In the centre is the double *Tomb of João I and Philippa of Lancaster* (transferred here from the Capela-Mór on the completion of this chapel). The recumbent figures of the king (died 1434), armoured, and of his English wife (died 1416) lie hand in hand, each beneath an octagonal canopy on which is carved the arms of Avis and Lancaster, while round the margin of the tomb their mottoes 'Por Bem' (Pour Bien; see p 153) and 'Yl me plet' (Il me plait) are many times repeated. (Colonel Leach admitted to having cut off a button from the royal robes, when the embalmed body had been exposed by troops during the retreat from Busaco in 1810.)

On the S wall are the restored altar-tombs of their four younger sons, each decorated with their individual devices, and the Order of the Garter, founded by Philippa's grandfather, Edward III, will be noted. Farthest to the left lies *Fernando*, Master of the Order of Avis, the 'Infante Santo' (died 1443), rashly left as a hostage for the surrender of Ceuta, which was never made, by the ill-fated expedition against Tangier in 1437; his remains were brought back from Fez and

interred with great pomp in 1472. That of *João*, Master of the Order of
São Tiago (died 1442) has a representation of the Passion behind. The
tomb of *Henrique*, Duke of Viseu and Master of the Order of Christ,
better known to the English as Prince Henry 'the Navigator' (died
1460) bears an indifferent effigy; next to which is that of *Pedro*, Duke
of Coimbra and Regent of Portugal (died 1449; at Alfarrobeira).

The tombs on the W wall are modern imitations: they contain the remains of
Afonso V (died 1481); João II (died 1495), and his only son, Afonso (died 1491;
see Almeirim).

The apsidal *Capela-Mór* is notable for its early 16C stained-glass
windows (ascribed to Francisco Henriques), which represent the
Visitation, Adoration of the Magi, the Flight into Egypt, and
Resurrection.

From the N aisle we enter the *Claustro Real* (55m by 50m),
originally built by Afonso Domingues, the arches of which were later
embellished for Dom Manuel (attributed by some to Mateus Fernandes, by others to Boitac) and were filled with elaborately convoluted
'vegetable' tracery of varied patterns (in which Sitwell observes the
poppy, cardoon, and artichoke), including his emblem, the armillary
sphere, and the Cross of the Order of Christ. The supporting
colonettes are likewise lavishly adorned.

From the E walk we enter the *Chapter House** through a massive
yet graceful arch between two fine double windows. The E window,
also of good design, contains 16C glass, while the vault, 19m square
without any central support, is remarkable.

On the N side is the *Tomb of the Unknown Soldiers* (one from Africa, and one
from the Flanders front), perpetually guarded, above which is the 'Christ of the
Trenches', found at Neuve-Chapelle.

Continuing round the cloister, we pass an elaborate Manueline door
to the long vaulted cellar. At the NW angle of the cloister projects the
Well House, or *Lavabo*, where the foliation of the tracery surpasses
itself. The diagonal view across the cloister, with its four secular
cypresses, to the upper parapet and to the clerestory of the church,
and of the small spired tower (rebuilt in the mid 19C), is
memorable.—Adjacent is the *Refectory*, now containing a miscellaneous military museum and objects left at the Tomb of the Unknown
Soldiers.

Hence, passing the *Kitchens* on our left (at present closed), we enter
the *Claustro de Dom Afonso V*, austere in comparison to the Claustro
Real. By traversing its S walk and continuing ahead we reach the
vacant site of João III's cloister, cleared after its virtual destruction by
French troops in the Peninsular War, and turn right to approach the
entrance to the **Capelas Imperfeitas**, which have no direct communication with the church.

The original plan of Dom Duarte's mausoleum can be seen in the
comparative simplicity of the main arches of the seven chapels which
surround the central octagon, now open to the sky. Note also the
descending keystones over three of the chapels. Mateus Fernandes,
Dom Manuel's master of works, planned an upper octagon with a
vault supported by massive buttresses built up from the six smaller
intervening pentagonal chapels, but work was abandoned before the
piers had risen more than a short distance above the rich cornices of
the main storey. Part of the latter, which had not been commenced on
some chapels, was added in the late 19C.

Some idea of the intended elaboration may be gauged from the profuse ornamentation of the truncated bases of the upper storey, and from the remarkable exotic *W Portal* (1509), 15m high, a masterpiece of lace-like tracery in stone. The obsessively repeated inscription on the arch is the motto of Dom Duarte: 'leauté faray tam yaserey' ('loyal I shall ever be'). Above is a double-bayed Renaissance loggia or tribune, added c 1533, attributed to João de Castilho.

The chapels now contain the tombs of (left) a Duke of Aveiro, whose escutcheons have been effaced; that of an infant son of Afonso V; and, opposite the portal, those of Dom Duarte (died 1438), and of his queen, Leonor of Aragón, mutilated by the French in 1810. These lay originally in the apse chapels, which have been attributed to both João de Castilho and Boitac.

Beckford, for one, did not admire all this exuberant ornamentation, but as the enthusiastic prior showed him round, he realised that 'to entertain any doubts of the supreme excellence of Don Emanuel's scollops and twistifications amounted to heresy'.

Santa Cruz, SE of the village centre, retains a fine Manueline portal.

11km. **LEIRIA** (11,200 inhab.), an episcopal city (from 1545) and capital of its district, lies among attractive country on the river Lis (or Liz), crossed by a Roman bridge, and is dominated by its imposing castle.

Situated on the road between Olisipo and Bracara (Lisbon and Braga), Leiria occupies the site of the Roman station of *Collippo*. In 1135 Afonso Henriques set up an advance post here, but it was recaptured by the Moors and its garrison massacred. It changed hands various times during the next few decades, being rebuilt by the Portuguese in 1144 and again in 1191. In 1254 Afonso III held a Cortes here, the first such assembly in Portugal at which the Commons were represented, and later Dom Dinis (who promoted the afforestation of the area to the W) and his wife St. Isabel chose it as a residence. A printing-press established here in 1492 (or possibly earlier, in 1466) was noted for the printing of works in Hebrew.

A rising here in 1808 against the French was savagely repressed by Géneral Margarot. English troops retreating through Leiria after the battle of Busaco broke down the doors of a convent, as the French were close, and out came the nuns 'as thick as a flock of sheep and set off for Lisbon', some of them jumping up behind the dragoons, clasping their saviours tightly round their waists. The town was severely damaged by the French during their retreat (March 1811).

It was the birthplace of the poet Francisco Rodrigues Lobo (1590–1621).

From the central PRAÇA RODRIGUES LOBO we ascend to the plain *Cathedral* (1550–74), attributed to Afonso Álvares. The vault is borne on flat ribs resting on square piers. The cloister lies behind the apse, as with the Sé at Lisbon.

From its W front steps mount past the detached belfry to the gateway of the old town. Beyond is the 18C *Bishop's Palace*, now containing a library and small museum; and near by, on the right of the ascent to the castle, the Romanesque portal of *São Pedro* (c 1140).

Passing through the main outer gate of the curtain wall of the *Castle, and climbing left, we first reach (right) the apsidal chapel of *N.S. da Penha* (c.1400), erected by João I and bearing his monogram, a crowned Y. To the left is the restored *Royal Palace*, with an imposing hall, the loggia of which commands a good vista; and higher up, the *Torre de Menagem* (1324), providing a more extensive view, of Monte Junto to the E, and across the *Pinhal Real* (or d'el-Rei) W to the sea.

Just outside the town is the high-lying chapel of *N.S. da Encarnação* (early 17C), with its large porch, approached by a long monumental flight of steps.

A small *Ethnographical Museum* may also be visited, on application to the Tourist Office.

For the road from Leiria to *Figueira da Foz* see Rte 20.

The great pine forest (PINHAL REAL) to the W of Leiria was first established by Dom Dinis in the 13C to anchor the encroaching sand dunes, and now covers an area of almost 10,000 hectares.

11km W of Leiria, and almost surrounded by the forest, lies the straggling industrial district of **Marinha Grande**. Here are the glass-works founded in 1748 by John Beare, an Englishman, and from 1769 developed by William Stephens, subsidised by Pombal. Stephens died in 1802, and his brother bequeathed it to the State in 1826.

Stephens had fitted up an opera house here, where performances were given each month, many of the parts sung by his employers, whom he had instructed in music and dancing; concerts were frequent. Lord and Lady Holland were hospitably received there for three days in February 1805. Mr Stephens then employed 24 workman. The sand principally used was brought 'from ye Isle of Wight, and the barilla from Alicant, and the potash from Russia or North America; so that except the pines and salt of tartar from Oporto, none of the rude materials are the produce of Portugal'.

Some 4.5km after leaving Leiria a left-hand turn leads via *Pinheiros* to approach the Baroque church of *Milagres*, of 1732, with azulejos of 1795. The architect was José da Silva, of Juncal, and his grandson designed the tiles, which describe the miracle of a local peasant restored to health after being paralysed by a fall.

23km. **Pombal**, by-passed, a market town with a partially restored *Castle* built c 1174 by Gualdim Pais. It is principally famous for having given a title to the 'Gran Marquês', Sebastião José de Carvalho e Melo (1699–1782), who retired here in disgrace in 1777 on the accession of the reactionary and priest-ridden Maria I; he died bed-ridden at his residence in the main square. His remains were first buried in *N.S. do Cardal* (1703). The place was sacked by the French on their retreat in 1811. An earlier peculiarity of Pombal was the fact that one of each of its three parish churches concentrated on baptism, marriages, and funerals.

At *Santiago da Guarda*, c 20km NE, was born the 3rd Conde de Castelo-Melhor (1636–1720), minister of Afonso VI for five years, until his temporary disgrace in 1667.

15km. A left turn leads 5km to *Soure*, with the ruins of the Knights Templar's first castle in Portugal (1128), and a 17C *Misericórdia*.

The road continues to undulate to (14km) **Condeixa-a-Nova**, a pleasant small town preserving the 17C *Casa Sotto Maior*, among other mansions.—*Ega*, c 3km SW, contains a small Manueline church with a Renaissance pulpit, and a good *anon.* 16C triptych.

3km SE of Condeixa is the site of ancient *CONÍMBRIGA*, the largest Roman settlement excavated in Portugal. Its approach is signposted off the main road.

Conímbriga, although a pre-Roman site (from c 800 BC), lay on the Roman road from Lisbon to Braga via Tomar, and as such it became a station of considerable importance. It remained so until its destruction by the Suevi in the mid 5C, after which the Visigothic kings transferred their seat to the more easily defended town of *Aeminium*, present-day Coimbra, although its bishops still retained the name of Conímbriga.

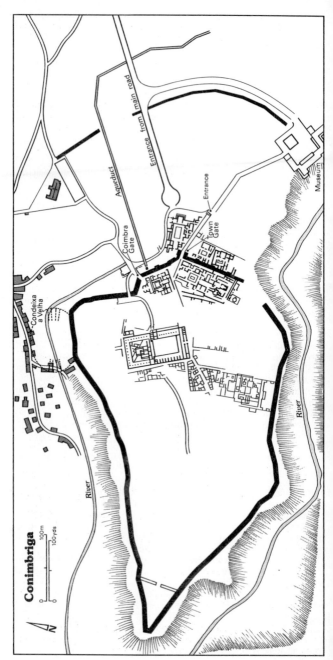

Although the presence of ancient remains had been previously noted, it was not until 1898 that any survey was undertaken, and in 1912 the first diggings were carried out by Dr Virgílio Correia, who was also responsible for the more systematic excavations of the extensive site after 1930.

The new site **Museum**, opened in 1985, contains numerous artefacts discovered in the area since 1874.

From the main entrance vestibule we turn left into the first of two rooms, concentrating on the smaller artefacts found on the site. They are well displayed and give a good idea of the importance of Coním- briga. The collection of coins, glass, ceramics, domestic utensils and tools, cameos, jewellery and metalwork is extensive. The second series of open-plan rooms is devoted to epigraphical collections, stelae, sculpture (or fragments; much of it carved from marble from Estremoz/ Vila Viçosa), bronze statuettes, mosaics (one of the Minotaur in his labyrinth, and another geometrical composition), carved capitals and other architectural elements, including decorative stucco-work, etc. Some larger pieces of sculpture and a huge capital found in the Flavian forum may be seen in a third exhibition area, a patio, which might suggest a Roman peristyle.

Reproductions of several objects displayed are for sale, and the building also accommodates a small Restaurant.

Conímbriga lies on a triangle of land between two gorges, and much of the *Walls*, some 1500m in extent, circumscribing this area of 13 hectares, still exist, with an outer defensive wall further to the E, crossed by the approach road and *Aqueduct*, which provided the city with water from a reservoir at *Alcabideque*, some 3km distant.

Part of the site of Conímbriga

To the right of the irregularly flagged Roman road which approaches the main *Town Gate* is the site of a large villa surrounding a peristyle, retaining a number of mosaic pavements. In the centre is a large pool, with numerous fountain jets of bronze (reconstructed by copying surviving pieces, and again in working order).—To the left of the road are some smaller houses, also preserving mosaics and thermae.

Passing through the main gate and bearing to the right, we reach the entrance of the aqueduct into the walled enceinte, leading to a distribution cistern, beyond which is the 'Coimbra Gate'.—To the left of the main gate is another villa containing more than one ornamental pool, in the largest of which five skeletons were found when it was excavated, probably of men slain there when the place was sacked in 468.—Further S are its private baths, with interesting installations, with the usual arrangement of *frigidarium, tepidarium* and *caldarium* over a hypocaust. Some lead piping from the first can be seen: it provided a complete water supply and sewerage system. Beyond are more skeletons (in situ) of the Visigothic period.—Further W is the recently excavated *Forum*, S of which is a commercial area abutting the *Temple of Flavius*, on the slope beyond which, reached by a flight of steps, is the *Palaestra*, and the *Public Baths*, etc., which await consolidation. An *Amphitheatre*, just beyond the N wall, is to be excavated, while excavations in other areas are continuing.

Regaining the N1, we shortly reach the entrance to the motorway by-passing Coimbra and driving N towards Oporto. After 4km the road skirts (left) *Cernache*, with a Nottingham alabaster of the Coronation of the Virgin in its church.

After 10km we reach and cross the Mondego, with a good view of **Coimbra** on the far bank as we approach it: see Rte 25.

B. Via Torres Vedras, Peniche, Óbidos, and Alcobaça

Total distance, 261km (162 miles). N8. 15km *Loures*—17km **Mafra** lies 9.5km W.—33.5km **Torres Vedras**—N8-2. 19km *Lourinha*—N247. 18km *Peniche*—N114. 23km **Óbidos**—7km **Caldas da Rainha**—26km **Alcobaça**. **Nazaré** lies 13.5km NW.—21km **Batalha**—N1. 11km **Leiria**—27.5km **Pombal**—29km *Condeixa*, for **Conímbriga**—14km **Coimbra**.

Follow the N8 sign at the N end of the *Campo Grande*. Shortly after traversing *Lumiar* (see last part of Rte 1F) the road veers right.

A left-hand fork at this junction leads in 2km to **Odivelas**, where the portal and apse is preserved of the church and convent built by Dom Dinis in 1295-1305, the rest of which was destroyed in the earthquake of 1755. It contains the founder's tomb (much restored), and that of his natural daughter, Maria Afonso (died 1320). Queen Philippa of Lancaster died here of the plague on 18 July 1415, and in October the following year was buried at Batalha: see Rte 18A.

Here resided the nun known as Madre Paula (da Silva; 1701-68), who, amongst other inmates, was a mistress from 1718 to 1728 of João V, the *'freiratico'*. The philoprogenitive king had the right of entry to the nunnery, and the results of his peculiar penchant (as commented on by Voltaire) were three bastards, known as the 'Meninos de Palhavã' (not 'palha', straw). They were Dom José, born 1720 to Madre Paula, later an Inquisitor-general; Dom Gaspar, born 1716 to Magdalena Máxima de Miranda, later archbishop of Braga; Dom António, born 1714, son of a French nun. It was the last two sons who were visited by Beckford in 1787. Sitwell suggests that Madre Paula, who when not otherwise occupied—for the nuns also had a reputation for their marmalade and quince jams—was an excellent musician, and may have been a pupil of Domenico Scarlatti, who was in Portugal in 1721-29. But in general they were a turbulent lot. In October 1713 there was even a rebellion of nuns here 'only subdued by the Duke of Cadaval after a pitched battle', so reported the British consul.

5.5km. *Loures*—which may be by-passed by a dual-carriageway under construction—just to the W of which is the 18C *Quinta do Correio-Mór* (Post-master General), erected for Luís Gomes da Mata, containing interesting features, but suffering from decades of neglect.

17km. **Mafra**, see Rte 3, lies 9.5km to the W.

20km. *Turcifal*, with a large 18C church.

13.5km. **TORRES VEDRAS** (10,700 inhab.), an important wine-growing centre, was frequently a royal residence until the 16C. Although it was the scene of a sanguinary combat during the troubles of 1846, its name is more famous as being the headquarters of Wellington's lines of defence for Lisbon during the early stages of the Peninsular War: see below.

The town itself is of slight interest, preserving the fort of *São Vincente*; a ruined *Castle*; a Gothic fountain, the *Chafariz dos Canos*; the Manueline church of *São Pedro*, and that of *Graça*, containing some azulejos and Portuguese primitives.

Some 4km W of the town is the hamlet of *Varatojo*, with the large *Convento de Santo António* (late 15C, with later additions), with a Gothic cloister, and a sacristy lined with 17C azulejos.

Some 3km E is the complex of prehistoric fortifications known as the *Castro do Zambujal*, which may well have given the town its name (*Turres Veteres*).

The so-called **Lines of Torres Vedras** were basically two bands of hilltop redoubts and batteries extending across the neck of the wide peninsula on which Lisbon stands, and were some 40km long. The first ran from the mouth of the Sisandre on the Atlantic c 12km W of Torres Vedras, to Alhandra, on the Tagus just S of Vila Franca de Xira. The second line of defence extended from Ribamar and a point just N of Mafra through Bucelas, to just N of Póvoa de Santa Iria, on the Tagus.

The remains of what were some 130 masonry and earthworks are still recognisable along the more northerly line, and their exploration can provide interesting excursions for the energetic. In certain areas the defensive positions provided what is virtually a third line.

Wellington, traversing the area after the battle of Vimeiro (see below) had already remarked on its suitability for defence, and the construction of these extensive bands of earthworks had been progressing secretly since October 1809 in preparation for any eventual retreat necessary in the face of superior French armies. The area enclosed behind the Lines was over 500 square miles (1300 sq km). Wellington had also ordered a 'scorched earth' policy to be put into effect N of the Lines. The local population, with their livestock, was moved S, so that when in October 1810, after the Battle of Busaco, the British retired into secure and well-provisioned territory, Masséna and his huge army found themselves in a comparative desert. But he had learnt his lesson, and warily did not even attempt to attack the Lines. The fact that the French were able to subsist near them for so long, being cut off from their supplies, is remarkable, but in the following March sheer starvation forced them to retreat from their own positions between Rio Maior and Santarém. This continued until 3 May when just across the Spanish frontier, between Vilar Formoso and *Fuentes de Oñoro*, they turned on their pursuers. It has been estimated that Masséna lost between 25,000 and 30,000 men during his disastrous campaign.

Detailed maps and descriptions can be found in Wyld's 'Atlas' (1841), William Granville Eliot's 'Treatise on the Defence of Portugal', and Jones' 'Journal of Sieges, etc.' (see Bibliography); while maquettes of the ground may be seen in the museum at Óbidos, and the Military Museum at Lisbon.

The N248 leads E and then SE from Torres Vedras past *Matacães*, with a well-carved retable and azulejos of 1736 in its church, to (6km) *Runa*, with the *Asilo dos Inválidos*, founded for old soldiers in 1792.—At *Dois Portos* (5km beyond), the church preserves a 16C artesonado ceiling; and 5km further, S of *Sobral de Monte Agraço*, the church of *São Quintino* preserves a curious baptistry of 1592.

FROM TORRES VEDRAS TO ÓBIDOS VIA BOMBARRAL (38km). The N8, although the direct road, was (in 1987) in a deplorable condition, full of pot-holes. It winds through country of slight interest to (26.5km) *Bombarral*.—7km SE, at *Cadaval*, is the Iron Age fort of *Castelo de Pragança*.—The next right turn beyond Bombarral leads to *Carvalhal*, with a quaint Mannerist retablo in the *Igreja do Sacramento*, and good azulejos of 1733 in *N.S. do Socorro*.—Continuing N from Bombarral, we shortly descend from the rim of hills defended by the French at the battle of **Roliça** (see p 219), named after the village by-passed to the left. The road from Peniche enters from the W as we approach **Óbidos**: see below

Our route briefly follows the N8, turning left just N of Torres Vedras onto the N8.2 for *Lourinhã*. Climbing down through woods, we shortly turn left again for *A-dos-Cunhados*, there bearing right to adjacent *Vimeiro*.

Neither the village of **Vimeiro** (with its monument to the battle: see below), nor *Maceira*, some 3km to the W, are of great interest in themselves, other than historical, but the drive along the N bank of the river to its mouth (unfortunately spoilt by the erection of an ugly hotel), and back through the defile near the S bank, is worth the short detour. One can well imagine the troops and their mounts coming ashore through the breakers, in which some were drowned, as so brilliantly described in Commissary Schaumann's 'On the Road with Wellington'.

Wellington, after the engagement at Roliça (see p 219), had originally taken up a defensive position along the hills just S of the Maceira river, at the mouth of which his reinforcements were to disembark. He later transferred them to other hills S and NE of the village of Vimeiro, where they awaited the combined French armies of Junot, Delaborde, and Loison advancing from Torres Vedras. The resulting battle of 21 August 1808 was the first and a classic example of Wellington's defensive tactics, which were later to serve him in good stead at Busaco and in other battles during the war. The massed French columns, which for years had been successful elsewhere in Europe, disintegrated before the superior firepower of the sheltered extended lines of their disciplined foe, whenever the two formations came together. The French were heavily defeated, their casualties being 2000 compared with some 720 British, and they also lost at least 13 pieces of artillery. Géneral Kellerman proposed a truce, which Wellington was forced to agree to by his elderly superior Sir Hew Dalrymple, who with Sir Harry Burrard had just landed to supersede him in command of the victorious army. They preferred to draw up the unpopular *Convention of Cintra* (see p 156) rather than risk further fighting.

We regain the main road some 4km NE of Vimeiro, and turn left along a ridge, its fields protected from the wind by reed hedges, to **Lourinhã**, with a restored *Igreja Matriz*, preserving a Gothic portal and rose-window; a *Misericórdia* with a Manueline portal and containing paintings by the Master of Lourinha (early 16C) of St. John on Patmos and St. John the Baptist; and *N.S. da Anunciação*, with a small cloister.

18km. **PENICHE** (15,600 inhab.), whose name, a corruption of the Latin for peninsula, well describes its rock-bound site, once a rabbit-infested island, still almost cut off from the mainland except by a narrow sandy isthmus, and protected by a line of 16C fortifications (on which, when visited by General d'Urban in December 1809, 'nearly 100 heavy guns' were in position). The place was raided by Norris and Drake in 1589, when in Spanish hands. It contains a number of fish canneries.

Passing through the gate, we skirt (left) the inside of the wall, past gardens, to the important deep-sea fishing harbour and dockyard, in the process of enlargement, to approach the *Fortaleza*. During the Salazar regime this was one of the main prisons of his repressive secret police, the PIDE, from which the Communist leader Álvaro Cunhal escaped in 1960. From near its entrance the Rua José Estevão leads into the town to *São Pedro* (16C), some distance to the W of which (behind the apse) is *N.S. da Conceição*, with azulejo panels and a good painted ceiling. The *Misericórdia*, adjacent to the gardens, preserves 55 painted panels on its ceiling of scenes from the Life of Christ, etc.

A road leads away from the gardens across the peninsula to the chapel of *N.S. dos Remédios*, lined with azulejo panels, and providing a good view of the offshore archipelago lashed by the Atlantic, the ***Berlengas**.

The largest and nearest of these rocky islands (12km out), has a lighthouse and fort. The ruins of a monastery founded in 1513, but later abandoned owing to its inaccessibility, may be seen. For information regarding boats and ferries to the islands, with their picturesque caves and coves, enquire at the Tourist Office in Peniche.

Cabo Carvoeiro, the W headland of the Peniche peninsula, also has a lighthouse. Bearing N along the coast past canning factories, we regain the gate, beyond which (left) is the main beach.

Hence we follow the N114 to the E through the village of **Atouguia da Baleia**, once of importance as a port, preserving a Gothic fountain, and the interesting early Gothic church of *São Leonardo*, with its belfry topped by twin pyramids. It contains Romanesque capitals, a well-carved stone Nativity (14C), and the tomb of the 1st Count of Atouguia (1452).—We next traverse *Serra d'El Rei* (retrospective views), with relics of a palace of c 1360 built for Pedro I, beyond which, on approaching *Óbidos*, we have a good view to the right (S) of the battlefield of **Roliça**.

The engagement which took place here on 17 August 1808, was the first of the Peninsular War fought by British troops, who, commanded by Wellington, had landed some days previously at the mouth of the Mondego. Géneral Delaborde's small force was at Roliça, a village a short distance S of Óbidos within a horseshoe of low hills; while Loison with a larger army was approaching from Abrantes, which if they joined forces would outnumber the British, who decided to attack immediately. Delaborde was soon obliged to withdraw to a ridge further S to avoid being outflanked by the two wings of Wellington's army, which had been divided into three columns. But when they repeated the initial manoeuvre, at the same time advancing up the gullies of the hillside in a frontal attack, the French had little alternative but to give way again, and although the fighting was hard, Delaborde then retired SE, his position having been carried.

Next day Wellington received a dispatch informing him of the arrival of reinforcements awaiting instructions where to disembark from their transports off the coast, and therefore proceeded SW towards the mouth of the Maceira, near the village of *Vimeiro*, the site of a more serious engagement on the 21st: see above.

On regaining the N8, turn left for ****ÓBIDOS** (*Pousada do Castelo*). Tastefully prettied up, and with a reputation for its apples, this ancient walled town, taken from the Moors by Afonso Henriques in 1148, and once marking the S extremity of the domains of Alcobaça, remains one of the most attractive and picturesque sights in Portugal. It is therefore best visited when not overrun by groups on the Alcobaça–Batalha–Nazaré circuit.

Unless staying at the *Pousada* in the Castle, it is preferable to leave one's car near the *Porta da Vila* (note its tiled oratory) at the S end of the walled enceinte, close to which is the *Aqueduct*, built at the instigation of Dona Catarina, queen of João III.

The castle, Óbidos

Follow the Rua Direita (with the Tourist Office) to approach the imposing *Castle, built by Dom Dinis on a height dominating the N end of the town. Pedro López de Ayala (1332–1407?), the Spanish chronicler, while imprisoned here after the battle of Aljubarrota, wrote his 'Libro de las Aves de Caça' (or 'Libro de la Cetrería'), a treatise on hawking. Adjacent is the uninteresting church of *São Tiago*.

The main square is flanked by restored ***Santa Maria** (late 17C, with a Renaissance portal), on the site of an earlier church. The interior contains *albarrada* azulejos (early 18C); the fine Renaissance **Tomb of João de Noronha*, by Chanterène (1526–28; left-hand wall); good retables, that over the Altar-Mór with late 17C paintings by João da Costa; to the right are paintings depicting the mystic marriage of St. Catherine, by Josefa 'de Óbidos' (Josefa d'Ayala, born in Seville c 1630. She spent much of her life in a convent here, where she died in 1684, and was buried in *São Pedro*). Note also the series of paintings (School of Josefa de Óbidos) around the ceiling, and the *Organ*.

Adjacent to the church is the **Museum**, established here by the Gulbenkian Foundation in the old Town Hall. Among the somewhat miscellaneous collections of paintings, mostly 15–16C martyrdoms, are an *anon*. St. Francis (late 17C Portuguese); N.S. de Misericórdia, *School of Bento Coelho da Silveira*; and a Portrait of Faustino das Neves, attributed to *Josefa de Óbidos*. Also to be seen are a collection of polychromed statuettes; a room devoted to the Peninsular War, specifically Roliça, and the Lines of Torres Vedras (maquette), with French and English arms, etc; and other displays, including architectural and archaeological relics.

About 1km N of Óbidos, beyond the bridge and to the left of the main road, standing rather like a huge white elephant, is the curious unfinished hexagonal church of *Senhor da Pedra* (1747), the interior of which is of little interest.

6km. **CALDAS DA RAINHA** (16,900 inhab.) remains a frequented spa. Its warm sulphur springs have been reputed for many centuries, having grown up round the Hospital of Dona Leonor, queen of João II, established for invalids in 1486, and restored in 1747 by João V, who, it is said, derived much benefit from its waters. Southey, in 1801, found it a 'little clean town on sand amid fir groves', even if the Irish house there was expensive. It is also a garrison town, from which on the 16 March 1974 a detachment marched prematurely towards Lisbon, only to be turned back. It was also a temporary forced residence of refugees from occupied Europe during the Second World War. It has a reputation for its cakes, and one cannot well miss its crude green and yellow pottery. The factory of the artist and potter Rafael Bordalo Pinheiro (1846–1905: see p 151) was established here.

Its monuments are few. The chapel of the hospital, *N.S. do Pópulo*, has a curious Manueline cupola, 14C font, 17C azulejos, and a triptych attributed to Cristóvão de Figueiredo cut to fit the chancel arch.

In the park stands the *Museu de José Malhôa*, named after the local painter (1855–1933). His canvases, among those of his contemporaries, including Columbano (1857–1929), may be viewed here by those who have time to kill.

On the coast 10km NW is the beach of *Foz do Arelho*, at the mouth of the LAGOA DE ÓBIDOS, a salt-water creek famous for its eels.

12km. *Alfeizerão*. For the road hence to **Nazaré** see Rte 19.

From Alfeizerão the main road ascends a range of hills to the NE. The route was described in 1929 as being 'almost impossible for cars, the road is being repaired': it is now somewhat improved. We traverse attractive country, with the bald Serra dos Candieiros to the E, before winding down to (14.5km) *Alcobaça*.

Alcobaça is a pleasant little town in the centre of a rich fruit-growing district, standing at the confluence of the rivers Alcoa and Baça. It once had a reputation for its cotton chintzes. In the mid 18C the manufacture of cambrics had been promoted there under the guidance of Scottish and Irish managers, but (reported William Stephens of Marinha Grande in 1787) its products were 'trifling altho every effort and exertion has been made by one of the Inspectors to improve it. The situation of this fabric near the Convent where the Monks encourage Idleness by example and by distributing their superfluous provisions, makes all efforts of the managers ineffectual, and weakens their command over the workmen'.

It is still famous for its magnificent although mutilated Cistercian *ABBEY OF ALCOBAÇA, considered by many as being the finest surviving example of medieval architecture in Portugal. Lady Holland, who visited it in 1805, wrote: 'by far the best and least disgusting convent I ever saw'.

The whole façade is some 220m long. The Baroque W Front of the *Church*, with its two cupola-topped towers, retains a deep-set but worn Gothic portal and rose-window, below which is a wide terrace. The two ranges of domestic buildings flanking it once housed guest rooms (N) and to the S, the cells, formerly accommodating some hundreds of monks (while, according to Southey, the rabbit-yard contained 4000 rabbits).

It was founded by Afonso Henriques c 1153 as a thanks-offering for the capture of Santarém, and the original structure, started in 1178, was completed in 1223. Its mitred abbot, the senior of his rank in Portugal, was a personage of great influence, being ex-officio high almoner and precentor to the king. One of the figures in the São Vicente altarpiece in the Museu de Arte Antiga, Lisbon, has been identified as Vasco Tinoco. The W Front was cloaked by indifferent Baroque reconstruction in 1725, and the interior was adorned with rococo woodwork by William Elsden in 1770.

'Recollections of an Excursion to the Monasteries of Alcobaça and Batalha', Beckford's description of his visit there in June 1794, was not published until 1835. Here he found some 300 monks including servants 'living in a splendid manner', which is confirmed by his contemporaries. Twiss dined and supped with above 20 of the superiors in a private room '... and in the evening the bottle went as briskly about as ever I saw it do in Scotland; so that with the aid of some musical instruments, we spent a very agreeable day'; while the ill-informed and anti-clerical Major Dalrymple, having accepted their hospitality, ungratefully commented that it was a shame 'that the celestial pastors should possess so much worldly wealth, thereby wallowing in sloth and idleness, a nuisance to society'. In fact they were very good and 'improving' landlords.

Southey wrote that 'Perhaps no place contains so monstrous a medley as this huge convent ... a huge patched pile'. The French pillaged the place in 1810; the library, which was considerable, and contained 'many gifts from travellers and several from the inhabitants of the British Islands', according to Lady Holland, was ransacked. The monastery was again sacked during anti-clerical rioting in 1834. It has since been the object of the equally rigorous attentions of 'restorers',

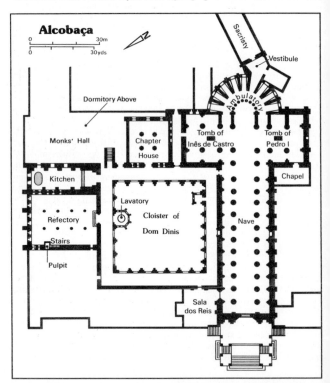

who in an attempt to re-convert the interior to its original Cistercian purity, have stripped it bare: 'one of the worst and most disgraceful works of vandalism of our times', in the words of Sitwell, perhaps too sweeping in his condemnation: 'All the magnificence of Alcobaça has gone, and the naked altars are the last stage in this wilful descent into disgrace'.

Alcobaça: the nave

INTERIOR. Nothing can now detract from the architectural impressiveness of the church, remarkable for its great length as compared with its width (109m by 23m; and 20m high), an impression accentuated by the great girth of the piers and the narrowness of the spaces between them, while the pier shafts have been curiously truncated some distance from the ground throughout its length. The general plan is modelled on the French Cistercian church of Cîteaux. Light is admitted only by the aisle windows and the rose-windows of the W front, and transepts.

The Tomb of Inês de Castro

In the S transept is the **Tomb of Pedro I** (died 1367); in the N transept the **Tomb of Inês de Castro** (died 1355), the royal lovers whose romantic tragedy is celebrated in Portuguese literature and history (see Rte 25C). They have been placed foot to foot, as it was traditionally said that the king had ordered this disposition so that at the Resurrection the first object before his eyes would be the form of his beloved: on their tombs are inscribed the words 'Até ao fim do mundo' (until the end of the world).

Both tombs are designed in the best traditions and with the highest craftsmanship of the 14C, and show the richness of imagination characteristic of Portuguese sculpture at its zenith. They are embellished by intricately carved scriptural scenes, martyrdoms, the Passion, etc. Note the line of musicians along the top of one side of that of Inês, and the Day of Judgement at the foot. The Wheel of Fortune may be seen at the foot of Dom Pedro's. Both are attended by six angels. Both tombs were damaged by D'Erlon's troops in search of treasure.

William Tomkinson, a cavalry officer, passing the monastery on 7 March 1811, noted that it 'exceeded anything I ever saw as a work of destruction. They [the French] had burnt what they could, and destroyed the remainder with an immense deal of trouble. The embalmed kings and queens were taken out of their tombs, and I saw them lying in as great preservation as the day they were interred. The fine tessellated pavement, from the entrance to the altar, was picked up, the facings to the stone pillars were destroyed nearly to the top, scaffolding having been erected for that purpose ...'.

In a chapel off the S transept are the tombs of Afonso II and Afonso III and their respective queens, Urraca and Brites. Here also is a mutilated terracotta group of the Death of St. Bernard, attributed to Frei Pedro (c 1687–90), which Southey, much prejudiced, condemned as one of 'the most execrable puppet shows of modern popery;— angels playing the fiddle at the nativity, and Portuguese washer-women coming to see the infant Jesus!'

Hence we may cross the ambulatory, off which is the vestibule, to the *Sacristy* (damaged in 1755), approached by a beautiful foliated Manueline doorway (c 1520).

It affords access to the circular *Chapel of the Relics* (1669–72), containing numerous painted reliquary busts, etc., long despoiled of their contents. Beyond the vestibule is the early 18C *Chapel of N.S. do Desterro*, with twisted columns.

A door in the N aisle admits to the **Cloister of Dom Dinis**, the lower storey of which, with double and triple arches surmounted by traceried circles, dates from 1308–11. The upper storey, with graceful arches, was added by the Card.-infant Dom Afonso (1509–40), son of Dom Manuel.

Off the E walk is the *Chapter House*, notable for its fine round-arched doorways and windows. A staircase adjacent ascends to the monks' *Dormitory*, its vaulting sustained by two rows of ten columns, extending over the Chapter-house and *Monks' Hall*. The latter, off the N wall of the cloister, is adjacent to the Kitchen.

The **Kitchen**, with an immense oblong pyramidal chimney and tiling of 1752, similar to those in the kitchen of the Palace of Sintra, has the rivulet (a branch of the Alcoa) mentioned by Beckford still running through its conduit. While still impressive in size, Beckford's 'most distinguished temple of gluttony in all Europe' now lies silent and empty; yet one can still imagine the pastry-making scene he so well described, 'which a numerous tribe of lay brothers and their attend-ants were rolling out and puffing up into a hundred different shapes, singing all the while as blithely as larks in a corn-field'.

Adjacent is the huge vaulted **Refectory**, with a flight of steps built into the thickness of the wall ascending to the lector's pulpit. This was the 'immense square of seventy or eighty feet; linen foul and greasy', which Beckford noted in his Journal of 1794. Earlier this century it was temporarily transformed into the local theatre! Beckford also referred to the young monks performing an opera in 'an extraordinarily spacious saloon ... normally assigned to holier purposes.' Opposite its entrance is a charming 14C *Lavatory* containing a hexagonal Renaiss-ance fountain.

Continuing the circuit of the cloister, we reach the *Sala dos Reis* (16C), containing royal statues and a group representing the coro-nation of Afonso Henriques, while the azulejos depict the Life of St. Bernard and the history of the monastery. A huge cauldron captured from the Spanish at Aljubarrota is preserved.

The rest of the much-debased monastic dependencies (including four other cloisters) has now been put to a variety of mundane uses, but entry may be gained to some parts by the persistent.

A little to the N is the attractive PRAÇA DA REPÚBLICA and, beyond, the converging rivers. A *Wine Museum* is passed (right) on the road to Leiria.

There is little else of interest in the immediate neighbourhood, except the remains of a Moorish *Castle*, to which—so Baron Taylor was informed by an old woman when he was sketching it early in the 19C—the Moorish chief to whom it belonged returned on one night of every year 'for the purpose of keeping a kind of witches' Sabbath, and of demanding twelve virgins as an annual tribute. "However", she continued, "there is not much danger in him now, for the *frades* prevent his injuring us; but still any young woman who visits the ruins by herself runs the risk of losing her senses, and I have even known some who have died from so doing'.'

Nazaré lies 13.5km to the NW: see Rte 19.

We bear E and then NE to (6.5km) *Aljubarrota*, with a 13C church. It gives its name to the decisive battle of 1385, which in fact took place some 10km further NE. In the village centre stood the house of Brites d'Almeida, the baker's wife, who, it is said, laid low seven Spanish soldiers with her oven-peel during the contest, whence the proverb: 'Endiabrado como a padeira de Aljubarrota' (as full of the devil as the baker's wife of Aljubarrota).

At 9km we join the main Lisbon–Coimbra road (N1: see Rte 18A), and c 1.5km beyond this junction reach a crossroad, 5km SE of which lies *Porto de Mós*: see Rte 18C.

The Battle of Aljubarrota, 1385

The **Battle of Aljubarrota**. At dawn on 14 August 1385 the Portuguese army heard mass at Porto de Mós before following the track thence and taking up a strong defensive position facing N. This lay between the hamlet and restored chapel of *São Jorge* (now by-passed by the main road, which veers to the W), and Batalha. It was here, in an area not then encumbered by pines, that João, Master of Avis, together with the Constable Nun' Álvares Pereira, redeployed their waiting troops, which included a small contingent of English archers. This movement had become necessary because the Spaniards, originally advancing from Leiria, had made a flanking march to the W before turning here for the attack, which in the event did not start until the late afternoon of that hot August day.

Although caution had been agreed, individual hot-heads amongst Juan I's undisciplined army forced the issue by indulging in harassing attacks, and soon both sides were generally engaged. The battle lasted hardly an hour, for although the Castilians were superior in numbers, they faltered when they saw their royal standard go down, the whole army disintegrating, Juan himself galloping off the field towards the castle at Santarém. João I was able to make the claim, without undue exaggeration, that 2500 enemy men-at-arms had been killed, apart from numerous members of the landed aristocracy of Portugal who had opposed his recent succession.

4km. **Batalha**, for which, and for the rest of the road, see Rte 18A.

C. Via Santarém and Tomar

Total distance, 225km (140 miles). E3 auto-estrada for 52km, there making our exit for (12km) *Cartaxo*—N3. 14km **Santarém**—40km **Torres Novas**.—After 8km turn left onto the N110 for (18.5km) **Tomar**—38.5km *Figueiró dos Vinhos* lies 16km E.—11km Fork left onto the E347 via *Penela* to (17km) **Conímbriga** and *Condeixa*—N1. 14km **Coimbra**.

For the first section of this route, see Rte 18A.

On leaving the motorway we bear NE to *Cartaxo*.

Some 6km short of this town, a road to the right leads to the ruined monastery of *Santa Maria das Virtudes*, where João II was visited by Columbus in c 1482 to discuss the possibilities of exploration beyond the Atlantic.

Cartaxo, an important wine-growing centre, contains a number of quintas, the most interesting of which is that of *Dos Chavões*. Note also the Manueline *Cruzeiro*. The Marqués de la Romana (1761–1811), the Spanish patriot, died here during the Peninsular War.—Some 7km NW, at *Vila Nova de São Pedro*, is an important prehistoric fortified *castro*, c 40m in diameter, discovered in 1936.—For *Manique do Intendente*, 5km beyond, see Rte 18A.—We cross the area occupied by Dom Pedro's forces prior to the evacuation of Santarém in the spring of 1834, at the close of the Miguelite War.

14km. **Santarém**: see the latter part of Rte 16.

FROM SANTARÉM TO BATALHA VIA PORTO DE MÓS (58km). After 4km we turn left onto the N362, and after 22km traverse *Alcanede*, with ruins of a *Castle* and a Roman bridge.—The road climbs (retrospective views) to (12km) *Mendiga*, with a church containing curious late 18C azulejos, beyond which we veer N, descending to (12km) **Porto de Mós**, with potteries and a 13C*Castle*, on a Roman site, altered in the mid 15C, and preserving a richly decorated balcony similar to that at Leiria. The Portuguese army heard mass here before the *Battle of Aljubarrota* (see above), fought some 5km NW.—8km. **Batalha**: see Rte 18A.

FROM SANTARÉM TO TOMAR VIA ALPIARÇA AND GOLEGÃ (61.5km): see the sub-route on p 202, in reverse, as far as *Golegã*, where we turn N to (7km) *Entroncamento*, and thence via *Atalaia* to (18.5km) *Tomar*: see below.

Continuing N from Santarém on the N3, we traverse (21km) *Pernes*, with relics of fortifications, S of which, on the Rio Alviela, are some slight Roman remains at *São Vicente de Paul*.

9km At *Alcanena*, 6km W, is the Bronze Age necropolis of *Marmota*.

10km **Torres Novas**: see p 203.

An ALTERNATIVE route (25km) to following the main road hence is to take the N349, turning left at the bottom of the hill beyond Torres Novas, off which after c 7km we fork right through *Paço*, with the 18C *Casa de Vargas*. Hence we veer right through most attractive country dotted with cypress trees, with a view (left) of the *Convento de Cristo* of Tomar, as we approach the town.

The main road continues E to (8km) *Entroncamento* (11,000 inhab.), there turning left onto the N110 through *Atalaia* (see p 203), then traversing undulating wooded country to (18.5km) *Tomar*, passing at

10km the right-hand turn for (10km) the *Pousada de São Pedro*, overlooking the Castelo do Bode reservoir on the Zêzere.

TOMAR (13,800 inhab.), although with some industry, is a charming small town on the Rio Nabão, overlooked to the W by the great Convent-Castle of the Knights Templar, for which it is justly famous.

Tomar's history is bound up with the fortunes of the military and monastic orders which have been its overlords. In 1157 Gualdim Pais, Grand Master of the Templars, was awarded the site of Roman *Nabantia*, which stood on the left bank of the river (some 2km downstream) where St. Irene was martyred in 653 (see Santarém, History), in recognition of his services in expelling the Moors. He is said to have begun a church (*Santa Maria dos Olivais*), and a castle, abandoned in 1162 for the better site on the hill opposite; and in 1190 the new fortress withstood the assaults of Almohad forces.

In 1314 the papal order for the suppression of the Templars was nominally enforced in Portugal; but Dom Dinis, mindful of their crusading enterprise in the past, decided to replace it by founding in 1319 the knightly Order of Christ, which succeeded to the extensive property of the Templars. In 1356 its headquarters (transferred from Castro Marím, in the Algarve) were at Tomar, and in 1417–60 its Grand Master was Prince Henry the Navigator. In 1492 the mastership (which afterwards always remained in the king's hands) fell to Manuel I, who set about enlarging the church.

Further impetus was given to the building operations by João III, who converted the Order into a monastic brotherhood, making the construction of living-quarters essential. The master of works (c 1523–51) was João de Castilho, who had already built the S Portal, and now added to the church and built the dormitories, and four additional cloisters. The main cloister, begun in 1557, was largely completed by Diogo de Torralva by 1562. In 1580 Philip II of Spain was proclaimed king of Portugal before the church door, and thereafter Tomar's political importance diminished, reflecting the decline in importance of the Order of Christ. Attempts were made to revive the town's commerce and in 1759 a Royal Hat Factory, and later a cotton-mill, were established.

In 1801 it was a military headquarters, and in 1809–10 Tomar was repeatedly sacked by Masséna's marauding troops—'fine paintings in the chapel torn in pieces, and many carried away; the organ broken, and altars thrown down, fireplaces made in all the cloisters, and every thing broken and defaced ... in wanton barbarity'—so wrote Colonel Frazer of the Royal Horse Artillery, continuing: 'The architecture of this convent is so fine, and the whole pile of buildings so noble, that I wonder I had never heard it mentioned'. In 1834 the monastic orders were suppressed, and it long remained in a sorry state of neglect, although partially restored in 1843. Murray's 'Hand-Book' of 1856 refers to the forecourt as being a wheat-field! Part of the convent is at present a military convalescent home, but it is hoped that they will be moved. The rest of the complex in being thoroughly restored.

To approach the ***CONVENTO DE CRISTO**, we ascend past the *Tourist Office* at the W end of the main avenue, and climb in zig-zags to the hill crest, leaving on our right the chapel of *N.S. da Conceição* (see below). The precincts are entered through the old gate beneath the ruined *Castle*. On the right of the terrace are the remains of the *Palace of Prince Henry*, where Dom Duarte died in 1438.

Ascending a flight of steps, dominated by the buttressed tower of the *Templars' Church*, we approach the SOUTH PORTAL, João de Castilho's addition of 1515, a brilliant combination of Flamboyant Gothic with Renaissance detail.

INTERIOR. On the right is the **Charola**, the original 16-sided church of the Templars, with the high altar enclosed in a central octagon, the typical plan of the Order, modelled on the Rotunda of the Holy Sepulchre in Jerusalem. On the ambulatory wall (right) are some paintings in the Flemish style attributed to Jorge Afonso (c 1510–20), and against the much-worn painted piers of the octagon are polychromed wooden figures of saints, probably by Fernão Muñoz, and the remnants of Oliver of Ghent's choir-stalls of 1511–14, largely des-

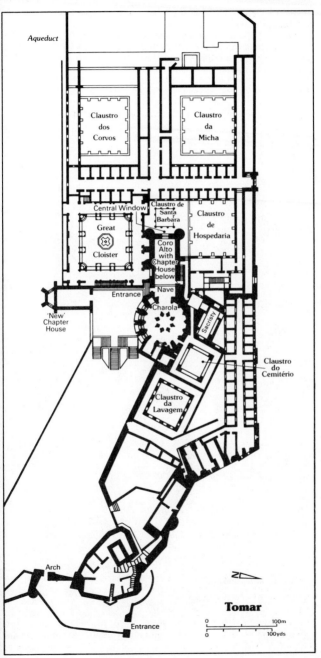

Aqueduct

Claustro dos Corvos

Claustro da Micha

Central Window

Claustro de Santa Barbara

Great Cloister

Claustro de Hospedaria

Coro Alto with Chapter House below

Entrance

Nave

'New' Chapter House

Charola

Sacristy

Claustro do Cemitério

Claustro da Lavagem

Arch

Entrance

Tomar

0 — 100m
0 — 100yds

troyed by the French invaders. Note also the faded coats-of-arms on
the ceiling.

From the E side a passage leads to the *Claustro do Cemitério*,
decorated with azulejos, and containing two 16C tombs, one of which
is that of Baltasar de Faria (died 1584), agent at Rome in 1542–51 of
the Infant Dom Henrique (Inquisitor-General since 1538). He was
later (1555) Visitor of Coimbra University. Hence we have a view of
the partially restored two-storey *Claustro da Lavagem*. On the left is
the *Sacristy* (1620).

Regaining the octagon, and the vaulted nave added to it in 1510–14
by Diogo de Arruda, we may first descend into the *Chapter House*
below the Coro Alto.

Tomar, the cental window

From the nave we enter the upper storey of the **Great Cloister**, its design attributed to Diogo de Torralva (1557–62), the Spanish son-in-law of Francisco de Arruda, but completed in 1587 by Filippo Terzi. Generally, though inappropriately, named the cloister 'dos Felipes', it is one of the most successful Renaissance works in Portugal, even if awkwardly abutting the chapter house, a window of which it partially screens. The main features of the design derive from two books of architecture by Serlio published at Venice in 1537 and 1540. Two spiral staircases descend to the lower level, in the centre of which is a Baroque fountain built by Pedro Fernandes de Torres; while in the SW corner is the unfinished *'New' Chapter-house* (1533–45).

A gallery off the upper cloister, overlooking the Manueline *Claustro de Santa Bárbara* and the *Claustro da Hospedaria* beyond, commands a fine view of the extraordinary **W Front** of the church, whose sensational central *Window* and supporting pinnacled buttresses comprise the outstanding example of the Manueline style at its most extravagant, an anonymous masterpiece designed while Diogo de Arruda was supervising work here (c 1510–14). The Cross of the Order of Christ surmounting the royal arms and the armillary spheres of Dom Manuel are connected by a writhing mass of ropework, seaweed and coral-stems with a profusion of pattern and foliation. Interesting details are the transverse rope with cork floats; the chain round one buttress, and the colossal buckled garter which binds the other, possibly symbolising the English Order of the Garter presented to Dom Manuel by Henry VII; and the head and shoulders of an old man supporting the roots of a tree-stump which protrudes from the base of the grated window. Above is a round window representing swelling sails held by spirally arranged ropes.

Parts of the other dependencies may be visited once their restoration has been completed. These comprise the Refectory and Kitchen; the Dormitory-corridors; and two further cloisters (*Da Micha*, and *Dos Corvos*), from the latter of which extends the *Aqueduct*: see below.

Before leaving the convent, visitors are advised to enquire for the key to *****N.S. da Conceição** (of the Immaculate Conception) on a spur overlooking the valley, on the left as we descend the hill. This is a plain and perfectly proportioned cruciform building with a low dome, and lined with Corinthian columns supporting barrel vaults in nave and aisles. Its construction, conjecturally assigned to the 1530s and certainly completed before 1572.

On regaining the foot of the hill, and before—or alternatively after—exploring the town, a short excursion by car is recommended to view the Aqueduct, known as the *****Aqueduto dos Pegões**. This is approached by following a track to the left (signposted) a short distance up the N113 climbing NW towards Vila Nova de Ourém. It leads through an almost Tuscan landscape before descending into a valley spanned by some of its total of 180 ogival arches constructed in 1593–1614 to bring water to the convent, and attributed to Terzi.
    Returning to Tomar, we pass (left) a lane to the chapel of *N.S. da Piedade* (1613; view), from which a long flight of steps descends to the porticoed octagonal chapel of *São Gregório* (16C), which we pass on regaining the town. Convenient parking may also be found here.

At the foot of the castle hill lies the attractive PRAÇA DA REPÚBLICA, the main square of the old town, preserving many 16–17C houses. Here the 17C *Town Hall* faces **São João Baptista** (1510), with Manueline doorways and an octagonal spire capped by an armillary sphere. Within are a carved stone pulpit, and 16C paintings, some attributed to Gregório Lopes (c 1460–1550), among them Salome with the head of the Baptist, and the Mass of St. Gregory (1538/9).

At No. 73 in the adjacent Rua Dr Joaquim Jacinto is the 14C *Synagogue, in use from the mid 15C until 1497, and the only one surviving in such good state in Portugal. It was recognised as such by a Polish Jewish refugee during the Second World War, and now houses the *Museu 'Abraham Zacuto'*. It is a square vaulted chamber sustained by four columns, and contains a number of tombstones and inscriptions in Hebrew collected from various sites in Portugal. The women's ritual baths, discovered below the floor of the adjacent house in 1985, may now be seen.

At the lower end of the street lie the late 18C buildings of a water-powered cotton-mill—once owned by Timoteo Lecussan Verdier (1754–1831), the editor, who was visited here in 1798 by Link, when touring Portugal, and Jácome Ratton—which in the 1850s employed 300 people.—Turning right here we approach the central roundabout, on the far side of which are remains of medieval buildings, and bear left across the river.

By turning right at the next crossroads, we soon reach, at a lower level, the much-restored church of **Santa Maria dos Olivais**, said to have been founded by Gualdim Pais (see History), but of this the basement of the detached belfry is probably all that remains. The church is a late 13C building altered in the 15C, its mutilated W porch surmounted by a large rose-window. Within are the graves of Pais (died 1195; 2nd S chapel), among other Templars; and the Renaissance tomb of Diogo de Pinheiro (died 1525; N side of chancel). He was first bishop of Funchal, but never visited his see.

Returning across the road junction, we shortly pass under an arch abutting (left) the Renaissance doorway of *Santa Iria* (1536), on the alleged site of that saint's martyrdom, and turn left across a 15C *Bridge*.—To the right is a pleasant riverside restaurant. Ahead is the main street of the old town (Rua Serpa Pinto), while to the right are riverside gardens flanked by a huge water-wheel.

For the road from Tomar to *Ourém* and *Leiria* see Rte 19 in reverse.

The N110 leads NE, after c 9km meeting the N238 from Sertã (see sub-route on p 206, in reverse), after another 5km by-passing (right) *Areias*, with a church attributed to João de Castilho (1548), and the ruins of a medieval tower.

12km. To the W is the ancient town of *Alvaiázere*, probably of Roman origin, with relics of a fort.

14.5km. **Figueiró dos Vinhos**, picturesquely situated, lies at a higher level among wooded hills 16km to the E, in the *Igreja Matriz* of which, with a Renaissance portal, are some 16C paintings and an organ of 1689; the convent of *N.S. do Carmo* dates from 1601.—Hence the road goes on to (20km) *Pedrógão Grande*: see p 206.

11km. The right-hand fork at this crossroads leads across country to Coimbra via (17km) **Miranda do Corvo**, an old town receiving its *foral* from Afonso Henriques in 1136, but much damaged by the French in the Peninsular War.—8.5km to the E is *Lousã* (see Rte 17). From Miranda the road continues N over a ridge to (8km) *Semide*, preserving the church (1697; rebuilt after a destructive fire) of the monastery of *Santa Maria*, founded by Afonso Henriques, lined with 18C azulejos, and preserving a large organ.

The N110 bears left and continues N over the hills via *Castelo Viegas* (right) to (32km) *Coimbra*.

We shortly turn left off the N110 onto the N347, by-passing **Penela**, an old town with a *Castle claimed to have been erected by 1087, but later rebuilt.

Our route climbs NW over a ridge, later descending towards (17km) *Condeixa*, passing (left) just prior to it, the important Roman site of **Conímbriga**, for which and for the rest of the route to **Coimbra**, 14km NE, see the latter part of Rte 18A.

19 Óbidos to Tomar, via Nazaré, Alcobaça, Batalha, Leiria and Ourém

Total distance, 126km (78 miles). N8. 7km **Caldas da Rainha**—12km *Alfeizerão*—N242. 4.5km *São Martinho do Porto*—12km **Nazaré**—13.5km **Alcobaça**—N8. 21km **Batalha**—N1. 11km **Leiria**—N113. 16km *Fátima* lies 6km S.—9km *Vila Nova de Ourém*—20km **Tomar**.

This composite excursion endeavours to follow a convenient cross-country route taking in some important monuments, which some travellers, pressed for time, attempt to visit in a day. As the main monuments have been described in detail in other routes, cross references are given whenever necessary.

For the road from Óbidos to *Alfeizerão*, see p 221.

Here we turn left to (4.5km) *São Martinho do Porto*, a small fishing village on a land-locked bay, beyond which we bear NE along an inland road, after c 9km veering left to follow the new road skirting the shore. Near by, at *São Gião*, is a church said to be of Visigothic origin.

3km **NAZARÉ**, an important and often-photographed fishing village. Its inhabitants, who are said to be of Phoenician descent, unconcernedly carry on their hard life in spite of the tourists who crowd the place during the season. The fishing boats, with their painted eyes, are indeed picturesque, even if they are now hauled up the beach by tractors rather than by teams of oxen; the sardines drying on their wire frames; the checkered shirts and black stocking caps of the men; the impassive groups of black-shawled women, with their thickly pleated skirts, and gold earrings: the scene is curious, and has great impact.

Its buildings are of considerably less interest. In the *Praia* or lower town, the narrow lanes of fishermen's dwellings lie at right-angles to the beach, near the N end of which a funicular ascends to the *Sítio* or upper town on the 110m-high cliff top (*View*; also approached by a road). The 17C chapel of *N.S. da Nazaré* replaces the hermitage founded in 1182 by Fuas Roupinho, the mayor of Porto de Mós, to receive an image of the Virgin, who miraculously saved him from riding headlong over the cliff when stag-hunting in a fog.

Marinha Grande (see p 213) lies 21km NE on the N242, off which after 13km the N356 turns right for *Batalha*, 13km E.

We turn SE for (13.5km) *Alcobaça*, after 10km passing a left turn for *Cós*, 6km NE, with the convent of *Santa Maria*, founded c 1279, but much transformed since, with interesting azulejos depicting scenes from the Life of São Bernardo de Claraval.

For **Alcobaça**, see p 221.

For the road from here to Batalha, 21km NE, and for **Batalha** itself, see p 208.

Leiria lies 11km N of Batalha: see p 212.

From Leiria we climb E and then bear SE on the N113 to (16km) the *Quinta da Sardinha* crossroads, 6km S of which lies *Fátima* (to which few—having seen Alcobaça and Batalha, and in expectation of visiting Tomar—will want to deviate).

Fátima, well-described as 'the Lourdes of Portugal', standing on a desolate high-lying plateau, is of little interest to the traveller unless he is curious to investigate the phenomenal growth of the religious souvenir industry and the massive commercialisation of the cult. The pilgrimage hither was described ten years after the apparitions occurred as being 'attended by real hardship, as the country is wild and accommodation practically non-existent'. The scene has changed. Under the Salazar regime, which imposed on the devout, vast sums were spent on the erection of a *Basílica* (consecrated in 1953), which is little less than an indefensible affront to the instinct of veneration. Its tower (65m high) is buttressed by a hemicycle surmounted by statues of sundry saints, below which, in the huge esplanade, occasionally thronged (on the 12-13th of each month), is a chapel on the site of visions of the Virgin said to have been witnessed on 13 May 1917 by three peasant children, two of whom did not survive the age of 12.

9km **Vila Nova de Ourém**, an important but decayed market town, to the SW of which stands the imposingly sited fortified enceinte of **Ourém Velha**, in which Sancho II's queen was held captive when carried off from Coimbra in 1246 by a band of barons headed by Raimundo Viegas de Portocarreiro, a brother of the archbishop of Braga, and very probably with her connivance.

The 15C *Igreja Matriz* (of Ourém Velha), rebuilt in 1756 and with a curious organ-loft, preserves in its crypt—similar to the Synagogue at Tomar—the drastically restored tomb of its founder. The *Castle* has unfortunately been the object of modern additions, which have not improved its otherwise remarkable bastions.

The road winds SE through attractive country to (20km) **Tomar**: see Rte 18C. A rewarding detour before entering the town is that to the *Aqueduct*, approached by a lane to the right just before we start to make the descent into the valley; see p 231.

20   Leiria to Oporto via Figueira da Foz and Aveiro

Total distance, 187km (116 miles). 53km **Figueira da Foz**—57km *Ílhavo*, and *Vista Alegre*—7km **Aveiro**—21km *Estarreja*—15km *Ovar*—18km *Espinho*—16km **Oporto**.

This route provides a pleasant alternative to the frequently congested N1. We drive almost due N parallel to the railway (left) to (38km) *Marinha das Ondas*, preserving the ruins of the *Monastery of Ceiça*, of ancient foundation, largely rebuilt in the 17C, beyond which we bear NW to cross the estuary of the Mondego, on the far bank of which lies (15km) *Figueira*.

FIGUEIRA DA FOZ (12,800 inhab.) is an important fishing port and frequented bathing resort of slight interest except for its sands, casino, and new museum. It lies at the mouth *(foz)* of the Mondego, crossed here by two bridges, one recently completed, which promises to ease communication between Lisbon and Oporto.

It was off the extensive beaches on both sides of the river-mouth that between 1–5 August 1808 Wellington's expeditionary force disembarked from its transports, with some losses of men and equipment in the pounding surf, preparatory to marching S towards Lisbon and its first encounter with the French at Roliça (cf.).

Wellington briefly occupied the late 16C fort of *Santa Catarina* at the SW corner of the town, built to defend the bar. Before reaching this we pass the Jardim Municipal, just behind which, to the right, is the *Casa do Paço*, its walls covered with several thousand 18C Dutch tiles said to have been translated here from a shipload destined elsewhere.

Some minutes' walk inland from this point is the *Museu municipal do Dr Santos Rocha*, installed in a modern building overlooking a park, and under the auspices of the Gulbenkian Foundation. The archaeological collection is important, with finds from dolmens in the region, funerary stelae (some from Faro in the Algarve), Phoenician inscriptions, and ceramics, etc. Other sections are devoted to furniture, numismatics, ethnography, and paintings (the last disappointing, except for the naïve ex-votos); and in a covered courtyard, a marine section, describing the fishing industry, salting, etc.

For the road hence to **Coimbra**, 44km E, see the latter part of Rte 24, in reverse.

Skirting the E flank of the SERRA DA BOA VIAGEM to the N of Figueira, the site of Neolithic settlements, we soon descend to the low-lying plain skirted by sandhills to the W, the coast being approached by roads leading off the N109 at (24km) *Tocha*, with good azulejos of 1763 in its church, and 13km beyond, at *Mira*; and from (15km) *Vagos*.

Some 5km beyond Vagos, in the S outskirts of *Ílhavo* (see below), a road turns left to **Vista Alegre**, with deposits of china clay in its vicinity, first traversing a village of workers' cottages. The manufactory here was founded in 1824 by José Ferreira Pinto Basto (1774–1839), whose wife, Bárbara Inocência Allen, was of English descent. It is said that the fragile china was at one time carried to Oporto and Lisbon on camel-back.

Adjacent to the large *Factory*, which may be visited on Monday, Wednesday and Friday from 16.00–18.00, is the *Museum*, well displaying the extensive range of glass and porcelain produced here during the last 160 years. Glass is no longer made, but Vista Alegre porcelain may be bought or ordered at the showroom next door.

Opposite is the chapel of *N.S. da Penha*, containing the dramatic *Tomb* of Manuel de Moura Manuel, Bp of Miranda do Douro (died 1699), by Claude de Laprade.

Ílhavo, an ancient fishing port until eventually virtually stranded by shifting sands, has a *Museum* containing models of fishing-boats, local costumes, examples of *moliceiros* (designed to harvest seaweed), etc., and a conchological collection.

7km. **AVEIRO** (29,200 inhab.) is an episcopal city and district capital sited on the edge of dull mud-flats adjoining the E bank of the marshy lagoon or Ria de Aveiro, fed by the Vouga, Águeda, and Antuã. It is an ancient and important fishing-port with a considerable trade in salt, obtained by evaporation, and with its few canals, dykes, and humpbacked bridges, it has a slightly Dutch appearance. It contains a museum of some interest in the Convento de Jesús, and has shipyards in the area; it is also noted for its *ovos moles*, an egg sweetmeat, its sardines, and its *mexilhões*, or preserved mussels.

Roman *Talabriga* became prosperous in the 16C, with the exploitation by João Afonso of the cod-banks of Newfoundland, and its fishing fleet at one time counted 60 vessels. The fish used to be taken into the interior in baskets carried on women's heads, many of them from the village of Ovar (see below), at the N end of the lagoon. In 1575, a year of drought, a violent storm helped to close the sand bar across the mouth of the Vouga, which overflowed its banks during winter floods, and inundating the low-lying area parallel to the coast, formed fever-breeding marshes, which reduced Aveiro's population from some 14,000 to 5000. In 1808, a canal, the *Barra Nova*, was cut through to drain the marshes, and only the salt lagoon now remains. In May 1809 General Hill, by transporting a brigade at a time by boats hence to Ovar, partially outflanked the French retreating on Oporto.

Its most famous native is José Estevão Coelho de Magalhães (1809–62), the political orator.

Aveiro will be at the western end of the transverse road under construction from the frontier at Vilar Formoso, passing near Guarda and Viseu, which will ease communication considerably in this direction.

Trips on the lagoon can be arranged with the Tourist Office, and individual boats, motor and otherwise, may also be hired.

Roads converge on the town centre, the PRAÇA HUMBERTO DELGADO, in fact a widened bridge across the central *Canal*, near which is a car park. The *Tourist Office* is a short distance to the SW, opposite the 16C *Misericórdia*. The *Harbour Master's house* (Capitania do Porto), to the E, appears to be built over an open drain.

To the SE a road leads up to the Praça do Milenário, with a Manueline Calvary and (left) the church of *São Domingos*, described as 'a squalid and tawdry room' in the 1850s by J.M. Neale, which, raised to the rank of cathedral, has recently been monstrously 'modernised'. Its only objects of interest are the ten paintings of the Life of St. Dominic placed over the choir-stalls, and an 18C organ.

To the W of the square is the former *Convento de Jesus* (15C; altered in the 18C), now housing the ***Museu Regional**, which although extensive, contains little of great merit. The principal objects are the richly decorated *Capela da Princesa Santa Joana, named after the daughter of Afonso V, who spent the last 14 years of her life here, dying in 1489; she was unaccountably beatified in 1693. A charming series of naïve 17C paintings describes her life from the moment of leaving her father's palace. Her *Tomb*, an ugly confection of marble marquetry completed in 1711 by João Antunes, stands in the Coro Baixo. Note the *talha dourada* by Antônio Gomes and José Coreia (before 1725), and in the *Coro Alto* the Chinoiserie panelling and ceiling (1731), and the two portable organs. The azulejos in the *Refectory*, the 16C Albuquerque tomb in the Cloister, and the *presépio* or crib *attributed to Machado de Castro*, are notable; and among paintings, one *attributed to Vieira Portuense* on copper, a Sienese Virgin and Child, and a Portrait of Santa Joana, *attributed to Nuno Gonçalves*, are of interest in an otherwise miscellaneous collection of ecclesiastical paintings and sculpture, etc.

A few minutes' walk to the W brings one to the Praça do Marquês de Pombal, with a *Carmelite church* of c 1650, preserving rich gilding.—Further to the S, adjoining a park, stands *Santo António*, founded in 1524, with an 18C façade.

By turning left on crossing to the N bank of the canal, and then over a hump-backed bridge, we reach the site of the *Fish Auction*, which takes place daily between 6.00 and 9.00 AM.

The only other building of interest is best approached by road, turning right on crossing the canal and following the main Av. Dr Lourenço Peixinho to the railway station, continuing past which, we turn left at the next T-junction. Below gardens on the right stands the restored octagonal chapel of *Senhor das Barrocas* of 1722–32, the design of which has been attributed to João Antunes, containing work ascribed to Claude de Laprade.

Leaving Aveiro, we follow the N109 NE, shortly passing (left) a particularly evil-smelling cellulose factory to reach (11km) a road junction; shortly beyond is an entrance to the A1 motorway for Oporto.

We turn N for (10km) *Estarreja*, preserving the 17C *Casa da Praça*.

The EXCURSION may be made hence to the *Pousada da Ria*, 22km SW, by turning left through the fishing village of *Murtosa* and across an arm of the Ria d'Aveiro by a new bridge to the long peninsula cutting it off from the Atlantic. The left-hand turn here—a humpy road—leads past (13km) the *Pousada da Ria*, overlooking the lagoon, occasionally dotted with the seaweed-harvesting *moliceiros*, and continues on to (7km) *Praia da São Jacinto*, on the N bank of the Vouga estuary. To the W, at the S end of a sandy beach over 40km long, the Atlantic breakers, with a strong undertow, crash against the shore.—The right-hand turn skirts the N arm of the lagoon to regain the main road just N of *Ovar*. The small resorts on the W side of the peninsula are sad little places, however much sand and sea they have to offer.

From Estarreja we continue N through (6km) *Avanca*, with a large mid 18C church, to (9km left) **OVAR** (9900 inhab.), an agricultural centre with light industries, once of importance as a fishing village in a somewhat sombre district, described at the turn of the 19C as being a wilderness 'so perfect and so destitute of any trace of civilization, that no part of Siberia or Africa could exhibit greater solitude'! Its short-skirted big-boned fishwives, known as '*Varinas*, sometimes still seen barefooted, found a living by taking their catch to sell in the hinterland, and even in Lisbon the local itinerant fishwives are still so named. There is a small ethnographical collection near the town centre.

From just N of the town the N223 bears NE to an entry to the motorway, and (11km) *Vila da Feira*: see Rte 26.

11km. A turning to the right leads shortly to *Rio Meão* (not to be confused with Rio Mau), with an early church remodelled in the 15C, and again later.

5km. **Espinho** (12,900 inhab.), with canneries, but more recently developed into a seaside resort, even boasting a casino to add to its distractions. A curiosity of the place is the fact that its streets are merely numbered, not named.

The road skirts other resorts, among them *Granja* and *Miramar*, before turning inland to approach (16km) **Oporto**: see Rte 33.

21 (Ciudad Rodrigo) Vilar Formoso to Coimbra via Guarda

Total distance, 208km (129 miles). *Fuentes de Oñoro* (Spanish Customs)—*Vilar Formoso* (Portuguese Customs)—N16. 42km **Guarda**—28km *Celorico da Beira*—N17. 39km *Seia* is 2km to the S.—19km *Oliveira do Hospital* is 3km to the N.—53km *Penacova* is 13km NW.—27km **Coimbra**.

For *Ciudad Rodrigo* (27km E), and *Fuentes de Oñoro*, site of the critical battle between Masséna and Wellington of May 1811, see *Blue Guide Spain*, and Rte 22B. We enter *Vilar Formoso*.

For the roads from Vilar Formoso to *Castelo Branco* see Rte 22; for that to *Vila Real* see Rte 27.

The new road, running roughly parallel to the old, part of the projected highway via Viseu to Aveiro, leads to a point just short of Guarda. When completed, it will bear NW, gradually descending towards Celorico.

After 10km we cross the rocky valley of the Coa, passing (right) near the ruins of the old frontier fortress of *Castelo Bom*. This area served as a base for part of Wellington's forces during the months prior to the siege of Ciudad Rodrigo in January 1812, and the Battle of Salamanca in the June of that year. And his lines of communication and supply passed through here during the winter of 1812/13 and before his advance to Vitoria. During two successive winters Wellington himself lived in a house opposite the church at *Freinada*, 5km S of the road between Vilar Formoso and Castelo Bom.

Castelo Mendo, an old town preserving relics of its fortifications, lies to the S of the old road. We traverse bare undulating country before obtaining a distant view of hill-top *Guarda*, passing (right) on its outskirts the Romanesque church of *Póvoa do Milea*, with a small rose-window. Adjacent to the church is the site of an ancient settlement; the objects excavated there are in the Regional museum.

GUARDA (13,100 inhab.), lying at just over 1000m, is the highest and coldest town in Portugal, standing as it does on a ridge commanding the entrances to the upper Mondego valley (W), the Zêzere (SW), and with a wide view to the E towards the wind-blown plateau of Spain.

According to J.M. Neale, writing in the 1850s, it was known as the city of the four Fs: Fria, Farta, Forte, and Feia (cold, well-supplied, strong, and ugly). This episcopal city has always been of strategic importance, and its name alludes to its foundation by Sancho I in 1197 as a frontier-guard against the Moors. Ruins of its early castle, dominating the area, are seen above the cathedral. It was also a base of Wellington's operations in 1811–12, after being pillaged by the French, who converted the cathedral into stables.

The partially arcaded LARGO LUIS DE CAMÕES in the centre of the old town is overlooked by the grey granite fortress-like *Cathedral, being restored, which replaced an earlier church on a different site, demolished c 1375 as being too near the walls for security.

The new building was not completed until c 1540. It is to some extent inspired by Batalha, being the only other church in Portugal with a clerestory and flying buttresses. Note the gargoyles (those facing Spain are stone cannon), and trefoil ornamentation. The narrow W front is constricted by two octagonal towers. The interior, in spite of the thick ribs of the vault, is imposing. Boitac worked on the building in 1504–17, and Manueline influence is seen in the pair of twisted colonettes near the crossing, and the keystone above. The somewhat static four-tiered retable, with its details and statues picked out in gilt, is attributed to Jean de Rouen (1550–52). In the **Capela dos Pinas** is an unusual late Gothic bishop's tomb. Admission to the cathedral may be difficult to obtain on Tuesdays.

From behind the apse we pass through the *Torre dos Ferreiros*, a medieval town gate, beyond which, by bearing right and then left, we reach the *Bishop's Palace* (rebuilt in 1601), now partly occupied by the **Regional Museum**.

The building has recently been gutted, and its collections are now well displayed in a series of rooms round the courtyard and in the open-plan first floor. Sections are devoted to the geology, flora and fauna of the area, together with archaeological collections, and also Roman, Suevic and Visigothic artefacts. The First Floor has sections concerning the life and productions of the District, and paintings, a number of them by Eduardo Malta, Eduardo Lapa, and T. Victoriano. A collection of militaria can be seen, with relics of the Peninsular War period, etc.

To the N is the Baroque façade of the *Misericórdia* (17C), containing a good Renaissance tomb to the left of the chancel.—Continuing N, we pass the *Porta da Estrela* and a stretch of the town *Walls* (*View*) to re-enter by the *Porta do Rei* and regain the central square.—A short distance to the N of the square stands *São Vicente* (18C), with contemporary azulejo panels.

For the road from Guarda to *Miranda do Douro* see Rte 31, in reverse; to *Viseu*, Rte 23; and for *Castelo Branco* via *Covilhã*, Rte 22A.

Shortly after leaving Guarda, the road bears round to the N, descending steeply into the upper valley of the Mondego, with magnificent *Views across to the N spur of the SERRA DA ESTRELA, and down into the valley itself. The scenery also changes once we leave the high central plateau of the Peninsula and drop some 500m in 10km, and we indeed appear to be entering another country.

The village of *Aldeia Viçosa*, down in the valley, was until c 40 years ago known as *Porco* after the wild boar that infested the area.—At *Açores*, to the right of the road at the valley floor, the church preserves some 16C paintings and a Latin funerary inscription referring to a Visigothic princess who died there in 666.

The main road bears left, by-passing Celorico, which may be approached by keeping right and crossing an old granite bridge.

Celorico da Beira, long at an important junction of roads, is dominated by the ruins of its *Castle*, possibly of Roman origin. The *Igreja Matriz* (18C; replacing one of the 13C) was used as a British hospital during part of the Peninsular War.

For roads hence to *Trancosa* (19km N) and *Lamego* see Rte 27A; for that to *Viseu*, Rte 23.

We veer SW parallel to the great dividing range of the SERRA DA ESTRELA, the Roman *Herminius Major*.

A worthwhile DETOUR, at the same time providing several wide views N, may be made by turning left before or at (11km) *Carrapichana* for (6km) hill-top *Linhares*, a village of ancient origin largely composed of 15C houses. The façade of a gutted mansion is passed near the village entrance. A narrow street leads up to the partly restored *Castle* ruins, displaying some remarkable stonework (return by the same street). Linhares, formerly *Leniobriga*, was the seat of a Visigothic bishopric, and it would appear from what monuments remain on the narrow road winding along the valley side here that this was formerly the 'main' road, later superseded by the present highway. We may continue along the older road by turning left before regaining Carrapichana. This road later traverses *Melo*, with the desecrated remains of a medieval palace, above which lies *Folgosinhos*, with relics of fortifications. The road may be followed SW through *Gouveia* and *Seia* (for both see below) before returning to the main road 2km from the latter.

The N17 drives through a particularly beautiful part of the country, with its orchards, and vineyards with their granite props, through (5km) *Vila Cortes da Serra*, with a number of old stone houses, to reach crossroads 9km beyond.

3km SE is **Gouveia**, above which towers the peak of *Santinha* (1593m.). Although a very ancient town, its main surviving monument is the 16C *Casa da Torre*. It was briefly Wellington's HQ before retiring on Busaco (September 1810).

Hence the N232 ascends to cross the range, passing the source of the Mondego before climbing steeply down to *Manteigas*, 38km to the S.: see Rte 22A.

13km. 2km S is **Seia** (5650 inhab.), taken from the Moors by Afonso Henriques c 1055 (then known as *Sena*), an attractively sited town containing several old houses, including the *Casa dos Obras* (18C), and on the site of its castle, the *Igreja Matriz*. It was the birthplace of the politician Afonso Augusto da Costa (1871–1937).

Hence the N339 ascends steeply to the SE to (29km) *Torre* (1991m), the summit of the SERRA DA ESTRELA, and the highest peak in Portugal, commanding—in good weather—superb panoramic *Views. The road descends even more steeply to *Covilhã* (18km beyond: see Rte 22A), passing the source of the Zêzere. It is as well to check on the condition of the road during winter months before attempting the climb.—Another longer road (80km) climbs S from Seia viâ *São Romão*, and likewise commands extensive views both on the ascent and as it climbs down to the E towards *Covilhã* via (59km) the tiny spa of *Unhais da Serra*.

13km *Póvoa das Quartas*, a hamlet of stone houses with exterior steps, lies to the right of the road, immediately beyond which (left) is the *Pousada de Santa Bárbara*, providing a fine *View* across to the SERRA DA ESTRELA, and a convenient base from which to explore the district.

6km. 3km to the right lies **Oliveira do Hospital**, a beautifully situated market town at the head of a valley settled since Roman times; a number of buildings in the vicinity appear to contain Roman masonry, while at the neighbouring village of *Bobadela* (3km W) there is a *Roman Arch*. Oliveira, as its name implies, belonged to the Hospitallers. Its *Igreja Matriz* (13–14C; later remodelled) contains tombs of the Ferreiros, above which a carved equestrian knight has been placed (comp. with that in the Museum at Coimbra); note also the 14C altarpiece.

5km. A left-hand turn leads to (4km) *Avô*, with the ruins of a *Castle* built by Dom Dinis, and the Manueline house of the poet Bras Garcia de Mascarenhas (1596–1656).—SE is the hamlet of *Aldeia das Dez*, probably built on the site of a Roman castro.

A track climbing from Aldeia das Dez (off which another turns to climb to the ancient village of *Piódão*, below the *Serra de Açor*, rising to 1340m) commands extensive mountain views, and later joins the N344 leading S to *Porta da Balsa*, among numerous small reservoirs in the centre of this beautiful, wild, district. Many of the village churches between, and including, Avô, *Arganil*, and *Góis* (46km SW), along the S flank of the luxuriant ALVA VALLEY, contain medieval remains. If following this road, we may regain our route 24km NW of *Góis* (see p 206), some 27km E of Coimbra.

Continuing W on the N17, the next left turn leads shortly to **Lourosa**, an old village, where the church of *São Pedro* is the only one of its kind surviving in Portugal. In 911 Ordoño II ordered that the limits of the ancient bishopric of Dume should be marked out, and in the following year this church was erected, presumably by Mozárab workman. It consists of a central nave with shorter aisles divided from it by broad horseshoe arches. The *ajimece* windows and the typical Visigothic decoration of the period in the entrance porch will also be noticed; and a baptismal stone and confessional seat are pointed out. The 15C belfry was removed to its present position when the church was restored in the early 1930s.

Regaining the main road, we continue W, frequently obtaining extensive views from the ridge we follow between the valleys of the Alva and Mondego.

5km A right-hand turn leads c 23km NW to *Tábua*, with a large 18C church, overlooking the Mondego, which we cross to approach *Santa Comba Dão*, on the direct road to *Luso* and *Busaco*: see Rte 24.

17km The late 13C chapel of *São Pedro* (*Arganil*) is 7km S.

9km The church at *Pombeiro da Beira*, some 5km S, contains the Manueline tomb of Mateus da Cunha, attributed to Diogo Pires the Younger.

We shortly cross the Alva, and at 17km reach the Penacova crossroads: *Penacova* itself (see Rte 24) lies over a range of wooded hills to the N.

The main road continues W, after 7km passing near (left) *Foz de Arouce* (frequently mis-spelled Aronce in contemporary descriptions), where in March 1811 Marshal Ney narrowly escaped capture. Some 500 of his troops, forming Masséna's rearguard, were killed or drowned in their precipitate retreat under strong British pressure, and some 200 mules were left hamstrung; the British loss was about 65. Ney, insubordinate to Masséna, shortly after returned to France in disgrace.

Lousã lies 7km SE; see p 206.

The road follows the winding valley of the Rio Ceira, a tributary of the Mondego, to (20km) **Coimbra**: see Rte 25.

22   Vilar Formoso to Castelo Branco

A.   Via Guarda and Covilhã

Total distance, 149km (93 miles). N16. 42km **Guarda**—N18. 25km **Belmonte**—20km **Covilhã**—18km *Fundão*—13km *Alpedrinha*—31km **Castelo Branco**.

For the road to **Guarda** see Rte 21. Here we turn S onto the N18.

FROM GUARDA TO COVILHÃ VIA MANTEIGAS (75km; the excursion up to *Torre* will add 12km to the route). Those wishing to visit the highest peak of the SERRA DA ESTRELA (and in Portugal) may conveniently make the ascent by this sub-route, should visibility be good, and the road not snowbound, as it occasionally is in winter. We bear to the right off the N18 some 5km S of Guarda onto the N18.1, shortly descending down a parallel valley to (23.5km) *Valhelhas*, with a church of 1262, and an old bridge in the valley to the SE.—Turn onto the N232 here, bearing W to descend to (17.5km) **Manteigas** (*Pousada de São Lourenço*, and *Hotel de Manteigas*), an old town famous for its butter (as its name implies), cheese, and trout. The main road climbs steeply in hairpin bends across the range, later descending to (38km) *Gouveia*: see Rte 21.—We bear SW via the small spa of *Caldas de Manteigas*, 6km to the E of which, approached by a rough track, is the cascade of the *Poço do Inferno* (Hell's Well). After 11km we reach the N339.—The summit of the range, the **Torre** (previously called *O Malhão*), lies some 6km up to the right, at a height of 1991m (6532ft), commanding wonderful panoramic views.—*Seia*, on the far side of the range, lies 29km NW: see Rte 21.—Descending from the Torre, we climb steeply down the flank of the Serra through the winter sports and mountaineering centre of *Penhas da Saúde* to *Covilhã*: see below.

The N18 shortly reaches a watershed, and commences the descent into the valley of a tributary of the Zêzere (*Views*): after 23km, as we approach *Belmonte* on its height, a road to the left leads almost immediately to (right) the *Torre Centum Cellas, a curious and interesting ruin, almost certainly of Roman origin, but no convincing answer has yet been advanced as to its precise purpose.

2km The ascent to **Belmonte** itself forks off to the left. The village, commanded by its granite *Castle* (late 13C; and at various times restored, the most recent being the most inept), providing extensive views. Opposite are the remains of perhaps a council house (as at Braganza), and near by is the old church of *São Tiago*, preserving a 14C pietà, and the chapel of the Cabral family. Pedro Álvares Cabral (c 1467–1526), the 'discoverer' of Brazil (1500), which he named Vera Cruz, was born at Belmonte (and is buried at Santarém). The statue of N.S. da Esperança, which travelled with Cabral round the Cape of

Good Hope on his expedition to India, is preserved in the more modern church at the far side of the village.

There are slight traces of Roman fortifications at *Caria*, 10km S, and further remains at *Capinha*, some 12km beyond.

We cross the Zêzere and continue due SW to (20km) *Covilhã*, also by-passed, on the steep lower slopes of the SERRA DA ESTRELA.

COVILHÃ (22,200 inhab.), a surprisingly large town developing as a resort for winter sports and excursions into the range, has long been an important textile centre, well known for its woollen blankets.

Sancho I, in resettling the area in the late 12C, granted it a foral guaranteeing the liberty and freedom of all Christian captives after a year's residence, while Afonso III encouraged trade by granting safe conducts on the roads to its August fair, where no fairgoer could be arrested for any past crime from a week before its commencement until 30 days after! Some crypto Jews later settled in the district.

In 1677 the English consul in Lisbon was reporting to London that the Portuguese ambassador there had apparently lured over nine men and two women from Colchester 'to teach their people to card and spin in the English way', and that they had gone to Covilhã in spite of him trying to persuade them to return home. Looms also were smuggled over, together with more English workers, and some months later the consul was reiterating that unless they were recalled the English exports of cloth to Portugal would soon be ruined. Colonel John Richards, visiting Covilhã in 1704, observed that the industry was not flourishing because of the Inquisition's interference with the New Christian entrepreneurs and artisans. Nevertheless by the mid 19C some 150 looms were in operation, manufacturing brown woollen cloth.

It was a cavalry base during the Peninsular War, with Sir Stapleton Cotton in command, and many dances were got up to enliven the long winter evenings, the local females being passionately addicted to balls: indeed Commissary Schaumann refers to 'barbarously brilliant' balls, at the same time contending that 'As regards morals' ... he had never come across 'such a Sodom and Gomorrah as that place was'.

It was the birthplace of Hector Pinto (c 1528–c 1584), the mystic.

Its remaining monuments are of slight importance, among them the relics of a *Castle*, and in the lower town (to the left of the Castelo Branco road, just before passing under a bridge), the Romanesque chapel of *São Martinho*.

We now descend to and cross the Zêzere again and traverse a fertile region known as the COVA DA BEIRA to (18km) **Fundão**, pleasantly situated amidst orchards below the N slope of the SERRA DA GARDUNHA.—There are important wolfram deposits at *Panasqueira*, not far distant.

An alternative to the main route is that turning S 6km SW of Fundão, and passing through the ancient village of *São Vicente de Beira*, to which Sancho I conceded a *foral* in 1195, and preserving a number of medieval houses.

Crossing the Serra, which commands some beautiful views, we pass (left) after 7km the village of *Alcaide*, with a 13C church, altered in the 16C; and with numerous chapels in its vicinity.

8km **Alpedrinha**, Roman *Petrata* or *Petratinia*, home town of the notorious 15C pluralist Jorge da Costa, Cardinal of Alpedrinha, Archbishop of Braga, Lisbon, and Évora (and also taking under his capacious wing the bishopric of Coimbra, the priories of Crato, and Guimarães; and the abbacies of São José de Tarouca, and even Alcobaça).

It conserves a number of old houses, a ruined 18C palace, an 18C fountain, a section of Roman road. Among the churches the *Igreja*

Matriz (16C; largely replacing the Romanesque original) and the *Capela do Leão* (early 16C) are of some interest.

After 3km a lane to the right leads 3km to *****Castelo Novo**, an attractively sited village refounded in 1202, preserving a number of 17C houses, and the ruins of a *Castle*.

The N18 continues S, following the line of a Roman road, after c 20km by-passing (left) *Alcains*, with some buildings of interest, before approaching (8km) **Castelo Branco**: see Rte 17.

For roads continuing S see Rte 14, in reverse. At (46km) *Nisa*, we bear SW on the N364 for *Lisbon*, joining the N118 11km beyond. *Abrantes* lies 45km further W: see Rte 16.

B.   Via Sabugal and Penamacor

Total distance, 133km (83 miles). N16. 15km. Turn S onto N324—36km **Sabugal**—12km. Turn left to (20km) **Penamacor**—20km *São Miguel de Ancha* crossroads—30km **Castelo Branco**. The recommended detour to take in **Monsanto** and **Idanha-a-Velha** will add 36km (22 miles) to the route.

An alternative to the first part of the main route to Sabugal is the N332 turning left almost immediately, traversing part of the battlefield of **Fuentes de Oñoro**, where on 3 and 5 May 1811 the French under Masséna made two powerful attacks in an unsuccessful attempt to dislodge Wellington, losing some 2200 men compared with 1550 of the Allies, who nevertheless were temporarily forced to withdraw the right flank of their line at *Nave de Haver*. The road continues S parallel to the frontier before veering SW through *Alfaiates*, with a ruined *Castle*, to *Sabugal*.

For the first section of this route see Rte 21. After 15km we turn left and follow the N234 to (36km) *Sabugal*, leaving on our right *Vila do Touro*, with relics of a *Castle*.

Sabugal, an early frontier fortress and the scene of a meeting in 1230/1 between Fernando III of León and his cousin Sancho II, was for some time under Spanish control, not being returned definitively to Portugal until 1393. Masséna withdrew through Sabugal when retreating from Guarda in 1811, and in a confused action here on 3 April, Reynier's rearguard was badly mauled (losing 760 men compared with the Allied loss of 180), and would have been annihilated but for the incompetence of Sir William Erskine's command. Sabugal preserves a medieval *Bridge* over the Coa, and an early 14C *Castle*.—Another *Castle* (13C) can be seen at *Sortelha*, 11km due W.

The road descends into the VALE DA SENHORA DA PÓVOA, after 12km turning S to (20km) **Penamacor**, on a commanding height. Although it retains some of its ramparts and gates surrounding ancient dwellings, and relics of its castle *Keep*, Penamacor preserves little else of great moment other than its steep lanes containing occasional Manueline windows, and a *Misericórdia*; the 16C convent of *Santo António*, just off the Castelo Branco road, with a two-storeyed cloister, is of some interest. It was at Penamacor that in 1584 the first of the false Sebastian pretenders briefly held court among the superstitious peasantry. It was the birthplace of António Nunes Ribeiro

Sanches (1699–1783), of Jewish origin, physician to Catherine II of
Russia.

The DETOUR to take in MONSANTO and IDANHA-A-VELHA may
conveniently be made from here, the main road being regained 20km
SW. We follow the N332 due S to (16km) *Medelim*, repopulated in
1200, but probably once a Roman station. 7km E of Medelim is
*Monsanto, a quaint village of granite dwellings built into a boulder-
strewn height crowned by a *Castle* (Views), below which is the relic of
a Romanesque church.—Hence the road continues E via *Penha
Garcia*, on another rocky outcrop, anciently fortified, to (23km)
Termas de Monfortinho (see Rte 17).

Returning to the Medelim crossroad, we turn left to (7km) **Idanha-a-
Velha**, just to the left of the road, the site of Roman *Egitania*, and
legendary birthplace of Wamba, elected king of the Goths in 672. It
was also the seat of a bishopric until the place was sacked by the
Moors. This was transferred to Guarda in 1199. The present village
takes up only a part of the massive walled enclosure, of which a
rebuilt Roman doorway is to be seen, while a tower has been erected
on the base of a Roman temple. The key should be requested from a
villager living near this tower, who will escort the visitor through the
partially excavated area to the restored Paleo-Christian **Basilica*, in
the three naves of which are preserved a number of interesting carved
and inscribed stones from the site, which is undergoing further
exploration. There is a Roman *Bridge* over the river Ponsul.—*Idanha-
a-Nova* lies 13km SW: see Rte 17. Returning to Medelim, we bear left
through *Proença-a-Velha*, with a partly Romanesque *Misericórdia*, to
regain the main road (N233) 12km W.

17km *Escalos de Cima*, which like *Escalos de Baixo* to the S and
Alcains to the W, was a Roman settlement, is traversed as we
approach (13km) **Castelo Branco**: see Rte 17.

23 Guarda to Viseu, for Oporto or Aveiro

Total distances, 194km (120 miles) to Oporto; 172km (107 miles) to
Aveiro. N16. 29km **Celorico** crossroads—32km **Mangualde**
crossroads—13km **Viseu**—22km *São Pedro do Sul*.
    Hence the N227 leads NW to (56km) *Val de Cambre*, 10km
beyond meeting the N1 at *São João da Madeira*—32km **Oporto**.
    The N16 continues W. from São Pedro do Sul through (8km)
Vouzela—8.5km *Oliveira de Frades*—25.5km *Passegueiro*—15km
Albergaria-a-Velha (on the N1)—19km **Aveiro**.

A new highway is under construction (completed between the frontier and
Guarda), which will run W from just S of *Celorico* and approximately parallel to
the N16, later passing 3km N of *Mangualde*. A by-pass is being built which will
circle to the N of *Viseu* to regain the N16. At the same time work is progressing
on an entirely new line bearing across country from Viseu at a higher level than
the present main road, which threads the valley of the Vouga. This will descend
to meet the N1 near *Albergaria-a-Velha*, shortly after crossing the A1 motorway
at a roughly central point between Coimbra and Oporto, to approach *Aveiro*.

Although these roads traverse very attractive country, they cannot be
taken at any great speed.

For the road to *Celorico*, see Rte 21.

We follow the S bank of the Mondego until we cross the river at
(11km) *Juncais* (left), shortly passing (right) *Fornos de Algodres* (to
the N of which are two dolmens), beyond which we follow a ridge

commanding extensive vistas, at 21km passing (3km left) **Mangualde**. It contains a number of old houses, including the late 17C *Palácio dos Anadia*; the 18C *Misericórdia* is also of interest.

Just W of *Penalva do Castelo* (12km NE), known as *Castendo* until 1957, stands the Baroque *Casa da Insua*, owned by the Albuquerque family.

FROM MANGUALDE TO COIMBRA (97km). The N234 leads SW through (13.5km) *Nelas*, a pleasant little town, and (4km) *Canas de Senhorim*, beyond running parallel to the Mondego, after 9km passing near (left) *Oliveira do Conde*, with a well-carved tomb in its church of Fernão Gomes de Góis (1440), and the *Solar dos de Albergaria*.—After 16km we reach a turning for (4km) *Santa Comba Dão* (see Rte 24) via *Vimieiro*, where António de Oliveira Salazar (1889–1970), the ci-devant dictator of Portugal from 1932 to 1968, was born and is buried.—We later cross the river near a dam and skirt the S bank, re-crossing at (22km) **Penacova**, an ancient and picturesque town commanding a fine *View over the Mondego, whence we may follow the N bank.—After c 4km a road leads to the right 5km up a narrow wooded valley to **Lorvão**, a village which, with Penacova, is the centre of the tooth-pick industry (*palitos*), much white willow-wood whittling being done in the vicinity. It was once famous for its convent of *Santa Maria*, founded in the 12C, which was almost entirely rebuilt in the 18C, and is now a sanatorium. The huge church contains the repoussé silver tombs (1713; by Manuel Carneiro da Silva) of Teresa and Sancha, daughters of Sancho I, who had been abbesses there in the 13C. The carved stalls (1745), iron grill of the nuns' choir, and the portative organ, are noteworthy.—Regaining the Mondego, we turn right for (18km) **Coimbra**: see Rte 25.

Near the road between Mangualde and Viseu lies the former convent of *Maceira Dão*, of earlier foundation, but largely rebuilt in the 17C and later altered.

18km **VISEU** (21,000 inhab.), capital of its district, and an episcopal city of very ancient origin, lies among wooded hills on the left bank of the Pavia, a tributary of the Mondego. Some distance to the SE rises the SERRA DA ESTRELA. It is a rich agricultural centre, and is well known for its Dão wines. It has grown considerably in recent decades (8250 inhab. in 1920), and there is a small airfield N of the town. Its main points of interest are the cathedral and the Grão Vasco Museum. It has also a reputation for its egg and chestnut sweets, and for the black pottery of *Molelos*, among other handicrafts of the region.

Although Viseu is traditionally connected with the last stand of Viriatus (see below) there is no historical evidence for this, nor for the fact that Don Rodrigo, the 'Last of the Goths', was buried here in 711. In 1028 Alfonso V was killed when besieging the place, but it was not occupied until 1058, by Fernando I. Being on one of the main routes into central Portugal from Spain, it was taken by Enrique de Trastamara in 1372; and by Masséna just prior to the Battle of Busaco in 1810.

Here were born Dom Duarte (1391–1438); possibly Vasco Fernandes (c 1475–1541), the artist usually known as 'O Grão Vasco'; João de Barros (1496–1570), the chronicler of the Portuguese conquests in Asia; the physician Gabriel da Fonseca (died 1668), and Baltasar Teles (1595–1675), the historian.

The old town lies huddled below a rock outcrop on which the cathedral stands, dominating the place. Although this may be approached by car (by the same route as described), it is perhaps preferable to park in the lower town somewhere near the central PRAÇA DA REPÚBLICA, or *Rossio*.

Hence we ascend due N along the Rua Nunes de Carvalho, shortly passing (right; entrance round corner) the small *Casa Museu Almeida Moreira* (named after the first director of the Museu Grão Vasco), with good wooden ceilings, and his private collections of furniture, 18C 'Mandarin' porcelain, etc., and containing an art school for young children.

Passing through a gate in the town *Walls*, the *Porta do Soar de Cima*, and (left) a chapel, we reach the large cathedral square (PRAÇA DA SÉ), on the W side of which is the remarkable and often-illustrated twin-towered *façade of the *Misericórdia*. It was begun in 1775 to the designs of António da Costa Faro, but the interior, except for its organ, is of slight interest. It is this church, painted by Tristram Hillier in 1947, which serves as the frontispiece to Sitwell's 'Portugal and Madeira'.

The **Cathedral** is a late Gothic and Manueline church dating from 1513, probably replacing an earlier building on the site of a mosque. At an even earlier period the church of *São Miguel do Fetal*, on the E side of the town, was perhaps more important. São Miguel do Fetal has the tomb said to be that of Don Rodrigo (see History). The W Front with its two towers (1641–71), but of no great merit, was added by Juan Moreno, a Spaniard. Sitwell refers to the fact that when he visited the cathedral it was 'undergoing furious and noisy restoration...an insensate example of how the Portuguese destroy their ancient monuments'.

The façade of the Misericórdia

However cluttered the INTERIOR may once have been, it is still remarkable for its fine *Vault*, the ribs of which are carved to represent knotted cables. The remaining paintings, by Grão Vasco, which once embellished the main retable, are now in the adjacent museum; they were replaced by a retable of 1730 by Santos Pacheco. Good 18C azulejos decorate the N Chapel; a portative organ is also preserved. The carved choir-stalls are notable.

Stairs ascend off the N aisle to the *Coro Alto*, containing a large lectern of Brazil wood. We pass through the Coro Alto to enter the upper cloister (c 1730), retaining attractive late 17C *albarrada* azulejos on two sides, off which opens the *Chapter House*, providing a good view, and also housing the cathedral treasure.

This includes a 13C Limoges enamelled coffer; a 12C Gospel, with a later silver cover; a 12C pectoral cross; a monstrance of 1533; a wooden box with a 12C painting in its lid; a 16C sculptured figure of Santa Isabel; a St. Raphael and Tobias, by Machado de Castro; azulejos of 1721, and an octagonal wooden ceiling of the same date. In the adjoining room, containing some anon. paintings, are a solid bronze pelican (16C Flemish); an 18C Bishop's sunshade; an altar frontal (18C), etc.

Before leaving the cathedral, pass through the lower Renaissance cloister of c 1550, in which one may see a Romanesque portal, and a carved Descent from the Cross of the Coimbra School. Note also the belvedere to the left as we make our exit.

To the right stands the granite four-square *Bishop's Palace*, now accommodating the *Museu Grão Vasco. The famous paintings, recently restored, of *Vasco Fernandes* (c 1475–1541), who Viseu claims as her own, are now on the SECOND FLOOR. Here (**R1**) we may see some of those paintings which originally adorned the high altar of the cathedral, outstanding amongst them being St. Peter, in fact a copy of that at São João de Tarouca, also *attrib. to Gaspar Vaz*. Adjacent are a Martyrdom of St. Sebastian; and Pentecost (in which the knotted cables of the cathedral ribs are depicted), very similar to that in Santa Cruz, Coimbra. Below each painting is a series of half-lengths of apostles or saints, by an inferior hand.—**R2** Death of the Virgin; Baptism of Jesus; and Crucifixion, with a predella of three small Passion scenes. —**R3** *attrib. to Gaspar Vaz*, a Triptych of the Last Supper, and Christ at the house of Martha.—**R4** contains a remarkable series of 14 Scenes from the Life of Christ of the *School of Viseu* (c 1520), among them a curious Adoration of the Magi, in which the traditional negro has been replaced by a Brazilian Indian.

FIRST FLOOR, on which collections of furniture and plate are displayed, together with later paintings, among them watercolours by *Alberto de Sousa*.— On the GROUND FLOOR are part of a retable from Oporto cathedral (1683); an *anon.* Annunciation; a collection of sculptured Virgins; a damaged Nottingham alabaster; Ceramics, including examples from Viana do Castelo; Arraiolos carpets; and, among other *anon.* paintings, a God the Father (14C) and two 15C representations of St. Peter are notable.

There is a pleasant square behind the museum, and also another to the S of the Praça da Sé, from which, by descending behind the cathedral apse through narrow alleys and steps, we shortly reach the thronged RUA DIREITA traversing the old town.

To the right at the N end of this street stands *São Bento*, containing 17C azulejos (apply next door), to the NW of which is the *Porta dos Cavaleiros*.

From a central point in the Rua Direita the Rua da Árvore leads SE through a medieval arch to gain the LARGO DE SANTA CRISTINA, with its fountain, and dominated by the *Igreja do Carmo* (1733–38), preserving 18C azulejos and Baroque carved and gilt woodwork. Behind it is the *Seminary*, with a 'suspended staircase' of which they are inordinately proud, but which is only of slight architectural interest.

We regain the Rua Direita by ascending the Rua Formosa. Just to the left in the Rua Direita is the *Casa de Cimo de Vila*, awaiting restoration, with attractive azulejos of hunting scenes on its staircase. The Rua Formosa then passes (right) the colourful covered *Market* before regaining the Praça da República.

To the S this square is dominated by the front and belfry of the *Igreja dos Terceiros*, or *São Francisco* (1773), approached by a flight of steps, and containing an octagonal chancel, azulejos depicting the Life of St. Francis, and an attractive organ.—Public Gardens lie behind the church.

Off the Oporto road (N16), leading NW, to the right just beyond the Rio Pavia and at a higher level, its edge defined by a line of trees, is the site of an octagonal fortified camp established here by Decimus Junius Brutus in 138 BC, the year after the death of Viriatus, whose last stronghold it was *not*, although still known as the *Cava de Viriato*.

For the roads from Viseu to *Busaco, Coimbra* and *Figueira da Foz* see Rte 24; and to *Lamego*, Rte 32, in reverse.

From Viseu we turn NW through attractive country to (22km) *São Pedro do Sul*, at the confluence of the Sul and Vouga, where the cloister of the Baroque convent of *São José* adjoins the Camara Municipal.

FROM SÃO PEDRO DO SUL TO OPORTO (98km NW). Turning right onto the N227, we skirt the S slope of the SERRA DA GRALHEIRA above the Vouga, deep in its valley to the S.—After c 16km we pass (left) the convent of *São Cristóvão de Lafões*, founded in the 12C, but altered since.—The road later bears away to the NW across the wooded hills, passing near (right) *Roge*, with an attractive mid 18C church, to approach (40km) *Vale de Cambre*. For the detour via *Arouca* see below.

Hence the main road leads NW to meet the N1 at (10km) *São João da Madeira*, a town of remote origin, where we turn right for (32km) *Oporto*: see the latter half of Rte 26, and Rte 33.

FROM VALE DE CAMBRE TO OPORTO VIA AROUCA AND ENTRE-OS-RIOS (91km). The N224 leads NE, climbing over a ridge to (21km) **Arouca**, a beautifully and remotely situated village among wooded mountains, where stands the famous Cistercian *Convent of Santa Maria*. The place existed in 716, but was destroyed by the Moors, and the convent was refounded in the early 10C. It was rebuilt after a fire and on a larger scale in 1704–18 by a Maltese, Carlos Gimac. It is interesting for its association with Mafalda (?1194–1256), daughter of Sancho I, who retired here after her marriage (in 1215, when she was 21) to the 12-year-old Enrique I of Castile was annulled; Enrique died accidentally in 1217. Her remains lie in a silver casket placed in the church in 1734 (not to be outdone by her sisters at Lorvão). A later inmate was a Clara Warre, visited here during the Peninsular War by her brother General Sir William Warre and Lord Beresford. Notable are the 108 stalls in the lower choir carved in 1722–25 by António Gomes and Filipe da Silva, of Oporto; the stone figures of female saints, etc., of the same epoch, carved by Jacinto Vieira, of Braga (not improved by recent coats of whitewash!); and the organ of 1739. The museum contains 15–16C Portuguese paintings.—Returning to the main road, we may turn right to make the steep descent from (27km) *Sobrado* (or *Castelo de Paiva*), crossing the Douro to (5km) *Entre-os-Rios* (see also p 267), near the Roman castro at *Eja*, and here turn left along the N bank of the river (N108) to (38km) **Oporto**.

From São Pedro do Sul we bear left through *Termas de São Pedro*, a spa known to the Romans, there crossing the Vouga to (8km) **Vouzela**, with a Baroque-façaded police-station, 13C *Igreja Matriz*, and a *Misericórdia*, the interior of which has been variously described, by the 'Selective Travellers' as 'worth the visitor's while' to enter, and by Sitwell as 'creepily unpleasant ... with horrid portraits of early 19C benefactors, fly-blown objects, and mange and ringworm in all around'! (When the present Editor passed that way, every road was up to introduce drainage, and he was forced to make a long but attractive detour to the SW through the high-lying village of *Vilharigues*, with slight remains of a *Castle*, and impressive views over the wooded valley and the SERRA DA GRALHEIRA beyond.)

The main road above the Vouga traverses (8.5km) *Oliveira de Frades*, later descending to and crossing the river at (25.5km) *Pessegueiro*, from which another road (N328) climbs N to (23km) *Vale de Cambre*: see above. Skirting the N bank of the river gorge, we later bear away to meet the N1 at (15km) *Albergaria-a-Velha*, founded as a hospice in 1120, and preserving at its S end the mid 18C *Casa de Santo António*.

Turning right and then left, one may continue W, soon crossing the motorway, to reach (8km) crossroads 11km NE of **Aveiro**: see Rte 20. For the *Pousada da Ria* see p 237.

24 Viseu to Coimbra and Figueira da Foz

Total distance, 141km (87 miles). N2. 40km **Santa Comba Dão**—N234. 12km *Mortágua*—13.5km **Busaco** lies to the left.—3km **Luso**—9.5km *Mealhada*—N1. 19km **Coimbra**—N111. 27.5km **Montemór-o-Velho**—16.5km **Figueira da Foz**.

We follow the N2 SW parallel to but some distance W of the Rio Dão, famous for its orchards and wines, to (24km) *Tondela*, with a good Baroque portal to the *Casa de Corso*, and a convenient point from which to turn NW into the SERRA DO CARAMULO.

The N230 climbs NW via *Campo de Besteiro* to (15km) **Caramulo** (*Pousada de São Jerónimo*), a good centre for the exploration of the range, the summit of which, *Caramulinho* (1062m; extensive *Views*) lies further to the SW, now reached by road. The village surprisingly sports two museums: one devoted to veteran cars (including a Rolls-Royce of 1911, among other earlier vehicles); and the *Fundacão Abel Lacerda*, a collection of a somewhat miscellaneous nature, including canvases attributed to Pourbus, Jordaens, and Rigaud, among others, and minor works by Picasso, Dufy, Dalí, Léger, Sutherland, Vieira da Silva. The five early 16C Brussels tapestries of the Portuguese in India are notable.

From Tondela, we continue SW to (16km) **Santa Comba Dão**, a small market town, where in a house in the Largo Alves Mateus Catherine of Braganza stayed in 1692, and Pedro II in 1704, according to the plaque. For the neighbouring village of *Vimieiro*, see p 245, and for the road thence to Coimbra via *Penacova*.

We turn W through *Mortágua*, with a view ahead of the long ridge of Busaco rearing up, which we may approach by turning left not far beyond the village of *Moura*. It is perhaps more conveniently approached via the next village, **Luso**, an attractively situated spa, whose bottled mineral water, sold throughout Portugal, gushes freely from its fountains.

From Luso we ascend to the *Porta das Ameias* (Battlement Gate), a convenient entrance to the walled State Forest (the *Mata do Buçaco*), which covers the N extremity of the ***Serra do Buçaco**. It is noted for its magnificent trees, both native and exotic, and is famous for the battle of 1810 (see below) in which the 'Valoroso e glorioso Duque de Wellington' inflicted serious losses on Masséna's army before retiring behind the defensive Lines of Torres Vedras. In the centre of the park stands the *Palace Hotel*, which we soon reach.

BUSACO (also Bussaco; in Portuguese *Buçaco*), or at least the estate of that name, was presented by the Abp of Braga to the Discalced (barefooted) Carmelites in 1626. They planted the area with a variety of trees, among them the rare Mexican cedar

(*Cupressus lusitanica*), extinct in its own habitat. Some have grown to a height of 35m, and are best seen not far NW of the hotel. By 1643 Pope Urban VIII was issuing a bull excommunicating any person damaging the trees, while his predecessor, in 1622, had prohibited the entry of women into the precinct prior to the advent of the monks. In 1667 Castelo-Melhor, the fallen minister of Afonso VI, sought shelter here and hid in the forest, which his pursuers would have set alight was it not for the entreaties of the monks. He later escaped to England. While afforestation proceeded spasmodically during the next 160 years, the E slope of the ridge was still comparatively bare in 1810. At the Dissolution, the convent buildings accommodated a School of Forestry, adjacent to which a summer place was built in 1887–1907 for the royal family, designed by one Luigi Manini, a scene painter for the São Carlos Opera-house in Lisbon. This pseudo-Manueline confection was later added to, and with the demise of the monarchy it was converted into a luxurious establishment known still as the *Palace* Hotel, to which General Spínola retreated during a crucial stage in his presidency (August 1974).

On the N façade of the hotel—which is surrounded by charmingly laid out and colourful gardens amid the forest—its entrance porch encrusted with black and white pebbles, is the remnant of the *Convent*, now totally engulfed, with its tiny church and few gloomy cork-lined cells, in one of which—first washed out and dried by lighting a fire—Wellington passed the night before his great defensive battle.

There are a number of similarly decorated *ermidas* or hermitages dotted around in the surrounding forest, and 17C chapels, which flank the numerous sign-posted footpaths from the hotel.

Continuing through the forest, we shortly reach the *Porta da Rainha* (Queen's Gate), not far beyond which (left) is a small *Military Museum* devoted to the Battle of Busaco, containing British, French and Portuguese uniforms, arms, maps, prints and models, etc.

Just to the S is a commemoratory *Obelisk* and *Viewpoint, commanding an even better view than the Cruz Alta (see below), providing an extensive panorama over the area through which Masséna's army approached the ridge, with the SERRA DA ESTRELA to the E; while to the N is the SERRA DO CARAMULO.

The **Battle of Busaco**. It should be emphasised that much of the mountainside—Wellington's 'damned long hill'—has since been afforested; it was still much more open earlier this century. Wellington, with some 49,000 men (including 24,500 Portuguese, largely untried recruits), and 60 guns, took up an almost impregnable defensive position along the line of the ridge (rising to c 550m), behind which they lay concealed, but deliberately showing a thin line of sentries: 'Every one expected and wished for a general attack at daylight. The army is in most beautiful order, and the Portuguese as fine-looking men and as steady under arms as any in the world', wrote William Tomkinson prior to the battle.

Wellington was faced by a force of 66,000 French, comprising three Corps commanded by Junot, Ney and Reynier, which had been deliberately deflected towards this point by the destruction of the road between Celorico and Abrantes. Masséna, as yet unbeaten, and undissuaded by the saner counsels of his subordinates, on 27 September 1810 drove his columns in a frontal attack up the steep and broken slope in a thick morning mist. Not surprisingly, by using such tactics (see Vimeiro), they were repeatedly hurled down again in confusion, and with a total loss of at least 4600 men compared with the Allied loss of 1170. Eventually the French were forced to work their way laboriously round beyond the N edge of the ridge before turning on Coimbra, which they sacked en route. Wellington had meanwhile been able to retire undisturbed through Coimbra, before proceeding at leisure towards his prepared 'Lines' N of Lisbon: see p 217.

FROM BUSACO TO COIMBRA VIA PENACOVA (c 40km), although longer, a more interesting and beautiful route. If visibility is bad, follow an alternative road further W, from Luso to Penacova. From the Obelisk we follow the road S along the top of the ridge towards the *Cruz Alta* (c 530m), another good viewpoint partly overlooking the coastal plain, with the Atlantic visible behind a line of dunes. A left fork off this road leads to Wellington's vantage post during the earlier part of the battle, but now shrouded by pines. A good forest track may be followed hence, eventually descending towards the main Luso–Penacova road, W of the ridge, on reaching which we turn left for *Penacova*: for which, and for the road beyond to **Coimbra**, see p 245.

From Luso (see above) minor roads lead SW through *Pampilhosa* and *Souselas* to Coimbra, avoiding some traffic.—We descend W to (9km) *Mealhada*, there turning S along the N1, following the Roman road, to (19km) **Coimbra**: see Rte 25.

At 14km S of Mealhada—if by-passing Coimbra, which may also be done by following the A1 S—we may turn right towards the N111, which we then follow along the N bank of the Mondego to its mouth.

Just after passing under the motorway, the N234.1 leads NW via *Ançã*, whose quarries are the source of so much of the stone used by Portuguese sculptors in the past, particularly of the School of Coimbra. The historian Jaime Cortesão (1884–1960) was born here—10km beyond is **Cantanhede**, an agricultural centre, which was the scene of Pedro I's solemn avowal of his marriage with Inês de Castro: see p 277. The *Igreja Matriz* contains a retable ascribed to Jean de Rouen.—Another attributed to the same sculptor may be seen in a chapel at *Varziela*, 4km further NW.

Some 4km beyond this same junction, a minor road climbs to the right, traversing a village, to (c 4km) the church of *São Marcos, a remnant of an Hieronymite convent (1452), burnt down in 1860; the present buildings, later Braganza property, are owned by Coimbra University.

The interior of the church, behind a façade of 1510, contains a wealth of sculptural monuments, among them the tomb of Fernão Teles de Meneses (1481), by Diogo Pires, the elder, with its Gothic curtained canopy held aside by hairy men; the two Manueline tombs of the Da Silva family, of 1522, and the Renaissance tomb of 1559; also the beautifully carved *Retable by Chanterène (1522–23), unfortunately repainted about a century ago. Also of interest are the domed chapel *dos Reis Magos* (1556) and the Renaissance pulpit.

Regaining the main road, we continue W, by-passing (10km right) *Tentúgal*, a village noted for its cakes (pasteis de Tentúgal); the *Igreja Matriz* contains a carved Renaissance retable.

10km. To the left rises the imposing *Castle of **Montemór-o-Velho**, the ascent to which is recommended. The fortress, rebuilt in 1088, once accommodated a royal palace. Its wall walks command attractive views over the ricefields of the lower Mondego valley, and of the old town below. The restored church of *Santa Maria da Alcáçova*, within the enceinte, contains twisted Manueline columns between its three aisles.

The village, of ancient origin, briefly recovered from the Moors by Alfonso V in 1017, was eventually reconquered in 1034. It was the birthplace of the poet and pastoral novelist of Jewish descent, Jorge de Montemayor (1519–61), author of 'Los siete libros de la Diana' (Valencia, 1559?); the traveller and chronicler, Fernão Mendes Pinto (1514–83); and the navigator, Diogo de Azambuja (c 1456–1518), whose tomb—ascribed to Diogo Pires, the younger—lies in *N.S. dos Anjos* (1498, with a façade of 1692). Note also the domed chapel, similar to that at *São Marcos* (see above). The *Misericórdia* of 1555 contains a Mannerist high altar.

We cross a dyke over the ricefields and ascend past the rebuilt *Quinta da Foja*, beyond, which (left) an Iron Age site has been discovered near the chapel of *Santa Olaia*.

The 18C *Paço de Maiorca* is passed before beginning the descent to (16.5km) **Figueira da Foz**: see Rte 20.

25 Coimbra

COIMBRA (71,800 inhab.), an ancient capital, the chief city of the Beira, and until the advent of the Republic the seat of Portugal's only university, is certainly one of its more interesting and animated cities. If some attempt was made to clean its streets and to provide better accommodation, Coimbra would be much more visited, for it contains many remarkable buildings, among them the magnificent University Library, while the Machado de Castro Museum is one of the finest in the country. Unfortunately much of the old university district, on a height overlooking the old town, was ruined by the erection during the Salazar regime of a number of vast architectural blocks which do little more than supply walls for the application of more political posters and student graffiti.

At the foot of the main hill of Alcáçova on which the town was built flows the Mondego, the entire course of which is in Portugal, unlike the Douro or Tagus, which merely cross the country. The Mondego is notable for the amount of sediment it carries, which has caused its bed to rise, and, being subject to sudden floods, it has silted up several old buildings near its banks in the past.

Coimbra has been identified with Roman *Aeminium*, although it took its modern name from the more important *Conímbriga*, which lies near Condeixa-a-Velha, some 16km S (see the latter part of Rte 18A), when the country as far S as the Mondego was wrested from Moorish occupation in 872. Its arms, a crowned lady between a dragon and a lion, are supposed to symbolise the alliance of the Suevi and the Alani by a marriage between their royal houses. It reverted to the Moors between 987, when overrun and sacked by al-Mansur, until 1064, when it was reconquered by Fernando I of Castile, aided by the Cid, during which time it was largely occupied by Mozárabs. In 1081, Paternus, its mozárab bishop, gained control of the churches of Lamego and Viseu, much to the consternation of Braga. It was again briefly surrounded by the Almoravids in 1116.

From 1139, when Afonso Henriques was proclaimed king of Portugal, until 1385, Coimbra was the capital, having supplanted Guimarães, and as such it was the birthplace of six kings: Afonso II (1185), Sancho II (1209), Afonso III (1210), and later Afonso IV (1290), Pedro I (1320) and Fernando I (1345), although Afonso III had transferred the main royal residence to Lisbon c 1250. Dom Duarte and Leonor of Aragón were married here in 1428.

The University set up here in 1308 was likewise transferred to Lisbon, not being definitively re-established at Coimbra until 1537. Dominated by its bishops, the town had meanwhile stagnated.

Idrisi, the Muslim geographer writing in the mid 12C, records that it was then 'a small city, flourishing and well populated, rich in vineyards and orchards of apples, cherries, and plums. Its fields are very fertile ... and the inhabitants, who are the bravest of the Christians, possess many cattle great and small: the Mondego moves many mills and bathes many vineyards and gardens'.

In the second quarter of the 16C an important and influential school of sculptors had established themselves in Coimbra, among them the French artists Nicolas Chanterène, Jean de Rouen, Jacques Buxe, and Philippe Houdart, apart from João and Diogo de Castilho.

After 1567 it was one of the three seats (with Lisbon and Évora) of the Inquisition in Portugal, who were particularly active here in the 1620s. The Jesuits (suppressed in 1759) controlled the place until in 1772 Pombal undermined their influence by reforming the University. In 1808 its students formed the Academic Volunteers, and taking over from the occupying French a small port near the mouth of the Mondego, enabled the British expeditionary force to land there before the battle of Roliça. Wellington and Beresford passed through the city in May 1809 prior to attacking Oporto. It was brutally sacked by Masséna after Busaco (September 1810), but the following March, when retreating from before the Lines of Torres Vedras, he veered NE, S of the Mondego, the crossing at Coimbra having been recaptured and held by Nicholas Trant and his Portuguese militia.

H.F. Link, passing the night here 180 years ago, remarked that 'in no large town throughout Portugal are the inns so bad, strangers being lodged in wretched apartments with miserable beds ...'; while Southey observed that, although on approaching it Coimbra had the appearance of a gloriously seated city, the delusion ceased on entry, when 'It was noise and narrow streets, and stink'. Regrettably little has changed.

It was the birthplace of Francisco Sá da Miranda (1481/95–1558), the poet, and the eldest of five sons of a canon of Coimbra; the sculptor Joaquim Machado de Castro (1732–1822); Carlos Seixas (1704–42), the composer; and Joaquim António de Aguiar (1792–1874), the radical statesman, whose nickname, 'Mata Frades' (kill-friars) exaggerates his measures for the suppression of the religious orders in 1833.

Early 18C view of Coimbra from the S bank of the Mondego

The main hub of traffic (which can make parking a problem) is the LARGO DA PORTAGEM, immediately opposite the N end of the *Ponte Santa Clara*. The *Tourist Office* is on its E side.

A. The Lower Town

The narrow main street, the RUA DE FERREIRA BORGES, flanked by the principal shops, and along which trams ran until recently, is continued by the Rua do Visconde da Luz. Steps ascend on the right of the former to the upper town: see Rte 25B.

Further along, on the left, is the truncated apse of *São Tiago*, preserving little of its late 12C foundation but the S door and the W portal overlooking the PRAÇA DO COMÉRCIO, flanked by tall houses, to the W and N of which, among a maze of narrow alleys, some of the cheaper little restaurants and bars of Coimbra may be found, often still only advertising their presence by a laurel branch above their entrances.

The street widens and ends at the PRAÇA 8 DE MAIO, on the right of which, at a lower level, stands the church of *Santa Cruz, historically the most interesting building in Coimbra.

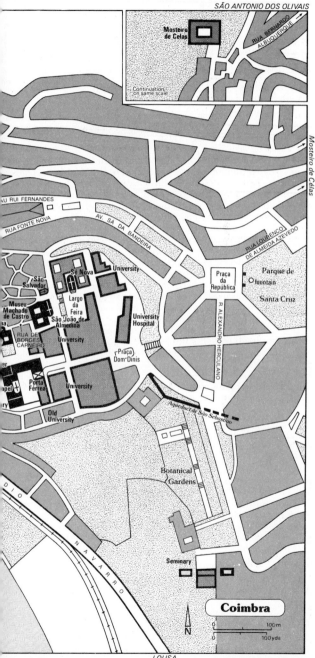

SÃO ANTONIO DOS OLIVAIS

Mosteiro de Celas

RUA BERNARDO ALBUQUERQUE

Continuation on same scale

Mosteiro de Celas

AU RUI FERNANDES

RUA FONTE NOVA

AV. SA DA BANDEIRA

RUA LOURENÇO DE ALMEIDA AZEVEDO

São Salvador

Sé Nova

University

Praça da República

Fountain

Parque de Santa Cruz

Museu Machado de Castro

Largo da Feira

São João de Almedina

RUA DE BORGES CARNEIRO

University

University Hospital

R. ALEXANDRO HERCULANO

Praça Dom Dinis

Porta Férrea

University

Aqueduct de São Sebastião

Old University

Botanical Gardens

Seminary

Coimbra

N

0   100m
0   100yds

NAVARRO

LOUSA

A priory of Austin canons was founded here in 1131 on a site known as the Banhos Reais, by Telo, archdeacon of the cathedral, and João Peculiar (later bishop of Oporto and archbishop of Braga), while St. Teotónio, the confessor of Afonso Henriques, was appointed prior. In 1502, the buildings no longer being adequate, Dom Manuel began its reconstruction, Marcos Pires (died 1524) being the architect, assisted by Diogo de Castilho, and Jean de Rouen (João de Ruão) and Nicolas Chanterène, French sculptors then in Portugal, among others. In 1539 João III made the priors perpetual chancellors of the University, a rank they retained until the Dissolution of 1834. Amongst its canons was Heliodoro de Paiva (died 1552), a composer of numerous masses and motets, etc. It was used as a British HQ during part of the Peninsular War.

The W Front, or *Portal da Majestade*, is a somewhat clumsy work by Diogo de Castilho (1524), with sculptures by Chanterène and Jean de Rouen, and the general effect is spoilt by the addition of an incongruous 18C doorway.

The INTERIOR, lined with 18C azulejos, contains (left) a corbelled *Pulpit*, now attributed to Chanterène (1522), with high reliefs of SS. Ambrose, Jerome, Gregory and Augustine. In the *Chancel* are the ornately carved **Royal Tombs** of (left) Afonso Henriques (died 1135), and (right) his son, Sancho I (died 1211), reinterred here in 1520. Various attributions have been made as to their sculptors, but it is now thought that Chanterène carved the recumbent figures, and that Diogo de Castilho was responsible for the general design.

The sacristan should be sought out for admission to the **Sacristy**, to the S of the chancel. This Renaissance room of 1622 contains an Ecce Homo, and Crucifixion, by *Cristóvão de Figueiredo*, a St. Vincent by *García Fernandes*, and a Pentecost by *Grão Vasco*.—To the N of the chancel is the entrance to the *Cloister* of two storeys (by Marcos Pires: from 1517), weak in design (with 'Mandorla-shaped' ribs), on three sides of which are worn altarpieces by Jean de Rouen. Southey found the cloister had been turned into a poultry-yard, when he visited the church. In its SE corner is the Manueline *Capela de São Teotónio*, with that saint's tomb (by Tomé Velho; 1582), and those of other priors.—Stairs ascend to the *Coro Alto*, containing Manueline stalls of c 1518, surmounted by a carved and gilt frieze of ships, castles, etc.; the red and gold 18C organ is under restoration.—Note also the vaulting in the abutting café.

From the adjacent *Câmara Municipal*, the Rua da Sofia leads NW past a number of convent-colleges of comparatively little interest, some of which are at present in military occupation. Among them (right) is the *Igreja do Carmo* (1597), with an earlier cloister containing azulejos; the *Igreja da Graça* (1555); and beyond (left) the cloister of *São Tomás* (1540), now part of the Law Courts; and the unfinished and ruinous church of *São Domingos. Santa Justa* (1710; right) lies further N.

Immediately behind Santa Cruz is the *Jardim da Manga*, once another cloister of the priory, in the centre of which is a curious domed *Fountain* surrounded by four subsidiary chapels joined to it by buttresses (completed 1535).

The main road ascending to the E from Santa Cruz, after passing a market, is continued by the Av. Sá da Bandeira to the PRAÇA DA REPÚBLICA, a hub of the upper town behind the university quarter: see pp 259 and 261.

B. The Upper Town

From the **Arco de Almedina** (*medina*, a city, in Arabic), the main pedestrian entrance to the upper town, above which was the town hall until 1878, we commence the steep ascent into the old university city of narrow alleys, first bearing to the left to ascend more steps.

From this point a lane (left) leads shortly past the **Casa de Sub-Ripas** of 1547, with a Manueline doorway.

This mansion was traditionally believed to be the scene of the murder of Maria Teles, who had excited the envy of her sister, Queen Leonor. She had also secretly married João (the eldest son of Inês de Castro) who was persuaded by the queen that Maria was being unfaithful, and that if he had been patient he might have married her own daughter. João, without further enquiry, hurried to Coimbra and stabbed the unfortunate lady. He was then conveniently hounded from Portugal, much to the queen's satisfaction, who had no intention of offering her daughter's hand to him.

Beyond an arch studded with medallions is the *Torre de Anto*, part of the old city wall, recently converted into a centre for the display and sale of regional handicraft, together with a small museum, for which it is hoped additional accommodation will be found (adm. daily in summer; closed on Sundays and holidays in winter). Among local manufactures is that of *palitos* or tooth-picks (see also *Penacova*), which was remarked on as flourishing some 200 years ago by Major Dalrymple, when passing through Coimbra: others have suggested that it was the main occupation of the students.

Almost adjacent is the *Colégio Novo* (or of *Santo Agostinho*; from c 1590), with a cloister of 1598 designed by Filippo Terzi and inspired by that at Tomar, which survived a later fire; it preserves some 17C azulejos. The whole fabric is undergoing restoration since housing the Misericórdia since 1842.

Returning to the main ascending street, we approach the *Old Cathedral, or *Sé Velha*, one of the finest Romanesque churches in Portugal (c 1162), in which Sancho I was crowned in 1185, as was João I in 1385 after eloquently demonstrating his claim before the Cortes. The *Sé Nova* (see below) replaced it as the Episcopal cathedral in 1772.

The fortress-like exterior has three doorways of very different character. The W Portal consists of a projecting bastion pierced by a deep round-arched doorway beneath a window almost equal in size. The Corinthian N Portal (or *Porta Especiosa*) is a Renaissance addition of the French School of Santa Cruz (see above), with a fine but worn Virgin in its tympanum. The door of the N transept was altered at the same time. The domed belfry dates from 1837. Above the apse is a Romanesque gallery.

INTERIOR. The *Nave* has massive square piers with semicircular pilasters, now stripped of the azulejos of 1508 once covering them. The bold triforium and central lantern should be noted. In the N aisle are the tombs of Bp Tibúrcio (died 1246) and of Dona Vetaça, daughter of the Count of Ventimiglia and a Greek princess, who was governess to Santa Isabel.

The *Capela-Mór* has an elaborate late Gothic retable (1508) of the Assumption, by Olivier de Gand (Ghent) and Jean d'Ypres, presented by Bp Jorge de Almeida (1483–1543), whose tomb lies in the chapel of São Pedro, in the N transept, beneath a *Retable* depicting the history of St. Peter, in the French style. On the left is the tomb of Bp Egas de

Faíes (1286). In the S transept is a semicircular retable containing figures of Christ and the Apostles, by Tomé Velho, presented by Bishop João Soares (1566), with a compartmented cupola above.

Beyond, is the entrance to the *Sacristy* (1593), erected by Bishop Afonso de Castelo Branco (died 1633), whose tomb, with that of Sisinando (died 1091; the first Christian governor of the city, who is said to have been a converted Moor) lies in the Chapter-house.— From the S aisle steps ascend to the *Cloister* (begun 1218) of the French Cistercian type, with canopied corners, which was at one time occupied by the university press. Here stands a mid 16C font.

Continuing the ascent behind the cathedral, we follow the Rua de Borges Carneiro, overlooked by the loggia of the old *Bishop's Palace*, now accommodating the *Museu Machado de Castro. Note the Moorish tower preserved by the main entrance, facing the LARGO DA FEIRA to the E.

Admission should also be requested to view the two attractive retables in the adjacent church of *São João de Almedina*, reached by a flight of steps to the right of the entrance hall, in which stands a bishop's coach. The church itself, although founded in the 12C, probably on the site of a mosque, was rebuilt between 1684 and 1704, but part of the Romanesque cloister is preserved.

The first section of the museum displays a collection of MEDIEVAL SCULPTURE, including a Visigothic angel; Santa Comba; Santa Agada; a Mounted Knight holding a mace; Santas Mães (15C); and The Sepulchre guarded by three knights in chain mail.—We now pass along the lower level of the two-storeyed *Loggia*, commanding a splendid view over the city, built c 1592 by Bp Afonso de Castelo Branco, before entering another wing, containing 17C polychrome sculpture; another bishop's coach; a Deposition *attrib. to Jean de Rouen*; and the retable from N.S. de Conceição; a Calvary and other works by *Olivier de Gand*; an early 16C Flemish carved and painted Nativity; and part of a terracotta group representing the Last Supper, by *Philippe Houdart* (c 1530).

PAINTINGS: among the more important works displayed are an *anon.* Flemish Crucifixion of c 1525; *Monagramist MN*, Assumption (early 16C); examples of the art of the *Master of Sardoal*, including an Assumption of Mary Magdalen, a rare subject; *Master of Celas* (early 16C), Descent from the Cross, and Nativity; *Quintin Metsys*, Virgin (part of a triptych), Flagellation, and Ecce Homo; The Retable of Santa Clara, with a row of apostles below (15C), and an *anon.* Christ in the Garden.—To the right, the Crucifixion of Santa Cruz, an emaciated black Christ (13–14C).—Adjacent, an *anon.* Santa Agatha (early 16C); *Garcia Fernandes*, Triptych of Christ appearing to the Virgin, SS. Cosmas and Damian; *Nogueira*, Repose on the Flight into Egypt (1590; note costumes); *Master of Santa Clara*, Christ appearing to the Virgin, and Deposition; *Morales*, Virgin and Child; *Cristóvão de Figueiredo*, Finding of the True Cross by St. Helen, and The Exaltation of the Cross (showing German influence).

This is followed by a section displaying a collection of dalmatics, pluvials, and other vestments, and fabrics.—Stairs ascend to a collection of FURNITURE, and examples of Castelo Branco embroidery. Here is a small *Oratory* containing a Magdalen by *Josefa de Óbidos*, and a Vision of St. Bernard.—The CERAMIC COLLECTION contains 18C Rocha Soares ware, and examples from Aveiro, Juncal, Brioso and Vandelli (both from Coimbra), from the Rato factory, Lisbon, and blue and white porcelain from Lisbon showing Oriental influence.—

Little of the important collection of Gold and Silverwork is at present on view.

One of the most interesting and surprising features of the museum is the *Roman Cryptoporticus*, to which we now descend, a grid of subterranean passages providing the foundations to the palace, below which is another floor (no admission). The passages contain a well-displayed collection of Roman sculptures and stelae, and Visigothic artefacts found on the site, and also some Neolithic and Bronze Age implements and weapons, etc.—Hence we make our exit.

In a side street to the left stands the small Romanesque church of *São Salvador*. The N side of the Largo da Feira is dominated by the unwieldy Renaissance front of the **Sé Nova**, probably designed by Baltasar Álvares, and built from 1598–1698 by the Jesuits (suppressed in 1759) as a church for the Colégio das Onze Mil Virgens, but used as a cathedral since 1772. Inside, to the left is an ornate white marble *Font* made for Bp Jorge de Almeida; also of interest are the coffered barrel vaulting and dome, the reliquarios in both transepts, a series of paintings of the Life of the Virgin (mostly copies of Italian originals) behind the choir stalls, and the repainted Baroque organs facing each other in the chancel.

To the NE are the buildings of the *Natural History Museum*, with a carved relief by Machado de Castro, and the *Chemistry Laboratory*, both designed by the English architect William Elsden.—To the right of these stand the *University Hospitals*, housed in the old Real Colégio das Artes and the Colégio de S. Jerónimo, both with degraded cloisters.

Further S is the PRAÇA DOM DINIS, the site of the castle, demolished in 1772, from which a flight of steps descends to the E. At the bottom, streets lead NE to the PRAÇA DA REPÚBLICA, and SE to the Arcos do Jardim, flanked by the Aqueduct 'de São Sebastião': see below for the Botanical Gardens and other monuments in this NE part of the city.

Of the other modern university buildings, the less said the better. Writing in 1954 Sacheverell Sitwell succinctly condemned them as being 'shaming in their blatant ugliness', and their sculptures 'of an insulting hideousness'. Much wanton destruction of the old (but perhaps not always so beautiful) took place under the aegis of Dr Salazar, who had himself been a student at the university.

All that remains of interest is the main quadrangle of the **Old University**, approached by a turning due W from the Praça Dom Dinis and entered through the *Porta Férrea* (Iron Gate), of 1634, in a wing formerly the Colégio de São Pedro. —Before entering, we may first visit (a few steps to the right) the *Casa dos Melos* (16C), now the Pharmacy Faculty building.

The University, founded in 1290 by Dom Dinis in Lisbon, was transferred to Coimbra in 1308 and installed in a building adjoining the royal palace, or Paço de Alcáçova. In 1338–54 and in 1377–1537 it was again in Lisbon, but in 1537 João III established it definitively at Coimbra, inviting the humanist André de Gouveia, then at Bordeaux, to collect together a competent body of scholars for the purpose, and housed it in the royal palace on the present site. George Buchanan was invited to lecture there in 1547. But Buchanan, a man 'of austere countenance, but mirrie, and quick in conference and awnswres to anie questioun', provoked jealousy and was imprisoned by the Inquisition at São Bento (Lisbon) in 1550–51. António de Mariz was printer to the University in 1556–99, publishing over 90 imprints. The University fell into the hands of mercenary priests in the 17C and doctorates were obtained for a 'fee' by students who never attended a lecture. Pombal sensibly expelled the Jesuits who controlled it, and established the system whose lines are largely followed to this day.

The head of the university, the rector (*reitor*), is assisted by the *Concelho dos Decanos* (deans of the faculties, and others), and some 300 professors (*lentes cathedráticos*) and lecturers. There are now some 12,000 students, who sport the following colours: violet (Pharmacy), yellow (Medicine), red (Law), light blue (Science), and dark blue (Philosophy).

Visitors first enter the *PÁTIO DAS ESCOLAS, on the right of which is the *Paço das Escolas*, preceded by a covered gallery known as the 'Via Latina', which contains the rector's residence, the principal lecture rooms, and the *Sala dos Capelos*, which is approached through the imposing central portico of 1701, embellished with sculpture by Claude de Laprade. This room, in which degrees are conferred, has a notable panelled wooden roof of 1655. One is also shown the *Sala do Exame Privado*, hung with portraits of rectors since 1537, and a guardroom with 17C azulejos. An exterior walk provides plunging views over the city.

At the NW corner of the patio rises the Baroque *Clock-tower* of 1733, known to the students as the *Cabra* (or goat) *tower*. In the W wing is the Manueline doorway (after 1517, probably by Marcos Pires) to the *University Chapel*, containing an impressive red and gilt Baroque organ of 1733, 17C azulejos, and a painted ceiling.

Adjacent is the imposing double-pillared entrance to the *Library, or *Casa da Livraria*, a very fine example of the 'João Quinto' style (1716–28). Its designer is not known with certainty, but it may have been Claude de Laprade. For admission press the bell to the left of door. The interior is divided into three main sections opening off each other, each containing an upper gallery with tapering supports. The whole is richly gilt, which, with the 'chinoiserie' japanning, is the work of Manuel da Silva, and the rooms are decorated in light green, a darker green, and an orange. Notice also the ceilings painted in perspective, and the rosewood and ebony tables. The principal treasures of the library are not at present on display.

At the far end (between curtains parted by putti) is the richly framed portrait of Dom João (attrib. to Giorgio Domenico Duprà), who—although also responsible for the Library at Mafra—being no great bibliophil, probably (or so Sitwell suggests) built the library merely in rivalry with his brother-in-law, Kaiser Karl VI, who was at the same time erecting the Hofbibliothek (completed 1737) at the Imperial Palace at Vienna, a work by J.B. Fischer von Erlach.

A good view over the Mondego valley and of the convent of *Santa Clara* (see Rte 25C) is commanded by the adjacent terrace.

Making our exit from the university, we may return to the lower town (if not visiting the district to the NE described below) by descending steps to the right, and then turning right, make our way through a series of narrow lanes, and keeping to the right, regain the old cathedral.

The Botanical Gardens: the Convent of Celas: Santo Antonio dos Olivais

A pendant to the previous route is the area to the E and NE of the University, which may be more conveniently visited by car by the less energetic.

Immediately SE of the PRAÇA DOM DINIS are the first of the 21 arches of the **Aqueduct** 'de São Sebastião', begun by Filippo Terzi in 1568 on the site of an earlier aqueduct, which then crosses the *Arcos do Jardim* and an entrance to the **Botanical Gardens**. These were laid

Interior of the University Library

out by Pombal in 1774 on a site chosen by William Elsden, and is the largest (20 hectares) in Portugal; the terraced gardens enriched with plants selected by Félix Avelar Brotero, the botanist, were only completed under Julio Henriques, director from 1873 to 1918.

On the far side of the gardens stands the the *Seminary*, the original part, designed by Francesco Tamossi, dating from 1748–65 but with late 19C additions. The octagonal domed church contains a fine organ of 1763, by Juan Fontana.

From the Arcos do Jardim we may descend the Rua Alexandre Herculano to the PRAÇA DA REPÚBLICA, the main square of the district. On its E side is the PARQUE DE SANTA CRUZ (or Sereia gardens), with a curious *Fountain* embellished by 18C azulejo panels.

By following the Rua Lourenço de Almeida Azevedo uphill on the N side of the gardens, we eventually approach, in a side street to the left beyond the Largo de Celas, the **Mosteiro de Celas**. It retains the circular Manueline church and part of the 14C cloister of the ruined abbey founded by Sancha, daughter of Sancho I, in the early 13C, but it is now of slight interest except for the capitals in the cloister. The key should be applied for at the house opposite the entrance.

Regaining the main street, continue uphill along the Rua Bernardo Albuquerque to reach the hilltop church of **Santo António dos Olivais**, approached by a short flight of steps flanked by chapels. The church, rebuilt in the 15C, is all that remains of the friary founded here in the 13C. Its terrace provides pleasant views over the surrounding countryside.

C. Santa Clara

Crossing the Mondego by the *Ponte de Santa Clara*, the third bridge on this site, we leave the main Lisbon road to our left, and by turning down the next lane to the left, reach the sad relics of the church of **Santa Clara-a-Velha**, the floor silted up by the Mondego floods, and with the remains of a fine W rose-window. This is all that is left of the convent founded in 1286 by Dona Mór Dias, and refounded by St. Isabel in 1330, six years before her death. Here both she and Inês de Castro were buried before their translation to their present tombs in the new convent (see below) and to Alcobaça, respectively.

The murder of Dona Inês, the subject of numerous romances, is said to have taken place by a water-tank in the garden of the *Quinta das Lágrimas* (an 18C building), some distance along the next left turn.

Inês Pires de Castro, the daughter of a Galician nobleman, was brought up with her cousin Dona Constanza, daughter of the Duque de Peñafiel, and went to join her in Portugal after Constanza's marriage in 1340 to the Infante Dom Pedro, son of Afonso IV. Pedro, however, conceived an uncontrollable passion for Inês on first setting eyes on this 'heron-necked' beauty. She was later exiled, but on Constanza's death in 1345 she returned to Portugal and set up house with Pedro at Coimbra.

During the next decade she bore him various children, and to legitimise them he married—or claimed to have married—Inês in 1354, at Braganza. Meanwhile a court faction, jealous of the Spanish influence they considered Inês had on the heir to the throne (for her brothers had political pretensions), eventually extracted from Dom Afonso his tacit permission for her 'removal', but the king, then residing at neighbouring Montemór-o-Velho, riding over to the Quinta das Lágrimas to see Inês, weakened at the sight of his grandchildren. The three nobles most concerned—Pedro Coelho, Diogo Pacheco and Álvaro Gonçalves—were not to be thwarted, and murdered her in cold blood on 7 January 1355.

Pedro raised the standard of revolt, but, influenced by the archbishop of Braga, was later ostensibly reconciled with his father. However, on his accession two years after, Pedro I had Coelho and Gonçalves executed at Santarém; Pacheco eluded him. At Cantanhede, Dom Pedro swore before the Cortes that his marriage with Inês was a reality, and had her body exhumed from her grave. According to Camoens, it was then enthroned beside him to receive the homage of his nobles before being placed in the royal tomb he had ordered to be constructed for her at Alcobaça.

Juana La Beltraneja (1462–1530; daughter of Enrique IV of Castile and Joana of Portugal) professed here in 1480.

The approach to the *new* convent of Santa Clara passes (left) a children's garden, beyond which a winding road climbs up to the early 18C chapel of *N.S. da Esperança* on Monte da Esperança, passing (right) the former monastery of *São Francisco* (1602), long transformed into a factory, before reaching the esplanade (good view of Coimbra).

Here stands the long barrack-like building—indeed much of it is now barracks—of the *Convent of Santa Clara, erected in 1649–77 by João Turriano, professor of mathematics at the university. The *Church* contains, in the *Capela-Mór*, six charming paintings showing the removal of St. Isabel's remains to her new tomb, the adjacent silver shrine, in 1696, and her life is depicted on a series of carved and polychromed wooden panels in the aisles.

Near the choir are two Gothic tombs, containing the bodies of Dona Isabel, daughter of Afonso V; and Dona Maria, daughter of Pedro I. In the *Coro Baixo* is the original tomb of St. Isabel (1271–1336), surmounted by her effigy, from which her remains were removed to the present shrine. The sacristan will also show some of her garments. Here stands a red and gold portative organ of 1745; another is in the upper choir. The large *Cloister*, possibly designed by Carlos Mardel, and perhaps inspired by that at Tomar, was given to the Poor Clares by João V, who (see Odivelas) had a penchant for nuns.

26 Coimbra to Oporto

Total distance, 116km (72 miles). N1. 19km *Mealhada*—23km *Águeda*—15km *Albergaria-a-Velha*—19km *Oliveira de Azeméis*— 40km **Oporto**.

The A1 motorway, which may be entered not far NW of Coimbra, will, when completed, provide a rapid and attractive route N. It is between 3km and 9km W of the N1, which is often congested. Exits are provided for *Aveiro*, *Vila da Feira*, etc., and for central *Oporto*.

This busy and uninteresting road leads due N to by-pass (19km) *Mealhada*, centre of the Bairrada wine region, and 4km beyond (left), *Curia*, a well-known spa, before reaching (5km) the road to *Anadia*, 3km NE, with the 18C *Paço da Graciosa*.

3km The direct road to *Aveiro*, 27km NW, N235, forks left.

15km *Águeda*, from which the N230 climbs 35km E to *Caramulo*: see Rte 24.

After 3km we pass (left) *Trofa*, where the church contains tombs of the Coimbra Renaissance School (c 1535). Some 5km beyond Trofa we cross the Vouga near *Serém* (*Pousada Santo Antonio*), and after 7km by-pass (left) *Albergaria-a-Velha*; see p 249. For the road hence to *Viseu* see Rte 23, in reverse.

19km *Oliveira de Azeméis*, a small town of ancient origin (referred to in a document of 922), was in 1832 a headquarters of Dom Miguel. It preserves few buildings of any significance apart from its 18C church.—Hence the N224 climbs 11.5km E to *Vale de Cambre* and, 21km beyond, to *Arouca*; see p 248.

4km. Just to the W is *Cucujães*, with a 17–18C monastery replacing a foundation of the 11C.

4km. **São João de Madeira** (16,200 inhab.) is by-passed, 2km beyond which a minor road leads NW to (3.5km) **Vila da Feira**, with a noble 11C *Castle* later much rebuilt, but with its four cone-capped towers, is picturesquely placed on a leafy hill. The 16C church of the monastery of *Espírito Santo*, its cloisters put to secular use, is of slighter interest. The N1 is regained 4km beyond.

The territory between this point and Oporto was long known as the 'Terras de Santa Maria', being the first to be wrested from the Moors by Afonso Henriques.

11km. A turning to the left leads shortly to the Augustinian monastery of *São Salvador* at **Grijó**, commenced in 1574 from the designs of Francisco Velasques. The two-storeyed cloister was completed in 1593; the hospice in 1605; but the Capela-Mór was not finished until 1629, with a Camarin added later in the century. It was briefly Wellington's headquarters prior to his 'passage of the Douro' in May 1809 (see p 285).

Regaining the N1, we continue N, shortly obtaining good views to the E, to approach (17km) *Oporto*. The main road forks right to *Vila Nova de Gaia*, on the S bank of the Douro, while the present motorway, turning beneath it, bears NW to cross the river by the *Ponte da Arrábida* (1960–63).

For **Oporto** see Rte 33.

Travellers wishing to *by-pass* Oporto are warned that the complex of roads attempting to ease communications is not yet completed, and bottle-necks may be experienced on reaching the N13 E of the Airport, at *Moreira*, and elsewhere.

27   Vilar Formoso to Vila Real

A.   Via Celorico, Trancoso and Lamego

Total distance, 202km (125 miles). N16. 42km **Guarda**—27km *Celorico* crossroads—N102. 15km, then turn left onto N226 for (4km) **Trancoso**—20.5km *Aguiar da Beira* lies 6.5km to the SW.—20km *Moimento da Beira*—21.5km **São João de Tarouca** is 3.5km S.—12km **Lamego**—N2. 15km **Régua**—25km **Vila Real**.

For the road to the crossroads just NE of **Celorico**, see first part of Rte 21. The N102, bearing NE, crosses the Mondego and ascends the narrowing valley to crossroads. For the road ahead see Rte 31, in reverse.

We turn left to (4km) **Trancoso**, an interesting walled town, well-sited for defence on a hill spur at a height of 900m.

It was of importance in the mid 12C and later. In 1283 Dom Dinis and Isabel of Aragón (later known as St. Isabel) were married here. In 1385 a battle took place here between the Portuguese and Spanish, when the latter were routed; and here two years later were concluded the negotiations by which John of Gaunt agreed to let his daughter Catherine (Catalina) of Lancaster marry the future Enrique III of Castile, in return for a large indemnity in money, and surrendering his own claims to the country.

Here in the 1580s Gonçalo Anes, a local cobbler, composed his 'Trovas' under the name of Bandarra, describing the return of Dom Sebastião, one of the first popular verses propagating the messianic cult of Sebastianism. The Inquisition was active here in the early 17C. João de Lucena (1550–1600), author of a 'Life of Francisco Xavier', was born here. General Beresford was given the title of Conde de Trancosa in 1810 after the battle of Busaco.

The ruined *Castle* of 1160 was several times rebuilt, and Trancoso's Romanesque churches have also been much altered, but the old town within its fortifications preserves a number of attractive corners.

A 12C church and ruined *Castle* can be seen at *Moreira de Rei*, 5km NE.

After 5km a right-hand turn leads 13km N to *Penedono*, with a curious well-machicolated 'toy' *Castle* of triangular plan, passing a turning (left) for *Guilheiro*, with a partly Romanesque church.

10km. A track to the left leads to a Neolithic site near *Carapito*. More interesting is *Aguiar da Beira*, approached by the next main turning, reached after 10.5km.

Aguiar, a pleasantly sited village, lies 6.5km SW. It preserves a granite clock-tower, what has been described as a medieval council-chamber, and a curious dry-stone fortification known as the 'castelo', but of doubtful denomination.

Some 12km W of Aguiar, reached by rough tracks, is *Ferreira de Aves*, the site of a Romanesque church and the later church of the ruined monastery of *Santa Eufémia*, founded in the 12C.

Continuing the descent of the Távora valley, after 5km we by-pass (right) *Sernancelhe*, with a church of Romanesque origin, and shortly skirt the S bank of the *Barragem da Vigia*, amid beautiful country, beyond which we traverse *Rua* and (15km) *Moimento da Beira*, with a church of 1594 containing 17C azulejos, and the 18C *Casa dos Guedes*.

FROM MOIMENTO VIA TABUAÇO TO THE N222 (36km), 6km W of *Pinhão* and 19km E of *Peso da Régua*. The N323 leads NE, later descending the W flank of the steep valley of the Távora, and passing (right at c 18km) a lane climbing down to the well-carved Romanesque chapel of *Granjinha* or *São Pedro das Águias*.—Bearing NW, at c 7km *Tabuaço* lies to the left, its church containing well-carved altars and painted ceiling panels.—To the W, at *Barcos*, are a Romanesque church and the hermitage of *Sabroso*.—The road descends steeply from Tabuaço to reach in 9km the road skirting the S bank of the Douro.

21.5km.—3.5km S up a narrow valley stand the extensive and impressive ruins of the monastery of **São João da Tarouca**, the first Cistercian monastery in Portugal, founded in 1124, but not commenced until 50 years later. The *Church* (key from house opposite) contains the tomb of Pedro, Count of Barcelos (c 1280–1354), a bastard of Dom Dinis, and author of the 'Livro das Linhagens', the 'Burke's Peerage' of its time. A fine painting of St. Peter, similar to that at Viseu, ascribed to both Cristóvão de Figueiredo and Gaspar Vaz, is normally here, among other works. Note also the organ.

A road opposite this turning leads down into the valley of the Barosa, where at *Ucanha* is a fortified *Bridge* (14C). The road leads in 5km to *Salzedas*, where an 18C church remains of a monastery founded in the 13C.—We regain the main road at *Ferreirim*, with painted panels by Cristóvão de Figueiredo and others in the Igreja Matriz.

12km. **LAMEGO** (8600 inhab.), an old episcopal city, and one of the most attractive of its size in Portugal, is a good centre from which to explore the region S of the upper Douro. It contains a wealth of Baroque architecture and an important museum. Much has changed since the Editor of Murray's Hand-Book of the 1850s described it as 'a very dirty, not particularly picturesque, and somewhat uninteresting city' ... but he also refers to an 'execrable' estalagem providing 'scanty fare', which may well have affected his opinion. Its wines and hams are reputed.

Lamego was re-occupied in 1057 by Fernando I. The Inquisition was active here, the home of many New Christians, even if its establishment was opposed by one of them, a doctor named Pedro Furtado, who had cured 'the mother of the sons of the Archbishop of Lisbon'. In 1827 it was visited by Lord Porchester, who considered it 'full of picturesque beauties and old remains of art', but one of the remains he was expecting to see, an ancient church, had been recently razed to the ground by its proprietor.

Convenient parking can be found around the gardens in the lower town, but it is recommended that one first drives up to the pilgrimage

The Largo dos Reis of N.S. dos Remédios

church of **N.S. dos Remédios** (1750–60), overlooking the town to the S, at the top of a double flight of over 600 steps, which invites comparison with that of *Bom Jesus* near Braga. The octagonal granite platform of the upper terrace, known as the LARGO OS REIS, is surrounded by dramatically placed if inelegant statues, and obelisks, etc., below which, on lower landings, are fountains and pyramidal roofed pavilions. The plunging *View* from the upper balustrade, of the town and of the hills above the Douro valley beyond, is very fine.

To the N of the gardens is the triangular LARGO CAMÕES, by which rises the **Cathedral**. Little remains of the Romanesque original except the belfry. The fine Gothic W front dates from 1508–15; the restored *Cloister*, with its belvedere, finished in 1557, is mainly Renaissance, with a few Gothic details. The interior preserves some damaged frescoes by Nasoni (1734–40). The retable painted by Grão Vasco in 1506–09 is now in the museum. The silver frontal (1758–68) in the Chapel of the Blessed Sacrament is notable; and the two organs should not be overlooked.

Facing the main avenue is the ***Museum**, installed since 1918 in the old episcopal palace reconstructed in the late 18C, recently restored after a fire, and in the course of being reorganised. It contains good collections of furniture, ecclesiastical plate, glass, azulejos, and, above all, 16C Flemish *Tapestries*. These last include the Temple of Latona, Music, and an Oedipus series. Outstanding among the paintings of *Vasco Fernandes* ('O Grão Vasco') are: Annunciation, Visitation, Circumcision, and Presentation, and his Creation of Animals.

On the GROUND FLOOR is the chapel of *São João Baptista*. On the floor above, the chapel of *São João Evangelista*, with its carved and painted panels and figures, was previously in the Convento das Chagas (see below) and moved here when it was demolished earlier this century. There are lapidary collections in the courtyard.

A number of mansions may be seen nearby, including the adjacent *Casa das Mores* (17C), and *Casa das Brolhas* (18C), further along the street; and at the top of the Rua da Pereira (S of the cathedral) the *Palacetes dos Vilhenas* and *de Santa Cruz*; the adjacent late 16C church and convent of that name are in military hands. Slightly further S at the next corner is the richly decorated *Capela do Desterro* (1640).

A lane leads downhill from this point to the picturesque riverside suburb of *Balsemão* (see below).

Proceeding down the main avenue from the museum, we soon reach (right) the old *Hospital*, now the *Theatre*. Here we ascend (right), passing through the *Porta do Sol* to enter the walled enceinte, and shortly bear left towards (left) an ancient vaulted *Cistern*. Turning right, the remains of the 13C *Castle* (views) are passed before approaching the *Porta dos Figos*.

Further N is the 17C *Casa dos Pinheiros*, and at the far end of the garden square, the *Igreja das Chagas* (1588).

A few paces to the W of the Porta dos Figos is *N.S. de Almacave*, said to have been once a mosque, or at least abutting a Moorish cemetery (*macab*). It preserves worn Romanesque S and W portals. Hence, by following the Rua de Almacave downhill past (right) *São Francisco* (1599) we regain the main avenue.

For the road S from Lamego to (70km) *Viseu* see the latter part of Rte 32.

FROM LAMEGO TO OPORTO VIA THE SOUTH BANK OF THE DOURO AND ENTRE-OS-RIOS (88km). This is a slow winding road, following the sinuosities of the steep Douro valley at some distance above the river but occasionally providing impressive views. The valley sides get increasingly populous as we drive W. We turn NW, past the *Miradouro da Boa Vista* (*View), and within a few kilometres reach a point above the S bank of the Douro, where we turn left on the N222, shortly traversing *Barrô*, with a curious Romanesque church, and enter the area of Vinho Verde vineyards. Beyond, to the left is *São Martinho de Mouros*, a fortified Romanesque church with a superimposed belfry.—13km *Resende*, where on a hill (views) stands restored Romanesque *São Salvador*, 3km beyond which a left-hand turning climbs c 5km to Romanesque *N.S. de Cárquere* (late 13C), part of a convent founded in 1099.—18km. **Cinfães**, reached after a steep ascent, is a centre for the production of Vinho Verde, and with the Roman bridge of *Covelas* over the Bestança. On the far side of the Douro (which may be crossed before climbing to Cinfães) is *Ancede*, see p 282.—The road climbs down steeply, bearing left near the *Barragem do Carrapatelo*.—9km *Tarouquela*, with the restored and partly rebuilt Romanesque church of *Santa Maria Maior*, once part of a Benedictine convent.—8km *Souselo*, beyond which is Romanesque *São Miguel*.—Crossing the Paiva, we shortly ascend to *Castelo de Paiva* (or *Sobrado*), from which we may climb S into the hills to visit *Arouca*: see p 248. The road descends steeply to cross the Douro for *Entre-os-Rios*, at its confluence with the

Tâmega. Hence the main but narrow road (N108) follows the N bank of the Douro to (38km) **Oporto**.

The main road from Lamego (N2) leads N.

5km A lane to the right (signposted) descends steeply to *Balsemão*, first crossing a reservoir and then turning right. The chapel of *São Pedro*, a Visigothic basilica built in the 7C and remodelled in 1643, contains the tomb of Afonso Pires (died 1362), Bishop of Oporto. Some difficulty may be experienced in finding the site, and it is advisable to enquire first for precise directions from the PT at Lamego.

Regaining the main road, we continue to make the steep descent into the Douro valley, crossing the river by a comparatively new bridge adjacent to the rusting remains of the old, to **Régua** (or *Peso da Régua*), a busy river port almost entirely occupied with the Port Wine industry, being the westernmost town in the demarcated area, and the nearest port to Oporto. Here is the *Casa do Douro*, headquarters of the Port Wine Institute: see also p 290. Otherwise the town is not of much interest.—To the W stands the *Casa dos Alambiques* or *Quinta do Salgueiral*, bought by the Bearsley family (which later became Taylor, Fladgate and Yeatman) in 1744, probably the oldest English-owned property in the Douro.

Some 12km N of Régua, between *Canelas* and *Covalinhas*, are excavations of the Roman settlement at *Fonte do Milho*, with remains of 1st and 4C villas, etc.

FROM RÉGUA TO AMARANTE (38km). The N108 skirts the steep N bank of the Douro, climbing steeply to (N101; 13km) **Mesão Frio**, whose *Igreja Matriz* is embellished with numerous painted ceiling panels, and ornate carved and gilt woodwork.—*Quintela*, with a 13C tower, is passed after c 6km before we descend the Fornelo valley. After c 14km we pass near (left) *Jazente*, with a late 13C church, before meeting the N15 and reaching the Tâmega at **Amarante**: see Rte 35A.

For roads from Régua to Penafiel, and to Oporto via the N bank of the Douro, see p 282.

From Régua, the N2 climbs steeply out of the main valley of the Douro, at c 17km traversing *Cumieira*, where the church of 1739 contains some sumptuous carving, before entering **Vila Real**, 8km beyond: see Rte 27B.

B.   Via Vila Nova de Fozcôa

Total distance, 163km (101 miles). N332. 17km **Almeida**—16km. **Castelo Rodrigo** is 1.5km to the right.—3km *Figueira de Castelo Rodrigo*—N332 and N222. 35km **Vila Nova de Fozcôa**—41km **São João da Pesqueira**—21km **Pinhão**—N322. 30km **Vila Real**.
The second part of this route is slow going, particularly on the descent to and ascent from the Douro valley.

We bear right immediately on leaving *Vilar Formoso* to (17km) **Almeida**, long one of the strongest fortresses on the Portuguese frontier, standing opposite its Spanish counterpart, *Fort Concepción*, on the far bank of the Turones.

It was refounded by Dom Dinis, and received its *foral* in 1296, confirmed by Dom Manuel in 1510, who strengthened the fortifications. These had been taken by Enrique de Trastamara in 1373, and by Juan I in 1381. It was here that John of Gaunt and Nun' Álvares took leave of each other after their invasion of Castile in 1387. It was briefly a base of operations against the Spanish in August 1704. In 1762 Almeida was forced to surrender to a Spanish force, but during the 18C it was rebuilt on a Vaubanesque plan, with strong bombproof casemates, etc.

It was in French hands from the beginning of the Peninsular War until evacuated after the Convention of Sintra, and was garrisoned by Portuguese under the command of Colonel William Cox when isolated by Masséna's advance in 1810. Crauford's Light Division fought a bloody battle against the superior forces of Ney and Loison on 24 July just S of the town, before retiring. The French did not attack until 26 August, when an unlucky shell lit a powder trail from a damaged keg, causing the strongly vaulted main church, then used as a central magazine, to blow up, killing some 500 Portuguese outright: Cox was forced to capitulate. It remained a French outpost until after the battle of Fuentes de Oñoro (May 1811); as they withdrew they blew up more as a parting shot. Here in the 1840s Baron de Bomfim briefly took up arms against Costa Cabral's administration. It was the birthplace of the historian Bernardo de Brito (1569–1617).

That there is still so much to see of the *Fortifications, the main gate of which is dated 1797, is remarkable. The town itself has not much else to offer except for the newly established *Pousada*.

We continue N through *Vilar Torpim*, where in January 1810 Colonel Leach spent his evenings smoking cigars 'over some Douro wine', dancing 'boleros, fandangos, and waltzes, with the good-looking daughter of an Israelite', in whose house he was billeted. It retains a Gothic church and an attractive mansion.

We approach the heights of *Marofa* (left; 977m) and after 16km (right) **Castelo Rodrigo**, a decayed village once of importance, with extensive remains of its circuit of bastioned *Walls*, *Castle*, and the small church of *Reclamador* (sic: N.S. do Rocamador). The village commands panoramic views.

3km *Figueira de Castelo Rodrigo* has only one feature of architectural curiosity: the interior arch supporting the coro alto of its church is composed entirely of S-shaped stones.

3km SE are the imposing remains of the 13C Cistercian convent of **Santa Maria de Aguiar**, now a farm (to which visitors should apply), possessing a large Gothic *Church* and finely vaulted Chapter-house. Note the Renaissance loggia of the adjoining house.—About 3km further to the E, N of the *Almofala* road, are the remains of a Roman temple known as the *Casarão da Torre*.

For the road NE from Figueira to *Freixo de Espada à Cinta* see Rte 28, in reverse.

At *Freixada do Torrão*, 5km W, are a medieval tower and a church preserving its Romanesque portal.

Terraced vineyards in the Douro valley

We now bear NW into 'Port Wine' country along a ridge (views) to (16km) *Almendra*, with a large Baroque mansion and fortified church, later passing (left) the ruined *Castle* of *Castelo Melhor*, before steeply descending to cross the Coa at its confluence with the Douro (right; views). Climbing out of the valley we meet (17km) the N102 just S of **Vila Nova de Fozcôa**, its *Church*, adjacent to a *Pelourinho*, with a good Manueline portal. The cant of its pillars, the stone pulpit, well-carved altar, and painted ceiling, are notable. For the cross road see Rte 31.

Turning left and then right after 4km, we climb over the hills, at 8km passing *Freixo de Numão* (3km N), taken from the Moors in 1055, with ruins of a *Castle* and a church of Romanesque origin, beyond which lies the famous *Quinta de Vesúvio*, founded by António Bernardo Ferreira. (On the opposite bank of the Douro here is the *Quinta da N.S. da Ribeira*.)

7km. There is an 18C mansion at *Cedovim*, 4km to the S of this last turning; and 4km to the N the circuit of fortifications of *Numão*.

22km **São João da Pesqueira**, a large viniferous village surrounded by Port quintas, on the plateau overlooking the Douro. Pombal is said to have spent part of his youth here. The Baroque *Casa do Cabo* is notable.

A road leads steeply down to the river and the *Barragem de Valeira* at the *Cachão de Valeira*, where the narrow gorge was until 1792 the highest point of navigation, being choked with granite slabs until cleared. Rapids still remained, and it was here that Baron Forrester met his death on 12 May 1862, when his boat capsized. High above the gorge is the shrine of *São Salvador do Mundo*, to the E of which is the *Quinta de Vargellas*.

From São João we climb down to meet the Douro again 19km NW, passing near (right) the *Quinta of Roriz* (originally owned by Robert Archibald until bought by Nicolau Kopke in the 1760s), and the 18C *Quinta das Carvalhas*. Opposite that of Roriz are those of *Tua* (*Quinta dos Ingleses*) and *Malvedos*; opposite Carvalhas those of *Roeda* (once owned by Mr Fladgate, created Baron da Roeda), and *Bom Fim*.

On reaching the river bank we turn right to cross the Douro at (2km) **Pinhão**, with Régua, the most important river port and transport centre of this region.

The N222 skirts the S bank of the Douro to (21.5km) *Régua*, see Rte 27A, passing near the *Quinta do Bom Retiro*.—After 4km a road climbing steeply S leads 9km to *Tabuaço*; see p 265.—On the N bank of the river just W of this deviation is the *Quinta da Boa Vista*, its vineyards possibly planted by Baron Forrester himself.

The N322 climbs steeply NE from Pinhão up a valley of the same name and past (right) the *Quinta do Noval* to (16.5km) high-lying *Alijo* (*Pousada Barão de Forrester*); the N212 continues N to meet the N15 after c 20km; see Rte 29A.

Our route climbs steeply NW from Pinhão on the N323 to (15km) **Sabrosa**, the birthplace of Fernão de Magalhães (Magellan; c 1480-1521). One ship of his fleet of five (commanded by Juan Sebastián de Elcano, a Basque) was the first to circumnavigate the globe (1519–22), Magellan himself having been killed in the Philippines.

2km to the N is a Bronze Age site, while there is a Luso-Roman rock temple at *Panóias*, to the right of the main road some 8km NW.—3km beyond that turning we enter the village of **Mateus**, on the E outskirts of Vila Real. The church at neighbouring *Moucós* contains the well-sculpted tomb of Fernão de Brito (1483). Mateus is well known for the Baroque finialed *Solar* built here for António José Botelho

Mourão in 1739–43 by Nicolau Nasoni (illustrated on certain rosé wine labels during recent decades).

The fabric is in a sorry state of disrepair, two exterior walls being shored up by wooden beams to stop them crumbling to the ground, and it is hoped that the present owners will be able to restore their residence before it is too late.

3km. **VILA REAL** (13,300 inhab.) is the largest town of the Trás-os-Montes and the capital of its district.

It was granted royal rights by Afonso III in 1272. Here the reactionary Count of Amarante established the headquarters of an insurrectionary movement in February 1823 prior to the *pronunciamento* at Vila Franca de Xira (cf.). It was the birthplace of Diogo Cão, the first navigator to reach the mouth of the Congo (1482).

In the wide central avenue, its S end retaining a few 17–18C mansions, is Gothic *São Domingos*, a monastic church now raised to the rank of cathedral, but of slight interest.

From the N end of this avenue a lane leads E to (right) the *Capela Nova*, or *Clérigos*, at the junction of two streets, with its curious narrow façade framed by a set of twin columns. Further to the N is *São Pedro* (from 1528), the interior of which contains some good Baroque gilt carving.

Vila Real is an important road junction and its communications will be improved when the new N15 highway is completed; see p 273. For the road to *Chaves* see Rte 32, in reverse; for *Oporto*, Rte 29A; and for *Lamego* and *Viseu*, also Rte 32.

28 (Zamora) Miranda do Douro to Guarda

Total distance, 189km (118 miles). N221. 45km *Mogadouro*—47km **Freixo de Espada à Cinta**—40km *Figueira de Castelo Rodrigo*—20km **Pinhel**—37km **Guarda**.

Miranda is 56km due W of *Zamora*, with Spanish and Portuguese Customs on their respective banks of the Douro. The recently-opened connecting road now makes it a convenient approach from the NE, in preference to Braganza.

Another road (C527) leads SW from Zamora to (65km) *Fermoselle*, crossing the Douro 9km beyond, at the *Barragem da Bemposta* (Customs), and meeting the N221 after 9.5km and 28km SW of Miranda.

Miranda do Douro (*Pousada de Santa Catarina*, with impressive plunging views of the Douro), once an isolated frontier outpost overlooking the Douro rapids, is now—with the construction of its dam across the gorge, surmounted by the road—one of the more important crossings from Spain into the Trás-os-Montes. Here, and in adjacent villages, a dialect known as Mirandés, in fact a Leonese *patois*, is spoken.

Miranda was the Roman *Sepontia*. It was raised to a bishopric in 1545, but in 1782 the see was transferred to Braganza. It was attacked by the Spaniards in May 1762, when the castle blew up, killing some 400 people. On 28/29 May 1813 Wellington, having ridden from Salamanca, was slung across the gorge here in a 'kind of hammock' suspended by ropes, to inspect 60,000 Anglo-Portuguese troops, assembled within Portugal in previous weeks under the command of General Graham. This composed the heavy-weight left wing of his army across the Esla, the movement of which next day was to outflank the French entirely, and which was perhaps the most successful single offensive manoeuvre of the

Peninsular War, the immediate campaign culminating in the great victory at Victoria (21 June) only three weeks later.

The *Castanilla*, or walled town, consists largely of 16C houses, or earlier. At the far end, beyond the central square, stands the former **Cathedral**, overlooking the ravine of the Douro. With its severe W Front, the edifice was built between 1552–76 by a Spaniard, Francisco Velázquez, to the designs of Gonçalo do Torralva and/or Miguel de Arruda. The retable of the Capela-Mór was carved in 1610–14 by Juan de Muniátegui at Valladolid and transported here. Note also the well-carved furniture in the Sacristy; the choir stalls and organ; the rich carving (of boys, birds, and grapes, etc.) of another altar (left), and (right) the curious puppet-like 'Menino Jesus da Cartolinha', dressed in an opera-hat and white bow-tie!

Behind the cathedral, an arcade remains of the unfinished cloister, and the ruined bishop's palace.

The town has a small ethnographical *museum* 'da Terra de Miranda'.

For the road to Vimioso and *Braganza* see Rte 29A.

We turn left just W of Miranda, and bear SW to (9km) *Duas Igrejas*, 3km S of which is a rock shelter with late Paleolithic carvings.

9km. A left turn leads 9km down to the *Barragem do Picote* on the Douro. From just N of Miranda to Barca de Alva (see below) it naturally divides the two countries, the river at this point passing through a precipitous gorge.

Another dam, the *Barragem da Bemposta*, may be approached by turning left after another 12km, but the views are less impressive. For the road from Zamora via *Fermoselle* to this crossing see above.

Passing (9km) a turning for *Algozinho* (c 8km SE, with a 13C church) we bear SW and then W over open country, to (6km) **Mogadouro**. A market town which was once an important frontier fortress, the ruins of which we may see, Mogadouro was a stronghold of the Távora family until crushed by Pombal. The 16C *Igreja Matriz* contains some good carved and gilt woodwork (18C); the church of the convent of *São Francisco* is of the same period.

At *Azinhoso*, 6km N, is a 12C church, 3km NE of which, at *Penas Roias*, is a medieval tower and ruined *Castle*. For the N216 leading NW to (49km) *Macedo de Cavaleiros* see Rte 29A.

From Mogadouro we climb S over the hills through (15km) *Castelo-Branco*, with the deteriorated *Solar dos Morais Pimentéis*, and after 18km reach a road junction high above the Douro valley (views). —The right fork leads due W to (26km) *Moncorvo*: see Rte 31.

We bear left, with the peak of *Pocinhella* (821m) on our right, to (14km) **Freixo de Espada à Cinta**, an old frontier fortress preserving a tall heptagonal tower of its *Castle*, and remains of walls. It may take its curious name—'ash-tree of the girt sword'—from a gesture of Dom Dinis, who, when he founded the town, buckled his sword round an adjacent ash-tree, but there are alternative guesses. It was the birthplace of Jorge Álvares, the navigator and chronicler of Japan, and of the regional poet Abilio Manuel Guerra Junqueiro (1850–1923). Its cheeses are reputed.

From the main road lanes flanked by medieval houses lead towards the main square overlooked by the **Igreja Matriz*, an imposing Manueline rebuilding of a 13C church, containing the *Retable* of c

1520–35 of 16 paintings ascribed to 'Grão Vasco'. Note also the tomb, and a figure of St. Peter to the left of the altar, the pulpit, and the lateral portal.—Opposite the church is the tower of the 16C *Misericórdia*.

On leaving Freixo, we pass a ruinous church (right) and shortly wind round the *Durão* (722m) the summit of which can be gained by a road leading to the right, then left before reaching the mountain. Both this, and the road as it descends towards the Douro at the *Barragem de Saucelle*, provide good views.

We turn W along the N bank of the river through a forest of almond-trees to (21km) *Barca de Alva*, once the upper limit of navigation, and a railway crossing into Spain. Here we cross the Douro and ascend the steep S side of the valley, with the *Garganta de Agueda* to our left.—12.5km *Escalhão*, some 5km SE of which, at *Mata de Lobos*, is a monument recording the Portuguese victory here over the troops of the Duque de Osuna in July 1664.

7km *Figueira de Castelo Rodrigo* (see Rte 27B), beyond which we pass (left) *Castelo Rodrigo* on its fortified height, and skirt the foot of (right) *Marofa* (977m), which may be ascended for the view.

After c 14km of winding road, we cross the rocky gorge of the Coa and climb S towards (6km) **Pinhel**, añ attractive old town and seat of a bishopric until 1882, commanded by its *Castle* (1312), the interior of one tower of which is supported by a single column. Near by stands *Santa Maria* (14C), containing a series of 17C paintings of the Life of the Virgin. In the central square is the 18C *Paço do Concelho*, with a small archaeological collection. The *Misericórdia* preserves a Manueline portal; the *Igreja Matriz* (*São Luís*), Baroque woodwork and 18C azulejos. The old *Bishop's Palace* housed the headquarters staff of Generals Graham and Picton at various times during the Peninsular War.

We continue SW, at (5km) *Malta* passing a turning for neighbouring *Souro Pires*, 2km right, with the 15–16C *Solar dos Távoras*, from which the road (N226) goes on to (27.5km) *Trancoso*, see Rte 27A

We reach the N16 after 24km, 6km from **Guarda**, on its height to the W: see Rte 21.

For the roads hence to *Castelo Branco* see Rte 22; for *Viseu*, Rte 23; and for *Coimbra*, Rte 21.

29 Miranda do Douro to Oporto

A. Via Mirandela, Vila Real, and Amarante

Total distance, 312km (194 miles). N221. 45km *Mogadouro*—N216. 49km **Macedo de Cavaleiros**—N216 and then N15 for (28km) **Mirandela**—33km *Murça*—38km **Vila Real**—47km **Amarante**—30km *Penafiel*—42km **Oporto**.

This somewhat tiring cross-country route promises to be improved in part when the new N15, at present under construction, is completed, running SW from Braganza to Oporto via Vila Real and Amarante. This highway will virtually replace the tortuous old road. It will by-pass Mirandela and Murça, and between Vila Real and Amarante it will run parallel to and N of the present road. Bearing W, it will then pass just N of Penafiel, and cross and re-cross the N15, to enter Oporto from the N.

FROM MIRANDA TO BRAGANZA (84km). The N218, bearing right just W of Miranda, shortly by-passes (right) *Malhadas*, an old village with a part-13C church, and continues NW to (29km) *Vimioso*, to the left of the road. Its *Igreja Matriz*, on the S slope of the village, dates from the 17C. Between its towers is an unusual cruciform window.—8km SW is the *Castle* of *Campo de Viboras* (views).—23km. *Outeiro*, where the 17C *Igreja Matriz* preserves a curious façade between its two towers.—At 10km we join the road from *Zamora* via *Alcañices* and descend towards *Braganza*, 22km NW (see Rte 30).

For the first part of this route, see Rte 28. From *Mogadouro* we turn NW, later climbing down into the valley of (18km) the Rio Sabor, and ascending its far bank.—19km. *Chacim*, with a good *pelourinho*. 5km E of Chacim is the abandoned convent of *Balsemão*, founded in the early 18C by Frei Casimiro Wiszynski, a Pole.—12km. **Macedo de Cavaleiros**, an agricultural centre, preserves the *Solar* of the Morais Sarmento de Vasconcelos family.

We shortly meet the N15 from Braganza, and turn left, after 15km passing (left) *Romeu*, one of the 'restored' villages of the VALE DE COUÇO, with a small *Museum* of mechanical curiosities, before descending towards (12km) **Mirandela**, with a long medieval *Bridge* of 17 arches over the Rio Tua, probably of Roman foundations. The town is dominated by the *Palace of the Távoras* (late 17C), now the town hall.

The N213 leads 50km NW to *Chaves* (see Rte 30) via (22km) *Valpaços* and *Vilarandelo*, with the *Solar dos Calainhos* of 1745, before crossing the SERRA DA PADRELA.

We start to climb, and skirt the S slope of the SERRA DO VILARELHO to (33km) **Murça**, in the gardens of which (right) stands the '*Porca de Murça*', a roughly sculpted boar of pre-Roman origin. To call someone such implies that he is a political turncoat. The *Misericórdia* retains a typical Baroque façade of 1692.

We now cross the Rio Tinhela and ascend in steep zigzags to a road junction from which Rte 29B leads NW.

We leave on our left, 3km beyond, the N212 bearing SW via *Alijó* to (41km) *Pinhão*, on the Douro.

28km **Vila Real**; see Rte 27B. For the road S to *Lamego* and *Viseu* see Rte 32.

From Vila Real we bear W, briefly on the improved road, climbing across the SERRA DO MARÃO to the *Alto de Espinho* (1019m), after 22km passing the *Pousada de São Gonçalo*, before descending to the Tâmega valley at (27km) *Amarante*.

AMARANTE, situated on the steep bank of the Tämega, here crossed by a handsome three-arched obelisk-embellished *Bridge* of 1790 by Carlos da Cruz Amarante (1740–1815), and a modern bridge, is a small but straggling wine-growing town. It has a reputation for the curious phallic cakes it bakes during the festival of its thaumaturgic patron saint, São Gonçalo, protector of marriages (but only beatified in 1561).

The name of Amarante is said to be derived from the Latin *Ante Moranam* (in front of the Serra do Morão), although others have preferred an origin in its fertility cult! The Roman bridge here is said to have been reconstructed by Gonçalo himself in the 13C, but his erection collapsed in 1763.

In 1809, Beresford and Silveira (later Count of Amarante: see *Vila Real*), holding the E bank of the river, effectively stopped the French from retiring E and NE after precipitately abandoning Oporto. Loison evacuated Amarante on 12 May, and, joining up with Soult, moved N towards Guimarães, jettisoning his wheeled transport and guns. But with Wellington entering Braga on the 15th, the

French had no alternative but to clamber across country towards Salamonde and Montealegre in full retreat.

The main monument of Amarante is the *Church and Convent of São Gonçalo, by the bridge. This was begun in 1540 under the supervision of Frei Julião Romero, architect of the Dominican Order, but was not completed until 1620. Its most obvious exterior features are its entrance façade; the arcaded loggia with its sculptures; and the cupola above the crossing. The interior contains some richly carved and gilt woodwork, particularly in the Capela-Mór, and the gutted organ-case with its supports is also notable; while to the left of the high altar is the tomb of the saint (c 1262), against which—so they say—husband-hunters past their first youth have only to rub their bare flesh to be granted one within the year. Its two Renaissance cloisters are being restored, and in due course its dependencies will house a *Museum*. The adjacent belfry will be noted.

Steps climb to *São Domingos* (18C), a round building (closed, but said to contain a fine organ-case and rococo woodwork). Further up the hill is *São Pedro* (1727), with a good Sacristy.

On the far bank of the river is a restored arcaded building.

For the road NW to (33km) *Guimarães*, see the latter part of Rte 35A, in reverse.
The N210 leads NE along the N bank of the Tâmega to (3km) *Gatão*, home of the poet Joaquim Teixeira de Pascoaes (1877–1952), with the church of *São João* of some interest, and, c 26km beyond, *Celorico de Basto*, with an early *Castle* (?11C), partly restored, and some 17–18C mansions.

A tortuous road (N210) leads SW above the bank of the Tämega to a junction at 16km. To the left here is *Tabuado*, with a good late Romanesque church. To the right, on a height, is *Marco de Canaveses*, with a small Romanesque church and the 17C *Casa da Ribeira*.—The main route may be regained 13km NW, passing near (left) *Vila Boas de Quires*: see below.

We follow the N15 NW, passing (left) at 6km *Freixo de Baixo*, with a 12C church (*São Salvador*); there is another of similar date at *Telöes*, to the right of the road.

After 3km we turn left; the right-hand fork leading NW via *Felgueiras* to (24km) **Guimarães**; see Rte 37. After 7km we reach a left turn descending to *Travanca*, where the 12C church of the monastery of *São Salvador* (founded 970–1002) has two good Romanesque portals, and an apse and a separate tower retaining interesting features. The monastery is now an asylum.

Regaining the main road, we follow the ridge W for 7km.

The left turn here, for *Marco de Canaveses* (see above), descends to (c 6km) a turning (right) for *Vila Boas de Quires*, with a 12C church, its interior modernised, to the left after c 1.5km. Of more interest, to the right some 700m along this turning (easily missed when approached from this direction) is the remarkable 18C *Façade* only of the so-called **Casa das Obras** (or *Obras do Fidalgo*, or *dos Portos Carreiros*). The rest of the building was never completed.

Regaining the main road, we approach (6km) **Penafiel** (until 1770 known as *Arrifana de Sousa*). It was founded in the 9C and retains a mid 16C *Igreja Matriz* on the site of an earlier building, a Doric *Misericórdia*. The Rua Direita contains a number of old granite houses, some with Manueline features; other may be seen in the Rua Serpa Pinto.

8km. *Mouriz*. A lane leads 2km S past (right) *Cete*, with a Benedictine monastery with Romanesque and Manueline features; and, beyond the railway, **Paço de Sousa**, where the Monastery of *São Salvador* preserves a fine Romanesque *Church (12C; damaged by fire in 1927) containing the tomb of Egas Moniz (died 1144), on which his legendary exploits are depicted in high relief. Adjacent are two 18C quintas, charmingly sited.

Regaining the N15, we continue W, shortly descending through increasingly populous districts on approaching the E suburbs of **Oporto**: see Rte 33.

B. Via Vila Pouca de Aguiar and Guimarães

Total distance, 343km (213 miles). For the road to (155km) **Murça** see Rte 29A. Beyond (c 7km) we turn right onto N212 for (37km) **Vila Pouca de Aguiar**—N206. 41km. *Cabeceiras de Basto* lies 4km N.—28km *Fafe*—13km **Guimarães**—N10. 22km **Santo Tirso**—27km **Oporto**.

Climbing out of the valley of the Tinhela, beyond *Murça*, we bear NW to **Vila Pouca de Aguiar** (see Rte 32), and after c 30km cross the Tâmega, passing near, on the slope of the SERRA DE ALVÃO, the dolmens of *Carrazedo*, artefacts from which were the subject of much discussion at the turn of the century.

11km *Cabeceiras de Basto* is 4km to the right, with the large Benedictine monastery of **Refóios**, founded in the 12C, but rebuilt in the 18C, with a large cupola and twin towers.

28km *Fafe*, site of an ancient fortified settlement, from which the artefacts and some primitive statuary have been moved to the Museu Martins Sarmento, Guimarães.—4km *Arões*, with the church of *São Romão* (1237) is traversed before we reach the N101 and turn right for (5km) **Guimarães**: see Rte 37.

Bearing SW on the N105, after 11km **Vilarinho**, with a good 12C church, lies c 4km SE on the far bank of the Vizela. Vilarinho is not far from the spa of *Caldas de Vizela*, where some Roman tessellated pavements have been found.—3km A left-hand turning leads 3km to **Roriz**. Above the portal of its restored Romanesque *Church* (1228) is a large rose-window.

To the SW is the Iron Age *Citânia of Sanfins de Ferreira*, preserving a number of stone huts and lines of defensive walls (cf. *Citânia de Briteiros*). Some artefacts excavated here are to be seen at *Paços de Ferreira* (further S on the N207), with a Romanesque church (with a large apse of interest, and separate belfry) of the monastery of *São Pedro de Ferreira*.—**Oporto** is 27km SW.

8km **Santo Tirso** (12,000 inhab.), a busy textile town on the Rio Ave, with the former Benedictine monastery of *São Bento*. The church, rebuilt in 1659 to the plans of João Turriano of Coimbra, preserves a late 14C cloister containing some archaeological relics.

From here we turn SW for (22km) **Oporto**: see Rte 33.

30 (Zamora) Braganza to Braga via Chaves

Total distance, 226km (140 miles). The frontier (*Customs*) is 84km W of *Zamora* on the N122 via *Alcañices*. **Braganza** is 31km NW on the N218.

N103. 31km *Vinhais*—67km **Chaves**—33km. *Montalegre* is 9km NW.—37km *Venda Nova*—30km. *Gerês* lies 16.5km N—14km *Póvoa do Lanhoso*—14km **Braga**.

For *Zamora* see *Blue Guide Spain*.—On crossing the Esla at 24km the left-hand fork leads directly to the new frontier crossing at *Miranda do*

Douro: see Rte 28.—Here we bear right for *Alcañices*.

On crossing the frontier, we shortly descend steeply, with views ahead of Braganza, after 22km traversing *Gimonde*, with a medieval bridge.

At the hamlet of *Babe*, c 5km NE of Gimonde, John of Gaunt confirmed in 1387 the surrender of all rights he and his wife might have to the throne of Portugal.

5km. A right turn leads 5km to (right) **Sacoias**, where the church (ask anyone near where the key is hidden) contains some damaged paintings formerly ascribed to 'Grão Vasco'; note also the naïve ceiling paintings.—The neighbouring village of *Baçal* was the parish of the Abade de Baçal, who devoted his life to the archaeology of the region: cf. the Museum at Braganza.

As we bear SW to enter the town, we see the ancient citadel on a height to the left.

BRAGANZA (*Bragança* in Portuguese; 13,900 inhab.; *Pousada de São Bartolomeu*), a high-lying district capital (680m), and ancient capital of the Tras-os-Montes, was the Celtic *Brigantia* and the Roman *Juliobriga*. It has always remained a provincial backwater, largely due to bad roads, which have hampered both the sale of its produce and the movements of foreign invaders.

The construction of the new highway to supersede the old N15 to Vila Real and Oporto, promises to ease communications (see p 83).

John of Gaunt and João I passed through in 1387 before the Anglo-Portuguese attack on León. It is also certain that in these remote districts some crypto-Jewish communities survived the persecutions of earlier centuries (a synagogue was opened in Braganza in 1927).

But its name, widely known as the surname of Charles II's queen, Catherine, has conjured up a different image, and some may be disappointed. The title of Duke of Braganza was created in 1442 for Dom Afonso, natural son of João I. His family, whose seat was at Vila Viçosa (cf.), and whose rights of succession were ignored by Philip II of Spain in 1580, came to the throne in 1640 in the person of João IV, the eighth duke. The male line became extinct in 1853, but descendants of the female line ruled until the end of the monarchy in 1910.

A small square in the town centre is flanked by the nondescript little *Cathedral*, from 1545 the church of São João Baptista, but the Sé since 1770, when the seat of the bishop was transferred here from Miranda do Douro. It contains a gutted organ-case and, in the Sacristy, 17 painted panels.

Hence we follow a street downhill to the right to the Largo de São Vicente, overlooked by the church of *São Vicente*, on a Romanesque base, and with a curious naïve ceiling of 1886. Traditionally it was here that the future Pedro I was clandestinely married to Inês de Castro (cf. *Cantanhede*).

A cobbled lane ascends to gardens below the main entrance to the *Walled Upper Town, commanded by the Torre de Managem of its *Castle, erected in 1187 by Sancho I and besieged, unsuccessfully, in 1199 by Alfonso IX of León. Adjacent is a *pelourinho*, its base driven through the back of an ancient granite boar (cf. *Murça*); and near by is 18C *Santa Maria*, said to contain a painted ceiling. Immediately abutting Santa Maria is the over-restored *Domus Municipalis, a rare example of Romanesque civic architecture, and built over a cistern. Its red tiles look incongruous. The key may be obtained at a house opposite.

The present municipality has a well-conceived plan to clear this quarter of its hovels, and generally to improve its appearance. It looks well from a distance, preferably from the hill to the SW, on the slope of which stands the *Pousada*.

Leaving through the town gate, we turn right towards *São Bento* (1590), said to contain a Mudéjar ceiling in the capela-mór, a painted barrel-vault of 1763, and a sumptuous retable, but access is not easy to obtain, the ecclesiastics of Braganza keeping up a running fight with the civic authorities over such matters as admission to its churches.— *São Francisco*, a few paces to the right, is of slight interest.

Bearing downhill to the W, we shortly pass an attractive old mansion (No. 39), and following the main street ahead reach the *Museu do Abade de Baçal, named after its instigator, Francisco Manuel Alves (1865–1947), who dedicated most of his life to the study of the region, and which is installed in the old *Bishop's Palace*. On the GROUND FLOOR are three bishop's litters, and the smaller objects from the important archaeological collection. The larger objects, including numerous stelae, may be seen below the porch and in the garden; some of the most curious have unfortunately been imbedded in a wall to the right behind a tree.

Stairs ascend to a landing below a cupola, off which, below carved compartmented ceilings (some of the gilt of which has been overpainted), opens a series of rooms, including a private chapel (with a painted wooden ceiling, and displaying vestments, plate, etc.). Other rooms contain miscellaneous paintings, among them Orpheus, by *Roelland Savery*; the *Marquês d'Oliveira*, Study of a boy's head; an *anon.* Annunciation; *Henrique Tavares*, Portrait of the Abade de Baçal; works by *Abel Salazar* (1889–1946); and watercolours of pelourinhos by *Alberto de Sousa* (died 1961). Among books and MSS on display are some early 16C charters, including that of Braganza (1514; the first had been issued by Sancho I in 1187), and Bulls of the foundation of the diocese of Miranda do Douro and Braganza (1545). Other rooms are devoted to a numismatic collection, and to Ethnography: local costumes, including that of the 'Pauliteiros', or stick-dancers of the region; metalwork, including a scold's bridle, weights and measures, etc.; and Ceramics.

At the corner of the second right-hand turn stands the *Misericórdia*, with a charming carved retable of the Virgin with her arms protectively extended.—Opposite the end of this short street is *Santa Clara* (16C), under restoration, preserving a painted ceiling.

For the road S to *Celorico* see Rte 31, off which, after c 45km, the partly improved N15 leads SW to *Oporto*: see Rte 29.

We proceed W on the N103, shortly passing a left turn—now part of the new N15—to nearby *Castro de Avelãs*, with the ruined 12C church of a Benedictine monastery, of interest as it is the only one in Portugal built of brick in the style of those at Sahagún, in Spain, with blind arcading.

31km. **Vinhais**, once 'much infested by custom-house officers', but no longer a frontier town, preserves the ruins of its fortifications, and the convent of *São Francisco* (17–18C), with two churches, the best features of which are their organs, and carved and gilt pelmets, etc.

A minor road leads 24km N to the remote villages abutting the Spanish frontier, the furthest, *Moimento*, on the flank of *Coroa* (1273m).

Shortly beyond Vinhais we bear SW along a ridge providing extensive views, to (25km) *Rebordelo*, where we turn W, by-passing (left) *Lebução* with an old church, after c 30km passing (left) the *Castle of Monforte de Rio Livre*, probably erected on the site of a Roman fort.—Approaching *Chaves*, we meet the road entering from the right, from *Verín*.

For **Chaves** and the road S to *Vila Real* see Rte 32.

Leaving Chaves, we cross onto the right bank of the Tâmega, shortly passing (left) the site of the Roman castro at *Curalha*, and traversing the bald TERRAS DE BARROSO, the original home of the lyre-horned oxen known as *'barrosã'* seen throughout the Minho.

At 21km a left turn leads via *Boticas* to (13km) the *Castro of Carvalhelhos*.

13km **Montalegre**, a small walled hill-top town standing at 966m below the SERRA DO LAROUCO, rising to 1525m, is 9km NW. It preserves its 14C *Castle* (restored).

Here Wellington spent the night of 18 May 1809, on giving up the pursuit of Soult's army after taking Oporto. Wellington's forces then moved S to Abrantes to re-group before the commencement of the Talavera campaign. Unfortunately the local *Ordenança* had refused to blow up a bridge at Misarela (see below), to the SW of Montalegre, as it was the only means they had of crossing the Cávado. The French were thus able, with the loss of only 19 men, to capture the bridge and escape being virtually surrounded. Even so, the invaders were forced to jettison their baggage and artillery, and one eye-witness counted about 100 horses and mules they had hamstrung. They had also set fire to every place they passed through in their headlong retreat from Braga.

A minor road leads directly S to regain the N103, passing a castro (*'dos Mouros'*, or *'dos Duques'*) near *São Vicente de Chã*.

The main road now skirts the N bank of the huge *Barragem do Alto Rabagão* before descending the valley and circling the S bank of the *Barragem de Venda Nova*, and traversing (37km) the village of that name.

The road continues to wind above the S side of the Rabagão valley, in which lies the ancient *Misarela Bridge* (restored), while nearer *Salamonde* is the site of another bridge likewise crossed by the French in their precipitate retreat in May 1809. It was then apparently spanned by only two huge wooden beams, the planking between them having been removed.

At the E end of the Salamonde reservoir is the confluence of the Rabagão and the Cávado. Further W. is the many-armed reservoir of *Caniçada*, while to the N rises the SERRA DO GERÊS.

28km. A right-hand turn descends steeply past (right) the *Pousada de São Bento*, providing extensive mountain views, with the reservoir in the valley below.

At the crossroads on the valley floor, the road to the right leads up a narrowing thickly-forested side valley to (9.5km) the village of **Gerês**, a small spa. The whole area to the N of the Cávado abutting the Spanish frontier, and including *Castro Laboreiro* (see Rte 34B), has since 1970 been named the **Parque Nacional da Peneda-Gerês**, a nature reserve of c 70,000 hectares. The track beyond Gerês continues to and beyond the frontier (Customs; for Bande, Celanova and Orense), here the *Portela do Homem*, to which a Roman road, retaining several Roman miliary columns, ascends from the SW, above the S bank of the *Barragem de Vilarinho*.—For the road (N308) leading W from this crossroads down the Cávado valley, and that descending the Homem valley from *Covide* (c 10km N), see sub-routes off Rte 34B, in reverse.

The N103 continues SW to (16km) **Póvoa do Lanhoso**, with the ruins of a 12C *Castle*, and to the SE the **Church* of a Benedictine monastery founded in 1067 at *Font' Arcada*.

This village probably supplied the title for the reactionary insurrection against the government of Costa Cabral in April 1846, which began with a conflict of village women (personified by 'Maria da Fonte') and the local civic authorities over the (insanitary) right to be buried *in* churches rather than merely in consecrated ground away from villages.

At **Taíde**, some 7km SE, to the right off the N205 for *Arosa*, and on the N bank of the river, is the sanctuary of *N.S. do Porto de Ave*, of 1736 (preserving twin organs, painted ceilings, and an octagonal chancel), *above* which rises a series of garden terraces and statues in the style of Bom Jesus at Braga.—The N310 descends the Ave valley from Póvoa. At 9.5km a right turn leads up to the *Citânia de Briteiros*: see p 318. At *Caldas das Taipas* we reach the N101 between Braga and Guimarães: see Rte 35A.

The main road from Póvoa do Lanhoso continues W, later passing (left) the road ascending to the sanctuary of *Bom Jesus*, before (14km) entering **Braga** itself: for both see Rte 36.

31 Braganza to Celorico da Beira

Total distance, 182km (113 miles). The N15 now leads due W for 4km before turning S, there forking left onto the N102 for (6km) **Macedo de Cavaleiros**—59km **Moncorvo**—16km *Vila Nova de Fozcôa*—40.5km **Trancoso** lies 5.5km to the W.—21.5km **Celorico da Beira**.

The new and much improved N15 (which formerly crossed the railway line no less than five times in the first 20km) turns left past *Castro de Avelãs* (see Rte 30) and bears S and then SW.

At 39km we turn left.—For the continuation of the N15 see Rte 29A.

6km. *Macedo de Cavaleiros*: see Rte 29A, beyond which we cross the SERRA DE BORNES (at c 30km entering the Port wine region).

After 43km a right turn (N215) climbs NW to (11.5km) *Vila Flôr*, with the 18C *Solar de Diogo do Lemos*, a 17C church, and one remaining gate of its fortification.—Some 18km W of Vila Flôr, approached by the N214 (2km NW), is *Carrazeda de Ansiães*, some 6km S of which, at *Ansiães*, are relics of its walls and the ruins of Romanesque *São Salvador*, among other Romanesque chapels in the vicinity.—The road from Carrazedo later descends steeply to *Tua*, at the confluence of the Rio Tua with the Douro. From Tua the N212 climbs steeply to *Alijó* (see Rte 27B).

The road skirts (left) a rocky ridge. At 7km a by-road leads left to *Adeganha*, with an isolated Romanesque church.

We cross the Rio Sabor, a tributary of the Douro, and climb to (9km) **Torre de Moncorvo**, among orchards, on the N slope of the SERRA DO ROBOREDO (906m). It derives its name from an 11C senhor, Mendo Curvo, although the site of Roman *Valarisa* is in the neighbourhood. It preserves slight ruins of its fortifications; a massively buttressed Manueline *Igreja Matriz*, its imposing interior containing a polychromed triptych and a Renaissance *Misericórdia*. The town itself, once described as 'very ill-built and filthy', has not changed much. There are some iron-mines further E.

We turn SW, descending to and crossing the Douro at (9.5km) *Pocinho*, not far S of its confluence with the Sabor. To the W of Pocinho is the *Quinta do Vale de Meão*.

6.5km *Vila Nova de Fozcôa* is immediately to the E, for which, and for the road to *Vilar Formoso*, 75km SE, see Rte 27B, in reverse.

15.5km. *Longroiva* (right), an ancient town preserving slight remains of its castle, is by-passed as we traverse a long valley, some 8km beyond passing another ruined *Castle* at (right) *Marialva*, a long-abandoned but now partly repopulated walled village.

At 17km a right turn leads to **Trancoso**, 5.5km W: see Rte 27A; likewise for the winding road to *Guarda*, turning left at the next crossroads, from which we descend into another valley to approach (18km) **Celorico da Beira**: see Rte 21.

32 (Verín) Chaves to Viseu via Vila Real and Lamego

Total distance, 172km (107 miles). C532. 17km **Chaves**—N2. 17km *Vidago*—19km *Vila Pouca de Aguiar*—28km **Vila Real**—25km **Régua**—13km **Lamego**—33km **Castro Daire**—37km **Viseu**.

For *Verín* see *Blue Guide Spain*. Hence we descend the Tâmega valley to cross the frontier (Customs) 10km N of Chaves.

CHAVES (12,000 inhab.), Roman *Aquae Flaviae*, was a station on the road between Braga and Astorga. Its hot springs were reputed, as are its smoked hams (*presunto*).

Hydatius, its bishop in the 5C, compiled annals describing the Suevic occupation. It grew into an important frontier fortress opposite Spanish Verín, its canting device being keys (*chaves*), and as such was occasionally occupied by invading forces, among them those of the Spanish General O'Reilly in 1762. It later fell to Soult, whose retreating columns were followed this far by Beresford in 1809. Even as recently as 1912 it was briefly occupied by a monarchist faction rising against the infant Republic.

The Tâmega is here crossed by a Roman **Bridge** of 16 arches (AD 104), spoilt by the addition of a metal parapet. The bridgehead is commanded by a *Castle* of the Dukes of Braganza, the imposing *****Torre de Menagem** of which now houses a small *Military Museum*. Adjacent is a miscellaneous archaeological collection, including Roman stelae, artefacts from the Castro de Carvalhelhos, columns, and carved escutcheons, etc.

Also facing the PRAÇA DE CAMÕES is the church of the *Misericórdia* (late 17C), with an attractive façade and porch, ornate retable, painted ceilings by Jerónimo da Rocha Braga (1743), and large azulejo panels.

The adjacent *Igreja Matriz*, entirely rebuilt in the 16C, and since over-restored, retains part of its Romanesque portal below the belfry, also with Romanesque features, while the interior preserves relics of an organ. Here Afonso de Braganza (died 1461), natural son of João I and founder of the ducal dynasty, was first buried.

To the N is the *Fort of São Francisco*, part of the 17C Vaubanesque fortifications; and further N, that of *São Neutel*.—To the left of the S end of the bridge stands the 18C *Igreja da Madalena*, with an octagonal nave.

Some 4km N, approached by the road leading off the N end of the bridge, is the restored Romanesque church of *N.S. da Azinheira*, at *Outeiro Seco*, with interesting exterior corbels and faint 16C frescoes (enquire at neighbouring houses for key).

W of *Abobaleira*, 4km NW of Chaves, at *Outeiro Machado*, is a large rock covered with prehistoric carvings, approached by a track (30-minute walk).

For the road hence to *Braga*, see Rte 30.

Leaving Chaves, we skirt the left bank of the Tâmega, with the SERRA DA PADRELA rising to the SE, after 14km bearing S to (3km) *Vidago*, a small spa.

After 8km we pass (right) *Sabrosa*, where a small ruined chapel commemorates General Ronald Macdonald (or Macdonnel), a reactionary Scot who met his death here in 1847 during a skirmish.

4.5km. *Pedras Salgadas* (right) is another spa, which we by-pass before traversing (6.5km) **Vila Pouca de Aguiar**, with ruins of its *Castle*. For the cross road here to *Guimarães*, see Rte 29B.—We soon enter the Port wine region.

28km. **Vila Real**: see the latter part of Rte 27B; and for the road hence to *Amarante*, Rte 29A.

The road now descends steeply, parallel to the Rio Corgo, to (25km) *Régua*: see the latter part of Rte 27A.

FROM RÉGUA TO OPORTO VIA ENTRE-OS-RIO (121km), a somewhat tortuous route above the Douro. The N108 skirts the N bank of the Douro, off which, after 13km, the N101 ascends to *Mesão Frio*: see Rte 27A.—We climb away from the river bank, and away from the Port wine vineyards into those of the Vinhos Verdes, the winding road providing a number of attractive views, and at 30km pass (left) a road climbing down to *Ancede*, with a ruined 13C convent. High up on the opposite bank is *Cinfães*: see Rte 27A.

The road descends to the river and continues W above the *Barragem de Carrapatelo*.—*Alpendurada e Matos*, with a large convent of early origin, much rebuilt after 1611, and again in the 18C, is passed before we reach *Entre-os-Rios*, just beyond which the Tâmega is crossed at its confluence with the Douro.

The N106 leads N, off which after 4km a minor road approaches (c 6km) **Boelhe**, where the 12C church of *São Gens* is a good example of rural Romanesque.—The N106 continues N, off which we can turn left for *Paço de Sousa* (see p 275) via (right of the road) *Cabeça Santa*, with a good 12C church.

From Entre-os-Rios the road follows the N bank of the Douro to (40km) **Oporto**.

The S bank of the Douro may also be followed from Régua, shortly meeting the sub-route from Lamego to Entre-os-Rios: see the latter part of Rte 27A.

Crossing the Douro, we climb in steep curves to (13km) **Lamêgo** (see p 265). A good plunging view of Lamêgo is commanded by *N.S. dos Remêdios*, overlooking the town to the S, a turning to which we next pass, before reaching a high-lying plateau, with the SERRA DO MONTEMURO, rising to 1382m. on our right.

33km. **Castro Daire**, of ancient origin, retains little of moment, but at *Paiva*, 6km W on the N bank of the river Paiva, is a 12C hermitage.

We cross the romantic gorge. From its far bank the N228, turning right, climbs SW to (25km) *São Pedro do Sul* (see Rte 23).—We ascend through attractive and thickly wooded country before descending to cross the Vouga, meeting the N16 some 3km NW of **Viseu** (see Rte 23).

For roads hence to *Busaco* and *Coimbra*, see Rte 24.

33 Oporto

The second city of Portugal, known as **Porto** by the Portuguese, but to the English as **OPORTO** (*O Porto*, the port), is famous for the export of the wines of the upper Douro, the business of which has been largely in English hands for the last 300 years. The episcopal see is of very ancient origin, but the university dates only from 1911. According to the 1981 estimate, its population was 330,200, but this is more likely to be in the region of 350,000, while the conurbation of which Oporto is the hub may contain c 800,000.

Like Lisbon, it is favoured by its magnificent site, rising on the steep N bank of the rock-bound gorge of the Douro near the river mouth;

and likewise much of it is very hilly: indeed Costigan remarked 200 years ago that 'To walk about this city is, I assure you, rather a violent exercise, not one street in it being on a level excepting that where the most part of the English inhabit'. The sprawling town is ill planned; nor does it contain very many buildings of great importance; but nevertheless it is a thriving city full of vitality, and of considerable interest and character.

Part of the population still seethes in squalid '*ilhas*', badly ventilated alleys leading off the main streets, particularly between the cathedral and the riverside, and one may well wonder just what conditions were like half a century ago, when it was stated that 'great progress has recently been made in the cleanliness of the place'. The Douro, unlike the Tagus, has no wide estuary, its narrow mouth being partially blocked by a sand bar, and in the past Oporto was liable to sudden destructive floods in Winter, the water rising some 4.5m above its normal level, and in 1909 to within 10cm of the lower level of the Ponte de Dom Luís.

On the S bank is **Vila Nova de Gaia**, where most of the *armazéns* or lodges of the wine-shippers are to be found (see Rte 33D, and the Introduction to Port and the Wines of Portugal).

Pleasant central accommodation at a reasonable price is not too easy to find, a situation it is hoped will be improved. Most of the monuments of interest are within walking distance of the city centre, once this has been reached, through a confusing maze of one-way streets.

History, and the English in Oporto. The name *Portucale* appears for the first time in the Chronicle of Bishop Idacio (456), and is applied to the site of *Miragaia*, near the present Custom House. A ferry crossed the Douro hence to *Cale*, a Roman castro said to have been established by Decimus Junius Brutus, and mentioned in the 'Antonine Itinerary' as a strengthened Lusitanian fort on the road from Olisipo (Lisbon) to Bracara Augusta (Braga). At this crossing of the Roman *Durius* a castle was later erected on the *Pena Ventosa* (where the Bishop's Palace now stands), and in the 6C a church was built alongside it by the Suevi.

The town which grew up around it, the *Burgo do Porto*, was razed by the Moors in the 8C, but in 868 it was in the hands of a certain Vimara Peres, who held the line of the Douro, although it was not definitively recaptured by the Christians until 982. Rebuilt, it became the capital of the county of *Portucalia* and of the 'Terras de Santa Maria', the newly-won area S of the great river towards Vila da Feira. Count Henry of Burgundy is said to have founded a cathedral, and his descendants granted many privileges, including the curious decree, which ostensibly remained in force until 1505, that no nobleman 'or powerful person' should own property or stay for more than three days within its walls.

In June 1147 a fleet, which had gathered together at Dartmouth bound for the Second Crusade, landed here, including an expeditionary force of English, whose reputation as 'plunderers, drunkards and rapists, men not seasoned with the honey of Piety' had apparently preceded them. Having patiently listened to the bishop's proposal that they 'move on' to the assistance of Afonso Henriques, intent on the capture of Lisbon, and no doubt fortified with good wine, they lurched back to their ships ten days later to follow up what sounded like a profitable escapade, taking with them as hostages both the bishop (Pedro Pitões) and João Peculiar (Arcbishop of Braga), just in case.

A later bishop (Martinho), who had incensed the populace of *O Porto* in 1209, remained penned up in his palace for five months. In 1237 the

Dominicans established a monastery in the town. Another boundary wall, of which there are slight remains, was later built, being completed c 1376; while in 1387 João I and Philippa of Lancaster ('Filippa de Alemcastre'), daughter of John of Gaunt, were married in the cathedral. Their son Dom Henrique (Henry 'the Navigator'; 1394–1460) was born in the old palace. From this time on the life of Oporto became progressively and inextricably involved with the English, although their interest in the wine now known as 'Port' did not mature for another 300 years.

In 1415, when the fleet of Dom João was preparing for the Ceuta expedition, the people of Oporto considerately sent their best meat, suitably salted, to the ships, reserving the offal for themselves, thus earning the ungrateful nickname of *'tripeiros'* or tripe-eaters; but they retaliated by calling the inhabitants of Lisbon *'alfacinhas'*, lettuce-eaters.

The Inquisition was only briefly established in Oporto, one auto-da-fé taking place in 1543, and it was suppressed four years later. But in 1618 many of its 'New Christians' were arrested. In 1628, in the 'Revolta das Maçarocas' (the spindles), the women of Oporto attacked the minister responsible for a tax on linen and woollen goods; in 1661 occurred another anti-tax riot. In 1757 the 'Tipplers' Riot'—said by Pombal to have been instigated by the English against his wine monopoly—was put down by that minister with some ferocity.

Although in 1668 Robert Southwell in Lisbon was promising to send some 'white Oporto wine' to Arlington in London, after the vintage, it is unlikely to have been what is now known as 'Port'. The first British merchants in Oporto were not then engaged in the wine trade, the centre of which was at Viana do Castelo, and it was not until about a decade later that wines were being exported thence by the two sons of a Liverpool (or Yorkshire) wine merchant, being sent down the Douro from Lamego. Peter Bearsley (son of Job Bearsley of Viana) was one of the first shippers to move to Oporto, and he was visited there by Thomas Woodmass of Kettering in 1704, by which time the small English and Scottish community was well established under their consul, John Lee. Hunt, Roope and Company had had premises at both ports for some 50 years, shipping dried cod and oil from Newfoundland, and wheat and wool from England; and in exchange exporting wine, cork and fruit, etc.; but this bartering of cod and cloth for wine had been going on since the 15C or earlier.

Woodmass, who lodged with Mr Page in the Rua Nova, noted that the shippers kept very much to themselves, even employing English-speaking negro servants, some from Carolina, so that they didn't have to converse in Portuguese with their cooks. These vitiated viticul-turalists were even said to compel the peasants to sacrifice the honour of their daughters if they wanted to sell their wine, for 'they...only bought from growers who allowed their daughters to dance with them', which Trend suggests was merely making political capital out of old-time vintage customs.

Luckily, the Lisbon earthquake of 1755 did not physically affect Oporto. Building had gone on rapidly. Nicolau Nasoni, an Italian, did much to embellish the city during the years 1730 to 1763, when the bell-tower of the Clérigos was completed, and he died in Oporto (where he had married a local girl) in 1773. In 1770 work started on the new Hospital de Santo António. According to Alexander Jardine (1779), the author of 'Letters from Barbary', Oporto had been 'much improved and beautified' by João de Almada, the governor, 'with the assistance and advice of our good consul' (Whitehead). Jardine was then about to take up the post of consul at La Coruña, which he was to hold until 1795, when the outbreak of war caused him to move to Portugal—perhaps Oporto—where he died in 1799.

In June 1808, Lisbon having been occupied by the French, Oporto defiantly proclaimed the Prince Regent; a provisional junta under its bellicose bishop was set up; and the Royal Lusitanian Legion was raised there by Captain Robert Wilson. But in March 1809 Oporto was unable to resist Soult's assault, and many citizens were killed or drowned as they sought to escape across the bridge-of-boats which was then tethered to both banks. Within two months, however, Wellington's brilliant 'Passage of the Douro', took place, and they were relieved.

The Passage of the Douro, 1809

The French, warned to expect a seaward attack, had nevertheless broken up the bridge-of-boats, and secured all vessels, including barges, on the N bank. Their complete surprise was effected by Wellington, at first using the one small skiff which had slipped over to the S bank during the cover of darkness to ferry across a landing party. This, invisible to Soult's sentries, then installed itself in the buildings of an unfinished seminary surrounded by a walled enclosure running down to the water's edge. Meanwhile another force crossed the river further SE, at *Avintes*. Some barges were then collected from the N shore, and further troops ferried across. Having thus gained a fortified foothold, there was little Soult could do in a hostile town to stem the tide, for the area to the W of the seminary was now raked by artillery fire from the commanding Serra. With increasing numbers pouring across on more craft ferried over by high-spirited civilians from Oporto, and with their flank turned to the E, the French precipitately retreated, Soult himself hospitably leaving his dinner in the Palácio das Carrancas to be eaten by Wellington and his staff. Sir Nicholas Trant was later the military governor.

A revolt of radicals broke out in Oporto in 1820. In 1832–33 the city was besieged again, this time for 18 months, during the Miguelite War. On 9 July 1832 Dom Pedro landed from the Azores with some 7500 men on the beach at the mouth of the Mindelo, just N. of the city,

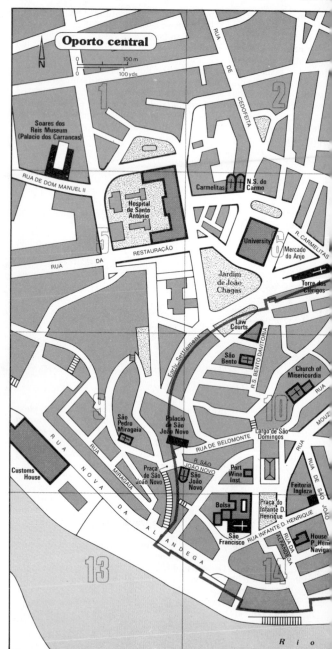

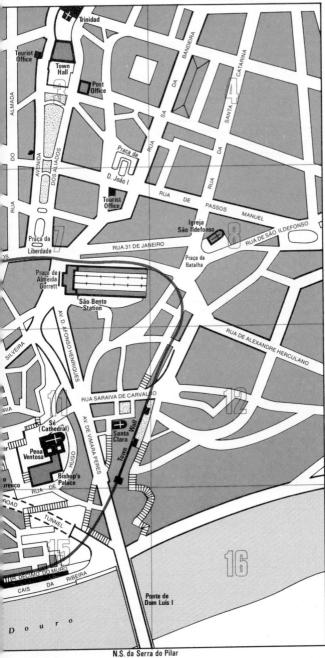

Trinidad

Tourist Office

Town Hall

Post Office

RUA DA BANDEIRA

SANTA CATARINA

Praça de D. João I

Tourist Office

RUA DE PASSOS MANUEL

RUA DA

Igreja São Ildefonso

RUA DE SÃO ILDEFONSO

Praça da Liberdade

RUA 31 DE JANEIRO

Praça da Batalha

Praça de Almeida Garrett

São Bento Station

RUA DE ALEXANDRE HERCULANO

AV. D. AFONSO HENRIQUES

SILVEIRA

RUA SARAIVA DE CARVALHO

AV. DE VIMARA PERES

Sé (Cathedral)

Santa Clara

Town Wall

Pena Ventosa

Bishop's Palace

RUA DE

TUNNEL

ROAD

R. DECIMO DO MURO

CAIS DA RIBEIRA

Ponte de Dom Luís I

16

Douro

N.S. da Serra do Pilar

which he entered, while its besieging force of some 13,000 briefly retired. These 'Voluntários da Rainha' were welcomed with relief by the citizens, who one way and another had suffered three years of Miguelite oppression, their stubborn defence against the usurper's attacks in late September and October being stiffened by a motley 'international brigade', consisting largely of an out-of-work Glaswegian and Cockney contingent under the command of Charles Shaw, plus a sprinkling of Peninsular War veterans. After ten months the opposing forces had increased to 17,800 Liberals, closely invested by 24,000 Miguelites, while Captain Nugent Glascock RN, with a small flotilla, patrolled the river-mouth, keeping a weather eye on British interests, and Colonel Lovell Badcock remained in Oporto as the British Government observer.

Cholera raged. Although a soup kitchen was set up by the British merchants, cats and dogs (including Colonel Shaw's pets) soon became the common ingredient of stews. The Miguelites continued to bombard the city in a desultory way, causing some damage and even hitting the British Factory house. The wine lodges stood in Miguelite territory. In June 1833 Captain George Rose Sartorius was replaced by Charles Napier as Pedro's naval commander, who shortly after captured Miguel's 'fleet'' at Cape St. Vincent. Eventually the Miguelites retreated, but not before they had blown up and set fire to the stores of the Old Wine Company at Vila Nova de Gaia. Gallant Captain Glascock, with a party of marines, stopped the fire from spreading to other lodges, but some 27,000 pipes of wine ran into the river, turning it a muddy red.

Oporto flourished and continued to be a stronghold of liberalism throughout the century, being the scene of opposition to reactionary regimes in 1846, 1851, 1890 and 1891, while in 1878 the first Portuguese Republican deputy was elected there. Its population also continued to grow. In 1864 it was 86,750; in 1900, 167,950; in 1920, 203,100; in 1960, 303,400.

Among those born here, apart from Henry the Navigator (see above), were: Francisco Vieira ('Portuense'; 1765–1805), the artist; Almeida Garrett (1799–1854), the poet, novelist and liberal; 'Julio Dinis' (Joaquim Guilherme Gomes Coelho; 1839–71), novelist and author of 'Uma Familia Inglesa' (1868), analysing Anglo-Portuguese relationships: another more anglophobe description was published in 'Epístola a John Bull' (1887), by Ramalho Ortigão (1836–1915), also from Oporto. Antonio Teixeira Lopes (1866–1942), the sculptor, was born at Vila Nova de Gaia.

Useful addresses: *British Consulate*, Av. da Boavista 3072; *British Institute*, Rua do Breiner 155; *English Church* (St James's), Campo Pequeno; *Associação Luso-Británica do Porto*, Rua do Breiner 155; *Câmara de Comércio Luso-Britanica*, Rua Sá da Bandeira 784; *Oporto Cricket & Lawn Tennis Club*, Rua Campo Alegre 532.

A. Central

One of the main centres of Oporto is the PRAÇA DA LIBERDADE (Pl.7), embellished by an equestrian statue of Pedro IV (1866), which lies a short distance N.W. of *São Bento* railway station. Hence the gardens of the AVENIDA DOS ALIADOS slope uphill to the *Town Hall* (begun 1929), with its tall belfry. Immediately to the W of the town hall is the *Tourist Office*, and behind it is the large 18C *Igreja da Trindade*.

From the SW corner of the Praça da Liberdade the Rua dos Clérigos ascends steeply towards the church and *Torre dos Clérigos* (see Rte 33B), one of the most conspicuous landmarks of the city.

By descending to the left almost immediately, we shortly reach the Rua das Flores, partly flanked by silversmiths, and turn right. Towards its far end (right) stands the *Church of the Misericórdia* (1559; but largely rebuilt in 1749–54 by Manuel Álvares Martins and Nicolau Nasoni).

Adjacent (No. 15) is the entrance to the Misericórdia offices, where one should apply to visit the council-chamber. In it is preserved one of the finest paintings in Portugal, the *Fountain of Mercy*, by an anon. Fleming (1520) of the School of Van Eyck. Figures of Dom Manuel, founder of the Misericórdia, and his queen Dona Maria, are seen kneeling with their family and a group of nobles and ecclesiastics beneath the central subject of Christ crucified between the Virgin and St. John.

The ceiling is notable. A collection of silver may also be on display.

On reaching the adjacent LARGO DE SÃO DOMINGOS, we follow the ancient Rua de Belomonte (note No. 49) to the right to approach the **Museum of Ethnography and History**, installed in the imposing *Palácio de São João Novo* (Pl.9), with its curiously shaped granite-framed mezzanine windows, built in 1723–33 for Pedro da Costa Lima, a wealthy magistrate, by Nicolau Nasoni. A double flight of stairs rises from the entrance hall, from the landing of which a single flight continues the ascent. Some rooms may be temporarily closed while the fabric of this interesting building is being restored.

GROUND FLOOR. Apart from a wine-press, and a machine for bruising hemp, the lower part of a statue of a warrior from Monte Mozinho, Oldrões (Penafiel), of the Castreja culture, is displayed. In the yard to the left of the entrance is a collection of stelae, and sun-dials, etc.—On the stairs are two paintings displaying genealogical tables of the Augustinians.

FIRST FLOOR. Reconstruction of a regional Kitchen, with furniture and domestic utensils; Plans and Prints of Oporto; an interesting collection of ship models, including (on the floor above) those of the various types of vessels peculiar to the Douro, previously used to transport wine from the upper reaches of the river to Oporto, etc., among them the *barcos rabelos*; the *catraias*, single-sailed passenger-boats, sharp at both ends; the *barcos de toldo*, like clumsy gondolas; flat-bottomed *caíques*, for ferrying the Douro; also the high-prowed *moliceiros* from Aveiro, and the three-masted *rasgas* from the S of Portugal, etc.; costumes; and silver filigree work from Gondomar. Here also are Palaeolithic and Bronze Age implements; ceramics, including amphoras from Póvoa do Varzim; glass and amber objects from Monte Mozinho; and a gold diadem and ring from Beiral, Ponte de Lima. Also a number of naïve paintings; ceramics from Vila Nova and Massarelos (note the violin and 'cello players); a collection of pen-holders; pharmacy vases; and two close-stools, etc.

SECOND FLOOR: a collection of ox-yokes; arms; locks; fishing equipment; Presépios; fireworks for St. John's Day, etc., and an early five-floor lift (18C) from the Largo de São Domingos.

On the opposite side of the PRAÇA DE SÃO JOÃO NOVO stands the church of *São João Novo*, started in 1552 and finished a century later. Note the organ-case. The adjacent cloisters now accommodate law-courts.

From the SW corner of the square a lane descends steeply to 18C *São Pedro de Miragaia* (ask at grocers opposite for key), with an elaborately carved and gilded chancel, and with a small 'museum' containing a 16C Flemish triptych.

By turning downhill from São João Novo to the E, and then bearing right and then left, we reach the N entrance of the glass-domed court of the *Bolsa* or *Stock Exchange*, of 1834–42, built on the site of the old Franciscan convent. It contains a particularly hideous ball-room in a pseudo-Moorish style which cost a great deal to construct, and of which the commercial hierachy has therefore always been inordinately proud.

Uphill to the left, opposite the relic of a covered market, are offices of the **Port Wine Institute** (*Instituto do Vinho do Porto*; founded 1932), containing a portrait of Joseph James, Baron Forrester (born Hull, 1809; drowned 12 May 1862 at the Cachão da Valeira, on the upper Douro). This organisation sets out to supervise and regulate the Port wine trade, instituting quality control, and issuing Certificates of Origin, etc.

Turning downhill beside the gardens of the PRAÇA DO INFANTE DOM HENRIQUE, we reach (right) steps ascending to **São Francisco (Pl.14),* a late 14C building with a good W window, its interior in the mid 18C elaborately festooned with gilded carving in late Baroque and Rococo

The interior of São Francisco

styles, including the ceiling. On the S side is the altar of the Martyrs of Morocco; to the N a richly carved Tree of Jesse. Also noteworthy are the 18C organ, and the Renaissance tomb of Fernão Brandão Pereira (1528) to the right of the organ.

Above the riverbank here is the Rua Nova da Alfândega, some distance along which stands the *Customs House*. To the left is a medieval tower-house.

Following the broad Rua do Infante Dom Henrique, formerly the Rua dos Ingleses, to the E, with its shipping offices and warehouses, etc., we pass the Rua da Alfândega Velha, in which is the heavily restored and rebuilt *House of Prince Henry the Navigator*, a royal palace once accommodating the old Customs House, and said, traditionally, to be the site of the birthplace on 4 March 1394 of the illustrious fifth child of João I and Philippa of Lancaster. It is now used for temporary exhibitions, and houses the city archives.

At the far end of the old Rua Nova dos Ingleses stands the imposing granite façade of the **Feitoria Inglesa**, or *Factory House of the British Association* erected between 1786–90 by John Whitehead, both bibliophile Consul at Oporto from 1756 to 1802, and amateur architect, possibly advised by John Carr.

It was not *officially* opened until 11 November 1811, and it is said, on very slight evidence, that Joseph Camo, an American citizen remaining in the town during the brief French occupation acted as caretaker, and its confiscation was thus avoided. Whether it is this new building or an earlier one Lady Holland refers to is uncertain, when she stated (December 1808) that with her husband they moved from 'their wretched *posada* to the inn built in the Factory House for the accommodation of English travellers; spacious, clean, and possessing the comforts of fireplaces'.

Major William Dalrymple, who passed through Oporto in 1774, 'feasted most voluptuously with the consul and factory, who were remarkably civil and attentive; the only thing that I disliked amongst them'—he added—'was their supercilious treatment of the Portuguese, from whom they derive their wealth and opulence'. The building in which he had feasted so well would have been its predecessor, but the consul would have been the same John Whitehead, who with his passion for the sciences and astronomy had erected a lightning conductor on his residence, which had caused consternation among the Portuenses, and even occasioned a visit from commissaries of the Inquisition.

H.F. Link, who visited Oporto a few years later, commented that among the English merchants were several who possessed 'both knowledge and the love of science, particularly a gentleman named Warre'. Consuls continued to be granted offices in the new building until c 1835. When not working, the British were playing, even indulging in a game called cricket on a field near the Palácio dos Carrancas, which quite bewildered the watching Portuguese.

Membership of the association has always been rigidly confined to firms which have been connected with the Port wine trade since the 18C, and the member firms (with the date of foundation of their original establishment in brackets) are: Cockburn Smithes (1815); Martinez Gassiot (1790): Croft (1678); Delaforce Sons (1868): Guimaraens (1822); Taylor, Fladgate & Yeatman (1692): W. & J. Graham (1814); Silva & Cosens (1862); Warre (1670): Robertson Brothers; Offley Forrester (1729); and Sandeman (1790).

Among these have been amalgamated a number of old firms, such as Quarles Harris (1680); Morgan Brothers (1715); Butler & Nephew (1730); Hunt Roope (1735); Smith Woodhouse (1784); Dow; Fonséca; and Gonzalez Byass.

The intricacies of their actual ownership—by such organisations as Messrs Harvey; International Distillers & Vintners; and the ubiquitous Symington family, among others—lie beyond the scope of this guide.

A considerable number of Port shippers are *not* members of the association, among them: Kopke (1638); Ferreira; Osborne; Borges; Barros, Almeida; Cálem; Ramos Pinto; Manuel Poças; and António José da Silva (Quinta do Noval, Van Zeller brothers).—See also the Introduction to Port and the Wines of Portugal.

British wine-shippers in the Rua Nova dos Ingleses in 1834, by J.J. Forrester (detail)

Permission to visit the interior of the building, which is normally closed to the public, may be courteously granted by a member of the association of the British Port Wine Shippers, to whom interested parties may apply.

The Ground Floor *Loggia* is some 24m long, containing seven openings, and leads to an entrance hall. Hence a newel staircase ascends to the main assembly rooms, consisting of *Dining* and *Dessert Rooms*, a *Drawing Room*, and *Ballroom*. The old *Kitchen* and *Library* are also of interest, and likewise the collection of china, and much of the furniture.

Among portraits are those of John Page (born in Oporto in 1699, whose father had also been in the wine trade) painted by Richard Wilson; of General Sir William Warre; Sir Robert Newman; George Glas Sandeman; Sir John Croft; and John Whitehead, among others associated with the Port Wine trade and the factory in previous centuries. Also to be seen is a painting by Francisco Vieira (Portuense) of Queen Eleanor sucking the poison from a wound inflicted on Edward I during the Crusades, being a variation on Angelica Kauffmann's study of the same theme.

Hence we may descend the Rua de São João to the PRAÇA DA RIBEIRA, once the centre of the waterside traffic of Oporto, and still often providing an animated scene. The *Cais da Ribeira* (left) is flanked by an arcaded walk containing shops and restaurants built into the old town wall, above which runs the Rua Cima do Muro. It was from this quay that the old bridge-of-boats crossed to the far bank (see History). It is now dominated by the **Ponte de Dom Luís I,** a two-storeyed bridge, designed by Teófilo Seyrig, thrown across the chasm of the Douro in 1886. Its upper level is some 172m long, and 60m above low water level.

A view E from the Cais a Ribeira, now dominated by the Ponte de Dom Luis I, c 1820

The lower level is approached by traffic from a tunnel, the entrance to which we pass (right) when re-ascending the Rua de São João or Rua dos Mercadores. The former leads into the wide Rua Mouzinho da Silva, which bears NE back towards the central station: the latter shortly enters a warren of steep and noisome alleys, of which the narrow Rua da Bainharia ascends to steps below the cathedral: see below.

A turning to the right off this latter alley leads to the Jesuit church of *São Lourenço*, better known as *Dos Grilos*, dating from 1577, and one of the earliest of its style in Portugal, attributed to Baltazar Álvares (who later built the new cathedral at Coimbra). Hence steps climb towards a 14C *Tower* above which stands the *Sé*.

Of the granite **Cathedral** (Pl.11), founded in the 12C by Count Henry and Dona Teresa, parents of Afonso Henriques, little remains except the foundations on which the church, with its high barrel-roof, was reconstructed in the late 13C, and in which João I and Philippa of Lancaster were married in 1387. This was drastically and ineptly 'modernised' in the 18C, by among others, Nicolau Nasoni, who added the *Porch* beside the N door in 1736. He also designed the grand staircase off the main cloister, and the completion of the famous silver altarpiece (see below). The W Rose-window (13C) and the W Front generally, with its twin buttressed towers (capped by cupolas), is typical of the medieval church architecture of N Portugal.

In the N transept is seen the silver altarpiece, largely composed by

The marriage of João I and Philippa of Lancaster

nine different silversmiths between 1632–83, but only completed after Nasoni's design in the 1750s. It is said to have been hidden behind a plaster wall in 1809 to protect it from Soult. It is likely that Nasoni was responsible for the design of the railings and gates of the chancel arch. On either side of the Baroque altar, with its spiral columns of 1610, by Gonçalo de Morais, are the organs of 1727, the design of their cases also attributed to Nasoni.

In the S transept is the statue of the Virgin said to have been brought from France by the Bp of Vendôme, when accompanying the Gascon fleet in 982, but probably of later date. Adjacent is the main *Cloister*, of the French Cistercian type (1385), decorated with 18C azulejos. Off its SE corner is seen the remains of the *Romanesque Cloister*.

Immediately SW of the cathedral, on the rock outcrop of the PENA VENTOSA, stands the former *Bishop's Palace*, with a façade 58m in length, designed by Nasoni before 1734, but which took more than a century to be completed, before its conversion into the Town Hall. It contains a fine granite staircase.

To the SE of the cathedral is a house of 1730–46, attributed to Nasoni, containing a museum devoted to the poet Guerra Junqueiro (1850–1923), with collections of furniture, ceramics and silver, etc., and recently reformed.

Hence we may gain the Av. de Vimara Peres, approaching the upper level of the Ponte de Dom Luís I (see above), while by turning N we regain the Praça da Liberdade.

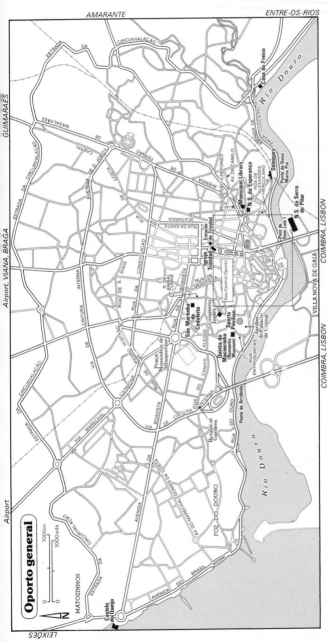

Oporto general

1000m

1000yds

N

B. Eastern

The Av. Dom Afonso Henriques leads S from the PRAÇA DA LIBERDADE to the **Ponte de Dom Luís I** (see p 293) off which the Rua Saraiva de Carvalho turns left to approach, at the lower end of a small square (right) the convent church of *Santa Clara*, founded in 1416, but rebuilt in the 17–18Cs. It contains a wealth of carved and gilt woodwork of c 1730, by Miguel Francisco da Silva, but its cleaning is overdue.

Immediately to the E of this church, approached from the next right turn, is the best-preserved section of Afonso IV's *Town Walls*, with several towers, but usually known as the 'muralha fernandina'.

Bearing NE, we shortly reach the ugly PRAÇA DA BATALHA, from which the Rua da Santa Catarina, one of the principal shopping streets, continues N, while the Rua de São Ildefonso, passing the 18C church of that name, leads NE towards gardens flanked to the E by the monastic buildings of *São António* (1783). These now accommodate the *Municipal Library* (preserving some rare illuminated MSS and incunables), its cloister lined with 16–17C azulejos. To the S the gardens are overlooked by the façade of the orphanage and church of *N.S. da Esperança* (1724–31), by António Pereira, to which Nasoni added a portal in 1746–63.

Besides this, the Rua das Fontainhas descends towards the ALAMEDA DAS FONTAINHAS, with a good view of the Ponte de Dom Luís I, and of the somewhat similar railway *Bridge of Dona Maria Pia*, but without a lower level; it was Eiffel's first important construction (1876–77). Adjacent to the latter bridge stands the *Seminary* which played such an important part in the capture of the town in 1809 (see History).

Some distance beyond, but now in a sorry state, is the relic of Nasoni's *Casa do Freixo* (1754), built for Jerónimo de Távora e Noronha, but sold by that family to the first Baron Freixo in 1850, who degraded it.

We may return towards the Praça da Batalha from the Alameda by ascending the Rua de Alexandre Herculano.

From opposite the Igreja São Ildefonso, the Rua 31 de Janeiro descends to regain the Praça da Liberdade, with a good view of the tower of the *Clérigos* (see below), while from a short distance further N the Rua de Passos Manuel descends past the PRAÇA DE JOÃO I, at the SW corner of which is another *Tourist Office* (Pl.7), to gain the Av. dos Aliados.

C. Western

From the SW corner of the PRAÇA DA LIBERDADE the steep Rua dos Clérigos climbs towards the *****Torre dos Clérigos** (Pl.6; 75m high), which, together with the adjoining church, was designed by Nicolau Nasoni. The *Church*, reached by a series of steps decorated by stone vases, and facing E, was the first part to be completed, in c1750, a curious oval-shaped, high-domed, building, to which a House of the Clergy, accommodating the brotherhood, was added in 1754, linking it with the famous *Belfry*, completed in 1763. Those wishing to make the ascent (240 steps) should apply at the N entrance.

Immediately to the N of the Clérigos is the *Mercado do Anjo*, beyond which is the main building of the *University*, founded in 1911, previously that of the Academia Politécnica. Facing it is the JARDIM DE JOÃO CHAGAS, to the S of which is the imposing façade, with its trophies, of the *Cadeia da Relação* (Law Courts), and Prison, of 1766–96, by João de Almada e Mello, but now tenements.

In the Rua São Bento da Vitoria, adjacent, stands the church of *São Bento*, by Diogo Marques. It was erected between 1597 and 1646, on a site said to have been that of a synagogue. It contains a remarkable high altar of c 1704, and its organs are notable.

Beyond the NW corner of the University are the twin churches of *N.S. do Carmo* (or *Terceiras do Carmo*, on the corner, of 1756–68), and the *Carmelitas* (1619–28, but remodelled after 1756 by José de Figueiredo Seixas).

To the W is the long colonnaded façade of the *Hospital de Santo António* (Pl.5), an unfinished edifice started in 1770 after the designs of John Carr of York. Alexander Jardine (visiting the place in 1779) rightly suggested it could not be finished 'in less than an hundred years; and perhaps never'.

Bearing along the N side of the building, we continue W along the Rua de Dom Manuel II, shortly passing (right) the former royal palace *'das Carrancas'* (by José Lima Sampaio; 1795), headquarters of Soult in 1809, which he had to leave so precipitately (see History).

In 1942 the *Soares dos Reis Museum* was inaugurated here, named after the sculptor (1847–89), and the most important museum in Oporto. See Pl.1.

GROUND FLOOR. To the right is the CERAMIC COLLECTION, including examples from the Fabrica do Cavaquinho (Vila Nova de Gaia); Bandeira; Fervença ware; from the Rato factory, Lisbon; and others from Coimbra, Viana, Estremoz, and Massarelos.

To the left of the entrance hall are collections of Sculpture and Painting, including, among the former, an early Crucifixion. Among Portuguese primitives: St. Helen and the discovery of the True Cross (*anon.* early 16C), and other scenes from her life; *Frei Carlos*, a small Virgin and Child, and St. Jerome with his lion; *Cristóvão de Figueiredo*, The Trinity; *Gaspar Vaz*, Annunciation; *Vasco Fernandes (Grão Vasco)*, St. Catherine, St. Lucy, &c.

Stairs ascend to a landing, with Views of the market of the Praça de Figueiroa, by *Delarive*. SECOND FLOOR. A large room here contains the COSTUME COLLECTION, and accessories. Among paintings are Views of Oporto, by *Jean Pillement* (1727–1808); *Giuseppe Troni* (1739–1810), Portrait of Carlota Joaquina, and a Self-portrait; *Sequeira*, Junot 'protecting' the city of Lisbon, and other sketches; *J.G. Ströberle* (1708–92), Portrait of José Moreira da Cruz.

Rooms to the right contain more costumes of the Romantic period; more paintings by Pillement; and a collection of small anon. paintings, among them a charming Holy Family; *Josefa de Óbidos*, Mystic marriage of St. Catherine; an *anon.* Calvary (? German); and two *anon.* Adorations; *J.A. Backer* (died 1651), Male portrait; Portrait of Martin Rychaist, *attributed to Van Dyck*; *Vieira Portuense*, Landscape, Flight of Marguerite d'Anjou, and a copy of a Seascape (?by Vernet); *Domingos Vieira*, Pastoral Scene, and Latona and Metamorphosis; also furniture, including an ivory *Contador* or box of drawers.

The SMOKING ROOM, decorated by Pillement, contains more of his paintings, and a remarkable *SILVER COLLECTION, including a 15C German silver-gilt chalice; a 16C Crucifix from Goa, and a filigree box; 18C silver from Oporto, among them two monstrances; *anon.* French Portrait of a woman wearing a veil (18C); 26 Limoges enamels of the Life of Christ (late 16C); a Watch, and a silver Triptych from Nuremberg (16C); Tortoiseshell and silver boxes, and two jugs, from Goa; a coral, filigree, and gold Pyx; an agate, jade, and gold Cross; the Reliquary of St. Stephen; and other fine examples of English and Portuguese silverwork.

DINING ROOM. Further collections of GLASS AND CERAMICS, including Vista Alegre glassware; Portuguese painted glass; and French Opaline ware; also a Portrait of a naval officer, by *Ströberle.* Among the porcelain is a Bishop's service in green and gold; enamelled copper (Chinese; 16C); chinoiserie Desk (English), surmounted by a Figure on a frog (Japanese); collections of Worcester, Crown Derby, and Vista Alegre ware; Japanese Screen (17C); Chest of drawers from Portuguese India, and further rare examples of Oriental porcelain.

Unfortunately the Portraits of Marguerite de Valois and of Henri II, by *Clouet*, are not at present on view.

Continuing along the street, we shortly pass (left) the JARDIM DO PALÁCIO DE CRISTAL, named after a building of 1865 replaced in 1952 by a domed *Sports Pavilion.*

Just beyond the gardens, by following the cobbled Rua de Entrequintas downhill to the left, we reach the *Quinta da Macieirinha*, in which Charles Albert, the abdicated king of Sardinia, died in 1849, some months after the battle of Novara (W of Milan). It now accommodates a small **Romantic Museum**, containing furniture and decoration of the period, and providing attractive views over the river. In the ballroom stands a William Collard piano. Among portraits are those of Admiral Charles Napier, and Baron Forrester. In the entrance hall are Views of Oporto, by *Batty*, etc.

The 'English' gardens of the adjacent *Quinta do Meio*, laid out by Alfred William Tait (1847–1917) after 1881, contain a huge tulip-tree and other notable specimens of magnolia, japonica, and wisteria, etc. The gardens may be visited by prior appointment.

The *Botanical Garden 'Dr Gonçalo Sampaio'* lies over 1km further W, between the Rua do Campo Alegre and the Cintura Interna, approaching the concrete *Ponte da Arrábida* (1960–63; designed by Edgar Cardoso).

The Rua da Boa Nova, at the corner of which is an old tower-house, leads NE from the Jardim do Palácio de Cristal, shortly passing (left) the **Cemitério Inglês**.

In the late 17C the English community had problems. The Rev. Samuel Burton was told in 1682 that he must leave the country, as only one chaplain was allowed—at the Lisbon embassy. It was thought that this move had originated with the Inquisition and four or five merchants who had turned Catholic (including Pickering and Wrothsly of Houblon's London-based firm), abetted by the Jesuits of the English Seminary in Lisbon. However by 1785 the situation had changed. In that year Consul Whitehead acquired a suitable site for a Protestant cemetery, in which he was buried in 1802; and a chapel was allowed to be erected in 1817–18 on condition that it had no external ecclesiastical appearance. Indeed it is of similar dimensions to the ballroom of the Factory House, in which church services may have well been held during the previous decade. The chapel, dedicated to St. James, was not in fact consecrated until 1843, by the Bishop of Gibraltar, on the occasion of which ladies were for the first time condescendingly invited to dine at the Factory House.

According to Southey, writing in 1797, until ten years before that date the English clergyman at Oporto never officiated at a funeral, such were the prejudices of the natives. The body was carried about a mile up the Douro, and buried in a common grave on its banks without any monument. 'The funeral service was read by the Consul, till at length he thought it beneath his dignity, and appointed the Vice Consul; this office was frequently held by a foreigner, and he deputed it again, so that at last it devolved upon a watchmaker. This poor fellow drank very hard, and one evening at the grave he mumbled at the service, and turned his book first this way and then the other, till a bystander had the curiosity to look over him, and found that instead of a prayer book he had brought the History of the Late War!'

But in the mid 19C matters improved. The Rev. Edward Whiteley, chaplain from 1825–71, also ran a private school for boys for several years. Of him it was said that he was 'probably better acquainted with the scenery of the N of Portugal than any other person now living, and whose courtesy in communicating his information to tourists is beyond all praise': so wrote the compiler of an earlier *Hand-Book.*

Near the monument to Consul Whitehead are the graves of four members of the RAF and two of the Royal Canadian Air Force whose planes crashed in Portugal during the Second World War.

The Rua Maternidade continues N, extended by the Rua da Boa Hora.

Some distance further N, approached by the dull Rua de Aníbal Cunha, stands the 12C church of **São Martinho da Cedofeita**, much altered and rebuilt, and erected on the site of an earlier building (mid 6C), marking the place of conversion from Arianism to Orthodoxy of Theodomir, king of the Suevi. It was said to have been run up in a hurry (thus its name) to house relics of St. Martin, sent from Tours. Some interesting capitals are preserved at the Romanesque W door and the early Gothic N door, and in the modernised interior.

By turning to the right down the Rua da Cedofeita, a short distance to the E, we eventually regain the University, and the Clérigos.

A short distance N of São Martinho is the Rua da Boavista, extended to the W by the long AV. DA BOAVISTA to the Praça Mousinho de Albuquerque, an important road junction providing access to the new *Ponte de Arrábida* (c 500m long) now spanning the Douro between Oporto and its mouth at **Foz do Douro**. This residential quarter, with a 17C *fort* guarding the sea approach, is reached by the Av. do Marechal Gomes da Costa, forking SW off the Av. da Boavista, which continues W to meet the Atlantic at the Praça de Gonçalves Zarco and the 17C *Castelo do Queijo*. Foz was referred to as 'the Brighton of Porto' in the mid 19C, but it was noted that 'The English ladies have a bathing-place to themselves at some distance from the rest'.

Some 2km NW of the Praça Mousinho de Albuquerque stands the restored *Casa de Ramalde*, now housing the new *Museu Nacional da Literatura*.

2km N of the Castelo is the industrial suburb of **Matosinhos**, on the S bank of the river Leça, which with *Leça da Palmeira* on the N bank have a combined population of over 37,800. Matosinhos was the birthplace of the 'cellist Guilhermina Suggia (1878–1950). Two moles enclose the adjacent harbour and docks of *Leixões*. It was near *Perafita*, further to the N, that Dom Pedro landed to relieve Oporto (see History). The church of *Bom Jesus* at Matosinhos was largely rebuilt by Nasoni in 1743–50, and contains the Saviour of Boucas, a cult image moved here from a neighbouring church c 1550. There are a number of quintas near the banks of the Leça attributed to Nasoni, among them those of *Fafiães* (1732–36), and *Chantre* (1743–46), which may be discovered by the persevering.

Further N, c 12km from the centre of Oporto, is the *airport of Pedras Rubras.*

D.   Vila Nova de Gaia

This transpontine suburb, with a population in the region of 61,000, is approached with ease along the lower level of the *Ponte de Dom Luís I* (see p 293), its quays providing a good view of old Oporto. Here, among a warren of lanes, stand the numerous *armazéns* or wine-shippers' lodges, in which the Port is stored before its export. Many of the shippers advertise their whereabouts by painting their names on their roofs. Most of them may be visited, and many hospitably provide facilities for the tasting of the varieties of Port: see the Introduction to Port and the Wines of Portugal.

We may ascend from the quays to **N.S. da Serra do Pilar**, which may also be approached directly by the upper level of the bridge (not particularly recommended to pedestrians likely to suffer from vertigo). This secularised convent is now in military hands. It was Wellington's post of vantage at the taking of Oporto in 1809 (see History). In 1832 it was held against the Miguelites by Sá da Bandeira, who lost his right arm in the bombardment which shattered most of the building.

It claims descent from one founded at *Grijó* (see Rte 26) in 912. The present building occupies the site of an earlier church containing 13C tombs, and was erected by João Lopes and Jérónimo Luís between 1576 and 1583, and consists of a round *Church* connected by a square chancel to a little Ionic *cloister*, also circular in plan.

The adjacent terrace provides a good view over Oporto.

In the *Gardens of the Conde de Campo Bello* in Vila Nova de Gaia (prior appointment essential) was planted the first Camellia japonica in Europe, brought here from Japan in the mid 16C. Some fine specimens may be seen in flower in February and March, among other trees and shrubs.

34   (Tui) Valença do Minho to Oporto

A.   Via Viana do Castelo

Total distance, 125km (77 miles). N13. 27km **Caminha**—24km **Viana do Castelo**—24km *Esposende*—19km **Póvoa de Varzim**—4km **Vila do Conde**—27km **Oporto.**

From *Tui* (see *Blue Guide Spain*), spelt thus by the Gallegos in preference to *Túy*, we pass Spanish and Portuguese Customs and cross the 333m-long *International Bridge* of 1885, constructed by Eiffel, to **Valença do Minho** (*Pousada de São Teotónio*). Adjacent to the modern frontier town is the older town, entirely enclosed within its 17C ramparts, which are in a perfect state of preservation, commanding the S bank of the river. Its previous name was *Contrasta*, until the fortress here was rebuilt in 1262. It sustained two minor sieges by the Decembrists in 1837 and in 1847.

The streets of the old town are pleasant enough, when not entirely given over to the display of souvenirs, etc. At the far end of the main street is the *Pousada*, providing a good view across to Tui. The church is of slight interest.

For the road along the S bank of the Minho to Monção see Rte 34B.

We drive S, after some 4km veering SW some distance above the Minho, in 2km by-passing (right) *São Pedro da Torre*, with a restored Roman bridge.

For the road climbing to the left for *Ponte de Lima* see Rte 34C.

7km *Reboreda*, with the 14C *Torre de Penafiel*, is passed, and 2km, beyond, **Vila Nova de Cerveira**, with an early castle with later additions, now accommodating the luxurious *Pousada Dom Dinis*.—3km *Gondarém*, with the 18C *Casa da Loureira*, and (3km) *Lanhelas*, with the *Casa da Torre* with its partly 12C fortifications, are traversed as we approach the widening estuary towards the mouth of the Minho. There are some attractive views ahead towards *Monte Santa Tecla* on the Spanish bank.

6km. **Caminha**, once an important river-port at the mouth of the Coura, still preserves its fortifications and a number of 17C houses. The attractive central praça is overlooked by a 16C *clock-tower* on an 11C base, and *Misericórdia*, with a good portal (and an organ open to the wind, as seen from an exterior balcony). Passing through an arch under the tower, a gateway of the medieval enceinte, we follow the Rua Direita. At its far end stands the ***Igreja Matriz** (1488), the finest in the district, with a later tower (1556) and two good doorways with Renaissance carving showing the influence of the Coimbra School. The apse and gargoyles deserve inspection. The artesonado ceiling, the carved granite pulpit, the Tree of Jesse of 1704, azulejos, and the organ-case, are also noteworthy features.

At the mouth of the Minho is the island fort of *Insua*, which we pass as we bear S through *Moledo do Minho*, and skirt the Atlantic shore, later traversing *Âncora*, NE of which is a well-preserved dolmen, to approach the mouth of the Lima.

23.5km. **VIANA DO CASTELO** (15,100 inhab.; *Hotel de Sta Luzia*), whose brochures have boasted of 'unpolluted beaches with a high iodine content', is a well-sited fishing port and prosperous holiday resort on the N bank of the Lima, preserving several old buildings of interest. It is dominated to the N by MONTE SANTA LUZIA, surmounted by an ugly early 20C neo-Byzantine Basilica of the Sameiro variety, and faces thick pine woods on the far bank of the river.

Known to the Romans as *Velobriga*, and standing on the banks of the Lethe itself, Livy's 'Flumen oblivionis', the river of forgetfulness, it was afterwards called *Diana*, which was eventually corrupted to Viana. It later had a considerable trade in *bacalhau*. It was raised to the rank of city in 1847, for resisting the revolt of the Septembrists. The military engineer and architect Manuel Pinto de Vilalobos (died 1734) was a native of the town.

A British community had been exporting Minho wines hence to England before 1580, when they were expelled by the Spanish, but by 1700 a British Factory was established here, with Christopher Battersby as Consul. They later moved to Oporto, with the growth of the Port wine trade, and the silting up of Viana's harbour. Thomas Woodmass, when passing through at that time, was entertained here by Job Bearsley and the consul, and after dinner 'some Portugal cockerels did engage in battle. Ye Minister directing'—presumably the latter was the chaplain from Oporto. John Page was building a house here in 1703. Coopers had been sent out from England to supervise the manufacture of casks, and Woodmass reported that they were a drunken lot, 'but ye natives now know how to make casks'.

The main street from the railway station to the river bank is of slight interest, and it is better to follow the Rua Candido dos Reis, further E, with the *Palace of the Távoras* (or *Condes da Carreira*) on the corner, rebuilt in 1714 and decorated in 1720 with a painted ceiling by Manuel Gomes and azulejos by António de Oliveira Bernardes (1684–1732). It now houses the *Tourist Office*. The church of *Santa Ana*, just to the N, is said (by the 'Selective Travellers') to contain 'lovely' things.

Further down the street we pass (left) the entrance to the church of the **Misericórdia**, a curious building of 1598 facing the triangular PRAÇA DA REPÚBLICA, with a *Façade of three superimposed loggias, the upper storeys supported by caryatids of original design, by João Lopes the Younger.

The Praça da República, Viano do Castelo

Adjacent is the restored *Town Hall* (*Paços do Concelho*; 1502) above an arcade. The Rua de Sacadura Cabral leads S, passing an elegant fountain, to a small square retaining some 16C houses (right), and the *Igreja Matriz* or *Sé*, with a 15C Gothic W door (between Romanesque towers), bearing figures on the archivolts. The sculptures on the towers are also remarkable.

The Rococo façade of the *Capela dos Malheiros Reimões*, in the nearby Rua 8 de Março, is notable, as is one in the Rua São Pedro, further S in this pedestrian precinct. Beyond is the river front.

Returning to the square and turning left, we cross the main avenue and follow the Rua Manuel Espregueira, at the far end of which (right) is the *Municipal Museum*, installed in the 18C palace of the Barbosa Macieis family (attributed to Vilalobos).

It contains some good furniture, and a ceramic collection, and among the paintings a number of naïve late 19C watercolours of Viana; paintings on glass; examples of the work of Vieira Lusitano, and Vieira Portuense; drawings by Sequeira, etc. The azulejos of hunting scenes by Policarpo de Oliveira Bernardes (1721) are notable.

Adjacent stands the large classical church of **São Domingos**, built by Frei Julião Romero for Abp Bartolomeu dos Mártires of Braga (died 1590), who attended the Council of Trent, and is buried in the church. He was an indefatigable visitor of his diocese, penetrating into its wildest recesses where certainly no bishop had ever been seen before, and it is recorded that he once met a procession of villagers chanting 'Blessed be the most holy Trinity, and her sister the most pure Virgin'. The church also contains a retable by José de Álvares de Araújo (died 1762).

To the SW, beyond the Praça General Barbosa and near the port, is the *Fort*, or *Castelo de Santiago da Barra*, built by Philip II of Spain to guard the mouth of the Lima and later strengthened. There is a project to accommodate a museum of the rich folk art of the Minho in its dependencies, together with a maritime museum, hotel school, etc.—To the NW is the small Baroque pilgrimage church of *N.S. da Agonia*, site of a *festa* during the third week of August, when Minhoto costumes are displayed.

From NE of the railway station a road and a funicular ascend to the above-mentioned basilica, behind which is the Hotel de Santa Luzia (*View*), and nearby the Celtic *Citânia of Santa Luzia*, preserving a defensive wall, circular stone huts and paved alleys.

FROM VIANA DO CASTELO TO PONTE DE LIMA (23km). The N202 leads E above the N bank of the Lima, at c 7km passing near *Nogueira*, with a church dated 1183. 6km beyond is the 18C *Solar de Lanheses*.—5km. On the left is the imposing *Solar de Bertiandos*, largely 18C, but with a tower of 1566. After another 4km we reach the modern bridge over the Lima, with the 17–18C church of *N.S. da Guia* (1528) to the left at the far end. From the bridge there is a good view of the ancient *Ponte de Lima* which gave its name to the town (see Rte 34C).

Crossing the Lima by a bridge of 1895 designed by Eiffel, to the right at the far end of which is the 18C *Casa do Cais Novo*, we traverse *Darque*. After 6km we bear SW; the left fork here (N103) leads to *Barcelos*: see Rte 35A.

As we approach Esposende we pass the ruins of a *Fort* (1704) converted into a lighthouse. *Esposende* itself is a small resort on the N bank of the Cávado, both sides of its estuary flanked by pinewoods, which we cross to *Fão*, with the resort of *Ofir* on the coast.

19km. **PÓVOA DE VARZIM** (22,500 inhab.), a fishing port and resort, and the birthplace of José Maria Eça de Queiroz (1845–1900), the novelist, who in 1874–88 was Portuguese consul in various parts of England. It retains an 18C *Fort*, an *Igreja Matriz* of 1743–57, and *N.S. da Lapa* (1772), but few other buildings of interest.

From just S of the fishing harbour, the N206 runs inland to (7km) **Rio Mau** where to the right of the road stands *São Cristovão* (1151), with well-carved capitals and sculpture of the period; and 2km beyond Rio Mau, a left-hand turn leads 1km to **Rates**, where *São Pedro* (12C; restored in 1940) is one of the more impressive Romanesque churches in Portugal, with remarkable carved capitals, among other features. It may have been built by Count Henry of Burgundy on the site of the martyrdom of the sainted Pedro de Rates, first bishop of Braga, who, said to be a Jewish convert of St. James the Greater, was also born here.

Almost contiguous with Póvoa do Varzim is **VILA DO CONDE** (20,200 inhab.), another resort and fishing port, at the mouth of the Ave, with shipyards and other industries. It is also reputed for its lace.

The Convent of Santa Clara

The town is dominated by the impressive bulk of the **Convent of Santa Clara**, begun in 1777 by Henrique Ventura, but founded in 1318 by Afonso Sanches, natural son of Dom Dinis. The 16C *Church* contains the elaborate tombs of the founder and his wife, Teresa Martins, and their family; and that of Brites Pereira, daughter of Nun' Álvares and wife of the first Duke of Braganza. Noteworthy is the organ, and the panelled ceiling. In the cloister walk is a fountain fed by a 5km-long *Aqueduct* of 1705–14, now partially ruinous. Adjacent is an attractive 18C mansion. Santa Clara, now a reformatory, is approached by turning E on the N bank of the river.

Also of interest in the town is the *Igreja Matriz* (*São João Baptista*; c 1514), with a later tower and a Plateresque portal by João de Castilho. There is a 17C *Fort* by the river mouth.

Near the confluence of the Ave and Este, some 5km inland, is the site of *Bagunte*, a pre-Roman settlement abandoned by the 6C.

At *Azurara*, on the S bank of the Ave, is a large Manueline church, the vaulting in its chancel completed in 1552, abutted by a later belfry. The road now veers away from the coast, at 14km reaching *Moreira*, with (right) an Augustinian *Convent* (1588–1662) with an elaborate altar-mór.

Here the N10 turns right past (right) the *airport of Pedras Rubras*, to cross the Douro by the new *Ponte da Arrábida*; the N13 continues ahead into central **Oporto**; while the left fork leads past *Leça do Bailio*; see below.

The Leça is crossed by a number of small Roman bridges, among them the *Ponte de Pedra*, the *Carro Bridge* and the *Guifões Bridge*, but the most important monument on the river is the fortified Romanesque *Church* of the Monastery of **Leça do Bailio**, once the headquarters of the Knights Templar in Portugal. The severe granite building dates from 1336 but preserves an earlier cloister. The crenellated parapet surrounding the church; the tower, corbelled at each corner; and the rose-window above the entrance portal, are obvious features. The well-proportioned interior, with well-carved capitals, contains the tomb of João Coelho and a font, both by Diogo Pires the Younger (1514–15); the tomb of Cristóvão de Cernache (1567), showing the influence of Philippe Houdart; and the brass epitaph of Estêvão Vasques Pimentel (died 1374), who was responsible for the rebuilding. It was here that Dom Fernando announced his marriage with Leonor Teles in 1372. The whole was heavily restored in 1940.

For **Oporto** itself see Rte 33.

B.   Via Monção and Braga

Total distance, 144km (89 miles). N101. 18km **Monção**—39km **Ponte da Barca**—33km **Braga**—N14. 18km *Vila Nova de Famalicão*—36km **Oporto**.

We follow the N101 to the E from the crossroads at Valença (see Rte 34A). The road ahead climbs to the summit of (7km) *Monte do Faro* (566m), commanding extensive views.

Our road winds parallel to the S bank of the Minho, providing attractive vistas across towards Spain. We shortly by-pass (right) *Ganfei*, with a Romanesque church (partly rebuilt), preserving good capitals. The ancient monastery was rebuilt in the 18C.

At 7km a turning leads shortly to the church of *São Fins* (12C), likewise with well-carved capitals.—*Friestas* is skirted, beyond which we pass *Lapela*, with a medieval defensive tower (left) before reaching (11km) *Monção*.

Monção, founded by Afonso III, and fortified in the 17C, remains an attractive little town overlooking the Minho opposite Salvatierra de Miño in Spain (to which there is a ferry service).

It is now better known for its *vinho verde* and *bagaceira* than for its red wines, exported at the turn of the 18C by English factors who settled there and called the place *Monson*. It is also reputed for its medicinal springs and lampreys. It preserves a ruined *Castle* of 1306, and a Romanesque *Igreja Matriz*, in which, among many tombs, is that of the local hero Deuladeu Martins, who successfully defended the town against the Spaniards in 1368 by the expedient, it is said, of throwing them loaves of bread to confirm how well supplied they were. It held out for four months in 1658, again besieged by its neighbours, commanded by the Marquês de Viana, when the starving inhabitants eventually capitulated on advantageous terms.

FROM MONÇÃO TO (24.5km) MELGAÇO AND CASTRO LABOREIRO, 28km beyond. It was at the neighbouring hamlet of *Ponte de Mouro*, a little E of Monção, that on 1 November 1386 John of Gaunt met João I to discuss the marriage of the latter with Lancaster's daughter Philippa, and to plan the invasion and dismemberment of Castile.—2km. *Longos Vales*, 3km SE, preserves some interesting capitals and carvings in the Romanesque part of its church.—Continuing along the upper slope of the Minho valley, we shortly pass (right) *Barbeita*, with a Romanesque *Bridge*, and then the *Casa do Amioso* (18C) at *Valadares*, before reaching **Melgaço**, which in the mid 13C had the privilege of choosing its own governor. It is reputed for its hams and for the numerous mineral springs in the neighbourhood. It preserves the *keep* of its castle, but the most interesting building is the church of *N.S. da Orada* (1245), standing on the right of the road 1km further NE.—The road goes on to (8.5km) **São Gregório**, on the frontier (Customs), here the Rio Trancoso, a tributary of the Minho.—*Celanova* lies c 40km E, and *Ribadavia* c 30km N: see *Blue Guide Spain*.

Some 5km E of Melgaço are relics of the convent of *Fiães*; and at *Paderne*, c 2km SW, a Romanesque church containing 13C tombs.—The N202 climbs S from Melgaço to (28km) a high-lying and remote village of Roman origin, **Castro Laboreiro**. The ruins of its *Castle* (1033) command extensive views, while the Romanesque church preserves features of interest. The district is known for a special breed of ferocious sheepdog. The SERRA DA PENEDA range here rises to 1335m to the E, and 1415m (*Outeiro Maior*) to the SW, the highest peak of the Serra. The village now lies within the PARQUE NACIONAL DA PENEDA-GERÊS: see p 279.

From Monção we turn S on the N101, after 3km passing (right) at *Pinheiros* the huge granite mansion of *Brejoeira* (1806–34), erected in the style of the Ajuda palace, Lisbon, with its own chapel, and gardens surrounded by its vineyards.

The road continues to wind up the boulder-strewn valley, with attractive retrospective views to the *Portela do Extremo*, commanding wide vistas S over the Lima valley, which we approach by descending the side valley of the Vez to (31.5km) **Arcos de Valdevez**, which suffered from a destructive fire in the 17C. Here in c 1140 took place an inconclusive tourney between Afonso Henrique's knights and those of Alfonso VII, which was an earnest of later claims to independence. The 18C church of *N.S. da Lapa* is perhaps its most architecturally interesting building, apart from the 18C *Casas da Andorinha* and *do Terreiro*.—To the E lies *Giela*, with the 14C tower of the later *Paço de Giela*, and the remains of the 18C *Casa do Requeijo*.

FROM ARCOS DE VALDEVEZ TO PONTE DE LIMA (c 22km). The N202 winds above the N bank of the Lima, passing near the castro of *Cendufe* and a number of attractive quintas, among them, at *Jolda*, the *Paço da Glória*, and beyond, at *Calheiros* (right) its imposing Paço of 1700. Before reaching Calheiros we pass (left) the convent of *Refóios do Lima* (1122, but much modernised), containing good woodwork and azulejos.—We later turn left to **Ponte de Lima** (see Rte 34C). The return journey—from Ponte de Lima to Ponte da Barca—may be made along the S bank of the river, providing several beautiful vistas, and passing, S of *Gândara*, the *Torre de Beiral* (1733), and *Bravães*: see below.

4.5km. **Ponte da Barca**, with its ten-arched *Bridge* over the Lima of 1543 (restored 1761 and 1896), was the birthplace of the poet Diogo Bernardes (c 1530–c 1595) and his brother Agostinho da Cruz (1540–1619).

Hence the N203 ascends the S bank of the wild upper Lima valley past *Ermelo*, whose church retains Romanesque features, to (25km) **Lindoso**, with its much rebuilt but imposingly-sited 14C *Castle* guarding the frontier 6km further E, beyond which the road continues to (32km) *Bande, Celanova*, or *Ginzo de Limia*: see *Blue Guide Spain*. The numerous *espigueiros* on the hill below the castle of Lindoso are a curious sight.

6km W of Ponte da Barca on the N203 lies **Bravães**, with its fine Romanesque *Church (ask for key at a house to the N of its apse), with well-carved W and S portals (noted the griffons on the latter), while the naïve capitals on either side of the windows in the interior, the rose-window, and remains of murals (St. Sebastian on left; the Virgin and Child on right) are all notable.

Near *Nogueira*, S of Ponte da Barca, are a number of quintas and solares, among them, to the left, the *Casa da Agrela*. At *Crasto*, beyond to the right, is a church of Romanesque origin.

We climb S.—After c 11km a left turn leads to *Aboim da Nóbrega*, with a church of some interest.

Detail of the portal of the church at Bravães

W of (10km) *Vila Verde*, at *Carreiras* are the *Torre de Penegate* (1360) and a *citânia*.

From just short of Vila Verde a road ascends NW up the thickly wooded Homem valley to *Covide*, and thence down to (c 40km) crossroads on the Caniçada reservoir SW of Gerês: see p 279, first passing near (left) *Couceiro*, with an interesting Romanesque church preserving curious sculptures, before crossing the river at *Caldelas*.—To the SW of Caldelas is the Benedictine monastery of **Rendufe**, largely 18C, with elaborate Rococo decoration and sculpture, some ascribed to Frei José de Santo António Vilaça.

4.5km beyond Vila Verde a right-hand turn leads SW to (21.5km) *Barcelos*; see sub-route on p 312 in reverse.

We cross the river Homem.

From the N bank a road ascends the Rio Cávado to (31.5km) the Caniçada crossroads via *Carrazedo*, with the 15C *Casa do Castro*; *Besteiros*, with a number of 18C mansions; *Ferreiros*, with the ruined *Solar dos Vasconcelos*; *Amares*; *Figueiredo*, with a medieval bridge, the *Ponte do Porto*, on Roman foundations (on the road from Braga to Astorga, in Spain), and old mansions; *Dornelas*, with the ruined *Torre*, possible birthplace of Gualdim Pais, and the *Casa do Outeiro* (late 17C), before reaching (20km) **Bouro**, with a ruined Cistercian monastery (*Santa Maria*), which existed in 1148. It was transformed in the 17C, and more recently despoiled of its lead and ironwork, since when it has rapidly deteriorated. The curious statues on its façade will be noted, as will the azulejos in the Sacristy (key from house opposite?).

Link, who visited it in 1798 noted that the 'feeble old abbé suffered all the young monks to run wild; which rendered them as ungovernable as they were ignorant; and a young lay-brother, the apothecary, was the only one who shewed any desire of knowledge', continuing: 'In all the portuguese monasteries, the monks eat an astonishing quantity, and we always had four courses at dinner. All their dishes, however, are dressed without art, and consist, in great measure, of joints of meat of various kinds'. The monks showed sufficient curiosity to handle—in his absence—Link's barometer and thermometer, both of which they broke, to his great irritation.

Above Bouro lies the 18C sanctuary of *N.S. da Abadia*.—The road continues up the valley, shortly skirting the *Caniçada reservoir*, to (12km) the crossroads below *Caldas de Gerês*, and (right) the *Pousada de São Bento*: see p 279.

Crossing the Cávado, we pass (right), on approaching the N outskirts of Braga, the hamlet of *Dume*.

Here, in the mid 6C, Carriaric, the Suevic king, converted to Catholicism during the illness of his son, Theodomir, founded a church, its priest eventually becoming St. Martin of Dume, who directed the activities of the second Council of Braga in 572, and died in 579.

A short distance further W stands the Visigothic church of *São Frutuoso de Montélios*: see p 310.

For **Braga** (first reaching its by-pass) see Rte 36; and for the road on to *Guimarães*, Rte 35.

We now bear SW on the N14, after c 12km passing (right) *Arnoso*, where the 12C church of *Santa Eulália*, on the site of a convent founded in 642 by St. Frutuoso, is of interest.

6km. **Vila Nova de Famalicão**, with paperworks, is by-passed, just E of which is the Romanesque church of *São Tiago d'Antas*, containing some curious 17C pink azulejos.

7km *Lousado* (left), with the medieval *Ponte da Lagoncinha*, possibly on Roman foundations, beyond which we pass near (right) the Roman castro of *Alvarelhos*.

Maia (left), just S of which is the Romanesque church of *Leça do Bailio* (see last part of Rte 34A), beyond which we approach the N outskirts of **Oporto**: see Rte 33.

C.   Via Ponte de Lima and Braga

Total distance, 125km (77 miles). N13. 6km—N201. 32km **Ponte de Lima**—33km **Braga**—N14. 54km **Oporto**.

For the first part of this route see Rte 34A.

At 6km we turn left, climbing steeply, with good retrospective views, to crossroads at (8km) *São Bento*, 8.5km SE of which is the high-lying village of *Paredes de Coura*, with an ancient church rebuilt in the 18C.—The main road briefly descends to cross the Rio Coura, with its Roman bridge, and climbs again past (4.5km) **Rubiães** and, left of the road, its fine Romanesque **Church*, preserving well-carved capitals and corbels. Note the adjacent Roman miliary column.

We shortly start the the long descent, probably along a Roman road, providing several attractive vistas over the valley of the Lima, to approach *Ponte de Lima* on its far bank.—For the road to *Arcos de Valdevez* or *Ponte da Barca* along its N bank see p 306, in reverse.

Turning left in its transpontine suburb, we approach the ancient *Bridge* of 31 arches. It is of Roman origin, but rebuilt in 1360 and restored in the 15C. At its N end is the chapel of *São António da Torre Velha* (1814). The bridge provides a very picturesque view across the river to the far bank, the site of a Monday Market, founded in 1125 and the oldest in Portugal, existing under a charter of Dona Teresa, Countess of Burgundy.

*PONTE DE LIMA, on the S bank of the Lima, has been praised for its beautiful situation by many travellers, among them Colonel Landmann and Lord Porchester. It is also a pleasant centre from which to explore the area. Accommodation is available in many private homes in the vicinity: see *Turismo de Habitação* (p 89); enquire also —preferably in advance—at the Tourist Office.

The Lima itself was assumed by the Romans to be the *Lethe*, the River of Oblivion, its beauty having the effect of the lotus, in making the traveller forget his own country and home. It was at this point that Decimus Junius Brutus had such difficulty in persuading his soldiers to cross, having already traversed the greater part of Iberia. Seizing the standard, and once more exhorting his men, he waded into the river, and the whole followed after. It was later known to the Romans as *Forum Limicorum*, and it is probably the *Lemici* where the Suevic annalist Hydatius was born in 394. A number of English archers played a vital role in João I's capture of the place in 1385.

Ponte de Lima, c 1839, by George Vivian

Near the bridgehead are the remaining towers of the town's fortifications, and behind them the *Igreja Matriz* (*Santa Maria dos Anjos*; 1359). Among the several mansions of interest are the *Paço of the Marquêz de Ponte de Lima*, originally of 1464, but much changed since, with Manueline windows; the *Paço da Alcaideria* (overlooking

the Tourist Office), and the former *Paço do Concelho*. Some of them
have been restored. There are a number of other old houses and
streets in the place, which, as Sitwell remarks, 'is pleasant to walk
about in but there is little to see': that is, in the way of important
monuments; nevertheless it is a delightful town.

The riverside alameda of huge plane trees leads W to the Renaissance church of *São António dos Frades*, part of a convent founded in
1480, and adjacent *São Francisco*, containing a collection of sacred
art.

The *Quinta da Tapada*, near here, was the home of the 16C poet Sá de Miranda
(see Coimbra).

Among the monuments of interest in the district are the 12C chapel of
Espirito Santo at *Moreira*, reached by turning right off the N202 after
Santa Comba, W of Ponte de Lima; Romanesque *Santa Marinha* at
Arcoselo (off the N306, turning off the N202 NE of the town), and,
further N, the 18C monastery of *N.S. do Socorro* at *Labruja*: but see
also the roads from *Arcos de Valdevez* and to *Ponte de Barca*, etc. The
summit of *Monte de Santa Maria Madalena*, c 3km SE, commands a
panorama over the valley.

The N203 leads along the S bank of the Lima via (13.5km) *Bravães* to *Ponte da
Barca*; see p 306.

FROM PONTE DE LIMA TO BARCELOS (31km). We follow the N204, leading
SW, through *Correlhã*, near which are the 18C monastery of *N.S. da Boa Morte*
and the Romanesque chapel of *Santa Abdão*, and (8km) *Facha*, with the 17C
Casa das Torres and *São Estevão*, and (10km) *Balugães*, with a church dated
1162. The road later passes close to *Cossourada*, with a church dated 1714;
Quintiães, also with an 18C church, and the abandoned *Torre de Aborim* (1650);
and to the E, *Couto*, the church of which contains some 15–16C tombs, before
entering *Barcelos*: see Rte 35.

From Ponte de Lima we proceed SE on the N201, as did Major
Dalrymple 200 years ago, who was enchanted that the vines 'twining
round the oaks, and other trees in the hedges, formed most beautiful
festoons'. We cross the hills into the Cávado valley, traversing
attractive wooded country, but passing near no places or buildings of
any great interest. After 23km we approach the Cávado, with a view
to the SW of the monastery of *Tibães*, standing out against the wooded
hillside.

After crossing the river and the next village, a right-hand lane leads
between high walls to approach the huge and ruinous monastery and
church of *São Martinho*, **Tibães**, seen from some distance away.

Little remains of the Romanesque period. The present *Church*, by Manuel
Álvares, is dated 1624–61, and contains a mass of mid 18C gilt woodcarving by
the *entalhador* André Soares; choir-stalls of 1666–68; and a Baroque organ of
1785. One of the four cloisters, long derelict, is under restoration; others have
been put to more rural uses, while the chapter-house retains some azulejos of
1785. There is usually someone about with a key. A water-staircase in the
abandoned formal gardens behind—visited by Lord Porchester in 1827, when
the roses were in full bloom and the garden was described as enchanting—is
said to have been an inspiration for the stair at Bom Jesus, Braga.

Very soon after regaining the main road, a left-hand turn leads shortly
to the early 18C church of *São Francisco*, abutting which is the tiny
Visigothic chapel of *São Frutuoso de Montélios*. Apply at adjacent
house for key. Steps ascend from the church to the interior of the
chapel (2nd half of 7C), built on a Greek Cross plan, with a
reconstructed central dome and barrel-vaulted apsidal arms. The
vaulting in each bay is supported by two marble columns. An

ornamental frieze is preserved, but the whole was remodelled in the 11C, and has received the more recent attentions of restorers. The exterior is lightened by Lombardic blind arcades terminating in alternate pointed and semicircular sections, and is also surrounded by decorative bands of marble.

Regaining the main road, we climb round a hill to reach **Braga** itself: see Rte 36, below.

For the road beyond to **Guimarães**, see the latter part of Rte 35A.

For the road to **Oporto** see the latter part of Rte 34B.

35 Viana do Castelo to Guimarães for Amarante via Barcelos and Braga

Total distance, 75km (46 miles). N13 for 11km, then N103 for (20km) **Barcelos**—22km **Braga**—N101. 22km **Guimarães**.

For **Viana do Castelo** see Rte 34A.

After forking left off the N13, we traverse (5km) *Forjães*, with the ruined tower of the *Casa dos Pregais* (c 1100), possibly the birthplace of the 15C navigator Gonçalo Velho.—5km to the E, at *Fragoso*, is the 18C *Casa da Espragueira*.—12km. *Abade de Neiva*, with (left) a charmingly sited church of 1152 with good capitals, and a restored tower. To the N is the 16C chapel of the *Quinta da Silva*.

4km. **BARCELOS** (10,800 inhab.), an attractive and ancient town on the N bank of the Cávado, crossed here by a restored 15C *Bridge* abutted by a *Chapel* capped by a pyramid, and surrounded by a colonnaded porch, which stands on the suburban bank of *Barcelinhos*. Lampreys swarm in tanks below the bridge. It is noted for being the centre of handicraft in a region rich in such, while its Thursday *Market* is still one of the most interesting in Portugal, selling everything from its characteristic regional pottery to its lyre-horned cattle. Unfortunately, little of the ceramic ware is of the imaginative quality of the productions of the late Rosa Ramalho.

Immediately above the bridge-head is the *Archaeological and Ceramic Museum*, installed in the ruins (retaining its chimney) of a palace built by Afonso, natural son of João I.

On his marriage in 1401 to Brites, daughter of Nun' Álvares Pereira, Afonso received the county of Barcelos from the king, the last count of the old line (Meneses family) having been killed at Aljubarrota. (Another of Dom João's bastards, Beatriz, was married off by Philippa of Lancaster to Thomas Fitzalan, earl of Arundel, in 1405.)

Among the crosses to be seen is that depicting the 'Cock of Barcelos' just below the 14C *Crucifix O Senhor do Galo*, which is associated with a legend in which a roasting rooster miraculously crowed in protestation of an innocent Galician being sent to the gallows ('I'll be hanged if the cock don't crow'), and which has almost been taken up as a national symbol: this gaily painted fowl is certainly reproduced often enough as a representation of Folk Art.

Behind is the *Igreja Matriz*, rebuilt by Afonso, preserving the 13C door of an earlier church, with a rose-window above. Near by is a late Gothic *pelourinho*, and to the W the 15C *Solar dos Pinheiros*, with its twin towers. To the N of the church is the *Town Hall* housed in an 18C palace, behind which in a little square is the *Casa de Nun' Álvares*.

Hence we follow the main street of the old centre to the **Torre Nova**, a tower of the 15C ramparts, now housing a 'Centro de Artesanato', a display of regional handicraft, which may also be bought here.— Beyond, to the right, are the Baroque MUNICIPAL GARDENS, embellished with a multitude of fountains and obelisks, etc.

To the left is the 'round' or octagonal church of *Bom Jesus (or Senhor da Cruz* (c 1705), possibly designed by João Antunes on the site of an earlier chapel. The interior is of interest, with a ground plan combining a Greek cross with a cylinder, covered by a granite cupola; it preserves a good organ.

Here is the large open space known as the CAMPO DA REPÚBLICA (or Campo da Feira, or Praça da Feira), on which the animated and colourful market takes place each Thursday. To the E is a wooded park, and a *Misericórdia* installed in a Capuchin monastery of 1649.

To the N stands the church of *N.S. do Terço*, formerly the nunnery of St. Benedict, whose life is described on the ceiling panels and on the azulejos of 1713 surrounding the carved and gilt pulpit, which features the crowned double-headed Habsburg eagle, which remained a popular decorative element even after the Spanish domination.

From the adjacent Campo 5 de Outubro, a lane leads NW towards an imposing 18C *Mansion* facing the decrepit Largo do Bonfim.

For the road from here to *Ponte de Lima* see p 310, in reverse.
At *Gilmonde*, 7km SW on the N205, is the 17C *Casa de Fervença.*

The N205 leads NW along the N bank of the Cávado (views) to join the Ponte de Lima—Braga road at (17km) *Prado*, close to which a Miguelite force was severely defeated in 1826, passing at (5km) **Manhente** where Romanesque *São Martinho* of 1117 has a well-carved portal, and a medieval tower adjacent.— 4km beyond, at *Lama*, is another tower, 'dos Azevedos', of 1536; and to the left 4km further E, at *Cervães*, the ruined *Torre de Gomariz* (15C).

Crossing the Cávado at Barcelos, we bear left through attractive country, passing near (7km) *Vilar de Frades*, with a Baroque church preserving both a Manueline portal and one which has survived of the former Romanesque church of c 1070. The conventual buildings, damaged by fire in 1898, now house an institution.

4km. *Martim*, whence a left-hand turn leads to *Tibães* (see Rte 34C).

For **Braga** see Rte 36.

Leaving Braga, we follow the N101 to the S, shortly climbing a ridge of hills before descending to (14.5km) *Caldas das Taipas*, a small spa known to the Romans, and cross the Ave.—The N310 leads NE parallel to the N bank of the river to (7km right) *Souto*, where the monastic church of *São Salvador* preserves good Romanesque details. We pass en route a turning (left) for the *Citânia de Briteiros*: see p 318.

7km. **Guimarães**: see Rte 37.

The N101 circles to the E round the *Penha*.—11km. A right turn leads to the church of *Pombeiro de Ribavizela*, partly rebuilt, but an interesting relic of a Benedictine monastery. To the E the road is dominated by *Monte Santa Quitera* (482m).—5km *Felgueiras.*

FROM FELGUEIRAS TO PENAFIEL (21.5km). We follow the N207 SW, to the right of which after c 3km is the partly Romanesque church at *Sousa*; to the S, at *Airães*, is another Romanesque church.—After c 8km a left turn leads to the church of *Aveleda* (13C).—At *Lousada* we turn left onto the N320, shortly traversing *Meinedo*, site of the Visigothic settlement of *Magneto*, with a 13C church, and *Bustelo*, with a Benedictine convent founded in the 12C but rebuilt in the 18C, shortly beyond which climbing up to **Penafiel**: see p 275.

We meet the N15 8km SE of Felgueiras and, descending steeply into the valley of the Tâmega, reach **Amarante** 10km beyond: see Rte 29A.

For the roads hence to *Vila Real*, and to *Régua* and *Lamego*, see Rtes 29A and 27A, in reverse.

36 Braga

BRAGA (63,800 inhab.), one of the most ancient towns in Portugal, which long disputed with Tarragona and Toledo the primacy of the Peninsula, and which continues to contend with neighbouring Guimarães for being the most interesting large town in Portugal N of Oporto, is a straggling and growing industrial and agricultural centre. Although the creation of the Lisbon patriarchate in 1716 reduced its ecclesiastical pre-eminence, it still retains some of the bigotry of an episcopal city, as reflected in the local proverb: 'Every good house has its cattle and its tonsure'. Regrettably, as most of its numerous churches were 'modernised' in the 18C by prelates with more money than taste, the interiors of comparatively few—apart from the cathedral—merit the attention of the visitor.

Bracara Augusta, claiming to have been founded in 296 BC, was later the main Roman station in North Lusitania, being an important centre of communication. In 411 it became the capital of the Suevian kingdom of Gallaecia. In 456 it fell to Theodoric II, and the conversion of the Visigoths later from Arianism to orthodox Catholicism at two synods held at Braga in 563 and 572 marked the beginning of its ecclesiastical hegemony. From c 730 until conquered by Fernando I of Castile in 1040 it was under Moorish occupation, and later virtually abandoned, and the see was only restored in 1070. In 1103 Diego Gelmírez, the ambitious bishop of Santiago, determined not to be dependent on Braga, forcibly carried off the relics of St. Victor and St. Fructuosus, after which St. Gerald, a Cluniac monk from Moissac, then metropolitan, after recourse to Rome, was confirmed in his supremacy over all sees in the W of the peninsula as far S as Coimbra. Some stability was provided by João Peculiar, who was archbishop for 37 years from 1139, but ecclesiastical wrangles persisted over the centuries.

Significantly it was from reactionary Braga that in 1926 General Gomes da Costa addressed an appeal to all citizens 'of dignity and honour' in his successful attempt to overthrow the Democratic regime, precipitating the quasi-hierocratic dictatorship which lasted the next half century. And it was in Braga in August 1975 that the archbishop instigated a mob to attack the local Communist headquarters during the recent revolutionary period.

The first buildings of the new *University of the Minho* are expected to be completed by 1991.

From the gardens (and parking space) just E of the central PRAÇA DA REPÚBLICA, providing a distant view of *Bom Jesus* on the hill to the E (see p 317), and with the *Tourist Office* adjacent, we may take the Rua do Souto to the W. Almost immediately we pass (right) the *Torre de Menagem*, a relic of the fortress-palace of 1378 guarding the NE corner of the medieval enceinte, which is crossed by the transverse street we continue to follow, later changing its name to the Rua Dom Diogo de Sousa (commemorating the archbishop from 1508–32).

In the first street to the left stands the 16C *Casa dos Crivos*, a rare example retaining its windows covered by latticed shutters (*Mushrabiyas*).

Beyond the next cross street, we pass (right) the LARGO DE PAÇO, the courtyard of the former *Archiepiscopal Palace*, with its 18C façade, and a castellated fountain of 1723. The building, part of which dates from the 14C, suffered a disastrous fire in 1866, and has been

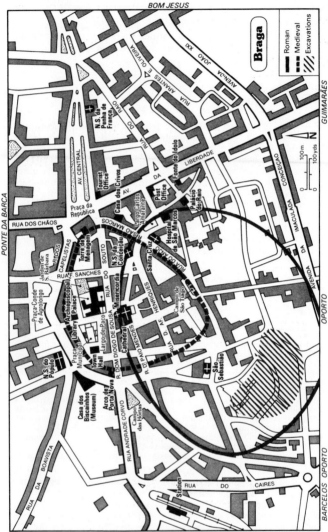

rebuilt and put to a variety of secular uses since. For the present it accommodates part of the *University*, and the important *Public Library*, formed from the spoils of 20 convents, and that part of the archbishop's collection not destroyed in the fire.

The ***Library**, one of the richest in Portugal, vying with that at Évora, now contains some 300,000 volumes and 10,000 MSS, among them one dated 1128 confirming Afonso Henriques as king, the Testament of Afonso II (1218), the Codicil of Dom Dinis (1299), and an interesting topographical study of the city in 1750 entitled 'Mappa das Ruas de Braga'.

Almost opposite are the miscellaneous outbuildings (see below) of the **Cathedral**, which is approached by bearing across the courtyard into the *18C Cloister*, there turning left. By turning left again we enter the N aisle. Little remains of the original Romanesque building of c 1100 except the S Portal and part of the W doors, now sheltered by a late Gothic porch (1532), added by Abp Diogo de Sousa when the E end was rebuilt, and later screened by a fine iron grille (1722). Above are two belfries, incongruously surmounted by basket-work pinnacles.

The interior was tastelessly modernised at the end of the 17C, although the chapel to the right of the Capela-Mór and the crossing are not too spoilt. Among those buried here are St. Pedro de Rates, the first bishop (see the Chapel of St. Geraldo, below; and *Rates*), and the third, St. Ovidius, a friend of the poet Martial. Beneath the coro alto is the bronze tomb (damaged) of the Infante Dom Afonso (died 1400), son of João I, while the *Coro Alto* itself (no admission at present), preserving some coarse but effective 15C stalls, is dominated by its magnificent carved gilt *Organs of 1737–38 (restored), certainly played upon—according to Sitwell—by Carlos Seixas (1704–42), a pupil of Domenico Scarlatti and a composer of some 900 toccatas, largely unpublished.

From the SW corner of the cloister, a flight of steps ascends to the extensive but badly displayed chestnut-floored **Treasury** (fee), which deserves the attention given to the similar collection in the Museu de Alberto Sampaio at Guimarães. The treasures include the usual assortment of rich vestments, silver plate, crowns, and crucifixes, among them an 11C Byzantine cross, and a fine 12C Romanesque example, and another of ivory; a silver and gilt archbishop's crozier of 1521; a Manueline chalice of 1509; another crozier said to have been that of St. Ovidius, but 11C; the 11C chalice 'of St. Geraldo', said to have been used at the christening of Afonso Henriques; an Hispano-arabic ivory casket (10C), and other carved ivories; a painted Christ on the Cross (13C); and a japanned portative organ (17C), which the Sacristan enjoys *kicking* into action, just to prove that its still works. On the stairs is a curious sculpted tomb.

The sacristan will also escort the visitor across the cloister to the 14C **King's Chapel** (*dos Reis*; or *N.S. do Livramento*), containing the tombs of the founder, Count Henry of Burgundy (died 1114; the legs of the count were once truncated to allow the tomb into a constricted space), and his wife Teresa (illegitimate daughter of Alfonso VI of León), parents of Afonso Henriques, the first king of Portugal; and the mummified body of Abp Lourenço who, after confessing João I and his troops at Aljubarrota, took a prominent part in the battle, in which he was seriously wounded on the cheek: the scar was later carved on his effigy.

At the E end of the adjacent courtyard is the restored *Chapel of São Geraldo*, containing the tomb of the first *arch*bishop of Braga (died 1108), from which we enter the ***Capela da Glória**, built in 1330 by Abp Gonçalo Pereira, whose tomb rests here. The Mudéjar decoration of the chapel is noteworthy.

Making our exit from the courtyard, and leaving the *Misericórdia* of 1562 on our left, it is convenient to cross the road into the PRAÇA MUNICIPAL, with the W façade of the Archbishop's Palace on our right (see above), and, left, the *Town Hall* (1753–56; attributed to André Soares da Silva), with a staircase lined with azulejos. Crossing the square diagonally, we turn right towards the church of *N.S. do Pópulo* (from 1596, but rebuilt c 1775–80 by Carlos da Cruz Amarante).

The entrance hall of the Casa dos Biscaínhos

Now turning left, we reach the ***Casa dos Biscaínhos**, an imposing mid 17C mansion, now accommodating an interesting and charming *Museum*, well deserving a visit. From the entrance hall, embellished by statues, two of which are in 18C costume, stairs ascend to the FIRST FLOOR, with a series of rooms, some with painted or plaster ceilings, and some containing azulejos of c 1725. The collections are mainly devoted to the decorative arts. On the GROUND FLOOR are sections on ethnography and archaeology, and artefacts excavated from the Roman city (see below). A passage leads past (left) *Stables*, to the *Gardens*.

Turning right on making our exit, we shortly pass (left) the pinnacled 18C *Arco da Porta Nova*, and ascend a gentle hill to the S, soon forking right past *São Sebastião*, to reach the present area of excavation of the **Roman City**, known as the *Colina de Maximinos*. Although some 60 years have passed since the possible importance of the site was brought to public notice, it was not until 1977, after destruction had already been caused by the erection of blocks of flats, that the site of *Bracara Augusta* was first seriously excavated, and yielded numerous artefacts of interest. Meanwhile a wide belt of land between this point and the Av. da Liberdade to the E is being protected from the further encroachment of property speculators. The area of the ancient city, which is overlapped by the medieval town, is probably centred on the CAMPO DE SÃO TIAGO, slightly to the E, with the cathedral forming its N boundary.

Three necropolises have been discovered to the SW, NE and N of this enceinte. The results of continuing excavations, which have already brought to light the extensive *Thermae*, are awaited with interest. Visitors wishing to study the site should apply to the Campo Arqueológico da Universidade do Minho.

While one may turn directly NE via the Campo de São Tiago towards the Largo Carlos Amarante, perhaps the better approach is by returning downhill and then turning right along the Rua Dom Paio Mendes towards the W front of the cathedral, skirting its S side, and then following the lane behind the *Apse* (before 1511; by João de Castilho), which will bring one to a small square.

On the E side stands *São João do Souto*, abutted by the Chapel of *N.S. da Conceição* (1525), with a well-carved Entombment and quaint statues of SS. Antony of Padua and Paul the Hermit. Adjacent is the relic of the Manueline *Casa dos Coimbras*, largely demolished in 1906, and rebuilt in 1924.

On the W side of the adjacent LARGO CARLOS AMARANTE stands the large church of *Santa Cruz* (1624), with a Baroque organ and loft; while the S side of the square is taken up by the unkempt 18C façade of the *Hospital de São Marcos*, with its twin belfries surmounted by statues, and containing a late 18C Baroque pulpit.

In the street flanking its E side stands the Baroque mansion known as the *Palácio do Raio*, or *do Mexicano* (1754; attributed to André Soares da Silva), with a granite and too brilliant blue azulejo façade.

From here a street leads E to the main thoroughfare of the Av. da Liberdade. To the right as we approach this avenue, is a gate, beyond which at a lower level is the *Fonte do Ídolo*, Roman or earlier, with a figure wearing a toga, and a female bust carved into the rock.

By turning left in the main street, we soon regain the Praça da República.

Ardent ecclesiologists may also visit the churches of *São Vicente* (1691) with its scrolled frames, some distance to the N; the Chapel of *N.S. da Penha de França*; *São Vitor* (Victor), E of the latter, with a façade of 1686, and superseding a Romanesque church: all preserve azulejos.

Those with time on their hands and curious to see to what depths the taste of some Portuguese was able to sink during the Salazar era may visit the building and collection left to the municipality and named the **Museu Nogueira da Silva** after this Maecenas, cynically preserved as a 'sociological warning'. It lies a short distance along the N side of the gardens of the Praça da República.

Environs

Apart from the excursion to *São Frutuoso* and *Tibães* (see the latter part of Rte 34C), easily approached from **Braga**, two slightly longer excursions may as conveniently be made, the second an extension of the first, and which may be followed as an alternative route hence to *Guimarães*, and as such is so described. The main objects are *Bom Jesus*, and the *Citânia de Briteiros*. It is best made in fine weather and in the late afternoon.

We turn left some distance down the Av. da Liberdade, and traverse residential suburbs, after c 4km starting the climb to the lower end of the first section of the monumental double flight of steps ascending to the sanctuary of *Bom Jesus*, which stands high above us on the thickly wooded slope of MONTE ESPINHO. The road continues the ascent. These steps were laid out in 1723 by Abp Rodrigo Moura Teles (1704–28). Each landing was subsequently embellished with grotesque wall fountains symbolising the Five Senses, and flanked by statues of biblical figures. The second section of the stairway, of the Three Virtues, is flanked by 12 chapels containing figures and fountains. The gardens at the summit may be visited, and plants and shrubs may be bought.

Jardine, writing in 1779, remarked that: 'It must have been attended with great labour and expence. Where despotism has left no other power but the church that is capable of great works, the public is obliged to her when she chuses to employ a numerous poor, though in useless labour: and still more, when she employs them in works of taste'.

The *Church of Bom Jesus* (1784–1811), by Carlos Luís Ferreira Amarante (1748–1815), built on the site of a late 15C sanctuary, is of no great interest in itself, but the wooded esplanade commands a wide *View. The *Hotel do Elevador* (named after the funicular of 1882—at present out of commission) provides a similar panorama from its restaurant.

Some 2km SE, at a slightly higher level, is the ugly sanctuary of *Monte Sameiro*, attempting to vie with Bom Jesus, but which has nothing to recommend it except the views obtained by the lantern tower above the dome (613m; fee) of the church of 1904.—The road hence follows the ridge of the SERRA DA FALPERRA to (4km) the church of *Santa Maria Madalena* (1753–55; designed by André Soares da Silva), from which we may return direct to Braga.

The excursion from Bom Jesus should be continued by climbing SE c 8km through attractive wooded hills to one of the most impressive archaeological sites in Portugal, the *Citânia de Briteiros*.

Part of the Citânia de Briteiros, showing the two reconstructed dwellings

From a lay-by, we follow a path (right) to the guardian's house (where, towards sunset, when visited by the Editor, a gentle and solitary old man, who to all appearances was a direct descendant of the Celtiberians, was sitting singing to himself), from which a succession of signs direct one round the extraordinary remains of the ***Citânia de Briteiros** straddling the slope of the boulder-strewn hill of São Romão. It is supposed to have been the last stronghold of the northern Celtiberians against the invading Romans, and consists of the ruined walls of over 150 stone huts with a vestibule or porch, separated from each other by paved causeways, and skirted by stone conduits. A few houses contain more than one compartment, some rectangular; and a larger meeting-house is also seen. Towards the summit are some sarcophagus-like remains, together with two round houses reconstructed by Dr Francisco Martins Sarmento, who was responsible for excavating the site in 1875. Most of the numerous objects, artefacts, and ornamental portals, etc. discovered here may be seen in the Museu de Martins Sarmento in Guimarães (see Rte 37), which certainly should be visited.

Some 64 kinds of coin (from 149 BC to Constantine the Great), largely bronze and silver, were found on the site, mostly issued by the municipalities of Roman Spain, but also from the Lusitanian cities of Mérida and Évora.

The rebuilt hermitage commands fine panoramic views over the district. The prehistoric settlement—dating approx. to 300–200 BC, but probably abandoned by AD 300—was surrounded by terraces and three defensive walls, partly reconstructed, with an additional wall to the N across the neck of land connecting it with the adjacent hill.

A very short distance beyond the lay-by, to the right of the road, is a *Funerary Monument* in the form of a passage grave, discovered in 1930, with its 'house-shaped' portal stone.

Martins Sarmento (1833, in Guimarães–1899) is buried in the churchyard of the lower hamlet of *Briteiros*, through which we soon pass. On reaching the next road junction we turn right to (4km) *Caldas das Taipas*, a pleasant little spa whose hot springs were used by both the Romans and by João I. **Guimarães** is 7km SE: see Rte 37.

An alternative to the main road back to Braga is that turning right just prior to Taipas, ascending towards the SERRA DA FALPERRA and *Santa Maria Madalena* (see above). After 2km a track to the right leads to the smaller 'castro' of **Sabrosa**, also excavated by Martins Sarmento (in 1878). It is surrounded by a single but more massive wall than those at Briteiros, contains only 35 circular houses and three rectangular, and was probably abandoned at an earlier date.

37 Guimarães

GUIMARÃES (22,100 inhab.; *Pousadas N.S. da Oliveira* and *Santa Marinha da Costa*), attractively situated, and noted for its linen, cutlery, and other manufactures (apart from its football team), contends with Braga as the cradle of the Portuguese monarchy. The old town preserves some charming corners, while the collections of the museums of Martins Sarmento and Alberto Sampaio are of particular interest.

Alfonso II of León convened a council of counts and bishops here in 840, with a view to the restoration of Braga after its abandonment by the Moors, and 28 years later one Vimara Peres, calling it *Vimaranes* or *Guimarais*, established it as a centre for the reorganisation of the old Suevic territory: a burgh in the Germanic tradition. A monastery was founded, and a castle built; and in 1095–96 Henry of Burgundy, who made it his court, granted the burghers a charter of privileges.

It seems likely that his son Afonso Henriques was born here in 1110, and it is in a document of 1127 that he was first referred to as king of *Portucale*. The following year he successfully defended his independent position against his mother and a faction supporting Alfonso VII on the field of São Mamede, nearby. An alliance with England, prior to the Treaty of Windsor, was signed at Guimarães in July 1372.

It was the birthplace of St. Damasus, Pope in 366–84; Gil Vicente (1470–1540), the dramatist; and the archaeologist Martins Sarmento (1833–99).

The curving gardens of the ALAMEDA DA LIBERDADE are immediately S of the old town centre, with a *Tourist Office* at its SW corner. To the S of these gardens, at a lower level, stands **São Francisco**, founded in 1220 by Dona Urraca, wife of Afonso II, but reconstructed in the 18C. It preserves little 13C work beyond the W door and the entrance to the Chapter-house on the ground floor of the Renaissance *Cloister* (c 1600, by João Lopes) adjoining. To the right of the wide barrel-vaulted nave is a Tree of Jesse. The grisaille ceiling, the elaborately carved Capela-Mór, and the azulejos of St. Francis preaching to the Fishes, are noteworthy. The whole building has been much restored.

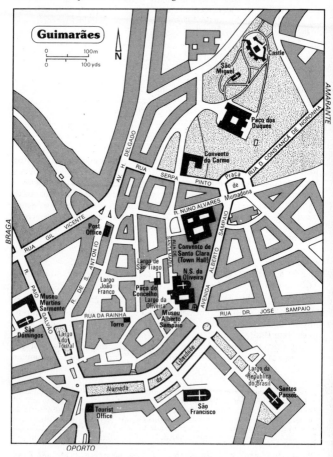

Turning right on making our exit, we shortly reach a roundabout. To the right at the end of the leafy LARGO DA REPÚBLICA DO BRASIL, stands the *Igreja dos Santos Passos* (1767–89; by André Ribeiro Soares da Silva), with a bowed façade between two belfries surmounted by obelisks. The view of the exterior is of more interest than the interior.

Continuing uphill along the Av. Alberto Sampaio, flanked by medieval ramparts, we soon reach the PRAÇA DE MUMADONA, and turn left. At the *Convento do Carmo*, on the next corner, we bear uphill to the right, passing the pretentious fake *Paço dos Duques* (see below) to the little Romanesque chapel of *São Miguel* (12C), containing a font in which, it is claimed, Afonso Henriques was baptised.

Beyond rises the **Castle**, with its massive keep and granite towers with pointed monolithic battlements, emerging from a rock outcrop on the summit of a grassy hill. It was the original fortress here that Count Henry reconstructed c 1100, which was later added to. In the early 19C, being still in a good state of preservation, it served as a debtors' prison. The whole was restored in 1940.—Hence we can see to the E the former monastery of *Santa Marinha da Costa* (see p 323), above which rises *N.S. da Penha*, the NW peak of the SERRA DE SANTA CATARINA.

Returning downhill past the chapel, some may wish to enter what was the 12–15C **Paço dos Duques** (of Braganza), with its brick chimneys, a granite block surrounding a large courtyard, and all too thoroughly reconstructed during the Salazar regime as an 'official residence' of the Head of State, etc. when visiting the N of Portugal. Various have been the objections published, from the 'piteously rebuilt' of the 'Selective Travellers', to the 'hideously restored' of Sarah Bradford, while Henry Myhill refers to his visit as being 'one of the least satisfactory' of all he had made to the monuments of Portugal. Most travellers will agree that it would have been wiser to leave it as a romantic ruin than to have erected such a bogus building. The Ministry of Finance lays claims to it, and well it might. It does however contain some good pieces of furniture and porcelain; canvases attributed to Josefa de Óbidos, and, among tapestries, a modern copy of the famous 15C series recording the taking of Arzila in 1472 by Portugal, the originals of which are at Pastrana, in Spain.

Continuing downhill we follow ahead the Rua de Santa Maria, shortly passing (left) the façade of the 17C *Convento de Santa Clara*, now the Town Hall, and passing below an arch, enter the LARGO DE SÃO TIAGO, at the S end of which is the former *Paço do Concelho*, a battlemented building over massive arcades. Beyond is the LARGO DA OLIVEIRA (with the *Pousada of N.S. da Oliveira*), dominated by the *Colegiada de N.S. da Oliveira* (founded in the 10C by Countess Mumadona), preceded by a curious Gothic canopy (c 1343) sheltering a *Cruzeiro*.

The church takes its name ('of the olive-tree') from the legend of Wamba the Visigoth who, when chosen king in 672, drove his staff into the ground here, swearing that he would not accept the office until it sprouted, which of course it did immediately, olive-branches shooting out in all directions. Wamba, his attempts at uprooting his potent staff being fruitless, fell on his knees and prayed for strength to govern, at least.

The good W Portal is surmounted by a door-like window (now blind), both dating from a rebuilding by João I. The Manueline tower on the N, with a fountain at its base and good plain grilles, was rebuilt after 1515 by Pedro Cogominho, whose tomb, with that of his wife (note head-dress) is in the chapel in its lowest storey. The interior, with fluted pilasters at the crossing, and a classical organ over the entrance, was entirely modernised earlier this century.

Adjacent to the S is the **Museu Alberto Sampaio**, tastefully installed in the conventual buildings surrounding the beautiful Romanesque *Cloister*, rebuilt by João I, and recently well restored, and preserving good capitals. The *Chapter-house*, off the E walk, is lighted by a door with flanking windows all with slightly horseshoe arches, and at the SW corner is the Gothic chapel of *São Brás*. Among the well-displayed works accommodated here on the first floor are the rich monastic *Treasure*: outstanding is a magnificent silver-gilt *Triptych of Juan I of Castile, traditionally taken with that king's travelling chapel at Aljubarrota and given to João I, but perhaps executed for the latter after the battle for presentation to this church in thanksgiving for his victory. Also of interest is the tattered 'loudel' or tunic said to have been worn by Dom João at the same engagement. The ceramic collection is notable, while among numerous paintings, those of *Frei Carlos* of St. Vie, and the Martyrdom of St. Sebastian, and a Virgin and Child by *António Vaz*, should not be overlooked; nor the charming sculptured group of the Flight into Egypt by *Ambrosio Coelho* (18C).

Retracing our steps, follow the lane opposite the colegiada entrance, bearing right at a tower, along the Rua da Rainha, flanking the Largo de João Franco, to gain the popularly known LARGO DO TOURAL, just beyond the NW corner of which is the Museu Martins Sarmento. On the S side of the Rua da Rainha stands the imposing *Casa do Lobos Machados* (18C).—The left-hand lane at the tower traverses another pleasant square to approach the S end of the Largo do Toural.

The *Museu Martins Sarmento, named after the archaeologist who started the excavation of the Celtiberian settlement of *Citânia de Briteiros* in 1875, and later that of *Sabroso* (see pp 318–9), some 12–15km N, preserves the objects discovered on these sites, among other collections. While archaeologists will wish to spend time studying the artefacts, etc., most visitors will wish to gain further insight into the culture of the peoples which occupied the area 2000 years ago. Many of the larger objects are to be seen in the 14C cloister of the adjacent secularised church of *São Domingos*, behind the main building, to which stairs descend (embellished by carved escutcheons from demolished mansions in the district). The floriated capitals of the cloister itself should be noted.

Among objects of interest to the non-specialist, apart from the collection of Roman votive altars, sepulchral and other inscribed stones, miliary columns, sarcophagi, etc., is the so-called *Pedra Formosa, a large carved stone slab curiously similar in shape to the traditional design of the *cangas* or ornamental wooden yokes of the lyre-horned Minho oxen. It undoubtedly served as a decorative front to a mausoleum, as with the *Pedro Formosa-II* found in situ at the Citânia in 1930—*not* a sacrificial altar, as was once assumed. Also important are the two statues of headless Lusitanian warriors, protectively holding their round shields before them; the so-called *Colossus of Pedralva*; and the numerous geometrically ornamented door-jambs and lintels, from Citânia de Briteiros, Âncora, Sabrosa, and elsewhere.—Among the smaller objects on display are a bronze votive coach; bronze dolphins; a bull; and a hermaphrodite figure holding a bunch of grapes; collections of fibulae; and coins found on the same sites. ·

The other collections are of slight interest, but include Chinese coins; and in the Ethnographical section, an 18C litter, an 18C Psaltery made in Brazil, and costumes; while among the somewhat miscellaneous paintings, mostly 19C, are portraits by August Roquemont (1804–52), of Swiss origin, who died in Oporto. The important *Library* of the Sociedade Martins Sarmento is also housed in the building.

The Rue Dr José Sampaio leads E. Off it a turning ascends towards the *Penha* (617m), overlooking the town to S. On the lower slope is the former monastery of **Santa Marinha da Costa**, founded in 1154, probably on the site of a 4C sanctuary. The whole was entirely rebuilt in the 18C and a new church was started in 1748. The prior of Crato (cf. Crato) was educated here. The azulejos by Policarpo de Oliveira Bernardes are notable, while the belvedere known as the Varanda de Frei Jerónimo is also of interest. The well-restored buildings now accommodate the luxurious *Pousada de Santa Marinha*.

A minor road leads NE from Guimarães via *Azurém*, with the medieval *Casa de Pousada*, passing (6km) a 19C church, beyond which at a higher level is the Igreja Matriz of *São Torcato*, preserving some 12C features, and the cloister of the Benedictine convent of *Santo Agostinho*.

For the road from Guimarães to *Amarante*, 34km SE, see the latter part of Rte 35.

INDEX

Topographical names are printed in Roman or **bold** type; the names of eminent artists and architects (together with their dates) are printed in *italics*. Subject entries are in CAPITALS. Barragems (reservoirs) and Serras (hills or mountain ranges) are sub-indexed.